THE SUPERVISOR'S BASIC MANAGEMENT GUIDE

THE SUPERVISOR'S

New York
San Francisco
Toronto
London
Sydney

BASIC MANAGEMENT GUIDE

**An A-Z Manual
on Supervisory Effectiveness**

CARL HEYEL

Management Consultant

McGRAW-HILL BOOK COMPANY

This is a book about problems all supervisors run into—in plant and office, in government, in institutional organizations—with practical pointers on how to handle them.

You will note that the problems turn out to be largely "people problems." This is because it is only through people that a supervisor can get the work of his department done. Problems of a technical nature are not overlooked—budget preparation, cost accounting, quality control, methods improvement—but here again the orientation is to people, since the supervisor's management problems in connection with them revolve around getting his people to cooperate with staff specialists, or interpreting and communicating information up, down, and sideways, or persuading people to see the significance of such information and react in a desired manner to it.

The material is assembled in alphabetical order because the intent is to provide a ready reference to which you can turn when you are confronted with a particular problem situation.

An index is added as a look-up aid, since you may think about a particular problem in terms of a different key word from the one used in the entry heading.

However, the author hopes that you will find the book interesting to read straight through from A to Z on your first go-around. The accident of alphabetic location means that the entries are actually in random order as far as subject matter is concerned, with quick changes in pace as to substance, relative urgency, and relevance to a given type of operation. This makes for a certain "you-don't-know-what-will-happen-next" sequence—which is exactly the way in which people problems turn up in real life, rather than in orderly compartments as presented in textbooks.

For additional insight, a glossary of traits, behavioral characteristics, and related psychological terms is given in Appendix A. These are expressions which a supervisor is likely to hear at meetings of professional personnel-management groups he may have occasion to attend, or which he may come across in articles and books on management subjects. Some of these terms are often bandied about loosely, and if you feel you should use any of them in a merit rating or appraisal discussion, or in an employee counseling situation, you should be sure that you know their meaning. Here again it is suggested that you read these straight through to get an insight into the "infinite variety" that goes into the making of a human being.

Appendix B lists certain sources of additional information. This opens the door to further self-development in any areas where special interest may have been stimulated by entries in this Guide.

Carl Heyel

ACKNOWLEDGMENTS

It is obvious that in a book of this sort, the author must draw from a wide variety of sources in addition to synthesizing his own direct experiences. Where material in the following pages is directly quoted or heavily drawn upon, acknowledgment of source is given. However, during the course of compiling this "A–Z" guide, special assistance was tendered by certain individuals and organizations for which the author wishes to record his appreciation separately here:

Lawrence J. Benninger, Ph.D., Professor of Accounting, University of Florida, Gainesville, Fla., for his review of the entries pertaining to accounting.

Willard A. Lewis, Ph.D., LL.B., Management and Industrial Relations Professor, School of Commerce, New York University, and Member of New York Bar, New York, for his review of entries having to do with labor legislation and collective bargaining.

W. C. Zinck, Plant Manager, Arbogast & Bastian, Inc., Allentown, Pa., for collaboration on the Work Simplification and related entries; and to Reinhold Publishing Corporation, New York, for permission to draw upon Mr. Zinck's book, *Dynamic Work Simplification*, published by that company in 1962.

The following organizations kindly permitted the author to review manuals and other materials published for supervisors, or supplied extensive information by correspondence or interview. Where these have been drawn upon, source is indicated in the pertinent entry:

A.C.F. Industries, Inc., New York
Aluminum Company of America, Pittsburgh
American Airlines, New York
American Arbitration Association, New York
American Management Association, New York
American Telephone and Telegraph Company, New York
Armco Steel Corporation, Middletown, Ohio
Connecticut General Life Insurance Company, Hartford, Conn.
Detroit Edison Company, Detroit
Iowa Power and Light Company, Des Moines
Kordite Corporation, Macedon, N.Y.
Long Island Lighting Company, Hicksville, N.Y.
National Board of Fire Underwriters, New York
National Council on Alcoholism, New York
Rural Electric Cooperative Association, Washington
Joseph Schlitz Brewing Company, Milwaukee
Seiberling Rubber Company, Akron, Ohio
Thompson Ramo Wooldridge, Inc., Tapco Group, Cleveland
Trans World Airlines, Inc., New York
United Shoe Machinery Corporation, Boston, Mass.
U.S. Department of Health, Education, and Welfare, Vocational Rehabilitation Administration, Washington
U.S. Department of Labor, Manpower Administration, Washington
Veterans Administration, Washington
Westinghouse Electric Corporation, Pittsburgh
Whirlpool Corporation, Benton Harbor, Mich.

C. H.

CONTENTS

A

ABSENCES

1. Who Are the Chronic Absentees?

What do you know about the records of absenteeism in your department? Large companies have found that in some departments the average number of absences per employee is almost three times as much as in other departments. *The attitude of the supervisor* appears to be the controlling factor. In large departments about one third or one fourth of the employees may be producing most of the absenteeism. This is the group you must control.

Connecticut General Life Insurance Company reports that when the responsibility for control of absenteeism, especially a tough-minded check into the reasonableness of individual absences, was placed squarely upon the supervisors rather than upon a more remotely oriented medical department, there was a dramatic reduction in chronic absenteeism. (It defines chronic absenteeism as eight or more absence periods during any twelve months, regardless of total number of days absent.) Connecticut General tells its supervisors not to encourage absentees to "stay out until fully recovered." (They will do this without urging!) Rather, they should be encouraged to "get well quick; we miss you here!"

Related Entries *Absences—2. Emergencies Caused by Unexpected Absences; Early Leavers; Tardiness.*

ABSENCES

2. Emergencies Caused by Unexpected Absences

If you have an emergency caused by an unexpected absence, you will have to "play it by ear"—all we can do here is to discuss ways to prevent such emergencies. For example:

1. Insist on prompt notification at all times when someone in your department must be absent unexpectedly. Be hard-boiled about this—in this age of telephones there is hardly ever an excuse for no notification. Be sure everyone knows *whom* to notify in the department.

2. Make it clear that you will be understanding of personal situations. This will encourage prior discussions about needed absences, rather than thin fictions.

3. Be sure that operating procedures in your department are up-to-date, that all concerned understand them, and that the manual, inserts, and supplements are readily available.

4. Set up a clear procedure for reviewing any absentee's work to pick up matters which require prompt handling. Where appropriate, set up standard backstop procedures —who is to be kept informed of what details, who is to pinch-hit for whom.

5. Insist upon prompt notification of customers or other departments affected by any delays that may be caused by absences.

6. Keep a good record of absences to identify anyone who is becoming absence-prone.

7. Is *your own* base covered? Who is your understudy?

Related Entries   *See listing under preceding entry.*

ACCIDENTS

1. Reporting

Always insist that your employees report any accidents in which they are involved, no matter how slight. Prompt reporting of even slight injuries will greatly lessen the danger of infection. Don't accept the excuse that the employee considered that no damage was done, or that the damage was slight. Whether damage was slight or not is a matter of judgment, and management should know about *all* accidents.

What about the employee who refuses to report accidents, no matter how often you ask him to? You have a right to get tough. Be sure all employees of your department have a copy of the company's regulations and procedures about accident reporting, post a copy on bulletin boards, and keep emphasizing the importance of reporting at employee meetings. If the employee persists in his conduct, you should see your own superior about recommending suspension, and for continued violations, even dismissal. In cases of this sort brought to arbitration, management has been upheld on discharge.

Notes Don't bandy about the word "carelessness." A power company arranged a series of weekly meetings of foremen and assistant foremen to analyze the reports of accidents that had occurred during the past year. The purpose was to make sincere attempts to determine causes and to develop ways to avoid accidents in the future. One of the first points brought out by these meetings was the extremely loose use of the word "carelessness" in ascribing causes. Apparently there had been a tendency to use that term because it served to remove all blame from the foreman. Analysis soon showed that, in addition to "carelessness," a great deal more usually had to

be said before a remedy could be suggested to prevent repeats. A rule was established, prohibiting the use of the term
"carelessness" in accident reports unless it was accompanied
by very complete additional information. This led to the
accumulation of much more reliable data. Better still, it made
the foremen much more careful in their safety supervision.

• In one plant, the foremen appoint a secret "Unsafe Committee" each month, consisting of three members. No one
else knows the make-up of this group, and so no one can ever
be sure that some slip-up of his went unobserved.

Related Entries *Accidents—2. Accident-Prone Employees;
Fire Prevention; First Aid; Horseplay; Housekeeping; Lifting
and Carrying; Office Accidents; Office Machines and Safety;
Safety—1. Safety ABC's; Safety—2. Be Your Own Safety
Engineer; Safety—3. Dramatization to Employees; Safety—4.
Safety and Hand Tools; Safety—5. Safety for the Physically
Handicapped Worker; Women and Girls—3. Safety and
Women Workers; Workmen's Compensation.*

ACCIDENTS

2. Accident-Prone Employees

Are some people accident-prone? There are differences of
opinion as to whether, scientifically speaking, it is proper
to use this term—that people so designated are merely
manifesting other characteristics of lack of interest, carelessness, etc. The mere fact that one employee has more
accidents than others is not enough to label him as accident-prone, and The National Safety Council discour-
ages use of the term as implying a specific personal characteristic, saying that a worker may have more than his
share of accidents because he has not been trained properly or simply because he needs new glasses or is working
in cramped quarters. Obviously, the physical conditions

surrounding a job are the first thing a supervisor should look into if he suspects accident "proneness."

Whether or not having frequent accidents is really the manifestation of other attributes rather than a characteristic in itself, psychologists have been able to devise tests which seem to screen out poor performers in this regard. In a transit company, for example, it was found that the highest tenth of the drivers measured on a composite profile test had 21.2 per cent less chargeable accidents than the lowest tenth, and using this test in selection brought about a 28.8 per cent improvement in accident rates.

Dr. Flanders Dunbar, an authority in industrial medicine, studied 160 workers who were treated for broken arms. Her study of accident-prone individuals is considered one of the most complete and comprehensive ever made. Correlating what she had observed with the findings of other investigators, she characterized the typical accident-prone individual as follows:

He is impulsive. He is apt to act on the spur of the moment. . . . He likes excitement and adventure, but he seldom plans ahead. . . . He usually comes from a family with strict discipline. . . . He has developed a resentment of authority. He even subconsciously resents his own reason, which would act as a restraining influence on him! He is normally intelligent, and knows this attitude is wrong, so he has a guilty feeling about it. . . . The accident-prone individual is always seeking for a way to change his surroundings. . . . a new wife, a new job, or a new thrill.

Note Dr. Dunbar's work is cited by D. H. Robinson, M.D., in his article, "Your Safety Is Up to You," in *Management Quarterly*. He also tells of the medical director of a trucking firm, who compiled the accident statistics for each driver. He found that moving an accident-prone driver from one job to another rarely cured the condition. The accident-proneness moved right along with him! When the doctor "grounded" these drivers, the result was spectacular. The accident rate was cut to one fifth the former rate and the length of time between accidents lengthened five times.

Related Entries   *See listing under preceding entry.*

ACCOUNTING

See *Budgets; Overhead; Standard Costs; Time Standards —Standard Minute (Standard Hour).*

AFTER-HOURS RELATIONS WITH SUBORDINATES

Every supervisor will sooner or later come up against the knotty problem of just how friendly he can afford to be with any of his subordinates *after hours*. This problem is usually most acute for the newly made supervisor, because he has just taken the long step from being "one of the boys" to being part of management. However, when once you have established a policy for yourself—probably involving the pang of gradually cutting off some old relationships—you should not have any significant problem on that score again, no matter how far up the ladder you go.

There is a "fact of life" which a supervisor must accept at the very start, and which has been recognized by every leader throughout history—the loneliness of command. You can't have it both ways: you can't be one of the old gang after hours, and a responsible and effective head of the department during the day.

This does not, of course, mean complete standoffishness and isolation. At company affairs—picnics, social gatherings, etc.—every executive should be able to mingle and to be on terms of easy temporary familiarity: "shop talk" taboo, good-natured bantering accepted, and distinctions of title and position absolutely de-emphasized. In fact, as the personnel director of one company pointed out, positions may be completely inverted at company-sponsored recreational activities (the band-director's boss may play the drum in the band, the personnel manager may be bat boy on the baseball team, and the plant superintendent may have to take instructions on how to prepare hamburgers), but the point is that the effective executive knows how to snap back into his standard mode of demanding results and no-nonsense-or-alibis the day after the outing.

The formula is that you enjoy but you don't always join: You take part in an occasional evening of bowling, but you think twice about joining the team. Similarly, you may play a game of cards, but probably should not be part of a weekly card-playing group with men in your own department. You don't want to be entangled by after-hours relationships if the need arises on the job to take disciplinary action for carelessness, or to demote, or to pass over for promotion, or to lay off or discharge.

The same holds true with regard to social activities with the men and their wives. Every executive will want to have occasional social evenings to which department members and their wives or husbands are invited. But these are best infrequent occasions. You and your wife can't regularly play bridge with one of your men and his wife—and yet expect that you can be completely objective when a tough superior-subordinate situation arises.

Note   The story is told of Edward VII, the famous "playboy" Prince of Wales while Queen Victoria reigned, that when he ascended the throne, he sent a token gold piece to all of his up-to-then roistering companions, with a note saying that from now on he was to be King, and that, reluctantly, he was cutting all of his old ties. No one expects the newly appointed foreman or supervisor to take such dramatic action; but you can remember the story, and do some graceful withdrawing of your own.

Related Entry   *Favoritism.*

AGE

The Young Supervisor

A person who has been advanced to a supervisory position may be unusually young for such responsibilities. Most of the department's personnel, even including his own direct assistant, may be quite a lot older. Or it may happen that a young staff specialist in, say, operations research, may have frequent contact with older people in operating departments—or a brilliant young researcher may be put in charge of a research project to which older scientists have been assigned.

Such relationships call for special thoughtfulness and tact on the younger man's part—especially since he may have been advanced to his position because of his quickness and drive. . . . If you are in this position, keep the following in mind:

1. Try to develop an understanding and consideration for the slower tempo, more modest ambition, and reduced energy of the older people in the department.

2. Don't betray impatience because it takes some of the older, steady hands a bit longer than you think is neces-

sary to see the advantage of a point you're trying to get across.

3. If your direct assistant is older than you, go out of your way to discuss departmental matters with him, and to seek his counsel.

4. Be more than usually alert to all of the points of criticism, reprimand, suggestions, etc., covered in separate entries herein.

Note In this connection, you might well take to heart the following prescription set down for himself by Benjamin Franklin. In his autobiography, he says: "I continued in the habit of expressing myself in terms of modest diffidence; never using, when I advanced anything that could possibly be disputed, the words *certainly*, *undoubtedly*, or any others that give the air of positiveness to an opinion; but rather say, I conceive or apprehend a thing to be so and so; it appears to me, or I should think it so and so, for such and such reasons; or I imagine it to be so; or it is so, *if I am not mistaken*. This habit, I believe, has been of great advantage to me when I have had occasion to inculcate my opinions, and persuade men into measures that I have been from time to time engaged in promoting."

Related Entry *The Older Worker.*

THE ALCOHOLIC EMPLOYEE

According to the National Council on Alcoholism, more than 5,000,000 Americans are alcoholics, and 1,700,000 of these are employed in industries. Less than 3 per cent of the total, says NCA, are on "Skid Row." The overwhelming majority are people who have jobs, who have families, and who on the surface look like other people—only they have developed an uncontrollable drinking problem.

The important thing to recognize is that alcoholism is

an illness that can be treated, not a moral problem. It is a progressive disease which, if left untreated, grows more virulent year by year. All manner of people can fall victim: rich and poor, educated and illiterate, young and old, men and women.

Their drinking is not simply an emotional problem (worry, frustration, marital difficulties) plus liquor. "Alcoholics," writes a former alcoholic in *Personnel* (he is now successfully helping alcoholics help themselves), "have a physical response to alcoholism that more often than not creeps up on them—and once it does, they cannot control it by limiting the amount they drink or changing their attitudes or their living or working conditions. Just as the diabetic has to learn to live without sugar, so the drinker with a drinking problem has to learn to live without liquor. Any liquor."

Hundreds of large and small companies now have organized programs for coping with alcoholics in their employ, including counseling programs under the administration of the personnel department, special programs administered by the company's medical department, outside alcoholism clinics supported by the company, or special consultation arrangements with NCA.

Whether your company has a formal program or not, you as a supervisor should have an insight into the problem, and some guidelines as to how to deal with it. You should spot possible early symptoms and know what resources are available for helping the employee.

While the supervisor knows that the drinking is disrupting smooth production in his department, he will as a rule like to help the employee "straighten out," because he knows that if management finds out there is a drinking problem (and if the company is not one with an organized program for helping the man), dismissal may soon result. So he reprimands the employee. In each one of these episodes the employee promises faithfully that it will not happen again. "The trouble is," says NCA's industrial consultant, Lewis F. Presnall, "that an alcoholic promising never to take another drink is like a person with active tuberculosis promising he will stop coughing because it isn't polite."

Identifying the Problem

For the supervisor's purposes, a suspected alcoholic is someone whose drinking seriously and continuously interferes with his job. The supervisor should not attempt a formal diagnosis—that is up to the professionals whom the problem employee should be urged to see. But he should know when certain symptoms are present that indicate serious trouble.

Unlike "heavy drinkers" or even the "occasional drunk," the alcoholic's condition grows steadily worse. While the first two have some control over their drinking, and can even cut it out completely for a specified period of time without deep discomfort, the alcoholic becomes completely dependent upon drink, to the point in later stages when he must have a certain amount of alcohol in his system at all times. Whether the employee is medically defined as "alcoholic" or not, the supervisor has a right to step in when the drinking affects the work of the department.

Professor Harrison M. Trice of the New York State School of Industrial and Labor Relations, Cornell University, has reported on a study in a large Eastern company. The immediate supervisors of 72 employees who had been diagnosed as alcoholics by the company's medical department were given a list of 44 possible on-the-job signs of alcoholism, and were asked to select the first five signs of alcoholism they recalled noticing in these alcoholic subordinates. Here are 17 of the 44 items most often checked:

1. *Noticed early and frequently thereafter:*
   Leaving post temporarily. . . . Absenteeisms of half-a-day or a day. . . . More unusual excuses for absences. . . . Lower quality of work. . . . Mood changes after lunch. . . . Red or bleary eyes.

2. *Noticed later but frequently thereafter:*
   Less even, more spasmodic work pace. . . . Lower quantity of work . . . Hangovers on job.

3. *Noticed fairly early but infrequently thereafter:*
   Loud talking. . . Drinking at lunch time. . . . Longer lunch periods. . . . Hand tremors.

4. *Noticed late and infrequently thereafter:*
   Drinking during working hours. . . . Avoiding boss or associates. . . . Flushed face. . . . Increase in real minor illnesses.

Here are behavior and psychological signs pointed out by NCA which are not necessarily connected with the actual drinking periods, which can be evaluated: recurrent periods of tension, showing up as extreme irritability, flashes of temper, unreasonable ideas, and a general attitude of resentment toward the world. If these are noticeable along with evidences of excessive drinking, there is cause for suspecting alcoholism rather than mere heavy drinking.

If you have a problem employee who seems to have an unusual share of minor ailments, accidents, unexcused absences, disciplinary hearings, collection of sick leaves, etc., you may well be alert to evidence of excessive drinking.

Corrective Action

Find out if your company has a policy and procedure regarding alcoholics, how to make proper referral to the medical department or to personnel, and what resources you can draw upon within the company in motivating an employee to seek treatment.

A person with alcoholism should never be disciplined just because he has alcoholism. You do not discipline employees for having an illness. You may have to apply discipline if they refuse to seek medical attention, and if their work performance continues to suffer.

As soon as you notice signs that may mean alcoholism, you should do something about it. Don't wait until the only thing left to do is to warn the alcoholic that he will lose his job if "it" happens again.

Are there a few good people with whom you can meet to discuss the situation? If there is a direct foreman or supervisor in a level between you and the employee involved, he would form one of a logical group perhaps also including the union shop steward in the department. Union representatives are close to their people, and are in a position to help motivate an employee. They would rather work with you and the employee at the first sign of trouble than merely make a formal protest when a nearly unemployable last-stage alcoholic must be discharged. Is there a friend of the employee in the department who knows something of the employee's family situation and can throw added light on what the employee's drinking pattern is? Does the employee drink steadily or is he a periodic drinker? Does he drink alone or with people? Has he ever been approached about his drinking? By whom? What was his reaction?

As soon as possible after you have analyzed the situation, have a frank private talk with the employee to "lay it on the line." As the *Personnel* writer quoted above puts it, there is never a "right" time to discuss excessive drinking with an employee. "No matter what you say, the interview will be unpleasant. You may get excuses, rage, or lies. But if *you* don't weasel, the alcoholic is more likely to take what you say."

Don't pull punches. Put it on the basis that your sole concern is with departmental performance—and that the drinking problem *must* be overcome. If your company has a medical department, insist that he visit it. But before he does so, have a frank talk with the doctors there, so that the alcoholic can't minimize or explain away the whole thing. If your company has no medical department, insist that the employee give you the name of his own doctor, so that you can give the latter the same type of information you would have given a company doctor.

While you must be blunt and firm with the employee, don't concentrate exclusively on upbraiding him about past poor behavior. Place primary emphasis on treatment.

Notes Most larger communities have Alcoholism Information Centers operated by voluntary councils affiliated with the National Council on Alcoholism (whose headquarters address is the New York Academy of Medicine Building, 2 East 103rd Street, New York, New York). These centers provide a place where people can come for information about the problem, for limited counseling, and for referral to those who are skilled in handling alcoholism, such as doctors, psychiatrists, clergymen, family agencies, and hospitals in the community.

• The Alcoholics Anonymous groups in your area provide

a resource which NCA reports to be the best single approach to recovery. This is especially true for industry, since almost any firm will have a few employees on the payroll who have recovered through A.A. These individuals will be most helpful at all stages of rehabilitation.

• Most states have alcoholism programs, and most of them operate clinics and hospitals.

Related Entry *Employee Counseling.*

THE ALIBI ARTIST

The alibi artist is glib of tongue. . . . He has a quick answer for every failure to perform, which always turns out to be due to circumstances beyond his control. One problem is that alibi artists are quick-witted, and may by and large be able to turn out good work, fast. But they just won't admit they're in the wrong. In their worst form, they're lazy or slipshod, and in the back of their minds they are always preparing alibis and explanations ahead of time, just in case they're called to account. If you think you have an alibi artist on your hands, here are some guidelines for action.

1. First, examine your own actions. Are some of your men prone to alibi because you have a reputation of blowing up on the slightest provocation?

2. If it's the other fellow's fault, diagnose the seriousness of the case: (a) Is this a young employee who may have fallen into an alibi habit, but who can be helped, and is worth taking some trouble about? or (b) Is he an old, habitual alibi-er, who is cast in a mold that probably can't be changed?

3. If he is (a), take time out for a serious straight-from-the-shoulder discussion as soon as possible after a critical incident. Analyze, step by step, whatever it was that went

wrong. . . . not in a sharply critical tone, but with a view of having *him* tell *you* how he might handle the same or similar situation if it ever came up again. . . . Stress that you have to have results, not excuses, but that you don't hold mistakes against anybody if the mistakes are used as a basis for improvement.

4. If he is (b), and he is of a key-man level to receive annual performance appraisal, stress, in your appraisal interview, that you'll bear down hard on the "if-not, why-not." (See point 9 in *Development of Subordinates—1. Development-Appraisal-Development.*)

5. Be *doubly* sure that there's no room for misunderstanding in any instructions you give him: Ask him to repeat the key points about what and when and who. . . . If appropriate to the type of job, be more than ordinarily insistent upon "saying it in writing." Perhaps you have to confirm an oral instruction with a memorandum. . . . Set up special check points for follow-up. . . . Be specific on the limits of his authority, and at what points he must come to you for approval on deviations or extensions.

6. Don't lean on a weak reed: put him last on the list of those you'll rely on when the chips are down; and don't pull punches in any recommendations you're asked to make regarding his advancement.

Related Entry *Development of Subordinates—1. Development-Appraisal-Development.*

ALTERCATIONS

Even in the best regulated families, internal quarrels break out. Sharp differences—animosities—can break out in your department, more often than not over something not directly connected with the job. Fistfights have been known to break out, even between balding men with paunches who should definitely know better.

As supervisor, you will be drawn in as an adjudicator after the smoke has cleared. Where there has been physical violence—or even only strong vituperative language that has disrupted operations—there should probably be some penalty. To overlook prompt action will only set a dangerous precedent, and invite recurrence if not among the first two offenders, then among others.

Suspension or loss of privileges will depend upon applicable company rules and union agreements. The big point is that prompt action must be taken.

There is only one caution, or "caveat," as lawyers say: *Be sure you get the facts straight, and get ALL of the facts—and keep an open mind until you do.*

Note "Did you ever serve on a jury?" asks the Veterans Administration *Personnel Information Bulletin.* "First you listen to the prosecutor. He makes such a damaging case that you can't see how the defendant in the case could be anything but guilty. You're ready to give him the works! . . . But then along comes the defense lawyer, and lo and behold he makes such an eloquent argument that he completely crumbles the case. . . . *Moral:* It's up to you, who are going to act as both judge and jury, to hear *both* sides. Repeat: Be sure you get the facts straight, get all of the facts, and keep an open mind until you do!"

Related Entries *Discipline—2. Handling Critical Incidents; Friction.*

APPRAISING SUBORDINATES
1. "How Am I Doing?"

"How am I doing?" is an important question for every employee and "How is he doing?" is a question every supervisor should continually be asking about every member of his department.

Many companies have formal "merit rating" or "appraisal" plans, usually administered by the personnel department, in which a supervisor or department head fills out a merit-rating form which becomes part of an employee's personnel record. In more elaborate plans, covering at least key employees if not all rank-and-file, periodic "appraisal interviews" are conducted in which a subordinate's performance for the previous year is carefully reviewed with him, and suggestions are given for further development and improvement. (See *Development of Subordinates— 1. Development-Appraisal-Development.*)

But even if your company doesn't have a formal system, there's nothing to stop you from carrying on a systematic appraisal and rating on your own. You can work out the characteristics which you think are important in your department and assign maximum rating factors to them. You will then be in a position to evaluate an employee's progress in tangible terms.

The characteristics, and especially the maximum ratings, will depend upon your department's operations, but here is something to use as a starter:

Characteristics

Maximum Rating

1. Does he follow instructions willingly? 5
2. Is he clean and orderly? 5
3. Does he apply himself conscientiously during working hours? 5
4. Is his attendance good? Does he notify you promptly when he knows he will be absent? 5
5. Is he careful with company property? 5
6. Does he get along well with others? 20
7. Does he do good work? 25

8. Is he versatile—can you use him on a number of operations?   15
9. Does he frequently make good suggestions?   10
10. Does he work safely?   5

For each of your *key employees,* you can draw up the following type of check list for a written analysis (or at least detailed notes) as a basis for a meeting with him about his work which you may want to have once a year, or for a meeting you may have with your own superior to discuss possibilities in promotion or upward transfer of a particular employee. (This is based on a form originally prepared by Lawrence Appley, President of the American Management Association.)

1. *Results.* What has he accomplished in measurable results since his last appraisal? Have facts and figures wherever possible. Be specific.

2. *Methods.* How does this person go about getting his job done? How does he work with and through people? Does he attack new assignments in a logical and orderly manner?

3. *Personal qualifications.* List only outstanding points, those which are significantly above or below average.

4. *Strongest single qualification or characteristic.*

5. *Most noticeable weakness.*

6. *Potential.* What is the next logical step ahead for this key employee? Does he have further potential beyond the next step? Be specific.

7. *Action.* Recommend action for improvement, such as training, change of attitude, change in pay, encouragement, etc. Indicate a current rating as "Immediately promotable"; "Satisfactory plus"; "Satisfactory"; "Decision deferred because new"; "Questionable"; "Unsatisfactory—action recommended."

Related Entries *Appraising Subordinates—2. Appraisal Interview; Appraising Subordinates—3. "Best versus Poorest"; Development of Subordinates—1. Development-Appraisal-Development; "People Problems"—2. Employee Types; Personnel Audit; Problem Employees.*

APPRAISING SUBORDINATES

2. Appraisal Interview

Good supervision calls for periodic detailed review of the work of subordinates. The entry, *Development of Subordinates—1. Development-Appraisal-Development*, discusses the extent to which an executive will find it profitable to go in such a program with respect to subordinate supervisors and executives and key men. But even if such an intensive program is not followed with all rank-and-file employees, a yearly interview to look at the subordinate's job performance in broad perspective will be in order. Here are some ground rules to follow in such a meeting:

1. Schedule enough time—certainly an hour for any employee, and a half day to a day for a subordinate supervisor or key man.

2. Focus on the future—on what can be learned from any mistakes discussed, rather than on the mistakes themselves.

3. Call a recess on the superior-subordinate relationship—take the approach of joint problem solving.

4. Avoid personalities.

5. Give the subordinate a chance to talk.

6. Give him a chance to save face, if you're finding fault with performance. Often all the blame for disappointing results is not the subordinate's alone. If part of it can justifiably be laid on your own doorstep (unclear

instructions, insufficient facilities, etc.) lean over backward and perhaps take more than your share.

7. Don't bring in comparisons with others. Focus attention on performance standards set on the job.

8. Don't make promises lightly.

9. Don't let the discussion get into criticisms of *your* boss. A pitfall in the recess in the superior-subordinate relationship, point 3 above, is that the free-and-easy atmosphere established may lead to criticisms of company and divisional policies and activities. You may (you're human too) be drawn into making a remark that you will regret later. (One remark can lead to another.)

10. Don't pull punches where drastic improvement is called for. Follow the guidelines in our entries on *Criticism,* but don't leave room for misunderstanding of your appraisal.

11. "Play back" any important agreements reached, and end the interview on a positive and helpful note.

Related Entries   *See listing under preceding entry.*

APPRAISING SUBORDINATES
3. "Best versus Poorest"

What does a "best versus poorest" comparison of your workforce show? Psychological studies have indicated that among individuals ordinarily regarded as normal, in the average vocation the most gifted will be between three and four times as capable as the poorest. But don't let it go at that, for the simple reason that in most work situations, and indeed in most activities, people are not making use of the maximum aptitudes and skills they have.

The big point is, what can be done to bring the performance of the poorest up closer to that of the best? Training and coaching may be the answer (see appropriate entries). Or using something like the "buddy" system, especially with newcomers, to make a seasoned employee responsible for the development of another less skilled. And perhaps the best producers have developed some special knacks or method improvements which should be passed along to the others.

Additionally, there are five important self-examination questions to ask before making the best-poorest comparison:

1. Do you know more about your best employee than you do about your poorest—or vice versa?

2. Do you fail to note the good qualities of your worst employee and the bad qualities of your best?

3. Is your best employee "best" simply because you know more about him?

4. Do you know as much about your *average* employee as you do about your best and worst?

5. Are the average employees "average" because you haven't taken the trouble to know very much about them?

Related Entries *See listing under Appraising Subordinates —1. "How Am I Doing?"*

APPRENTICESHIP PROGRAMS

Apprenticeship training is a long-recognized system for producing skilled workers. There are companies in the machine-tool, railroad, and shipbuilding industries which have conducted outstanding apprenticeship programs continuously for well over 75 years. Many international craft unions have for generations placed special emphasis on apprenticeship as a means of entering their trades. There are approximately 160,000 apprentices in registered programs recognized by the Bureau of Apprenticeship and Training of the U.S. Department of Labor and by state apprenticeship agencies. In addition, there are at least 200,000 or more apprentices in unregistered programs—although many of these may not be providing adequate training in the light of criteria given below.

The number of registered apprentices has been declining in recent years, and this has been of some concern to the Bureau, which works closely with employers, labor, vocation schools, and other groups in almost every industry. However, with the imperative need for skilled craftsmen to meet the demands of our growing industrial population, the trend may well be reversed. In any event, it behooves the industrial supervisor to be knowledgeable about this form of training.

The Bureau of Apprenticeship and Training is charged by the U.S. Department of Labor with the responsibility of promoting apprenticeship and on-the-job training programs in industry. It cooperates with the U.S. Office of Education and with state agencies. The Bureau functions through its national office in Washington and through 12 regions with representatives in each of the 50 states. However, it does not administer or conduct apprenticeship programs. It does no actual training, serving rather as a programmer, promoting the establishment of apprenticeship programs and improving existing ones. The Bureau requires that apprenticeship programs meet nine standards before they can be registered with it and before it will award its Certificate of Completion to an apprentice at the conclusion of this apprenticeship. Thus:

1. The starting age of an apprentice to be not less than 16 years.

2. An established schedule of work processes in which the apprentice will receive instruction and experience on the job.

3. A minimum of 144 hours annually of organized instruction to provide the apprentice with knowledge in technical subjects related to his trade.

4. An established progressively increasing schedule of wages.

5. Proper supervision of on-the-job training with adequate training facilities.

6. Periodic evaluation of the apprentice's progress in both job performance and related knowledge—and maintenance of adequate records.

7. Employer-employee cooperation.

8. Recognition for successful completion.

9. The selection of qualified men and women for apprenticeship without regard to race, color, creed, national origin, or physical handicap.

Successful programs are usually operated and administered by joint apprenticeship committees composed of equal representation of management and labor when the workers are organized, and otherwise by management alone. The joint committee formulates the program, often helps select the apprentices, and sees that the objectives of the program are carried out. Job experience is obtained under journeyman supervision and related training is usually received in evening vocational classes in local schools. A number of correspondence schools will also provide the related training required by the Bureau of Apprenticeship and Training. (See note to *Self-Improvement— 2. Correspondence Schools.*)

Note Numerous publications are available from the Bureau of Apprenticeship and Training, U.S. Department of Labor, Washington 25, D.C. Specifically recommended are *The National Apprenticeship Program* and *Apprenticeship for Me?*

Related Entries *See listing under Development of Subordinates—1. Development-Appraisal-Development.*

ARBITRATION

More than 4,000 times every year, labor unions and company managements, invoking the labor arbitration clauses in their contracts, ask the American Arbitration Association to set in motion the machinery of its Voluntary Labor Arbitration Rules for the resolution of grievances. No law or government agency compels these parties to use AAA facilities. They do so voluntarily. Approximately 95 per cent of the collective bargaining agreements in existence contain arbitration clauses.

Definition: Arbitration is the reference of a dispute, by voluntary agreement of the parties, to an impartial person for determination on the basis of evidence and argument presented by such parties, who agree in advance to accept the decision of the arbitrator as final and binding.

In referring a matter to arbitration, the parties are presumed to have explored every avenue of negotiation and compromise. As a last resort, they call upon an impartial person for a *judicial* decision and agree to abide by the result.

The American Arbitration Association was founded as a nonprofit organization in 1926 "to foster the study of arbitration in all its aspects, to perfect its techniques and procedures under law, and to advance generally the science of arbitration." It is privately organized and financed and is nonpartisan and nonpolitical. For its arbitration tribunals, the Association maintains a National Panel of Arbitrators in more than 1,700 cities. The panel includes some 14,000 men and women, experts in all trades and professions as well as specialists in labor-management relations. (The fees of the arbitrators, agreed to in advance, are paid by the parties in the dispute.)

Throughout the years, the arbitration tribunals have heard foremen and supervisors as witnesses and have viewed them as people who establish precedents in areas not covered by contract. Attorneys and personnel directors recognize that a case can be won or lost by supervisors' practices and testimony; arbitrators' decisions also reflect the role of the supervisor in a large variety of cases. Obviously where there is an arbitration clause, the supervisors should inform themselves about the arbitration process. As representatives of management, they should be constantly aware that their activity under the labor contract, their interpretations of the contract, and even practices that in a sense are unwritten supplements to the contract, may be brought up for review by an arbitrator. Supervisors should be familiar with the entire process by which cases reach arbitration—not merely their part in the grievance procedure. The foreman is likely to be involved in many of the procedures.

Points of Procedure

Labor-management disputes are brought to arbitration in one of two ways: (1) by a *submission agreement*, which describes an existing controversy which *both* parties want settled by an impartial person, or (2) by a *demand for arbitration*, which is filed by *either* party to a contract containing an arbitration clause.

Either party may file a submission agreement with an office of the Association, provided it is signed by *both* parties. The submission agreement must include a brief statement of the matter in dispute and the relief sought. The demand for arbitration may be initiated by either party by serving notice on the other party, with a copy of the demand forwarded to the Association. The notice of intention to arbitrate must be given in a manner and within the limits described in the collective bargaining agreement. It is usual for contracts to require that notice of arbitration be given within a certain period after the final step of grievance procedure. The demand must include a brief statement of the issue to be arbitrated and the relief sought, and is signed by the complaining party. The AAA will supply demand and submission forms on request, but in the absence of forms, parties may initiate arbitration through ordinary letters.

On receiving the demand for arbitration, the Association will invite the "responding" party to file an answering statement within seven days. The demand and the reply are read by the arbitrator at the beginning of the hearing. They guide him in receiving and giving weight to testimony, and form the framework within which he will make his award.

The Supervisor's Role

An arbitrator's award is final and binding upon all parties. The supervisor should know more than the terms of the award. He should make it his business to know what attitude to adopt toward it. Often, if the company has won, the supervisor considers this a justification of his actions, and is naturally proud of it. But his behavior should not be such that even though management has won the decision it loses ground generally in its labor relations. *"This is no time for boasting of victory or rubbing salt into the wound,"* says AAA's Vice-President Joseph S. Murphy. "It is the time to accept the victory, making every effort to hurt as few people's feelings as possible. If the decision is adverse, it is equally important to accept it in good faith and with good sportsmanship."

What should the supervisor know specifically when he becomes a witness? Here are some pointers by Mr. Murphy:

1. Have an understanding of the entire case and your part in it. You should realize the importance of your testimony.

2. Be calm and objective, and testify only on those matters of which you have first-hand knowledge.

3. When asked to testify to the ability or incompetence of a person, be prepared to state the facts on which you base your judgment. The personal judgment of the supervisor is certainly admissible as evidence, but it is most effective when it is supported by specific facts or details.

4. Be prepared for cross-examination, and don't be intimidated by the occasionally belligerent tone of the cross-examiner. Avoid getting into an argument with the other side.

5. Remember that you must return to work with the men against whom you may be testifying. Therefore try always to give the impression of being fair, honest, and without prejudice against the man bringing the grievance, or against others in the department.

6. Since the supervisor himself may be a participant in the events leading to a grievance, he should be conscious that his actions are subject to review. He should act in a straightforward, honest manner, and do his job

without prejudice or favoritism. He should make notations in a logbook or diary of situations that may lead to later grievances. Whenever a supervisor deviates in any way from company policy or the collective-bargaining agreement, and whenever he makes a decision where there is no governing rule or contract provision, his actions tend to create a precedent. The exception should be clearly noted in his records, with clear reasons for the deviation.

Related Entries *National Labor Relations Act; Mediation and Conciliation Services.*

AUTOMATION

The push-button factory with no employees in sight is far from just around the corner. However, the personnel effects of automation as it is already unfolding are causing understandable concern. As a result of developments and refinements in traditional forms of mechanization and controls, and the availability of small-scale computers and tape-operated machine tools and other equipment, piecemeal automation is already under way in many companies, and is rapidly extending downward into smaller factories and offices.

Fortunately, the earlier fears of really catastrophic *overall* displacement of workers by automation (or mechanization—let's not argue over terms) have not been realized, although there have of course been serious individual and local hardships. The lack of immediate and widespread consequences has been due to a number of factors:

First, automation has been proceeding on a staggered basis: Workers displaced in one company could be placed elsewhere.

Second, while the country has experienced some business setbacks, the period since World War II has by and large been one of expanding business, and individual companies could absorb displaced workers in their own increased activities. This absorption has been aided by the rather long time span, sometimes eighteen months to two years, involved in any considerable factory or office automation program.

Third, in any given company the usual attrition or quit rate has worked along with the time span required by automation to lighten the burden of adjustment.

Finally, many companies have in recent years greatly stepped up their expenditures on research and development, so that innovations leading to new products and services and diversification of operations have created new job opportunities.

But there's another side to the picture. There is a persistent, nagging unemployment, and if there should be a business recession, the present absorption of personnel released from former tasks will cease, and the hard core of jobless will swell.

In addition, the growth of automation in office operations, and in service fields (e.g., automatic vending devices, automation in library information storage and retrieval, handling of plane reservations, etc.) has cut down opportunities in white-collar fields which heretofore soaked up a lot of people who were released as manufacturing and process industries automated.

Finally, of course, there is the hidden disemployment created by *invisible* layoffs—i.e., people not actually laid off, but rather not hired at all as a result of increased productivity of equipment and processes.

What does it all add up to for the foreman or supervisor? Obviously he won't have much of a voice in the basic management decision on investment in automation (piecemeal or otherwise). Fortunately in many companies he will have the benefit of an enlightened management, engaged on long-range planning designed to soften the repercussions of an automation program. Such planning will include employee and public relations programs to condition the workforce and community to change; retraining programs; placement of affected employees in jobs outside the company; severance pay and consideration of seniority and other factors in laying off workers; and accelerated retirement programs. Also, of course, in many companies agreements with unions on these points will come into play.

As to the supervisor's own job, automation for the most part adds emphasis to traditional supervisory responsibilities. Thus:

1. *Greater cooperaton with staff personnel.* This will be especially true during the conversion period, when analysts and systems planners will be developing integrated systems affecting all departments.

2. *Getting the day's work done and keeping costs down.* Highly automated equipment and processes will largely set their own pace, but the costs of delays and inadvertent stoppages may be severe. Such stoppages may be due to poor planning by the supervisor, and in a highly integrated system will have much more widespread effect than formerly. In addition, operators will be working with extremely expensive equipment, increasing the supervisor's responsibility to prevent costly damage by improper or careless operation.

3. *Responsibility for quality will increase rather than diminish.* Machine settings and control charts indicating

tool wear or other departures from optimum (see *Statistical Quality Control*) must be carefully watched. In many office departments, where the output will have to be in a form ready for entering into computer processing, special vigilance in prior editing for accuracy and proper form will have to be increased.

4. Personnel problems will not diminish and may well increase. For many levels of increasing mechanization, until almost the last stages of automation, the importance of vigilance on safety will increase. As to the general "people problems," studies have indicated that even in highly automated plants the supervisor may have to give more attention to the human factors of dealing with subordinates, because of the very fact that the work itself will be becoming more and more impersonal. He will have to redouble his efforts to get people to work well together, motivating them to do the best they can, giving recognition for conscientious attention to duties, and the like.

Here are some special check points for the supervisor:

1. Make an "automation implications" survey of your own. What information is available from relevant staff departments? Will your department be directly affected, or will your main function rather be to feed into or take output from other operations which have been automated?

2. Make a systematic "personnel audit" of your department. This in any event is a sound management practice. (See *Personnel Audit.*) How do your people classify in terms of skill and mental alertness? What is the normal attrition rate?

3. Be more selective in recruitment and transfers. Even in companies with highly functionalized personnel services, the supervisor usually has some voice in the selection process for his own department. In sizing up applicants, keep the factors of alertness and adaptability to change in mind.

4. *Keep the rumor mills from working overtime.* This will call for skills of communication. While it is up to top management to initiate the proper policy of keeping its organization informed on its automation plans, as a supervisor you will have to be a reliable transmission belt for information. (See *Rumors.*)

Related Entries *Appraising Subordinates—3. "Best versus Poorest"; Communicating—2. Answering the "Unanswerable"; Personnel Audit; Rumors; Staff Units—How to Work with Them Effectively; Statistical Quality Control; Training —1. An Audit of Needs.*

BACK TALK

How are you as a supervisor supposed to handle "back talk"? You're torn between two fires—on the one hand, if you countenance no expression of disagreement or criticism from subordinates, you are in danger of being accused of not having an "open mind," or of being supersensitive to implied criticism. On the other hand, there is the obvious problem of having to maintain discipline.

We're using "back talk" here as a sort of shorthand. The term, of course, essentially connotes flippancy and disrespect, but let's consider the broader question of any sort of objection by a subordinate to an order or instruction or suggestion by a supervisor. The human instinct is for you to resent the lack of compliance—perhaps even to flare up with some sharp back talk of your own. But as a "count-ten" procedure, let's step back and see what pointers you should "tape" and store in the back of your mind for a rapid run-through when a situation like this arises:

1. If the employee's comeback is *flippant or hostile*, you have an immediate disciplinary problem on your hands. You have to handle the situation in a way that leaves no question as to your authority. Two broad types of situations will obtain:

   a. *The employee is young* and perhaps relatively new in a work situation. Here you will be doing him a service by putting him in his place firmly and not too gently. Cut him short at once, with a "Do it this way—and watch your language," or "That's enough of that." When the time is appropriate, seek him out later (but not too much later) to discuss problems of departmental discipline, the need to adjust to the work environment, etc. Most people, later in life, will remember with gratitude the "tough" supervisors they had when they started out.

b. *The employee is an older worker*—perhaps even a number of years older than you. Here, biting your tongue will invariably pay off. In any event, there is not the justification of training a youngster by an immediate tough-talk response. A good response is: "I'm sorry you feel that way, but—." Then insist upon the original request, but, depending upon the urgency of action required and the importance of the episode in general, take some time out then and there to talk over whys and wherefores, or invite the employee to see you at a specified time. Handling from there on will depend upon your analysis of the personal background and relationships involved.

2. If the employee's objection seems sincere and not in any sense flippant, disrespectful, or hostile, ask yourself:

a. Is there something to this idea? Would it hurt anything to delay long enough to think about it?

b. Am I reacting negatively simply because I'm resenting some implied criticism?

c. If the objection is obviously impractical, how can I turn it down without seeming curt? How about "That's a good idea, but—"? Or "Maybe we should do it that way next time, but—"?

    d. Can the reasons for insistence be spelled out now, or should I indicate that I'll be back for some further talk about the matter?

    e. Should I arrange to have some further explanation by a key person in the department?

    3. Training and development is a continuing process, with older as well as new employees. Therefore, if an objection to your instruction as to how something should be done is raised by an older employee, remember the points made in the entry, *Oversupervision*. A good habit here (even to the extent of countenancing some mistakes for the sake of development) is to say: "All right, do it *your* way—but remember that *you* are going to be held responsible for results," and let him proceed on his own. (You may both learn something that way!)

Related Entries   *Age—The Young Supervisor; Criticism—2. How to Take It; Discipline—1. Day-by-Day Discipline; Reprimands.*

THE BOLD EMPLOYEE

This type of worker can be your "best man or your worst headache," says the Trans World Airlines' *Supervisor's Handbook*. It depends on how you match your firmness against his boldness. Note:

    1. He's usually most responsive to the request-type of order rather than the direct order.

    2. Watch out for rashness, ill-considered action, carelessness, and tactlessness on his part, and their effects on the team.

    3. Be low-pressure in your dealings with him. He's apt to overrespond.

    4. Reprimand him quietly. Be businesslike, matter-of-fact. Watch *your* temper. Avoid argument; always give

him a chance to save face. He may be the kind who thinks he just has to have the last word. Try ending with finality; turn and walk away.

5. He can be kidded—but in a man-to-man fashion. Appeals should be directed to his good sense.

6. Give him adequate work and responsibility. He can be a bad case of idle hands.

7. He's a good man to lead off a change, but watch his methods closely.

8. Handle his complaints with speed.

9. Never flatter; don't overpraise.

10. Help him plan. Lack of planning is usually his big weakness.

11. Don't go out of your way to ask his opinion unless you have very real need of it.

Related Entry *The Eager Beaver.*

BOTTLENECKS

Is your department getting the reputation of being a bottleneck? Is the backlog of work piling up? Have you been on the carpet recently because of hold-ups? Maybe an overall review of the departmental operations is in order. Here are things to watch out for (taken from the Veterans Administration's book of instructions on work simplification):

1. *See what activities take the most time.* Are these the ones that *should* take the most time?

2. *See if there is misdirected effort.* Too much time on relatively unimportant things is "misdirected effort."

3. *See if skills are used properly.* Is everyone doing what he can do best? It is wasteful to have employees working below or above their abilities.

4. See if there are too many unrelated tasks. Unrelated tasks mean waste motion. Few people can do everything well.

5. See if tasks are spread too thinly. Can one person do several related tasks more efficiently?

6. See if work is distributed evenly. Is there too much work on one employee and not enough on another?

7. Look at the details. Question and challenge every part of every job:

a. What is done? (*Why* is it done? Can it be eliminated?)

b. Where is it done? (*Why* is it done there?)

c. When is it done? (*Why* is it done then? Should it be combined with another operation?)

d. Who does it? (*Why* does that person do it?)

e. How is it done? (*Why* is it done that way?)

So much for causes lying in your department. Now how about turning the spotlight on yourself:

1. What is your record in planning for fluctuating workloads? Is the overtime record of your department out of line?

2. Do you work out definite deadlines by which designated phases of work are to be completed?

3. Do you have control points and measures by which you can "take readings" at specified intervals?

4. Have you trained people to permit adequate functioning when there are unexpected absences?

5. Do you remove unusual problems from the regular flow of work and set up special procedures for follow-up?

6. Have you trained a competent understudy?

Related Entries *Planning and Control Boards; Planning and Scheduling—1. Progress Charts; Planning and Scheduling—2.*

"Critical Path" and Other Network Plans; Workload Fore-casting.

BRAINSTORMING

Some departments, as in technical research, sales pro-motion, or advertising, are definitely in the business of constantly coming up with new ideas. But practically every department can stand some organized skull practice on ways of cutting costs or improving operations. So whether or not your department is classified as a "creative" one, you can probably profit from some applied "brain-storming."

The brainstorming method was developed by Alex Osborn and is described in his book *Applied Imagination.* In brainstorming sessions, a group, usually five to twelve in number, actively sparkplugs ideas for a period, say an hour, under the leadership of a chairman (who could be you). The chairman announces the problem as succinctly as possible—maybe the need for a name for a new product, or a slogan, or new uses for an old product, or how to simplify the product design without hurting its effectiveness. The group then is asked to come up with all possible ideas, adhering to the following ground rules:

1. Criticism of any idea advanced is absolutely barred.

2. But modification of an idea or combination with another idea is encouraged.

3. Quantity of ideas is sought—the more, the merrier.

4. Unusual, remote, or "wild" ideas are sought. (Wild ideas, of course are useful because they open up new directions for exploration.)

If you're chairman of a brainstorming session, be sure to enforce the rule to bar criticism; don't allow high-pressure "selling" of an idea. The ideas themselves are what are wanted—they'll be analyzed and evaluated later. Welcome *all* contributions, especially "hitch-hikes" on others' ideas; strive for quantity of ideas; and close the session when fatigue begins to show.

Related Entries　*Methods Improvement—1. The Questioning Attitude; Suggestions—1. Tapping the "Latent Resources"; Suggestions—2. Helping Make the Company Suggestion System Work; Work Simplification.*

BRIEFINGS AND PRESENTATIONS

A department head will have occasion to make presentations or conduct briefings of executive committees or other management groups. Do your presentations often miss the target? When you aim your ideas at an audience, do you have the uncomfortable feeling that they're missing the mark?

The following pointers are culled from guidance directives issued by the Department of the Navy on the art and technique of staging briefings and presentations. They should be of direct usefulness to any executive or staff personnel, in government and out:

1. *Your purpose.* Are you providing information. . . . a need for action. . . . a plan of action. . . . or seeking to inspire confidence in or support for an opinion. . . . or what? Adverse audience reaction may well result from neglecting to pinpoint precisely the specific decision, intention, thought, or mood you are seeking.

2. *Your audience.* "To whom am I making the presentation?" The answer to this question will give a clue to the kind of thinking represented by the listeners. . . . Are they at a high enough level to make decisions. . . . What language do they speak: technical. . . . business

. . . . man-in-the-street?. . . . Are there leaders who will sway the rest?. . . . Are they likely to be biased (pro or con)? Some of the human traits in your audience may be:

Vanity: Fear that somebody else might get credit or authority.

Timidity: The "let's not stick our necks out" type of thinking.

Pride: Unwillingness to admit need for improvement.

Prejudice: Unwillingness to see another viewpoint.

Ignorance: Lack of basic understanding of the subject under discussion.

It is obvious that an approach must be calculated to counter subjective reaction. Consider questions such as: Will my listeners be sympathetic and friendly, or unsympathetic and even hostile?. . . . Will there be opposition?. . . . Will there be debate?. . . . Does anyone's face need to be saved?. . . . Is my department on the spot for any reason?

3. Your facts. What does this audience need to know in order to reach a decision? Your responsibility is to save *their* time by speeding up the process of conveying needed information to them more clearly, more effectively, and more rapidly than by other means.

The greatest service your presentation can render is to screen out from a mass of statistical material or other data those things which are significant. Note that the *documentation* on which a presentation is based and the *visual material presented* are measured by entirely different yardsticks: Documentation must be complete, detailed, and accurate. A presentation, on the other hand, must distill out the significant facts and interpret their meaning.

No group can absorb a great many points at a single sitting. Therefore a clear and effective presentation must stick to related high spots. Management action almost invariably revolves around relatively simple relationships of *size,* of *distance,* of *time,* of *cost,* or of *movement.* The prime function of a presentation, say our Navy directives, is to marshal the facts in such a way as to establish and clarify these relationships.

No matter how complex or detailed the interrelated basic information may be, before decisions are made, the essentials of the situation must be isolated and reduced to simple terms. "Get there fustest with the mostest" is a Civil War classic. Another is Sir Winston Churchill's famous phrase, "too little and too late!" Note that in neither case were numbers mentioned, nor dates. . . . *Size* is nearly always considered in terms of "too big," "not big enough," or perhaps "just right"—and this applies not alone to navies, but just as well to inventories, sales, markets, factories, organizations. . . . Figures on *distance* must be interpreted in terms such as "nearer than," "within reach," "too far," or some other relative term expressing the significance of the basic figures. . . . *Time* must be interpreted as "on time," "not enough time," "ahead of schedule," "much too late.". . . *Cost* must be dealt with in such terms as "too expensive," "higher than," and "lowest estimate."

Management must think in terms of such basic relationships. Therefore, your translation into relationships must precede action. A good presentation takes over a large share of the function of translation of data into significant relationships.

4. *Your parade of points.* Your final question must be, "What is the logical order for presenting the facts?"

Whether the answer is difficult or easy will depend largely on the care exercised in the preceding step of reducing the data to a minimum and translating them into meaningful relationships. The points you have selected as the irreducible minimum to achieve the purpose of your presentation must be set down so that they follow in exactly the right order. To produce the desired end result, your presentation must be interconnected, and the tie that binds is the thread of logic.

Related Entries *Business Conferences: Communicating—1. Selling Ideas; Public Speaking—When the Supervisor Has to Make a Speech; Visual and Audio Aids.*

BUDGETS

Practically any company of any size today operates under some form of budget system. Details and degrees of refinement will differ, but the basic objective is the same—to develop a blueprint for a specific period ahead, in terms of dollars, so that management will be sure to have enough money on hand to meet its bills as they come up, and so that it will be able to estimate profits or anticipate losses.

In this form of control, the foremen and supervisors of all departments have a twofold responsibility: (1) to cooperate with those concerned with budget preparation to arrive at realistic estimates of needs for individual departments; and (2) to adhere as closely as possible to those elements of expenditures over which they have some control, or to call their superior's attention as soon as possible to any condition which will make "actuals" depart from "budgeted."

The entry, *Overhead,* discusses some basic concepts of

budgeting, and should be read in conjunction with the present entry. It can be seen that in addition to developing the items of overhead expense discussed there, it is a simple additional computational job for the budget setters to add budgeted figures for direct labor and direct materials required for the year's estimated production.

Flexible budgeting is the name given to the process of developing detailed cost and budget figures for various levels of production. As explained in the entry on overhead, some costs, such as taxes, depreciation, major supervision, and executive payroll, remain fixed for widely varying levels of activity. Others will vary with output. The supervisor has a definite stake in the budgeted costs for his department established for various levels of production, since they will form the bench mark against which his operations will be judged. Hence his need to understand the system, to ask questions about specific items if he doesn't agree with them, and to give correct estimates of his requirements when the figures are being prepared.

Depending upon the practice in his company, a supervisor will receive some sort of report, once a month or perhaps more frequently, showing how costs under his control compare with budgeted figures. If the company is using a flexible budget system, he may receive a report with budget allowances specified for the level of activity at which his department worked during the period covered. This provides a more refined breakdown of the "variances" for specific items of cost for which he is responsible. If the report is not based on a flexible budget, it may simply show actuals against whatever was budgeted for that month, as determined by the budget or cost department on estimates for the whole year, broken down

EXHIBIT B-1 *Flexible Budget, Department 15*

Items	Activity								
	80%	85%	90%	95%	Normal 100%	105%	110%	115%	120%
Standard productive hours	40,000	42,500	45,000	47,500	50,000	52,500	55,000	57,500	60,000
Direct labor allowance	$60,000	$63,750	$67,500	$71,250	$75,000	$78,750	$82,500	$86,250	$90,000
Direct overhead:									
Chief foreman's salary	$ 625	$ 625	$ 625	$ 625	$ 625	$ 625	$ 625	$ 625	$ 625
Assistant foremen's salaries	900	900	1,350	1,350	1,350	1,350	1,350	1,800	1,800
Indirect labor	6,300	6,775	7,050	7,500	7,700	7,950	8,450	8,800	9,000
Spoiled work	2,500	2,650	3,060	3,600	4,100	4,700	5,600	6,600	7,650
Perishable tools	750	800	1,000	1,300	1,600	2,000	2,500	3,100	3,900
Manufacturing supplies	2,040	2,160	2,280	2,400	2,520	2,640	2,760	2,880	3,000
Power	1,600	1,630	1,660	1,690	1,720	1,750	1,780	1,810	1,840
Total direct overhead	$14,715	$15,540	$17,025	$18,465	$19,615	$21,015	$23,065	$25,615	$27,815
Total budget	$74,715	$79,290	$84,525	$89,715	$94,615	$99,765	$105,565	$111,865	$117,815

by months, weighted for known seasonal differences in activity level, etc.

Whether the reports he receives are based on a flexible or static budget, the supervisor's responsibility is the same: he must be in a position to give a reasonable explanation for any significant variance between what was budgeted and what actually happened. Under a flexible-budget system his job of explaining may be a bit tougher, because the yardstick is more refined.

The accompanying exhibits show how such a system can work. Exhibit B-1 is the department's flexible budget as worked up by the cost analysts in cooperation with the supervisor of the department involved. Note that output is stated in terms of various levels of standard hours' worth of production (see *Time Standards*) at five percentage-point intervals above and below an established "normal" set at 100 per cent, in this case 50,000 standard hours. These hours are translated into dollars for direct labor. For each of the levels of production, overhead expenses are computed (i.e., those overhead factors over which the foreman has control).

For the months that follow, the foreman receives a report of budget against actual. One is shown in Exhibit B-2. Here standard hours originally budgeted were 50,000. However, more work went through the department than budgeted, namely 55,000 standard hours' worth of work, or 110 per cent of normal. All budget allowances for the month are therefore taken from the column for 110 per cent in Exhibit B-1. (Note: We chose 110 per cent to make our explanation easier. If the amount produced had been, say, 107 per cent, the department issuing the report would have adjusted variable entries by "interpolating," i.e., adding to figures for the 105 per cent column two-fifths

EXHIBIT B-2 *Operating Report, Department 15*

Current month: March			Items		Year to date
		50,000	Budgeted standard productive hours		158,400
		55,000	Accounted standard productive hours		166,320
		110%	Department activity		105%
Variance for month	Actual	Current allowance	Account		Variance
			No.	Name	
($1,270)	$ 83,770	$ 82,500	7.1	Direct labor	($1,538)
				Direct overhead:	
	625	625	8.1	Chief foreman's salary	
	1,350	1,350	8.2	Assistant foremen's salaries	(100)
(452)	8,902	8,450	8.3	Indirect labor	(1,064)
(410)	6,010	5,600	8.4	Spoiled work	(1,308)
52	2,448	2,500	8.5	Perishable tools	(250)
656	2,104	2,760	8.6	Manufacturing supplies	564
110	1,670	1,780	8.7	Power	450
($44)	$ 23,109	$ 23,065		Total overhead	($1,708)
($1,314)	$106,879	$105,565		Total department	($3,246)

Remarks

( ) = unfavorable

of the difference between those figures and the ones for the 110 per cent column.)

With this report in hand, the foreman or department head will be able to give his views and explanations concerning variances. Thus increased spoiled work may be

due to inferior materials added in prior departments. . . .
Why was more direct labor used than budgeted? Perhaps
somebody in the department was producing below
standard. Why? Or were there absences in the department, so that certain production lines were thrown out
of balance, making it impossible to meet standards?

Care must be taken to see that budgetary enforcement
procedures are not applied in such a manner as to secure
the attainment of short-term departmental objectives to
the detriment of the welfare of the company as a whole.
Meeting departmental expense budgets is little consola-
tion for the shipping of shoddy merchandise and the
consequent loss of customers.

BUSINESS CONFERENCES

Are you using business-conference techniques effectively?
Here we are talking about business conferences used in
day-to-day operations, not to be confused with the "conference method" often used as a technique in supervisory
and executive development. (See *Supervisory Training
Conferences.*) Admittedly, conferences and meetings can
become flagrant time wasters—but guided group thinking
can also be an extremely effective management tool, and
every executive, from supervisor on up, should learn how
to use it properly.

First of all, it will be well to define the term. A *business
conference* is a meeting whose purpose is the joint consideration of a common problem or set of problems by
persons qualified to have an opinion on one or more
phases of the subject. Note the phrase, "qualified to have
an opinion." *Everyone asked to a business conference
should be qualified by background, training, or seasoned
judgment to make a contribution.*

Pitfalls

Don't try to apply conference techniques where they shouldn't be used. A conference can't "do" anything: It can only *analyze, formulate,* and *recommend.* It's no substitute for executive action. Think about the "why" of a conference before you call it. Trying to apply conference techniques to a meeting which is actually for presentation may be a time waster and, more important, may lead to fuzzy results. A "conference" where a forthright statement of policy or line of action is called for may end up by a group's "yessing" something which will be violated in practice. . . . Finally, wasted time and positive damage may result from failure to follow up on a conference: If there's no explicit fixing of who is to do what, the whole matter at issue can peter out in a haze of "what's everybody's business is nobody's business."

When to Use Conferences

There are seven basic situations where conferences, if properly managed, are effective:

1. *Developing a policy or plan of action.* No one present is opposed to any major premise or intention. All are bringing specialized talents to bear on a common set of data to hammer out a policy or plan.

2. *Analyzing data.* This is usually contained in (1), but often analysis and interpretation are so important that they become a separate end in themselves.

3. *Developing an understanding of a policy or plan.* Here questions and discussion are elicited, but the plan is given as something already established. However, suggestions for changes are not ruled out.

4. *Reconciling conflicting views or interests.* As a leader of the conference, you are the umpire drawing up

a final recommendation or referring unalterable differences to higher authority.

5. *Coordinating an activity.* These are usually run by a staff man. Regularly held meetings under his leadership can keep the wheels of a specific project turning; adequately prepared minutes will keep everybody informed.

6. *Creative thinking.* These can be "brainstorming" sessions, where all ideas no matter how farfetched are brought out and batted around.

7. *Periodic review of operations.* These are the familiar regularly scheduled get-togethers of a department head with his key people to coordinate the forthcoming period's work.

Preparation and Techniques

1. *Frequency, duration, facilities.* Err on the side of using conferences too sparingly rather than too frequently. . . . Where the objective is coordination, it is usually better to schedule conferences at fixed intervals; for regular review of operations, the meetings definitely should be regularly scheduled. . . . Conferences should not exceed reasonable time limits, but they shouldn't be brief for briefness' sake. . . . End creative conferences when everyone is still in high gear. . . . Obviously, *begin promptly.* Obviously, physical facilities should be conducive to good discussion —and be convenient to reach by all.

2. *Protocol.* Be sure everyone has met everyone else and knows not only people's names, but also their connections. . . . Give reasonable advance notice. . . . If you invite a subordinate from some other department, be sure to clear with his department head first, giving specific information on purpose and probable duration.

3. *Preparation.* If research should be done ahead of

time, who should do it? Should there be advance distribution of data to participants?. . . . Should you have informa-
tive or preparatory discussions with certain key people?
. . . . Draw up, at least for your own use, a list of specific
points to be covered, and try to estimate the time to be
allowed for each point. (If an agenda is to be distributed,
it should be no more than a bare outline, since distributed
papers distract attention.)

4. Differences of opinion. Avoid stifling of discussion
when you disagree with a statement. . . . Phrasing as a
question takes away some of the bluntness: "But don't
you think that . . . ?" "On the other hand, isn't it true
that . . . ?" Prefacing disagreement with some such
phrase as, "However, I think it's possible to look at it this
way . . ." also helps avoid antagonism. Throwing an opposite opinion out to the group is often a good device:
"But doesn't anyone here think that . . . ?" Be sure
to let everyone know just how you intend to record sharp
differences of opinion. . . . Finally, be alert to the problems of "saving face." Criticisms should be of ideas and
methods, and not directed at individuals. (See note to
entry, *Age—The Young Supervisor.*)

Evaluation

It's a good idea, after every conference, to attempt an
evaluation (even if it is only a mental review), judging
objectively its general excellence or failings. Where possible, sound out some of the key participants to see
whether they are favorably disposed, basically, toward
spending the time required by the type of conference
just concluded. Here are nine specific evaluation check
points.

1. Were the right kind of persons present?

2. Were the physical facilities adequate?

3. Were most of the proposed points on your list covered?

4. Was participation in the discussion generally good?

5. Was any individual unfairly squelched?

6. Were there any breaches in the rules of protocol?

7. Where the conference decided that something had to be done, were the *what, who,* and *when* explicitly covered?

8. Did you, or someone you designated, make an adequate statement in summary?

9. Is there a good set of notes for adequate minutes?

Notes What are the hallmarks of a good business-conference leader? Observation of hundreds of successful managers confirms that an effective leader should have: (1) *an analytical mind:* to break the conference problem down into logical and manageable pieces and keep the discussion on the right track. . . . (2) *a quick mind:* to handle fast balls, especially if his objective is to reconcile conflicting views. . . . (3) *a sense of tact:* to elicit or cut off discussion gracefully. . . . (4) *a sense of humor:* to smooth things over with a joke or a josh if differences of opinion get edgy or verge into personalities. . . . (5) *a sense of timing:* to judge when tabling something will help in getting ultimate agreement; to keep things moving; to end a conference when there's nothing to be gained by more talk. . . . (6) *an open mind:* else why have a conference in the first place?

For a Robert's-Rules-of-Order type of guide on this subject, see *Standard Business-Conference Technique,* by Carl Heyel, Funk & Wagnalls Company, New York, 1948—also published as a special report by Motivation, Inc., Springdale, Conn.

Related Entries *Brainstorming; Briefings and Presentations; Communicating—1. Selling Ideas; Staff Meetings; Supervisory Training Conferences.*

C

CAR POOLS

Car pools are a pernicious contributor to the "early leavers" problem (see separate entry), making some people leave on the stroke of quitting time, come weal, come woe.

A commonsense policy should be adopted: In many locations car pools are necessities, and the supervisor must bend over backwards with respect to rank-and-file employees. However, it should be understood that with respect to all *key personnel* and all who have been promoted to supervisory responsibility, membership in a car pool will not be acceptable as an excuse to leave an important matter unfinished. . . . The rationale is simple: An employee promoted to a key position is undoubtedly being paid enough to be able to provide transportation to the scene of employment. . . . If for personal reasons he chooses to live in some remote area, then it is up to him not to let that interfere with all of the necessary attention his job requires. One proviso in his living thus remotely should be that he is expected to have his own transportation.

At the first sign that car pools are becoming an evil, the alert supervisor should arrange for some heart-to-heart talks with the offenders.

Related Entry   *Early Leavers.*

THE CARELESS WORKER

Everybody is careless from time to time. But here we are dealing with *habitual* carelessness. The causes of carelessness, as pointed out in the Trans World Airlines' *Supervisor's Handbook*, may be: (a) distraction—always thinking of something else; or (b) plain lack of interest. Here are points to consider about the habitual offender:

1. If the worker is disinterested, you may have to give him more responsibility to arouse interest in the job. If that fails, you may have to reassign him.

2. If he's the distracted type, avoid assignment to hazardous work, especially where the safety of others is involved.

3. He's not good on details. His work needs more than usual inspection.

4. When you talk to him, be sure you have his attention and hold it. Check his understanding of instructions carefully.

5. Be firm. Give clear, direct, detailed orders.

6. Such a worker is always a maintenance problem. Keep an eye on his equipment. Check his handling of the job from time to time.

Note The above is not intended to imply that carelessness is something you must accept in a worker, and adjust to it. If the worker is young and not "sot" in his ways, a tough supervisor will be the best thing that can happen to him.

Related Entry *Job Interest—How to Stimulate It.*

CHANGES

See *Resistance to Change.*

CIVIL RIGHTS

Federal Law

Title VII of the *Civil Rights Act* of 1964 regulates the employment practices of employers, labor unions, and employment agencies. The law bans discrimination because of race, color, religion, sex, or national origin in hiring, assigning, promoting, training, firing, or retiring employees. Employment agencies cannot refuse to refer, nor unions to include, any individual on the above grounds. The Act provides for the establishment of an Equal Employment Opportunity Commission to enforce these provisions.

The law covers employers in industries affecting interstate commerce with 100 or more employees working at least 20 weeks a year. Union locals with 100 members or more are also covered. From 1965 to 1970, coverage is to be extended until in the fifth year the Act will cover most employers with at least 25 employees or more.

Despite equal-pay-for-equal-work provisions, employers may apply different standards of compensation, terms, conditions, or privileges in conjunction with a bona-fide seniority or merit system. At this writing, many provisions will have to be tested in the courts; for example, whether pay differentials can be maintained for the same work in different locations within the same plant or in separately located plants within the same corporation.

Where a job can only be performed by a person of a specific religion, national origin, or sex, job recruitment can be so restricted. (As an example, Chinese restaurants can continue to hire only Chinese waiters.) However, the railroads' tradition of employing only Negroes as Pullman porters may turn out to be illegal, since neither race nor color can be construed as a qualification "reasonably necessary" in that occupation.

State Laws

Twenty-two states now have fair employment statutes, although these have not hitherto been enforced with vigor. In view of current unrest, it will behoove every supervisor to check with his personnel department to see just what the statutory provisions are in his locality.

New York State is representative of advanced practice in such legislation, and its coverage goes all the way down to employers with six or more employees. The law prohibits discrimination based on age, creed, color, or national origin in: hiring or firing . . . wages and working conditions . . . promotions . . . employment application forms . . . labor union membership . . . employment agency referrals . . . apprenticeship and other training programs.

Note Your state may have a commission on human rights or similar body. Such organizations, or your state department of labor or state employment office, will make available descriptive literature setting forth prohibited and desired practice.

COACHING

Coaching is a special form of on-the-job training and can go on as long as a senior in a department has a junior working for him—no matter at what level: A president may coach a vice-president, and a worker at a bench may coach a helper.

Coaching gives effect to one of the basic elements in education—*guided self-development*. Some do's and don'ts:

1. *Don't* be a crutch. Coaching isn't stepping in and doing the job yourself whenever the going gets tough. It's seeing to it that the junior is brought to the condition of being able to take the bit in his own mouth. So—

2. *Don't* oversupervise. (See separate entry on that.)

3. *Don't* be overly concerned about mistakes. A good man will learn more from a mistake than from hitting the nail on the head by a lucky blow. (Check the entry on mistakes—take a positive attitude, to see what can be learned from them.) But—

4. *Do* develop a "range of permissible error." That is, safeguard the junior against mistakes that can be a hazard to life or limb, to himself or others. And consider the range of dollar cost of possible errors.

5. *Do* keep an eye out for his weak points, and see what should be done to strengthen them.

6. *Do* use praise as a careful coin. (See entry on praise.)

7. *Do* taper off on detailed instructions as soon as possible. Feed responsibility, and determine as early as possible how much head you can give.

8. *Do* be sure that at all stages of his progress, the junior knows the limits of his responsibility and authority.

9. *Do* set up control check points, for a goodly time after he is on his own. *Always* have periodic appraisal and accountability sessions.

Note In bringing along a promising younger person, it's a good idea from time to time to load on just a bit more than he can take. This is perhaps one of the best incentives for *self-discovery* and *self-development* for anyone properly motivated. It is a well known technique in athletic coaching, where for example the crossbar for the high-jump is always placed a bit higher than the jumper has previously cleared. He knocks it down a few times, and then clears it—to be followed by a higher notch! And music analysts will tell you that Sousa's incomparable marches stimulate by being just a bit ahead of the heartbeat. A true teacher's offerings will be just a bit ahead of the pupil's understanding—a bit ahead, but never beyond.

Related Entries   *Learning; Mistakes; Oversupervision; Praise.*

COLLECTIONS FROM EMPLOYEES

How many times is the "bite" put on people in your department for collections—somebody's getting married, somebody died, somebody's in the hospital, somebody had a baby, it's somebody's birthday? Unless there's some attempt at control, collections can become a source of irritation and embarrassment. Whose birthday? If Joe's, why not Harry's? Birthdays come once a year, and in a largish department, there could be many collections for them. How much to give? "Give anything you like," or "We'll leave that up to you," can be worse than no help. The salary somebody makes often has no direct bearing on ability to contribute—who knows what personal drains somebody might have at home? It's a cruel choice to put someone to, to decide between a sacrifice at home, or appearing to be stingy in the office or plant.

The thing to do is to try to get some commonsense perspective and order into this situation. But hold on— don't do it by edict! This is something employee groups will be likely to consider their own affair, and will resent "high-handed" interference. So:

1. Arrive at a departmental policy through group participation. Here's a good opportunity to take advantage of the "informal leaders" (see entry under that head). Talk it over.

2. Arrange to have the employees, through some spokesman agreed upon, come back to you with a suggested set

of ground rules. Maybe birthdays are out. Maybe only funerals and babies are in. Or maybe flowers for a hospital case. Probably collections for a Christmas party are in. At any event, try to have them develop some sort of list. See what can be done to suggest ranges of amounts to contribute.

3. Have a memorandum go to everyone, or posted on the bulletin board, or have a statement drawn up for the departmental policy and procedural manual—whatever the mode of communication most effective in your department.

4. If a memorandum is used, or covers a formal statement of policy, be sure to indicate how the rules were arrived at.

COLLECTIVE BARGAINING

See *National Labor Relations Act; Union Organization.*

COMMITTEES

Unless you are head of a number of departments, the chances are that you will not be in the position of having to create numerous committees to carry on your department's work. However, it may well be that you will be asked to serve on a number of committees that have been created by your own boss or by others.

Are you, or higher management, "committee happy"? Maybe you should ask some penetrating questions, and discuss the situation with your superior. Thus:

1. How many formal committees does the major division or department of which you are a part have compared to a year ago? Two years ago?

2. How many formal committees have become inactive for all practical purposes, without ever having been officially dissolved?

3. Do you have numerous committees composed of practically the same people?

4. Are some of your committees ineffective because they are not made up of people with requisite authority?

Note   In one case, the time spent each month on developing overall production schedules was cut by 90 per cent by a change in the make-up of a committee. It had formerly been made up of the department heads and staff people who worked up the figures. As reconstituted, it comprised the top executives in sales, finance, and manufacturing, with the former members attending as expert advisers. A rule was established that when a top man could not attend, his delegate would vote for him—and the principal would have to stand by that vote. As a result, action could always be secured on the spot.

Related Entries   *Business Conferences.*

COMMUNICATING

1. Selling Ideas

What does direct mail advertising have to do with your work as a supervisor or department head (unless you happen to be working in an advertising or sales promotion department)? It has a lot to do with you, no matter what your job is, because there is a lot of good, hard, practical *communications psychology* that all of us can learn from the direct-mail experts. . . . The best communicators in the world are in the advertising business, and a good many of them are in the direct-mail end, where they've spent years perfecting ways to get their messages across to people who initially aren't especially interested in what they have to say. The D-M writers have to know how to catch their interest, and hold it, *and make them act.*

Isn't that the same problem you have with your employees, your fellow supervisors and department heads, and your superiors—whether you're instructing a newcomer, or trying to expedite something from another department, or selling a new idea upstairs?

According to the Direct Mail Advertising Association, there are a number of tried-and-true formulas and guides developed over the years to make direct-mail copy click. The essence of these formulas is given below. You'll find that they are just as applicable to internal communications as they are to a sales campaign for customers. You can start using them tomorrow—and it won't even cost you anything for postage!

A-I-D-A

This is the oldest of the formulas. AIDA means (A) attract *attention*; (I) arouse *interest*; (D) stimulate *desire*; (A) ask for *action.*

D-D-P-C

This says the message should start by being *dramatic*, continue by being *descriptive* of the product or service and by being *persuasive*, and end by *clinching* the sale.

Egner's Nine Points

The late Frank Egner, one of the nation's greatest copywriters, listed these nine points:

1. Write a lead to create desire as well as get attention.
2. Give an inspirational beginning.
3. Give a clear definition of the product.
4. Tell a success story about the use of the product.

5. Include testimonials and endorsements from satisfied customers.

6. List the special features of the product.

7. Make a statement of the value to the purchaser.

8. Devise an action closer that will make the reader want to buy immediately.

9. Conclude with P.S. rephrasing the headline.

Picture-Promise-Prove-Push

According to this precept, you start by painting a word *picture* of what the product or service will do for the reader; then *promise* that the picture will come true if the product is purchased; offer *proof* of what the product has done for others: and end with a *push* for immediate action.

Jack Lacy's Five Points

1. What will you do for me if I listen to your story?
2. How are you going to do this?
3. Who is responsible for the promises you make?
4. Whom have you done this for?
5. What will it cost me?

To the above, the Direct Mail Advertising Association has added:

6. How do I order from you?

Robert Stone's Seven Steps

1. Promise a benefit in your lead or first paragraph— *your most important benefit.*

2. Immediately *enlarge* upon this benefit.

3. Tell the reader *specifically* what he is going to get.

4. Back your statements with *proofs* and endorsements.

5. Tell the reader what he might *lose* if he does not act.

6. *Rephrase* prominent benefits in closing offer.
7. Incite action NOW.

Note "Show business" need not be confined to Broadway.
. . . One of the most effective ways to get objectives across
to employees is to dramatize them. *Examples:* A personnel
director (as recounted by Ordway Tead in his *The Art of
Leadership*) got nowhere with a mimeographed ballot in
employees' pay envelopes in an effort to secure a necessary
75 per cent vote in favor of a small pay deduction for a very
attractive group insurance plan. He then went to each department and called a meeting of employees where he showed
a blown-up copy of a check for $1,000 made to the widow
of a man who had recently died, and who had been an employee of a neighboring plant where the plan was in effect.
Result: 95 per cent in favor, at the next vote!. . . . A plant
superintendent in a radio plant had a set put together made
entirely of rejected parts, and displayed it with a sign, reading, "How would you like to buy this set at our regular $59
price???"

Related Entries *Briefings; Business Conferences; Listening;
Motivation; NO—NO—NO—How to Say No; Orders and
Instructions—1. Transmission and Reception; Orders and Instructions—2. Types of Instruction; Public Speaking—When
the Supervisor Has to Make a Speech; Suggestions—1. Tapping the "Latent Resources"; Suggestions—2. Helping Make
the Company Suggestion System Work; Visual and Audio
Aids.*

COMMUNICATING

2. Answering the "Unanswerable"

You may be stumped for an answer when some of your
people ask about something that you know the answer to,
but can't reveal for reasons of management policy: something about a new plant, or a government contract, or
shutting down an operation, or possible layoffs. Often it's
just a matter of time before the facts can be made public.

In the meanwhile, you can use the following means to parry questions, as suggested by *Supervisory Management* (American Management Association):

1. Explain why you cannot divulge the information, positively if possible. "You stand to benefit by the move, but . . ."

2. Emphasize the time factor. Set a date to reveal plans, but only make promises you can keep. If material is permanently classified, say so.

3. Acknowledge the right to ask questions, even though you know the answer must remain confidential. The holier-than-thou "You have no right to know that" attitude builds employee animosity. The "I'm glad you're interested, but in this case . . ." reply satisfies most workers.

4. Be honest. Straight answers, even those revealing nothing, are better than half-truths and lies which breed distrust.

"And," adds the publication, "you can't tell them everything." Here is how it classifies information for employees:

1. Information the employee *has to know* to do his job properly.

2. Information he *should know*, because he may be affected by the new development.

3. Information that *might be helpful* because it could increase his general knowledge of his part in attaining the goals of the company.

4. Information that the employee *should not know*: (a) when disclosure might be harmful to the company; (b) when data are covered by security regulations; (c) when management's plans are incomplete; and (d) when information must pass through channels.

Related Entries *Company Policy—When You Disagree with It; Rumors.*

COMPANY POLICY
When You Disagree with It

Management has the right to expect the performance of a very definite function by the foreman and supervisor— the proper interpretation and implementation of company policy. Most foremen and supervisors will have little to say on the determination of policy matters, although their prior opinions and suggestions may have been sought on many matters affecting personnel in general, and their department in particular. However, with respect to the policy as finally adopted, every supervisor is expected to be a salesman, to be sure employees understand it and adhere to it.

You may have heard it said that a salesman can only be successful if he is sold on his product. What about the supervisor's actions, if a policy is adopted that is contrary to his own views, and perhaps his own very emphatic recommendations to his own boss?

If a salesman thinks his product is poor, he has the option to leave the company—but if he stays on, he knows he'd better keep right on selling. He can, of course, continue to make suggestions regarding product improvement.

The same attitude must hold for the supervisor. Few policy decisions are of such world-shaking importance in your own department as to be worth making an "I'd rather quit" issue out of them. If they are, you of course have a problem of personal integrity to decide. But if you're going to go along, here are basic guidelines:

1. Be sure you have all the facts: Just exactly what has been decided?. . . . How will it affect your department,

and when?. . . . What specific lines of action are called for?
. . . . How final is the policy decision? Is this something
which management has indicated will be reviewed after a
specific time?

2. Get your lines of communications straight. If there
are further questions, just how and where are the answers
obtained?. . . . Are there to be any exceptions?. . . . Is there
a procedure for possible hardship cases?

3. Be firm in calling for adherence. If the matter has
been one of much controversy and discussion, you may
have to call your department (or at least your key men)
together, and say something like, "There's been a lot of
talk pro and con on this matter—*but the decision has
now been made*. We're going to carry on under the new
rules, and with a minimum of further palaver about it.
Maybe at some future time, the policy will be changed—
but in the meantime, let's get on with the main job." But
don't indicate that the policy is subject to review and may
be changed, unless you know for sure that that is the case.

4. Don't give an indication of half-hearted support, or
a shrug-of-the-shoulders implication that management
doesn't know what it's doing. Keep your own counsel.

5. Find out if in your department there will be any
hardship cases as a result of the policy, and arrange for
individual discussions with the persons affected.

6. If the matter is one on which your people feel very
strongly, arrange for a talk with your own superior, so that
he understands the situation. Be sure, however, to make
the point that you're going to follow through as instructed
—but that you want to be sure you're fulfilling your
obligation of upward feedback as well as down-the-line
communication.

7. After a suitable time lapse, make a follow-up ap-

praisal of the situation for yourself: Does the policy seem to be sound after all?. . . . Should you change your fundamental position?. . . . How is the general adherence in your department?. . . . Are there some still-unconvinced "washroom lawyers" who are keeping the original irritation active? Are some private talks with them indicated?

Related Entry *Policy Formulation.*

CONFERENCE TECHNIQUES

See *Business Conferences; Staff Meetings; Supervisory Training Conferences.*

CONSISTENCY

See *Self-Appraisal—What Is Your "PQ"?*

CONTROL TECHNIQUES

See *Planning and Control Boards; Planning and Scheduling.*

COOPERATION

See *Technicians and Specialists* regarding problems of cooperation with such staff or service representatives.

COORDINATION AND FOLLOW-UP

A practice generally followed in factory management is to conduct regular (usually weekly) meetings of foremen and department heads, where operating problems are brought up for discussion, misunderstandings between departments are ironed out, working schedules are assigned, etc. At such meetings, one of the most trying problems confronting the works manager, superintendent, or general foreman in charge is to keep the discussions *specific*—to nail problems down properly when they are brought up, to get at the underlying causes, and to assign definite responsibilities for solution and follow-through.

A good idea is to adopt a slogan, such as "Be Specific," and to draw up a special form for outlining a problem to bring up. The form can list six points, the first of which puts strong emphasis on the correct statement of the problem when it is first brought up. Thus:

1. *What is the problem?* Make an accurate statement of what is wrong—what it is you want to correct.

2. *What is the cause?* State your opinion as to the cause —the root of the problem, not the effect. Give all the essential facts.

3. *What is the proposed corrective program?* What must be done to eliminate the cause—be specific.

4. *Who will correct?* Propose assignments of specific responsibility to each individual.

5. *When will it be corrected?* Make as accurate an estimate as you can.

6. *Was it corrected?* Has the problem been licked? If not, the program is unfinished.

Signature————————

Now, when someone raises a question or complains about something at one of the operating meetings, he will not be permitted to take up the time of the meeting in generalized complaint or discussion. He can be handed one of the "Be Specific" forms and requested to get his problem down in writing, with as much preliminary thinking-through as possible on cause, workable corrective program, and who should do what and when. The reverse side of the form can be used for a Report of Progress, with entries initialed and dated. Thus the form, when filed, provides a ready case history of how the problem was handled.

Related Entry *Follow-up; Staff Meetings.*

CORRESPONDENCE SPEEDUP
"Correspondex"

"Correspondex" is a simplified system of letter writing developed by the Navy, offering large-volume correspondence offices these immediate benefits *without* an expensive investment in new equipment:

Consistency in replies
Better personnel utilization
Adaptability and flexibility
Increased economy of operation

A Better Letter—Overall

The principle is simple. You apply it every time you use an old letter to prepare a new one. A Correspondex is a file of preapproved and numerically indexed letters and paragraphs. Letter writers just tell typists the index numbers of the letter or paragraph to use.

Drafting and dictating time is eliminated; planning and typing time is cut. The result: a ready-made letter with a tailor-made appearance in half time!

Only a good hard look at your overall correspondence

needs can tell you whether you need Correspondex. Look for these rule-of-thumb indicators, says the Navy:

Large volume. 250 or more repetitive type letters written per week. (Note: The Navy talks in big numbers! We think Correspondex would be justified at a much lower figure.)

Low productivity. Less than 25 letters per day being written per full-time letter writer.

Inconsistencies. Different answers to the same question going out in different letters.

Related Entry *Letter Writing.*

CORRESPONDENCE SCHOOLS

See *Self-Improvement.*

COST ACCOUNTING

See *Standard Costs.*

"COST CONSCIOUSNESS" IN EMPLOYEES

Employees will often be careless or indifferent about company property. It's a good idea to remind them about the value of equipment and materials they use, so that they will take better care of them. One way to do this is to put price tags on all materials, supplies, tools, and machines. This brings home to workers the high cost of scrap, waste, misuse, and abuse.

Don't hesitate to try some "indirect punishment" on employees who are careless about equipment. It's probably not a dischargeable offense, but you can correct negligent attitudes by other means. Said one bank controller: "A woman becomes a lot more careful when she finds that if she puts her good typewriter out of commission, she's going to have to work at a second-hand one for a while—even after her good one is repaired."

A point to keep in mind: One characteristic of this day of advancing automation is that employees are operating more and more expensive equipment—some of it fantastically so, as for example, a multi-million dollar computer complex.

Related Entries *Waste*—2. *Dramatizing Avoidable Waste*; *Work Simplification*.

COST CONTROL

All sorts of staff specialists—timestudy men, methods analysts, cost engineers, cost accountants, budget analysts —are concerned with *setting* costs, developing ways of *measuring* costs, and drawing up reports showing *cost variations* from standard. But it is only the foreman or the supervisor himself who can actually *control* costs in his department. Despite all of the broad factory overhead costs that enter into the final cost of a product, and that are beyond the control of a foreman, it is still true that in a typical industrial establishment foremen are responsible for some 65 to 75 per cent of operating costs (excluding raw material).

In helping the specialists set standards, and in controlling costs against those standards, the foreman obviously can only deal with those which are directly within his jurisdiction. What are these in your department? Here are seven important outlays which *The Foreman's Handbook* lists as wholly within the foreman's bailiwick:

1. *Direct labor costs.* Often very high because of new help inadequately trained, giving slow, off-standard production. . . . or because direct labor is waiting around because of shortages of materials or parts to work on.

2. *Indirect labor costs.* Often too high as a ratio to direct labor, and usually so because of excessive handling charges.

3. *Spoiled work.* Untrained workers are the worst offenders in producing spoilage.

4. *Tool breakage.* Likewise caused in great part by new and inexperienced workers, also by too much "rush" effort.

5. *Manufacturing supplies.* One of the greatest sources of waste, and one calling for the tightest of controls, in normal times as well as when new supplies are difficult to acquire.

6. *Defective material.* This is a cost that usually goes back to the vendor; but a smart foreman will catch the defects quicker and thus save waste of labor and overhead.

7. *Power.* (Directly controllable by the foreman only if metered to his department.) This is a cost which if closely watched will show as high as a 30 per cent saving.

Related Entry *Waste—1. Reducible Waste.*

COUNSELING

See *Employee Counseling.*

CREDIT UNIONS

Credit unions are self-help cooperatives formed by employees to help solve some of their personal financial problems by making loans available at moderate interest rates. The Bureau of Federal Credit Unions estimates that one out of every 14 Americans belongs to a credit union—but there may not be one in your company. In that case, some of your employees might ask you about them, and about the possibility of establishing one, and so it will be a good idea for you to know something about them, and how you would go about forming one.

The formal definition of a credit union is that it is a cooperative corporation, chartered by a state or the Federal government, with powers basically limited to promoting thrift and extending credit to members. The field of membership is restricted to a specific group of people by the charter and bylaws. These groups must have a common bond of occupation, association, or residence in a well defined neighborhood, community, or rural district. Credit unions cannot do business with the general public, and they do not compete with each other. They are owned and controlled by their members, and each member has one vote regardless of the number of shares owned.

Each CU operates in accordance with the state or Federal law. Federal CUs are chartered, supervised, and examined by the Bureau of Federal Credit Unions, which is part of the Social Security Administration, Department of Health, Education, and Welfare. State-chartered CUs are supervised by a state agency—usually the banking department. Federal CUs are required to keep their books in accordance with forms and procedures prescribed in an accounting manual. Some states do not prescribe accounting procedures, but CUs in these states generally have adopted Federal procedures.

To obtain a charter for a Federal CU, a group must

have at least 100 persons with a common bond. Seven subscribers to the organization certificate are required. Some states issue charters to groups as small as 50, and others require a potential membership of 200 persons. Charter fees vary between states. The Federal charter costs $25.

CUs are managed by a board of directors elected annually by members. Responsibility for approving loans is placed with a credit committee, elected by the members under most laws. The credit committee is not compensated for its work. Another committee, the supervisory or audit committee, is required to make certain audits each year and report to the directors, members, and the government authority.

The principal source of funds is the regular savings of members in the form of withdrawable shares. In a few states CUs may accept deposits. Average savings in all CUs is a little over $400. Dividends on member shares in Federal CUs is limited to 6 per cent. Some states also limit dividends. Savings in CUs are not insured by any Federal agency. CUs may borrow up to certain percentages of their paid-in and unimpaired capital, as limited by bylaws and statutes.

Loans are made only to members, for "provident or productive purposes," such as education, medical bills, funeral expenses, durable goods such as appliances, and the like, not excluding vacations and other recreational expenses. Loan limitations vary from state to state, with unsecured limitations ranging from $300 to $1,000. The cost of CU borrowing is, as a rule, the lowest available to the average person from financial institutions. Interest is limited by law to 1 per cent per month on the unpaid balance, inclusive of all charges incident to making the loan. The vast majority of CUs insure the lives of borrowers for the amount of their loans at no charge to the borrower.

Reserves must be established from net earnings, before payment of dividends to shareholder members.

Note The Bureau of Federal Credit Unions, Washington 25, D.C., assists eligible groups to organize credit unions. The Credit Union National Association, 1617 Sherman Avenue, Madison, Wisconsin, publishes information and assists groups to organize.

CRITICISM

1. How to Dish It Out

You can't supervise without on occasion having to criticize—and sometimes you will have to find fault with a seasoned, valuable employee as well as with a newcomer whom you are training. Obviously no technique in criticizing will make you win popularity contests—but there are ways and ways. . . . We need not labor here the trite admonition about not pointing out somebody's weakness in the presence of others. But here are some finer points:

1. You can lead off with a remark that shows appreciation for some of the man's good points. Thus: "This job requires special care—that's why I gave it to you as one of our best men on this type of work. . . . but here's something we should be especially careful to watch out for in the future. . . ."

2. "Tell 'em when they're happy." If you have to criticize in the course of the general development of a man, point out his little weaknesses and faults at the time you give him a raise. He's definitely in a receptive frame of mind then. . . . The spurt the raise gives to his ambition will make him doubly attentive.

3. A phrase here and there to soften the blow won't

hurt your message, and will help the fellow on the receiving end: "I can see how this happened. . . ." "I'm sure that if this came up again, you'd do thus and so. . . ."

4. Don't beat a dead horse. (Enough said.)

Here are some common errors of criticism.[1] (Does the shoe fit?)

1. Blowing up as soon as an error is revealed.
2. Hoarding grievances until they become magnified beyond control.
3. Passing judgment without investigation, or on the run.
4. Focusing on the person instead of the act.
5. Exaggerating the error—for example, "You always . . ." or "You never . . ."
6. Generalizing instead of being specific. ("The whole job is botched up" offers no clue to where the mistake was made or how to correct it.)

Note One plant superintendent placed so much importance on the way his supervisors handled criticisms that he instructed them to draw up a special analysis, as shown in the accompanying exhibit, whenever a serious shortcoming had to be discussed with a worker. Using this as a guide, he said, the foreman could preface his criticism with a few good points about the worker, and then wind up with a few more good points, followed by a constructive suggestion. Here is a sample talk based on the exhibit:

"John, you're doing a good job for me around here, and I like the way you handle yourself. You're getting a good reputation as a motor winder. Lately we've been running into a number of shorts at test. I hate to see your good work going to waste. Do you suppose it's the way you slide your stators across the bench? Look into it, will you, John, and see if we can't get that percentage of good ones up?"

[1] From a listing by Benjamin Balinsky and Ruth Burger in "Don't Be Afraid to Criticize!", *Supervisory Management*, January, 1950.

EXHIBIT C-1

Preparation for Criticism	
Name John Doe	*Department* Motor Winding
GOOD POINTS	BAD POINTS
Good winder Always on time Confidence in himself Gets out production	Slides stators from one side to another, often tearing the winding, causing short when assembled into motor

Related Entries   *Criticism—2. How to Take It; Development of Subordinates—1.   Development-Appraisal-Development; Reprimands.*

CRITICISM

2. How to Take It

"They bleed—but they bleed inwardly." That is how a poet described the way most men endure criticism. Any supervisor (any executive, any person) who does anything at all is bound to run into criticism. The question is, how much bleeding—inwardly and outwardly—should he do? Even the most extrovert or "outgoing" among us resent criticism, since it is a blow to our ego. The pointers assembled below may be a collection of the obvious—but it's worthwhile to look at them in their entirety, because this is a subject we tend to grasp intellectually, and then violate emotionally.

1. *Learn to expect criticism.* President Harry Truman had a favorite motto for this: "If you can't stand the heat, get out of the kitchen." (You may have to grow an extra layer of skin!)

2. *Always consider the source.* Criticism by your superior or higher management is one thing . . . idle griping

or manifestations of jealousy by others are something else again. Resolve to react in the light of the source.

3. *Don't flare up under any circumstances.* Develop the knack of some inward bleeding. Even if the criticism is unjust, try to express gratitude for the idea. "Much of what you say may be true" is a gambit in conversation and correspondence which is at once disarming and non-committal. Then in a closed room, with the shades drawn, you can kick a chair or two and indulge in some appropriate opinions. It helps to let off steam, in order to follow points 4 and 5 below.

4. *Never ignore criticism, no matter what the source, no matter what the degree of justification.* You may ignore it as far as answering it is concerned, but don't ignore it as a subject for analysis. If it's unjustified, maybe a better job of communication is in order. And even if you consider the source unworthy, it won't hurt to think about how you can improve your "image." Think carefully about what might constructively nip further criticism in the bud, but don't fall into the trap of he "doth protest too much." (See 5, below.)

5. *Don't spend too much time explaining.* If a deep issue of morality or courage-of-conviction is involved, no one expects you to compromise your self-respect. But often the best form of an answer is proper operation and proper communication regarding future actions, which may speak louder than words and will not keep alive an unpleasantness that can otherwise be forgotten.

6. *Don't brood.* If the criticism is justified, and especially if it came from higher up, resolve to profit by it. A hurt feeling and nursing a grudge will interfere with efficiency. (See the first three pointers under *Mistakes.*) Remember the chances are that criticism by a superior is probably only one-tenth finding fault, and nine-tenths helping to improve you on this job, and readying you for a higher job.

Note Incidentally, you'll note that the foregoing, as it happens, concern criticism from people not subject to your direction or control. But how about your instinctive reaction when criticism is voiced by one of your own employees? What was your reaction the last time a subordinate disagreed with one of your opinions or orders? Would you be able to prove an assertion that you don't resent such implied criticism?

Related Entries *Backtalk; Mistakes.*

D

DEADLINES

Deadlines are part of every managerial job—whether you are running an entire plant or divisional office, or only a single department or section. The supervisor's deadline problems are of three types: (1) He must impose deadlines within his department in order to meet promises he has made outside; (2) he must accept deadlines from without; and (3) he must help establish deadlines in co-operation with planners and others who are setting up projects.

Imposing Deadlines

1. Be sure deadlines are set in full awareness of the problems of carrying them out. This means careful probing of the key people involved. Be sure you check with the *right* people.

2. It won't do any good to set time limits by "fiat" if there's no chance of meeting them. But be tough about making people back up any assertions about "impossible." Be realistic about time that will be required, but don't tolerate rubber.

3. Develop records that can be used as bench marks on similar jobs, so that guesswork is kept to a minimum.

4. Weigh alternatives and costs—time can usually be bought with money (more people, overtime, farming out,

etc.), or at the expense of inconvenience or delay on other jobs. Then make a realistic choice.

5. Set up check points and danger signals, to see how deadlines are being met. Don't live in a fool's paradise until it's too late to do anything about it.

6. Don't change deadlines lightly. Make your people realize that when deadlines are set they are meant to be kept. Be tough about causing inconvenience to subordinates to meet schedules which they themselves had a hand in establishing.

7. Don't sacrifice quality to meet a deadline, without a complete understanding with those for whom you are turning out the work or service. (There are occasions when it may be perfectly feasible to do without some gilding—but be sure it's done with everybody's eyes open.)

Accepting Deadlines

1. Don't make promises lightly. If there is a good chance that you can't live up to the proposed deadline, state the situation at the beginning. (But note "reverse English" here regarding rubber on *your* part—as per 2 above.)

2. Know special cost situations, and be sure that whoever is requesting the deadline knows what unusual cost factors may be involved.

3. Establish a reputation for keeping promises. Be sure of your facts regarding your internal departmental situation, and then make everyone in your department realize that you have a "religion" about the subject: Deadlines are sacred with you.

4. Set up check points and danger signals, as mentioned in 5, above, and be sure you alert other departments or work-requesters involved. (But keep your finger off the

panic button; exhaust every possibility of corrective action before raising alarms.)

5. Always question "Rush" deadlines and "Crash" jobs (see *Rush Jobs*).

Helping Establish Deadlines

1. Follow points 1, 3, and 4 under *Imposing Deadlines*.

2. Follow points 1, 2, and 5 under *Accepting Deadlines*.

3. Explore all practical alternatives with the planners. Be sure to determine how critical your own department's work is in the overall project completion. For example, if other, *collateral* operations are going to take three weeks, and subsequent steps cannot be undertaken until those have been completed, then there is small reason for disrupting your department's work to complete your portion in less than three weeks. (In this connection, review the reasoning used in "Critical Path" method as set forth in *Planning and Scheduling—2. "Critical Path" and Other Network Plans*.)

4. Offer realistic estimates, but be sure you and the planners for whom you are making them understand each other about "margins for error." Before you commit on a big job, take account of factors which may affect your performance and which are beyond your control.

Related Entries *"Learning Curve" in Estimating; Planning and Control Boards; Planning and Scheduling—1. Progress Charts; Planning and Scheduling—2. "Critical Path" and Other Network Plans; Rush Jobs.*

DELEGATION

How to delegate effectively is not a problem confined to high-level executives heading up large operations. Proper delegation is called for as soon as you are put into a position of having somebody reporting to you—even if you are heading up only a small department. As a matter of fact, one of the longest "first steps" that a newly created foreman has to learn is not to grab a wrench and do a job himself instead of seeing to it that somebody else does it. The same holds true in the supervision of office operations. "I'll do it myself" may be quicker in the first instance—but it's not *supervision*, and the tendency will inevitably bog down the department's work.

Of course, the problem becomes more important as you go up the ladder to bigger jobs, but it's worth thinking seriously about *now*, not only in terms of your present effectiveness, but because your ability to delegate, or the lack of it, as viewed by your superiors, may be the deciding factor in giving you heavier responsibilities.

Maybe you're not aware that you have a problem in delegation. Here are some questions on symptoms; they're worth asking, whether you're running a small section, or are heading up a 1,000-man division:

1. Are you satisfied with the amount of time you are able to devote to long-range problems, as against day-to-day operations?

2. Are important phases of your operations getting their proportionate share of your time and attention? How well are your key bases covered?

3. Are you spending too much time "putting out fires"? Are there constant emergencies that seem to demand your personal attention?

4. Do your projects suffer from repeated deadline crises —dates missed, inadequate completions? Are too many just barely getting under the wire?

5. Are you being "nibbled to death by mice"—continu-

ing irritating details or small problems that keep you from the main issues?

6. Are you bogged down with personal overtime and homework? Are you a "bulging briefcase" man?

If you have to give a significant number of unsatisfactory answers to the above, you had better take a new look at what can be delegated. For example, in reviewing your normal mode of operation, is there:

1. Anything anyone else can do *better* than you can? Are you taking full advantage of key people who have more direct knowledge, background, and experience in certain detailed phases of the work?

2. Anything someone else should do *instead* of you— even if not quite as well, at first? Try to limit yourself to explaining to the subordinate how you want it done, and within broad practical limits, run the risk of his making a mistake.

3. Anything someone else can do at *less expense* than you can? Should certain work be handled by the man on the spot instead of a trip by you? Or by someone whose total salary cost to the company is less than yours, even if it takes him longer?

4. Anything someone else can do with *better timing* than you can? A less than absolutely ideal action taken when it it needed may be more valuable than an otherwise perfect handling.

5. Anything that will contribute to *training and developing* someone? It may be worthwhile to set up a special program for this purpose alone, mapping out portions of the work for the year ahead in which key men can participate more fully—perhaps rotating them for further flexibility—and to plan ahead for eventual complete take-over of certain segments.

Note Failure to delegate is often an emotional problem. You may be attributing your frustrations and headaches to "short-handedness" or to "poor quality of help" when in fact you won't admit that you're afraid to delegate. Here are some searching self-analysis questions to ask yourself on this score: Are you afraid of somebody else getting credit? Are you afraid of admitting that others know more about a subject than you, or can do something better than you? Are you afraid of a subordinate's moving ahead too fast? Are you afraid to get tough with people who are not carrying their share of the load? These of course all have their roots in a basic sense of insecurity and inadequacy. There is only one answer: Bring them out into the open. Most of the fears will disappear when you examine them in true perspective, but they will fester if left in the dark. (For a detailed discussion of the above points on delegation, and the emotional factors underlying them, see the present author's *Organizing Your Job in Management,* published by the American Management Association.)

Related Entries *Organization—1. AMA's "Ten Commandments": Oversupervision; Understudy.*

DEVELOPMENT OF SUBORDINATES

1. Development-Appraisal-Development

Developing people is fully as important a part of the supervisor's job as getting out the day's work, and the higher up the ladder you go, the more important this phase of your job becomes.

In our heading, we link the words development-appraisal-development because the program must be carried out in a chain-reaction fashion—i.e., for every key employee: (1) an analysis and plan for individual development; (2) appraisal of performance over a specified period; and (3) further development.

Your company may have a formal program of executive

appraisal—which usually begins at the level of supervisor or department head. Whether or not there is such a program, you can use the following prescription to good advantage: *First*, apply the points *to your own job* and do a periodic review of your own work, even if the executive to whom you report does not have an "appraisal interview" with you at regular intervals. *Second*, use the procedure with respect to your key people, in your own department, in your own "home-made" appraisal and development program. (Note: The program may at first blush seem time-consuming to you. But how many subordinate executives or key personnel do you have reporting directly to you? In the important matter of developing people, you can undoubtedly afford to spend at least half a day or a full day a year on each one of them.)

1. Once a year (anniversary of employment date with the department is a good arrangement) meet *alone* with the key subordinate.

2. Emphasize that this is to be a "panoramic" review of performance—the *whole job* in review, not merely some critical incident.

3. Ask the key man (or woman) to bring a brief written statement of what *he* considers his job to be—the mission, responsibilities, limits of authority, etc. (For some types of personnel, not accustomed to desk work, an outline list of points may be requested, rather than a prose statement.) In many cases, the starting point can be the official position description or specification on file in the personnel office.

4. Carefully review this statement of the "routine job" and be sure that both of you are in agreement as to what is covered.

5. Before the meeting, ask the key man to come pre-

pared to highlight "key results" as he sees them which are expected on his job, and to discuss ways in which he feels his performance on them can be measured—in terms of meeting schedules, or units of output for which he or a group under him is responsible, etc. You and he should agree on these.

6. Ask the subordinate to discuss certain special targets he has in mind for improving operations during the ensuing year, *over and above the routine duties discussed above.* (Note: Obviously, you as a supervisor of a department or operation, will have greater leeway for special targets than will any key man under you. But *explore possibilities*: An idea for a method improvement which could be worked out? Better training of apprentices or new people? A work simplification program in the department? Cooperation in some activity such as the company bowling team or ball club, or, say the establishment of a credit union? The big point is that this phase of the program shows who can be real sparkplugs.)

7. Make it clear that if extra targets are agreed upon, the man will be held accountable for results a year hence, just as he will with respect to key points of the routine job. (This will put a restraint on eager beavers.)

8. Finally, ask the subordinate to discuss any special goals he has in mind for the coming year regarding his own *personal growth*: outside courses, getting a license, taking advantage of in-service programs, activity in professional groups, etc. (N.B.—What are you doing with respect to your own growth?)

And Now for the Payoff!

9. A year later, conduct the same type of meeting to plan for the following year, but prefaced by a review of

performance based on the foregoing points. Ask the following three hard-boiled questions:

    a. *What should he have done?*

    b. *Did he do it?*

    c. *If not, why not?*

Discussions can be on tangibles, not generalities. It can be seen that since he participated in developing the scope of his job, the key results expected, special targets and personal goals, he can have no excuse for not knowing what was expected of him.

Related Entries *Appraising Subordinates—3. "Best versus Poorest"; Apprenticeship Programs; Coaching; Development of Subordinates—2. How Do You Rate as a Trainer?; "Interns" and "Cadets"; Job Interest—How to Stimulate It; Learning; Motivation; Organization—2. Continuity through "Runner-Ups"; Oversupervision; Personnel Audit; Programmed Instruction; Promotions—1. Assessing Your People's Potential for Growth; Promotions—2. Assessment in Depth; Self-Improvement—2. Correspondence Schools; Suggestions—1. Tapping the "Latent Resources"; Suggestions— 2. Helping Make the Company Suggestion System Work; Supervisory Training Conferences; Training—1. An Audit of Needs; Training—2. Group Training; Training—3. How to Evaluate It; Understudy.*

DEVELOPMENT OF SUBORDINATES

2. How Do You Rate as a Trainer?

The preceding entry on *Development-Appraisal-Development* emphasized the supervisor's responsibility for developing his people. How do your immediate superior and others in higher management rate you on this ability? Here are the kinds of questions they will raise about you. . . . How many of them would you be able to answer to your satisfaction, about yourself, today?

1. Have discussions with him indicated that he recognizes his responsibilities as a trainer? Does he welcome trainees into his department? Does he make provisions for trainees in his personnel-requirements planning?

2. What do the records show about trainees that have had tours of duty in his department? As to his regular staff—are there any men elsewhere in the company doing outstanding work who are "graduates" of his department?

3. What use is he making of training aids and facilities made available by the company?

4. Do any of his subordinates ever go to association meetings, seminars, and the like?

5. What is his usual attitude about promoting people out of his department? Does he push for promotional opportunities for them, even at the cost of some inconvenience to his own operations?

6. What is his customary reaction to requests that he participate as a speaker or panel member in training programs conducted by the Company for departments other than his own?

7. How effectively is he using appraisal and interview techniques as a developmental tool?

Related Entries *See listing under preceding entry.*

DISCHARGING AN EMPLOYEE

Discharging an employee is no pleasant matter—which accounts for the fact that so many people are kept on even though they have amply proven their incompetency or for some other reason don't carry their weight. Every month or year added to their service on the job makes it more difficult to take the necessary separation step.

Let's look at the problem first from the general point of view, and then in the light of special problems occasioned by the presence of a union, and by the requirements of current labor legislation. (We are not here concerned with *layoffs*. See separate entry on that subject.)

I. *In the General Situation*

1. *Analyze the problem.* There are only three kinds of discharges: (a) for cause (infraction of rules, inability to get along with others, etc.); (b) for inability to do the work; (c) for economic or technological reasons, implying no fault whatsoever on the part of the employee. Your actions will be governed by the category into which the dismissal falls.

2. *Make the change in time.* An unfit employee should be transferred or dismissed before he has been on the job too long. If your personnel department has not laid down any rules regarding reports on new employees, develop a report form for your own information, and review it every month for the first three months. Cover his performance in safety, cooperation, willingness to learn, quality of work, and output. Make a special effort to correct any substandard performance shown during those early months. If a record such as this shows irrefutable evidence that the job-placement was unwise, discuss the situation immediately with your own superior and with the personnel department as required.

3. *Give proper warnings.* If an employee's work or attitude is unsatisfactory, tell him about it. For serious remisses, warnings should be in writing, to become a matter of record. There should be a reasonable period of time for the employee to demonstrate improvement.

4. *Make dismissal the last resort.* Remember that one

of your most important responsibilities as a supervisor is to develop people. "Habitual dismissers" are usually not the most effective supervisors. Before taking the dismissal step, ask yourself: How can I salvage this situation? Is there need for special training or coaching? Have I exhausted the opportunities of personal discussions? Am I acting impulsively or emotionally? Should I discuss this some more with my own boss? If I *do* let him go, have I planned properly for the take-over of his work? Have I laid the proper groundwork with the others in the department? What will be their reaction?

5. Do the dismissing yourself—forthrightly. As the direct supervisor, you should be the first one to tell the employee of his dismissal. You may, depending upon circumstances, want to arrange for the employee to have a last interview with your own superior, and there may be company rules regarding "exit interviews" (see separate entry) by the personnel department or others. Arrange for a private discussion, and follow as many as possible of the pointers given in the entry, *Exit Interviews.*

6. Avoid "lame ducks." For categories (a) and (b) under (1), above, it is usually the best policy to discharge "without notice." This means telling the employee on the last day of his time on the job, and having severance pay take the place of notice. (Of course, you'll have to be sure about company policy on this point.) Once the person is told that he is to be separated, his value to your department sinks rapidly, and any protracted period will simply compound your difficulties. Passive "moping" will have an adverse effect on other employees; but worse, for some types of employees a "lame duck" period provides time for "grousing" and undermining the loyalty of other employees, and even for physical sabotage. However, if discharge is for reasons beyond the employee's control, you should give as much notice as possible, and as much help as possible in relocating.

II. *In the Union Situation*

Under the Taft-Hartley Act (see entry, *National Labor Relations Act*), the supervisor has special responsibilities in discharging. You may be called upon to testify at a hearing before the Labor Board to prove that you did not discriminate against an employee because of his union activities. Or, in line with provisions of a union contract, you may be called upon before an arbitrator to substantiate a dismissal. Therefore:

1. *Follow to the letter all contract provisions* regarding disciplinary procedures. (See point No. 6 in *Discipline —1. Day-by-Day Discipline.*)

2. *Keep accurate records* about absences or violations of rules by employees, about occasions for serious reprimands, and about complaints made by customers or direct superiors of employees. Of course, retain a copy of any written reprimand or warning.

3. *Don't discharge unfairly.* You can get into trouble at a hearing if you discharge an employee for something which other employees under your direction have been guilty of *without* being discharged.

4. *State the full reason for the discharge to the employee.* If possible, have a competent person present as a witness.

5. *Be familiar with the employee's record* as to promotions, previous commendations, raises, etc., and be sure that your dismissal action does not show up as totally inconsistent with the employee's record.

Related Entries *Civil Rights; Exit Interviews; National Labor Relations Act; Reprimands.*

DISCIPLINE

1. Day-by-Day Discipline

You have to treat insubordination firmly and promptly. . . . "It is the *immediate firmness shown,* rather than the severity of the penalty which is the impressive fact," says Ordway Tead in *The Art of Leadership.*

However, as stressed under *Grievances—2. Handling Complaints,* be sure you have the facts, and be sure that the fault is in the motivation of the offender, and not in the defects of the organization—or in failure on your part to be sure that everyone knows the rules and regulations of the department. Other pointers:

1. Be sure all applicable rules and regulations are known and understood by all concerned, and make especially sure new employees are made aware of them. . . . Should some rules be posted?

2. Be fair in enforcing rules. . . . don't play favorites.

3. Don't single out an individual "to make an example of" if there has been a general slackening of discipline. A far better technique is to post a general, impersonal order, as by distributing a memo to all concerned, calling attention to a situation that needs tightening up on the part of everyone in the department.

4. Create a climate that makes discipline *self-enforcing,* as discussed under *Motivation* and related entries.

5. Here is a check list of *basic factors* to review in assessing penalties:

    a. Nature of the violation.

b. Record of prior conduct. This includes any formal and disciplinary actions that appear on a man's record, such as reprimands of disciplinary layoffs. Penalties should become more severe for each additional instance.

c. Length of service.

d. Intervening time since last penalty. A long period of good conduct following previous disciplinary action should be considered since it represents the aim of corrective discipline.

e. Local practice or policy.

f. Mitigating or aggravating circumstances. Mitigating circumstances might be exceptional stress or perhaps baiting or goading by other employees. An obviously aggravating circumstance is the repeated violation of the same rule.

6. Follow to the letter any union contract provisions governing disciplinary procedures. A union agreement may give certain representation rights in this connection, e.g., regarding layoff or discharge, the right to hold a private conversation wth his committeeman on company premises, or the right of representation during a disciplinary interview. Failure to accord such technical procedural rights may lead an arbitrator later to rescind or modify an otherwise proper disciplinary action.

Related Entries *Altercations; Criticism—1. How to Dish It Out; Discipline—2. Handling Critical Incidents; Early Leavers; Favoritism; Friction; Grievances—1. When the Employee Goes Over Your Head; Grievances—2. Handling Complaints; Horseplay; Informal Leaders; Manners; National Labor Relations Act; NO—NO—NO—How to Say No: Privileges; Problem Employees; Punishment; Reprimands; Sex; The Stubborn Worker; Talking; Tardiness.*

DISCIPLINE

2. Handling Critical Incidents

Run-of-the-mill discipline presents no special problems. Usually the rules and regulations in general force are followed with reasonable adherence. However, it's the *unusual* "critical incidents" which cause the real supervisory headaches—situations where the regular rules seem not to apply, or where, if they are applied, an obvious injustice will appear to be done. These include really serious, danger-breeding infractions: there is a flagrant violation of a safety rule (as when a power linesman decides to work a line "hot" instead of using rubber gloves, or a crane operator allows an unauthorized person to spell him on his job), or somebody shows up drunk or makes a pass at one of the girls, or a salesman goes AWOL and fakes a call report. These episodes are fortunately infrequent, but how they are handled will have far-reaching effect on departmental morale and on the respect your people will have for you.

If one of these critical incidents breaks in your department, use the following guidelines for your analysis and action:

1. Don't act in haste regarding disciplinary measures (but of course don't lose time regarding safety or other measures that have to be taken).

2. Review the standard TWI pointers on handling human-relations problems, as given in *"People Problems"* —*1. Pointers from the "J" Programs.*

3. Before taking any action, determine the precedent-setting nature of the whole episode. Is a similar situation likely to occur? Will an exception involve future risk?

4. What are the safety and health aspects of the situa-

tion to the infractor and to others? Do they add to the seriousness of the infraction? Are new rules required?

5. Who are the *informal leaders* in the group or groups involved? How can they aid in handling the situation? (See *Informal Leaders.*)

6. What sort of publicity should be given this incident? On balance, will the gain to the department as a whole outweigh the effects of the publicity on the individual?

7. What can be learned from this particular incident? Will a "post-mortem" help—with the person involved alone? with the department as a whole? with the informal leaders? (See *Emergencies—2. Post-Mortems.*)

Note In a talk on "The Foreman and the Worker," L. Clayton Hill, formerly executive vice-president, the Murray Corporation, had this to say: "When disciplinary action becomes necessary, the foreman will do well to follow the example of the judge in court. Over the centuries, the successful judge has followed this procedure religiously: He questions, he listens, he thinks. . . . He gets all pertinent facts and opinions. . . . He retires to the privacy of his chamber where he analyzes, weighs, and thinks all the way round the problem, checking against the law. . . . Then, and not until then, he renders his decision promptly and courageously. . . . He follows his decision with pronouncement of the penalty which fits the situation."

Related Entries *See listing under preceding entry.*

DISCRIMINATION

See *Civil Rights.*

E

THE EAGER BEAVER

An "eager beaver" is easier to recognize than to describe, because often a good man is so designated by somebody who is jealous of his progress. He has a lot of good qualities—ambition, enthusiasm, industry. He's not liked by his fellow workers, who think he's "pushy," and with respect to his boss he may be an apple polisher. We're not supposed to define something by using the same terms as the object defined—but let's face it: an eager beaver is somebody who is just too eager.

What to do?

If you're an eager beaver's supervisor, recognize that you may have a tremendous asset in getting out the work, and in keeping the others on their toes. Don't worry too much about the fact that the others are miffed by him. But if the eager beaver is a young fellow (or girl), as is usually the case, since eager-beaverishness is something that is later outgrown, you may on the proper occasion talk to him about some of the problems of rubbing others the wrong way. (An ideal occasion would be the regular appraisal interview—see the entry on that subject.)

As a supervisor and therefore as a trainer, the big thing to watch out for in eager beavers, and to correct, is a tendency to go off half-cocked in order to make a showing. Where the consequences will not be too serious, let him make a mistake or two due to moving too fast, or moving without thinking about the effect on others, and then hold a revealing post-mortem with him on the mistake.

Sometimes a supervisor has an eager beaver on his hands who he thinks is a threat to him. He may be gunning for the supervisor's job, and doing some apple polishing or attention-calling with respect to the supervisor's own boss. The way to handle this is definitely not to resent his apparent pushing for your job. Feed him opportunities to make a showing, and let him push you into a promotion. When he makes a showing, your department will gain—and your reputation as a trainer and coach will benefit. You can, of course, insist on his working through channels, and crack down on any indication of his not informing you of an activity on which he's supposed to keep you posted, or of going over your head.

If the eager beaver is somebody on your own level, with whom you are in competition, don't waste time on resentment. First, ask yourself honestly whether a little more industry and initiative on your part are called for—whether you're unfair in your designation of him. In any event, observe how he operates, and pick up all the good pointers you can while avoiding the eager-beaverishness itself.

EARLY LEAVERS

Early leavers are at the other end of the problem of *Tardiness* (which see). We're all familiar with the five-o'clock stampede—and (especially in offices), we're all familiar with the girls who are all primped and ready to go, hands on purses, five minutes before closing time.

How cope with this? A supervisor has the right to be firm on calling for active work on the job at hand up to quitting time, and to call for the necessary *plus* effort beyond the stroke of quitting time for emergencies, in return for the generous fringe benefits, sick leaves, time off for Christmas shopping, and all the rest which most organizations now provide. This fair give-and-take should be pointed out in a quiet talk with any employee who balks at occasional requests to finish something if it entails staying five or ten minutes longer.

Obviously, you can't abuse the idea. In general, the supervisor is responsible for planning workloads so that they can be handled in the normal working day. . . . but there will always be emergency situations, and "the mail must go through" spirit should pervade the department if there is the right kind of leadership.

Related Entries   *Car Pools; Tardiness.*

EMERGENCIES

1. Avoid and Prepare

No supervisor engulfed in an emergency will at that moment be inclined to look into a manual like this to find out how to handle it. But it is appropriate to include here some discussion on how to *avoid* emergencies, and how to *prepare* for them.

"Surprise," it has been said, "is the enemy of good management." Henry Dennison, the great American industrialist, put it this way: "In the steady running of an organization, the frequent need of great speed of decision is a symptom of lack of sufficient advance thinking." Following are some pointers. Note that steps taken in *preparation* for emergencies will automatically lead to *avoidance* of many of them.

1. Enforce safety and health rules. 'Nuf said.

2. Have Standard Operating Procedures. (See separate entry under this heading.) Your people can't always "go by the book," but to the extent that they do, emergency situations will be avoided or alleviated.

3. Have checklists. (As an example, see *Planning—Use of Checklists.*)

4. Practice preventive maintenance. (See *Maintenance Costs—Operating Departments.*)

5. Have an understudy. (See *Understudy.*)

6. Be sure all bases are covered. Have standard back-up procedures, and in general be prepared for unexpected absences. (See *Absences—2. Emergencies Caused by Unexpected Absences.*)

7. Be sure key men understand their full responsibilities. (See *Development of Subordinates—1. Development-Appraisal-Development.*) Do you allow sufficient authority to subordinates to handle special situations? Are key people designated to take charge in specific types of emergencies? Can these be reached at all hours? Does everyone concerned know who they are?

8. Develop versatility in your people. The more people who know how to do more than one job, the fewer your crises will be.

9. Check your communications procedures. Are the right people in your department, and in departments depending upon yours, adequately and *promptly* informed of changes, cancellations, new priorities, etc.?

10. Prepare for changes thoroughly. (See *Resistance to Change.*)

11. *Fix follow-up responsibilities.* This is especially important on nonroutine jobs and projects.

12. *Provide for danger-signal control.* Don't hesitate to delegate, but don't live in a fool's paradise, either. On any important project there must be predetermined check points for "how are we doing?" questions.

13. *Have a trouble-shooting set-up.* The exact form will of course depend upon the size and nature of your operation. It may vary from a "flying squad" in a large plant to the part-time responsibility of one assistant in a given department.

14. *Hold post-mortems.* A constructive analysis of an emergency just weathered may prevent its happening again.

15. *Keep a record of how you did it.* For example, the head of maintenance in one plant insists on a clear record of every kind of mishap and breakdown, no matter how trivial, as well as a detailed account on the way emergencies were handled. Now a big and ever-growing book in his office, carefully indexed, shows how hundreds of troublesome situations were handled, and by whom.

Related Enries *Emergencies—2. Post-Mortems; Maintenance Costs—Operating Departments; Planning—Use of Checklists; Understudy.*

EMERGENCIES
2. Post-Mortems

Every emergency situation or "critical incident," once weathered, should be subjected to a "post-mortem" to see what can be learned for the benefit of all concerned, and to see what should be done to prevent repetition, if humanly possible. Here are some evaluation guides:

1. Was there a breach of standard operating procedures? If not, was a "blind spot" in existing procedures revealed which should be covered?

2. Was the emergency due to an equipment breakdown which could have been avoided by preventive maintenance? (See *Preventive Maintenance Costs—Operating Departments.*)

3. Was this a case of panic—of somebody breaking down under pressure? If so, is this a personality problem —or a problem of poor placement? Or a greenhorn on a job that should have been held by a seasoned worker?

4. Does analysis reveal inadequacies in training?

5. Does analysis reveal errors or inadequacies in communication:

    a. From you to a subordinate?

    b. From a subordinate to you?

    c. Between subordinates, or between them and other departments?

    d. Improper liaison with other departments?

6. Was there a lack of pinpointing follow-up responsibilities?

7. If the crisis was one of not meeting promised dates, how realistic were time estimates given by key people? In general, what do records of actuals and revises show against original promises?

Related Entries   *See listing under preceding entry.*

EMOTIONAL REACTIONS

You may often have heard it said that "emotions have no part in business." Nothing could be farther from the truth. Business is conducted by and through people, and people are made up of emotions as well as bodies and intellects. A constant awareness of this fact, and of the fact that people differ widely in their emotional reactions, will go a long way in helping you with your "people problems."

In its booklet, *Emotions and Physical Health,* the Metropolitan Life Insurance Company points out that doctors base their recognition that emotions play an important part in many types of physical illnesses on facts with which we are all familiar. "All of us," says Metropolitan, "have experienced some of the effects of emotions on bodily functions. Most of us can recall blushing when embarrassed, or having a tight feeling in the chest or a weight in the pit of the stomach before an examination. Or having our heart pound or our hands perspire when we are excited or afraid. These are normal reactions of the body to specific situations, and are beyond the control of our will power; they generally disappear quickly once the cause is removed."

These bodily changes occur because emotion is really meant to make us act. Fear, for example, makes some of us tense. When this happens, it in turn leads to certain physiological and chemical changes in the body. Adrenaline is released which causes the heart to beat more rapidly. The muscles of the stomach and intestines contract, forcing the blood out into the general circulation. The rate of breathing is increased, and other changes occur which are meant to gear the body for action—either to run or fight.

Metropolitan says that almost 50 per cent of all people seeking medical attention today are suffering from ailments brought about or made worse by such emotional factors as prolonged worry, anxiety, and fear. Emotional tensions often play a prominent role in certain kinds of heart and circulatory disorders, especially high blood pressure; digestive ailments such as peptic ulcer and colitis; headache and joint and muscular pains; skin disorders; and some allergies.

Sometimes a person's emotional conflicts are so difficult for him to accept that he represses his feelings altogether, and is no longer consciously aware of them. Often what seems to be purely physical illness stems from a hidden wish to accomplish an end quite different from the one obviously demanded by the situation, and one which the patient is completely unaware of. The little boy who vomits before going to school, or the girl employee who develops an agonizing headache an hour before she is scheduled to substitute for Mr. Big's secretary who is going to be gone for the afternoon, may well be examples of the unconscious mind's protest against something the individual does not really want to do.

Related Entries *Employee Counseling; The Mentally Disturbed Worker; Tension and Stress; Women and Girls—1. ("God Bless 'Em"); The Worried Employee.*

EMPLOYEE COUNSELING

In his capacity as a leader, a supervisor will have to stand ready to discuss employees' personal problems—to the degree *they* desire (i.e., no prying on his part) and within limits which he himself should be careful to impose. Some large companies have gone to considerable lengths in setting up personnel counseling services, as part of the personnel department, staffed by trained interviewers and counselors. The supervisor with such a facility at his disposal is fortunate—but lacking it, he will be well advised to develop a practical way of handling himself in a counseling situation.

The biggest problem is to steer a proper course between practical, constructive advice and going over his depth on "amateur psychiatry." It is not possible to give an error-proof prescription—but here, at least, are some directions on general supervisor behavior when personal counsel is sought:

1. *General attitude.* Always show a continuing sincere interest in your people *as* people with homes and families, and not simply producers. If there is sickness at home, remember to ask about progress. . . . If someone's daughter is graduating from high school, show some interest in that. . . .

2. *Make yourself available.* If someone indicates that he or she wants to talk to you about a matter that has come up, answer by saying that if it's important to the employee, you'll be glad to take whatever time is necessary. The employee will probably be glad to have the interview after hours, when nobody else is around. In any case, it's obvious that you should make it possible to have the employee talk to you in private. Have the meeting *as soon as possible* after the request.

3. *Some meetings you will have to initiate*—despite what was said in our opening paragraph. This can occur, for example, when a usually competent and reliable person shows a marked falling off in interest or quality of work, or is unusually tardy or frequently absent, all indicating that some personal situation is interfering with efficiency. (See also *The Alcoholic Employee.*) Don't keep putting the meeting off. . . . it will never be any easier than right away.

4. *Be as prepared as possible*—for either kind of meet-

ing. If you have initiated it, be sure of your facts, with specific examples of the kinds of behavior that are giving you concern. If the employee has asked for the meeting, refresh your memory, if you are not sure, about the employee's general competence on the job, and any personal situations that had previously come to light about him. In either case, you may want to check discreetly with an older person in the department, or a close friend of the employee's in the department, about some of the surrounding circumstances, if you know the subject of the forthcoming discussion.

5. *Put the employee at ease.* You will already have achieved part of this by arranging for a private meeting. Maybe a cup of coffee or a coke is indicated.

6. *Be a good listener.* (Check the suggestions in *Listening*). If it turns out that his problem is a real or imagined grievance of his treatment in the department, let him get that off his chest without interruption. (See *Grievances— 2. Handling Complaints.*)

7. *Don't rely on pep talks.* If the employee's problems are serious enough to warrant the type of interview in question, they are too deep-seated for mere exhortation.

8. *Be wary of advice on personal matters.* On emotional and personal problems, your best contribution will be to serve as a sounding board for his own clarification. You can, of course, give advice as to any company policy that may be involved, avenues of financial assistance available through the company, Credit Union, etc., and other matters where you are sure of your ground. But on his personal problem, your main function as a counselor should be to help him analyze what the problem is, and to explore possible alternate solutions, *with final decisions left to him.* Always remember that in involved personal and emotional problems, you will rarely if ever be in possession of enough facts to take the responsibility for advising on explicit solutions, or for passing moral judgments and assessing blames. *Help him help himself*, perhaps by raising questions that may lead him to see areas where he may have been at fault, without telling him so yourself. Help him by suggesting sources of professional advice, if such advice seems called for.

9. *Avoid assuming the psychiatrist's function.* If you have reasons to believe that the employee is beset by more than the normal kind of anxieties, guide him to professional counsel. (See *The Mentally Disturbed Employee.*)

Note A good point to check: Is the person seeking your help so close a friend or relative as to make it unlikely that you can be objective in considering his problem? If this is the case, even if there are no symptoms of mental illness, you will be well advised to arrange for him to seek another point of view, in addition to whatever comments you may want to make. Discuss this with your own superior.

Related Entries *The Alcoholic Employee; The Mentally Disturbed Worker; Emotional Reactions; Tensions and Stress; The Worried Employee.*

EMPLOYEE EFFICIENCY

Research in industrial psychology and industrial medicine has shown that the average worker goes through a definite cycle each day, in terms of efficiency and energy expended —and this is something the supervisor should keep in mind in work assignments, in analyzing results of sample work measurements he may have taken, and in setting standards and developing estimates.

Work curves of output against hours of work have been developed for many different tasks in many industries. While these naturally vary depending upon specific conditions, they do conform to a general pattern. Thus:

Under normal circumstances, the employee comes to the job refreshed by a night's sleep. He is therefore presumably capable of doing his best at the very start of his work.

However, the curves usually show a "warm-up" period at the start, and the worker's output will usually be at a greater rate during the second hour than the first. Usually, contributing to this, is the make-ready involved in getting tools, equipment, and supplies ready, and in general the "warm-up" is needed to get into the full swing of the job.

There is then a "beginning spurt" during which output rate climbs. During the second hour he will probably level off to a steady rate.

As time goes on, he becomes physically tired or bored, and his output rate declines. Toward the end of the morning he will have reached a low point, with an increase in errors. Then, in anticipation of the lunch break, there will probably be an "end spurt." After lunch he will probably resume near the top of his efficiency, and go through the same general pattern—but with fatigue perhaps bringing his lowest point toward the end of the day, with again possibly an end spurt before closing time. Midmorning and midafternoon coffee or coke breaks will serve to interrupt the downward slope and provide to a smaller degree their own anticipatory end spurts and resumption at a good level of efficiency.

Related Entries *Fatigue; Music for Employees; Rest Breaks; Women and Girls—2. Special Physiological Problems.*

EMPLOYEE TYPES

See *"People Problems"—Employee Types.*

ESTIMATING

See *"Learning Curve" in Estimating.*

ETHICS

Perhaps governmental employment is a little more sensitive than private employment as regards the appearance of receiving favors from someone who may benefit personally from your goodwill. Federal departments, for example, have recently become quite strict in such relatively minor matters as accepting invitations to luncheons and trade-association banquets. However, the fundamental ethical criteria should be no different in public employment from what they are in private enterprise. Therefore, in the following Veterans Administration information bulletin headed *Employee Conduct,* simply substitute your own organization's name for VA:

Want your name in headlines?

It can happen to anyone working for the Federal government—even you. . . . if you aren't real careful. When we say it that way, you can see we're not talking about the nice headlines anyone would like. We're talking about the ugly ones—the muddy ones. How do you avoid them? Real easy. . . . exercise common honesty and common sense. Thus:

DON'T let your private economic interests carry over to your job. Keep your skirts real clean, and don't engage in any activity which even looks as though you might be mixing your private interests with your public duties.

DON'T accept any gifts of any kind from anyone doing business or seeking to do business with the Veterans Administration.

DON'T engage in any outside activities either for pay or gratis which would tend to embarrass the Veterans Administration or compromise your ability to perform your official duties, honestly, ably, and fairly.

DON'T give your supervisor a gift.

DON'T work for anyone on the outside who does business with the Veterans Administration.

DON'T lend any money to or borrow money from any beneficiary or claimant of the VA.

DON'T fail to pay your just debts.

DON'T ever, ever, disclose any official information which represents a matter of confidence or trust that you possess as a result of your employment, except as specifically authorized.

As we said before, and we will say again—use common honesty and common sense!

Related Entries   *Fraud by Employees; Integrity.*

EXCEPTIONS TO RULES

See *NO—NO—NO—How to Say No; Privileges (Point 2); Smoking on the Job.*

EXECUTIVE ABILITY

Every supervisor worth his salt considers his present job as simply an early rung on a ladder which in this country (praises be!) can reach all the way to the top.

How do those rungs look to you? For specifics, see *Self-Improvement—1. The Job Ahead*. Here we want to talk about management's-eye-view of you in their appraisal of your *executive ability*. This goes beyond technical competence on the job, and gets into some hard-to-measure traits involving judgment, leadership, reaction to responsibility, etc. Here are some key appraisal points used by higher management in deciding who are the "comers" and who are the "stay putters." Take some quiet time out, and see how you think you would stack up against them (and don't pull punches!):

1. *Sense of profitability.* Knowledge of what makes or will make for profitable operations and how to obtain them (a) now and (b) in the future.

2. *Ability to master details of a situation easily.* Then plans, organizes, delegates, and controls so that he can concentrate on only the most important phases of the situation, while remaining alert to other situations.

3. *Willingness and ability to weigh problems, decisions, and actions on the basis of the overall situation,* rather than solely with respect to his own department or specialty.

4. *Requires minimum direction.* Given the end results desired and told "why," seldom asks or must be told "how," and proceeds effectively on his own.

5. *Accepts and reaches for responsibility.* Doesn't cling to a "safety zone," but at the same time he recognizes established policy limits.

6. *Anticipates long- as well as short-range effects of decisions.*

7. *Makes dependable generalizations.* Whenever possible or practical, makes certain he has all available and importantly pertinent facts, but is not afraid to make de-

cisions, as required, based on sometimes incomplete or not fully reliable data.

Related Entries *Delegation; Leadership; Self-Appraisal— 1. The "Management-Eye-View of Your Planning Ability; Self-Improvement—1. The Job Ahead.*

EXIT INTERVIEWS

When a person leaves your department, either as a voluntary quit or as a discharge, it will pay you to schedule an "exit interview" with him (or her) before he leaves. *Do this even if your company procedure calls for an exit-interview conducted by the personnel department.* But don't schedule your interview for the last day, when he is busy checking out tools, cleaning his desk, signing forms, etc.

1. *If the employee has been discharged.* In the situation where an employee has been discharged for inability to do the work or for rules infraction, the prospect of a final interview may not be pleasant—but don't duck it on that account. As one superintendent put it, "I worry about the man I've fired. . . . His work and his wages end for us, but he himself goes on, and a definite relationship between him and the company goes on, even though he's been sawed off the payroll. . . . For a long time to come, he'll collar everyone he can get hold of, to chew the story over and over again. That story will, naturally, be told from his point of view, and if he is sore the company is pretty sure to be pictured as a soulless corporation. And Mrs. Ex-employee and the kids will be walking advertisements about the raw deal the old man got."

You should do all you can in the final, *private* discussion to show that you're sincerely interested in his personal welfare. (If a secretary or assistant shares your office be sure that you have arranged for them to be out of the room.) Point out that you're sorry things didn't work out on this job. If there are types of work for which you feel you can honestly recommend him, say so. Make it a point to check on whether he filled out all papers and did all other necessary things to assure that he will get all that is due him in severance pay, vacation-due pay, any returns due from a pension fund, etc. Assure him about such matters as forwarding of personal mail, etc.

If the person is no youngster, don't give any impression of "preaching," but if he is a youngster who got involved in some difficulty on this job, you may do him a good turn by discussing with him whatever constructive lessons can be learned from the episode. Let him see that there is nothing personal in the situation, and that he can call upon you later for any counsel or advice you may be in a position to give him on a new job situation.

2. *Discharge for economic reasons.* If the discharge is due to lack of work in the department, and not through any fault of the employee, be especially sure that all possible employee-goodwill is retained. Spend enough time in the interview to get the latest on the employee's new-job prospects, give him any leads you may have, and reassure him as to recommendations you stand ready to give about him. If there is any chance that he may be rehired, discuss that, but don't give any false hopes if you have nothing definite to go on. Again, be sure that he has complied with all procedures to get any pay and refunds due him. Be sure he understands about procedures for unemployment insurance payments. If you have anything constructive to suggest about further train-

ing, do so, but don't give the impression that he is being let go for a deficiency. Be sure that there is no feeling of unfairness or discrimination, and if there appears to be, do all you can to straighten the matter out. (See *Layoffs.*)

3. A *voluntary quit.* It is in this situation that you will get the most dividends out of the exit interview. Before the interview, review the employee's record if you are not completely familiar with it. Tell him that while you're sorry you're losing a good employee, if this is something that he wants and that is good for him, you're all for it. Then ask him if he has any suggestions about the job, the kind of replacement that would be best in this situation, and whether there was anything in your own relationship with him that unwittingly on your part might have led to his wanting to change jobs. Then say that you want him to be sure to tell you anything about his experience on the job that led him to leave, which might be of help to you in improving conditions for the next fellow. If he remains guarded in his replies, don't push for an answer—just be sure you opened the way by your questions. Also invite him to make suggestions about the work of the department as he sees it—you may learn something about roadblocks and bottlenecks you weren't aware of before!

Show an interest in his future plans, and assure him you'll always be glad to hear from him, and to help in any way you can on any future occasion.

Finally, *after* the interview, make a candid self-review: What can you learn from this particular quit? Were any of your attitudes or behaviors at fault? Was the quit a surprise—and if so, what was wrong with your supervisory tactics that you didn't know it was brewing? Was there friction in the department that you should have corrected, or that you hadn't even been aware of? Had you "over-hired" in the first place, so that the employee was dissatisfied because he wasn't using his talents? What guideposts did you develop for the selection of a replacement?

Related Entries *Discharging an Employee; Turnover.*

F

FAIR LABOR STANDARDS ACT

See *Minimum Wage Laws.*

FATIGUE

The symptoms of fatigue are a feeling of tiredness, inattention, and an impairment of productivity. The following pointers on the subject are largely culled from Dr. Howard W. Haggard's chapter, "Industrial Fatigue," in Heyel's *The Foreman's Handbook*:

The term "rest" is commonly used to mean the opposite of work. But in reality, the body, including the muscles, is never at rest and never ceases to work as long as it is alive. The heart continues to beat, the muscles of the chest continue to move, and various organs carry out activities necessary to the maintenance of life. In addition, the muscles attached to bones, as in the legs and arms, are continually making a static effort.

In vigorous manual work which can be continued for eight hours a day, as in the heavier jobs in farming, mining, etc., the average rate of energy expenditure may vary between four and eight times that of resting.

In doing heavy manual work, as described here, the rates of the heart beat and of breathing are increased.

However if the man is in good physical condition, both rates, after a few minutes of work, reach steady states well below their maxima. There is no strain upon the circulation of blood or upon breathing, and any symptoms of fatigue which develop cannot be attributed to the high rate of energy expenditure, as in the violent exertion of running or swimming.

In light and moderate industrial occupations, the rate of energy expenditure is less than three times the resting rate. In typewriting, the total energy expenditure may be only 50 per cent more than that of resting. Often in the "rest" period intended to relieve the feeling of fatigue from such occupations, the activity of the worker is actually considerably increased by walking about. Obviously, in light and moderate industrial occupations there is little strain on the circulation of blood and the other general functions intimately concerned in the expenditure of energy. However, in spite of these facts, several hours at a continuous light or moderate occupation are followed by tiredness and lowered output.

Such fatigue results from the sum total of "strain." The principal strains from light and moderate industrial occupations lie primarily in their continuity. They are tiresome, just as listening to a serious lecture several hours long is tiresome to the listeners, even though they are sitting in chairs and doing no "work." This is because of the effort to maintain continuous attention.

Here are nine summarizing points on fatigue for the industrial foreman:

1. Relief from the fatigue of continued strain can often be best obtained not by rest, but by changing the nature of the tasks performed.

2. Fatigue from one light task influences the fatigue

from another only to the extent in which the tasks are similar. If they are actually different, the change of work is beneficial.

3. Varied work can be continued without tiredness for a much longer working day than can a single variety of work.

4. A repetitive act which requires continued concentration of attention and which at first leads to fatigue may, with practice, become so nearly automatic as to require only occasional attention and permit conversation and pleasant social relations. The task then largely ceases to cause fatigue.

5. Poor physical condition, as from ill health, inadequate diet, or chronic infection, in itself constitutes a strain which is added to those from the occupation.

6. Diet especially is a point which deserves attention. Inadequacies, particularly of protective foods such as vitamins, may be a cause of tiredness, inattention, and lack of vigor and well-being.

7. The psychological make-up of the individual, his personality and temperament, are also important factors in determining the extent to which the nature of a given strain will affect him. A man who is "easy going" may be little affected by certain strains which may strongly affect and greatly add to the tiredness of a man who is by temperament excitable, anxious, or irritable.

8. The relation between fatigue and accidents is well established—people don't respond so quickly to stimuli when they are tired as when they are feeling fresh and alert. They grow careless in the operation of hazardous equipment, or don't jump out of the way rapidly enough when someone warns them by sight or sound.

9. Insecurity, frustration, pressure, and lack of adjust-

ment to the particular job are strains which may increase fatigue. Any psychological or sociological factor which is unfavorable and unpleasant, particularly if it disturbs the emotions and arouses anxiety, is a strain which contributes to fatigue. (See *Employee Counseling* and *The Mentally Disturbed Employee.*)

Related Entries   *Employee Efficiency; Lifting and Carrying; Monotonous Work; Music for Employees; Rest Breaks.*

FAVORITISM

We all have the human tendency to favor those we like, and very often the liking is not because of performance or ability. And often, of course, there is a strong temptation to favor somebody because of his "connections" or for some other advantage which he may be able to confer.

Favoritism breeds contempt among the more skilled operators. It usually involves many employees, and the ill effects are hard to overcome. It will affect your department's work in two ways, both bad: (1) employees favored become lax in their work; (2) employees discriminated against become dissatisfied, angry, resentful, or indifferent.

FIRE PREVENTION

According to the National Board of Fire Underwriters, each year more than 86,000 fires in business establishments in this country threaten workers' security. There's no mystery about how a fire starts: It starts when heat, fuel, and air (or oxygen) combine to produce combustion. A fire hazard is anything that causes or *could* cause that heat-fuel-air combination.

Every member of management should have a working knowledge of fire prevention and should know the basic features of his plant's fire protection. Fire prevention should be discussed at staff meetings, in the plant's newsletter or house organ, and through the circulation of fire safety bulletins or pamphlets (see *Note,* below.)

Every operating executive should be familiar with the fire codes and standards of the National Board of Fire Underwriters for the manufacturing processes and storage problems under his supervision. Similarly he should be acquainted with local fire prevention ordinances that pertain to any phase of his work.

Inspections for possible fire hazards in your department or departments should not be a one-shot affair, but should be done periodically, at least four times a year. (The National Board of Fire Underwriters makes available a detailed "Self Inspection Blank for Industrial Plants.") But inspection isn't enough—the hazardous conditions uncovered must be corrected. A follow-up inspection should be made to make sure that they have. Inspections should be made after any changes in operations or construction of buildings or additions, to see if they have affected fire protection in any way. Even if your building is noncombustible or fire resistant, periodic inspections are in order because the use or storage of highly combustible materials may require additional fire protection measures.

Do all you can to insure *fire prevention.* Here are some commonsense suggestions for detecting and removing the causes of fire that are most likely to be found in your plant: (Don't consider them as complete. Use them as a springboard for your thinking.)

General Order: Maintain good order and cleanliness. (See *Housekeeping.*)

Shipping and Receiving: Prevent accumulation of excess packing materials and empty boxes.

Packing Materials: Keep only a day's supply on hand of excelsior, shredded paper, straw, etc.—and keep only in a metal box or bin. The box should have a counter-weighted cover with a fusible link.

Waste and Rags: Use approved cans, with self-closing hinged covers for oily or soiled waste, rags, or excelsior, or anything used to rub down oil finishes. Oil paints usually contain linseed oil which will oxidize, heat, and set fire to such combustibles. Remove the waste, rags, etc., as soon as possible—at least once a day—and incinerate them.

Combustible Materials: Keep in as small stacks or piles as practicable.

Refuse Near Buildings: Don't allow.

Outside Storage: Provide at least 20 feet between exterior building walls and the outside storage of wooden boxes, packing cases, crates, pallets, skids, or lumber.

Locker Rooms: Secure metal lockers for the use of employees.

Gas Leaks: If the odor of gas is detected, ventilate the place before trying to find the leak. Get personnel out. Strike no matches. Summon gas company or plant maintenance men.

Stock: Don't pile stock so high that it will interfere with the operation of sprinkler heads.

Smoking: Forbid it except in designated areas.

Fire Doors: Keep closed when not actually in use unless they are automatic-closing, especially at night, and keep them free from obstruction.

Note The National Board of Fire Underwriters, 85 John St., New York, New York, will make available free copies of its booklet for employees—"Stop Fires—Save Jobs." Many fine industrial safety films are available for free loan or for purchase from the National Board of Fire Underwriters. Lists of other fire prevention films as well as posters can be obtained from the National Safety Council, 425 North Michigan Avenue, Chicago, Illinois. The publication, *The Sentinel*, will be sent free to interested companies and executives by the Factory Insurance Association, 85 Woodland Street, Hartford, Connecticut.

Related Entry   *Housekeeping.*

FIRST AID

On every shift in every department there should be several persons thoroughly trained in the principles of first aid. You, as foreman or supervisor, should be one of these. In most plants, the medical department is near at hand. But where your own first-aid kit is necessary as departmental equipment, it should be under the charge of a responsible individual, one of those trained in first aid.

General access to first-aid material should not be allowed, since general supplies can become contaminated; also, they may be drawn upon and not replaced. A serious emergency can result when supplies suddenly needed are missing. Thus the responsibility for the departmental first-aid service is a serious one.

First-aid courses are available from the United States Bureau of Mines and from the American Red Cross. Standard courses require 15 hours or more of instruction and produce a fairly well-trained first-aider. A short course in first aid has an additional advantage in that the mere teaching of first aid procedures tends to increase safety-consciousness.

FLEXIBLE BUDGETS

See *Budgets*.

FOLLOW-UP

Follow-up is one of the supervisor's most important managing functions. Good planning and scheduling are of no avail if there is no organized way of assuring that general directives are being carried out for alerting the right persons to impending problems of performance, and for doing the necessary expediting to see that parts, materials, and *information* are where they are expected to be.

Responsibility for outside follow-up of such things as purchased materials or components is usually in the hands of special expediters and not under the control of an individual department supervisor. However, the supervisor's operations may suffer severely from a poor company follow-up procedure. Accordingly, if he is pressed to make revisions in plans and schedules because of shortages, he is well within his rights to inquire about the kind of expediting that is being done.

Follow-up *within* the department is, of course, the direct responsibility of every supervisor. Perhaps good follow-up should more properly be considered an attitude than a skill—conscientiousness about taking the necessary trouble to make sure that things are going as planned. Broadly speaking, there are two types of internal follow-ups to be concerned about—those having to do with *general directives*, and those having to do with *specific operations*.

General Directives

Periodic check-up is required to be sure that general policies and standard operating procedures are actually being followed. Inserting a new directive into the departmental policy and procedural manual is not enough. Here are things to do:

1. Periodically review important operating procedures with key personnel—especially recent changed procedures. Does performance show that everyone concerned really understands what is called for? Is there any dragging of feet where changes have been directed?

2. What is the "exception" record? Are you being properly alerted when exceptions to established policy and procedures are made within your department?

3. If there are too many exception actions, maybe something is wrong with the established procedure. What "bugs," if any, have been found in the new procedures?

4. Are key people who have been provided with procedural manuals keeping them up to date? If these are loose-leaf manuals, are new pages properly filed—or are they just dumped in for "later" proper filing? (It may be a good idea to ask to see the manuals occasionally, without warning.)

5. Are suggestions in order about the format of the manual itself, to provide easier upkeep?

Specific Operations

1. Who does what and *when?* Are timetables and specific responsibilities clearly understood by all concerned?

2. When are regular "readings" to be taken as to

progress? What sorts of amber and red lights should be set up?

3. Which special projects or repetitive jobs should be controlled by progress charts and planning boards? (See *Planning and Control Boards* and *Planning and Scheduling—1. Progress Charts.*)

4. Are you becoming too "chairborne"? Are you tending to rely too much on records and reports and not enough on the sound "feel" for operations that only first-hand contact can provide?

5. Are all bases covered? What is your "loose-ends procedure" when somebody reports absent or goes off on vacation?

6. Who tends the store when *you* are away?

Related Entries *Planning and Control Boards; Planning and Scheduling—1. Progress Charts; Standard Operating Procedures.*

FORMS

See *Paperwork.*

FRAUD BY EMPLOYEES

All businesses are faced with the possibility of fraud on the part of some of their employees. Writing in *Bell Telephone News*, D. F. MacEachern, Chief Accountant of the American Telephone and Telegraph Company, points to the steps management should take to keep employee fraud down. Most of these, having to do with bonding of employees, establishment of a security organization, and operational auditing procedures, are beyond the province of most supervisors and department heads. However, some points are definitely part of supervisory responsibilities.

For example, MacEachern points out that it is "a fundamental managerial concept that the primary responsibility for safeguarding assets rests with the managers of the business." Managers in all levels of authority in all departments must be constantly aware of this responsibility and strive to conduct their operations in a way to make perpetration of fraud virtually impossible. Each operating routine should be developed with built-in control features that will enable management to maintain adequate control. Also, every department head must personally evaluate his operations in the light of these controls to guard against fraud. *Once this attitude of everyday supervisory control permeates the organization, every employee quickly realizes that the company is going to exercise specific controls to see that dishonesty does not occur.* No other form of control can ever match the effect of alert management.

Employee fraud prevention, as MacEachern sees it, is essentially a problem in human relations. If nobody seems to care, you can bet that employee theft will increase. It's unfortunate, but true, that the company must identify honesty as a condition of employment, in so many words. . . . There have been cases where an employee dismissed for a dishonest act was reinstated by a labor arbitrator on the grounds that the company had not explicitly forbidden the dishonesty. To be effective, the stimulus for honesty in business must come from the top, and it should be made clear that what is said is meant.

A booklet on the subject of honesty in the business is given to every employee of the Bell Companies, and is reviewed periodically with him by his immediate supervisor. The booklet covers thefts of services as well as goods, other dishonest acts, secrecy of communications, and the legal penalties prescribed for falsification of reports and records. There is a record in each employee's personnel file showing that he has been informed of this policy.

Your company may not have such a special booklet for distribution—but if your department is at all in a "sensitive" position with regard to opportunities for and temptations to fraud, there is nothing to prevent your thinking about the problem and setting down on paper the rules of conduct and the procedures of checks and balances that are going to be a must in your department.

Related Entries   *Ethics; Integrity; Money—Responsibility for Handling Company Funds.*

FRICTION

The effect of friction in human relationships upon efficiency is identical to that of friction in a machine. It not only causes an immediate loss of output, but also results in rapid wear at the point of greatest pressure. The big danger is that, unless the condition is brought to the surface, a breakdown may take place at the most unexpected and awkward time. Whenever it appears that employees are not getting along with each other, with their immediate supervisor, or with some other department with which they must deal, the underlying causes should be ascertained as quickly as possible, and corrected.

If there are complaints about a specific person, have him or her in for a chat. Check with key people in the department, to get added light on the situation. See what can

be done informally (check the entry, *Informal Leaders*).
See if changing the make-up of a particular group would
help. If the problem is serious, maybe a departmental
meeting is in order, to clear the air.

Related Entries   *Altercations; Discipline—2. Handling Critical
Incidents; Emotional Reactions; Grievances—2. Handling
Complaints; Problem Employees.*

G

GRIEVANCES

1. When the Employee Goes Over Your Head

The importance of the immediate supervisor in any grievance procedure is beyond question, and a company's announced grievance procedure will usually insist that the employee take the matter up with his foreman or department head before going farther. But it frequently happens that an employee will go over his immediate supervisor's head with some complaint. . . . Or, in a milder sense, he will go over his head with some question or comment.

Does this ever happen in your department? If so, it will be natural for you to get hot under the collar. However, before getting too burned up, it will be a good idea for you to stop and ask yourself the simple question, *Why?* Why did the employee go to your boss instead of to you? . . . Often when you try to answer that one, you'll begin to wonder whether the fault may not originally have been your own: If supervision had been right, would he ever have thought of going over your head? . . . Have you been "standoffish"? . . . Have you been open to suggestions? . . . Have you stalled in getting an answer to a legitimate complaint? . . . Have you played favorites?

Related Entries *Communicating—2. Answering the "Unanswerable"; Criticism—2. How to Take It; Grievances—2. Handling Complaints; Listening.*

GRIEVANCES

2. Handling Complaints

"Complaints spring up like weeds, and most serious grievances begin with unimportant trifles." Thus Thompson Products Company introduces its rules on handling of requests and complaints. Here are specific pointers from its *Supervisors' Manual:*

1. *Allow the worker to get things off his chest.* Deliberately take time out to listen to him. . . . If you are engaged with other pressing duties, make an appointment to see him as soon as possible. . . . If necessary, deliberately have him repeat his story to make himself clear. . . . At times nod your head or say "Yes" or "Un-hunh" while he is talking. (This doesn't mean you're agreeing with him, it means you understand what he's saying.) . . . Look straight at the employee while he's talking.

2. *Restate the request or complaint to the employee.* Repeat it word-for-word after him so that he knows *you* know what the situation really is. (This is perhaps the most important step in handling complaints.)

3. *Get the worker's opinion as to how the matter may be handled.* Talk it over with him and consider several answers to the question or problem. . . . Encourage him to tell you frankly what action he thinks should be taken. . . . If you don't have a ready answer, tell him you'll check into the matter and give him a definite answer at a specific time.

4. *Give the answer and convince him you have handled his case fairly.* Take action promptly. . . . Carefully explain the reasons for the actions you're taking. . . . Be sure he understands and is convinced that the answer is right.

Handling grievances is so important that we reproduce below the discussion given in the excellent booklet,

"Handling Grievances," produced by the Aluminum Company of America, even though some of the points parallel some of those given above. (On this subject, repetition won't hurt!):

TALKING ABOUT GRIEVANCES. . . .

We'd like you to meet Joe. He's been around Alcoa plants for a long time—almost 30 years. Joe is just about the best man we know when it comes to handling grievances. He's got the same know-how in handling people that he has in handling machines. . . . Let's go along with him and get his ideas. . . .

1. *Receive the grievance properly.* When a man stops to talk to me about a grievance, I give him my *entire* attention. Even if he is boiling mad, I keep my temper. Then we go into my office where we can talk in privacy. He has a chance to tell his full story without interruption and get it *all* off his chest. Then I calmly ask the man to repeat his story. This time, while he is speaking, I take a few notes, both to get the story accurately and to impress him that his complaint is being taken seriously.

After hearing the employee out, I repeat his complaint in my own words. Picking out the two or three essential points of the story lets the man know I have it straight.

If the answer to his complaint is obvious, it's a simple matter to give him the answer right there. But if there is any doubt whatever in my mind, I take time to check further. This means asking the man to come back at an appointed time. *It's important, too, to assure him of prompt action and tell him when he can expect an answer.*

2. *Get the facts.* Handle the case from the beginning as if you expected to defend your case before an arbitrator. After receiving the grievance, I collect additional facts. Here's how to get them.

First, I find out the *details* involved in the complaint. This means going over every angle of the story and talking to the people involved.

Second, I check the *master union agreement* plus any local agreement. It's also important for me to know whether the settling of a recent case has placed a new interpretation on the agreement. You just can't know your agreement too well. Even when I know every clause, I still check it again.

Third, I check *Company policy* with which the complaint is concerned. This means going as high as necessary to get information on previous practices, the current interpretation, and present Company policy. I also try to be sure, when asking for the opinion of my superintendent or personnel manager, that I tell the whole story, uncolored, *including any part which may reflect unfavorably against me.*

Fourth, I examine the *employee's record.* What is his production record? What are his absentee, safety, and discipline records? Is he constantly complaining? By checking on these points, I can pretty well tell whether a man has been dependable, stable, and productive. Since a grievance is settled on the facts in the case, *it pays to keep good records.*

3. *Take action.* If I'm wrong, I make the correction promptly. If the employee is wrong, it's up to me to give him a full and clear explanation. . . . If I am sure my decision is right, I stick to it. I don't allow myself to be bulldozed by threats to carry the grievance higher. It's my responsibility to remain calm and say nothing which can weaken my position. *In fact, I even tell the employee the exact steps he can take to get consideration at the next step in the grievance procedure.* This shows him I have confidence in my position and would be willing to have it reviewed.

Communicate the facts to your boss. I tell my boss the complete story, including the part, if any, which may be critical of me. My case is backed up with whatever factual records are available. If the case should go to arbitration, there is a written memorandum to support my findings, my actions, and my decision.

4. *Follow-up.* Here's what I do:
   a. Make sure my plan of action is properly carried out.
   b. Correct conditions which could result in a similar grievance happening again.
   c. Prepare a memorandum which describes the grievance and the action taken.

Note *On applying the facts:* If your employees belong to a union, remember that the union contract is your "law book." If you're uncertain about what it says, check to be sure. Technical or procedural mistakes may win a case for the shop steward. . . . On *attitude:* one executive says that he never feels the time is just right to discuss the details of a grievance with an employee until, by some means, he has won a smile from him. He claims that a smile is possible only after a person has regained a reasonably sound frame of mind.

Related Entries *See listing under preceding entry.*

H

HANDICAPPED EMPLOYEES

Very few jobs in any office, workshop, or factory require physical perfection. Many handicapped persons have special education, training, and skills which make them excellent workers on the right kinds of jobs. Handicapped workers constitute a reservoir of available manpower, and the millions of disabled workers constructively employed in industry, institutional organizations, and the government have proven their competence in almost every field of endeavor.

In cooperation with the President's Committee on Employment of the Handicapped, your company may have a policy of giving employment to a certain number of handicapped persons—and, of course, there may be people on the payroll who became handicapped as a result of an accident on the job, for whom the company is anxious to provide the proper job opportunity. In any case, you may find yourself with the responsibility for supervising a physically handicapped employee. You'll be interested to know that many surveys have demonstrated that the physically impaired worker has a record in production, absenteeism, and job-turnover that is, in general, equal or superior to his more able-bodied fellows. Apparently the courage, patience, and determination necessary for mastering a handicap are also applied to the jobs.

EXHIBIT H-1

FORM 1 — AN ANALYSIS OF JOB REQUIREMENTS FOR PLACING DISABLED WORKERS

PLANT A — JONES INDUSTRIES, INC.

Column legend

DOES THE JOB REQUIRE?
1. 100% STANDING
2. PARTIAL STANDING
3. 100% WALKING
4. ANY WALKING
5. TALKING
6. ANY KNEELING
7. ANY STOOPING
8. ANY CLIMBING
9. PULLING
10. PUSHING
11. NIMBLE USE OF FINGERS
12. USE OF BOTH HANDS
13. USE OF RIGHT HAND AND PARTIAL USE OF LEFT
14. USE OF LEFT HAND AND PARTIAL USE OF RIGHT
15. USE OF RIGHT HAND ONLY
16. USE OF LEFT HAND ONLY
17. RAISING RIGHT ARM ABOVE SHOULDER
18. RAISING LEFT ARM ABOVE SHOULDER
19. LIFTING FROM 10-25LBS.
20. LIFTING OVER 25 LBS.

VISION?
21. GOOD
22. FAIR
23. POOR ACCEPTABLE

HEARING?
24. GOOD
25. FAIR
26. POOR ACCEPTABLE

WORKING CONDITIONS?
27. HOT
28. COLD
29. WET
30. HUMID
31. SLIPPING OR TRIPPING CONDITIONS
32. DUSTY
33. FUMES
34. NOISY
35. OUTDOORS
36. SELDOM OUTDOORS
37. ARE POSSIBLE SKIN IRRITANTS USED

IMPOSSIBLE FOR THE JOB TO BE DONE BY?
38. WORKER WITH POOR COORDINATION
39. WORKER WITH NERVOUS INSTABILITY
40. WORKER WHO HAS FAINTING OR DIZZY SPELLS
41. A DEAF-MUTE
42. ONE LEGGED WORKER
43. ONE ARMED WORKER
44. A BLIND WORKER

JOB TITLE OR NUMBER

JOB	1	2	3	4	5	6	7	8	9	10	11	12	13	14	15	16	17	18	19	20	21	22	23	24	25	26	27	28	29	30	31	32	33	34	35	36	37	38	39	40	41	42	43	44
1 DRILL PRESS OPERATOR		✓		✓									✓				✓					✓				✓								✓			✓			✓				✓
2 BENCH ASSEMBLER											✓	✓									✓					✓											✓		✓				✓	
3 STOCK CHASER	✓	✓	✓		✓	✓	✓	✓	✓	✓											✓					✓								✓		✓				✓		✓		
4																																												
5																																												

NOTE: IF THE JOB'S DEMANDS DO NOT MATCH THE APPLICANT'S PHYSICAL CAPABILITIES, HIS PLACE-MENT REQUIRES A CONFERENCE BETWEEN THE PHYSICIAN AND PLACEMENT OFFICER

Your job will not be complicated by the employment of such persons, because through the work of interested public agencies, to say nothing of your own personnel and medical departments, a handicapped worker is placed at a *selected* job where his physical capacities will be equal to the job demands. If you have any doubts, you can make use of forms similar to Forms 1 and 2 shown in the accompanying exhibits, recommended by the Association of Casualty and Surety Companies.

Here are some pointers on supervising the handicapped:

1. The time to start assisting the new worker is the moment you extend your hand in greeting. Put him at ease. Ask him about himself and tell him about the company's and department's work and objectives. As with any new employee, tell about hours and rules, washrooms, locker rooms, tool crib, etc., and stress safety suggestions, both general and for the specific job assigned.

2. If the impaired worker has been transferred from another department, be sure he knows the reason. Don't let him magnify the reason, thinking it was solely due to poor workmanship resulting from his impairment, when in truth there may have been a totally impersonal reason.

3. Introduce the new employee to his fellow workers, as you would in any case. Don't make him feel any different from any other worker in the department. Always avoid referring to his impairment in his presence, but in the case of severe disability (those that are extremely noticeable and may be distressing to see), it may be advisable for you to prepare other people with whom the impaired person is to work.

4. As to training, use all of the techniques given in the entry, *On-the-Job Training*, but be doubly careful

FORM 2 — PHYSICAL CAPABILITIES ANALYSIS

NOTE: PLACE A CHECK (✓) IN EACH BOX DESCRIBING AN ACTIVITY THE EMPLOYEE IS NOT CAPABLE OF DOING UNDER NORMAL HEAVY WORK CONDITIONS

No.	Activity
1	100% STANDING
2	PARTIAL STANDING
3	100% WALKING
4	MUCH WALKING
5	MUCH TALKING
6	ANY KNEELING
7	ANY STOOPING
8	ANY CLIMBING
9	MUCH PULLING
10	MUCH PUSHING
11	NIMBLE USE OF FINGERS
12	USE OF BOTH HANDS
13	USE OF RIGHT HAND AND PARTIAL USE OF LEFT
14	USE OF LEFT HAND AND PARTIAL USE OF RIGHT
15	USE OF RIGHT HAND
16	USE OF LEFT HAND
17	RAISING RIGHT ARM ABOVE SHOULDER
18	RAISING LEFT ARM ABOVE SHOULDER
19	LIFTING FROM 10-25 LBS
20	LIFTING OVER 25 LBS

IS APPLICANT INCAPABLE OF ?

VISION CORRECTED?
21	GOOD (20/40 & 14/28)
22	FAIR (20/60 & 14/42)
23	POOR

HEARING?
24	GOOD (20/10)
25	FAIR (20/5)
26	POOR

IS THE APPLICANT INCAPABLE OF WORKING UNDER THESE CONDITIONS?
27	HOT
28	COLD
29	WET
30	HUMID
31	SLIPPING OR TRIPPING CONDITIONS
32	DUSTY
33	FUMES
34	NOISY
35	VISION
36	OUTDOORS
37	SELDOM-OUTDOORS
38	ANY SKIN IRRITANTS

DOES THE APPLICANT HAVE?
39	POOR COORDINATION
40	NERVOUS INSTABILITY
41	FAINTING OR DIZZY SPELLS
42	IS HE A DEAF-MUTE
43	IS HE ONE LEGGED
44	IS HE ONE ARMED
—	IS HE BLIND

COMMENTS: Applicant had severe injury to left arm and shoulder. Although he retired use of the number and it is advisable for him to use it in light exercise, he should not be given heavy work or job demanding that he raise the arm above shoulder level.

NAME: K. N. Smith   PLANT REG. NO. 39401   EXAMINING PHYSICIAN: A. R. Brown, M.D.

about the safety features. Before training, be sure you know what the impaired worker's physical capabilities are. You should be given this information when he is placed on the job. If for some reason you did not get this, ask your superior or the placement officer about it. (See Form No. 2.)

5. Don't permit any expression of maudlin concern or sentimental offers of assistance by the disabled man's co-workers. The physically impaired person should rely on his own abilities, just like any other worker in the department.

6. See the entry, *Safety—5. Safety for the Physically Handicapped Worker.*

7. Do a conscientious follow-up—check closely on the impaired worker's progress, and ward off any difficulties that might arise. Evidences of fatigue and strain, absenteeism, and all accidents should be noted and reported.

Related Entries   *The Mentally Disturbed Worker; The Mentally Retarded Worker; Safety—5. Safety for the Physically Handicapped Worker.*

HORSEPLAY

Horseplay is a manifestation of excess animal spirits that is apt to show up wherever there are relatively young men in the department, relatively inexperienced in business or work environments. You can't, of course, condone it—not only because of interruptions to the work (if indulged in during working hours) but because of hazards involved, especially if there is dangerous equipment nearby. Discouragement of it must be prompt and emphatic. Aside from making appropriate remarks on the spot, here are some general rules to follow, if it is a recurring problem:

1. Reexamine the workload of the department, and of the individuals concerned. Isn't there enough to keep them busy on work for which they're being paid?

2. Will reassignments serve as a preventive? A shifting of crew make-up may keep the ebullient ones apart.

3. Can you elicit the help of the older members of the department or crew? Can you definitely charge one of them with responsibility for preserving decorum?

4. Is safety properly stressed in the department? Should horseplay be the subject of a special safety session?

5. Is horseplay properly stressed in the indoctrination given all new employees?

Related Entry *Discipline—1. Day-by-Day Discipline; Safety —3. Dramatization to Employees.*

HOUSEKEEPING

Good housekeeping is one of the prime responsibilities of every supervisor and department head. A neat and orderly department is conducive of pride in workmanship, and an important element in accident prevention. Here are 17 housekeeping pointers set forth in The National Safety Council's *Supervisor's Safety Manual:*

1. *Set a good example in your own office or desk area.* Don't hesitate to pick up unused odds and ends or litter from the floor and put such trash in the waste can. Your concern will impress the people who work for you.

2. *Appeal to employees' pride.* Point out how attractive neat work areas look. Show how each employee can benefit by keeping his work space free from dirt and congestion.

3. *Explain the specific responsibilities each employee*

has for good housekeeping. Explain why such assignments are necessary if a clean department is to be realized.

4. *Make sure that instructions and directions to employees are complete and are understood.* Don't leave any chance for, "I didn't know you meant *that!*"

5. *Develop a definite schedule and procedure for making departmental inspections,* and stick to the schedule. The employees will then know you mean business.

6. *Keep a close check on general working conditions.* The *first* piece of trash on a window sill or under a bench invites employees to add to it. Take immediate action when necessary to keep heating, lighting, ventilation, and sanitation satisfactory.

7. *Keep aisles clear and clean.* Never let truckers leave a load in an aisle. If the storage area is full, truckers bringing in materials should check with the foreman before unloading.

8. *Make it easy for employees to keep trash off the floor.* Provide trash containers, plainly labeled, in strategic locations, and see to it that they are emptied promptly when full.

9. *Provide proper receptacles for empty milk or beverage bottles.* And make employees use them!

10. *Don't permit anything to be stored even temporarily on window ledges or hung from walls.*

11. Provide seats and benches for employees where needed. Discourage sitting on kegs and boxes.

12. *Eliminate the practice of keeping excess materials at work places.* This is one of the most prevalent of poor work habits.

13. *Check equipment using coolants to see that oil, coolant, and water are not allowed to leak directly on to the floor.* See that absorbents are handy for soaking up liquids spilled.

14. *Discourage employee habits of "calendart art,"* especially on walls and on cabinets in work areas.

15. *Be sure that flammable solvents are kept in ap-*

proved containers and used sparingly. Don't permit more than one day's supply to be stored in the department at any time.

16. *Encourage employees to report conditions which contribute to disorder.*

17. *Cooperate with materials-handling crews.* See that temporary storage areas are positively identified and easy to use.

Note Use *preventive* housekeeping. When you plan a housekeeping program, says Peter C. Reid (in a discussion of the price of poor housekeeping, in *Supervisory Magazine*), don't think only in terms of cleaning up—but in terms of preventing the need to clean up. It's easier to fix a leaking container once than continuously to mop up the mess it makes. Leaking pipes and containers, broken-down bins, defective trucks, and battered tote boxes all add to the housekeeping chore. . . . Preventive housekeeping makes sense, too, when you're installing a new machine or process. Consider the waste problem ahead of time, so that you can build in provisions for disposing of the scrap. For example, a new machine that produces a lot of waste might be placed so that the scrap can be dropped into a bin on the floor below. As much as possible, scraps, chips, cuttings, and dust should be dumped directly from a machine into containers, not allowed to accumulate on the floor to be cleaned up later.

Related Entries *Fire Prevention; Working Conditions.*

I

THE IMMATURE EMPLOYEE

Maturity means completeness in growth and development. With respect to adults, whose physical maturity is taken for granted, the term has come to imply behavior to be expected of a healthy, well-adjusted person. Note that this implies nothing with respect to formal education.

A mature employee is in command of himself. He is well adjusted emotionally and does not panic easily. He is usually calm under stress, displaying confidence and self-reliance. He does not let minor setbacks completely disrupt his ability to assess the changed situation or interfere with his ability to concentrate on other matters. His reactions are adult and not childish: He does not rely on tantrums and pouts to get his own way, has learned the value of persuasion and agreement, and is aware of the frequent need for giving in a bit to attain an end.

Maturity is not a matter of age. Some people are fully matured in their early twenties, while others remain essentially immature all of their lives. Fortunately, maturity is something that a person can build up over the years as a result of experience and discipline from both without and within. Many of us have known boys who were coddled at home—given their own way to a large extent and never asked to assume responsibility—

but who were transformed into mature individuals after a short period of military service. Therefore, in appraising a subordinate, a supervisor should not be influenced disproportionately by a rating of "immaturity" made several years previously; the employee may have grown considerably since then.

In connection with your problem of developing men, the chances are that your efforts to improve maturity will bring results only with your younger employees—the ones who haven't yet "solidified." The best help you can give in this regard, in addition to a tough-minded insistence upon high-standard performance, is in the annual "appraisal interview" suggested in *Development of Subordinates—1. Development-Appraisal-Development.* Analyze with each man pertinent "critical incidents" in the department during the previous year, with a view of what they demonstrated as to the maturity of the principal actors involved.

Note This and related traits and behavior characteristics are discussed in some detail in the author's *Appraising Executive Performance,* published by the American Management Association. Maturity is one of the significant rating points for executives—so be sure to turn the mirror upon yourself, as well as upon your subordinates, in considering the points made above!

INCENTIVE WAGES

A supervisor of industrial operations should be knowledgeable about modern *direct financial incentive systems* of wage payments, even if all workers in his company may be on straight hourly or weekly pay. Despite the fact that unions are generally somewhat negative toward such forms of payment, and despite the fact that many forms of *indirect* financial incentives (profit sharing plans, pensions and other types of "fringe benefits," etc.) have been gaining acceptance, piecework and similar types of direct plans are still very widely used. Thus the supervisor not immediately concerned may find that his company is contemplating installing a direct incentive system —or, in changing jobs, he may find himself in a company which has such a plan in effect.

Experience has amply proved that direct financial incentive plans which provide a direct monetary advantage to the employee for superior performance are a very strong stimulus for increased productivity. It is not at all unusual to find that output per worker doubles when going from a straight hourly form of payment to a *soundly designed and properly operated* incentive system. (The italics phrase is used because, as with so many procedures affecting people, the plan must be fairly conceived and fairly administered. Rates must be established on a sound industrial-engineering basis, not subject to arbitrary slashes once a job is under way.)

By far the most widely used plans today are one of two types—*piecework plans* and *standard minute (standard hour)* plans. Both of these are so-called "100 per cent premium" plans in that the worker's pay is in direct proportion to his output. Other types of plans pay the worker less than one per cent bonus for each one per cent increase in production, but these are increasingly in the minority.

Piecework plans are the oldest form of direct financial incentives. They are still in very common use, particularly in the needle trades and foundries. A piece rate is usually expressed in dollars and cents per piece produced. Its big advantage is that it is easily understood —by multiplying the number of pieces he produced in a day, the worker immediately knows how much money he has coming. However, there are administrative complications: The piece rate is dependent upon the time required to produce a unit of work, and upon the employee's *base pay*. Thus the piece rates have to be refigured whenever a general wage increase is granted. Moreover, in attempting to secure employee agreement to specific piece rates, the question of money immediately comes up, complicating what should be an objective engineering determination of how long it should take to produce a particular piece or perform a particular operation.

The *standard minute* plan retains the essential simplicity of piece rates, but divorces the emotion-laden negotiation of hourly wage rates from the factual, engineering determination of what should constitute a fair day's work.

Details of setting time standards under a standard minute (standard hour) plan are given in the entry, *Time Standards—Standard Minute (Standard Hour)*. Basically, all work is expressed in the standard amount of time it should take (e.g., "standard minutes"). This is determined objectively and scientifically. Then, the worker's output is expressed in terms of the number of "standard minutes worth of work" he produced in a day. He is paid for these standard minutes *at his base rate of pay*, no matter how many actual "clock minutes" he worked. Thus if, in a 8-hour day, he turns out 600 standard minutes of work, he is paid for 600 minutes, not for 480 minutes, and thus he has earned a 25 per cent bonus. It can be seen that this is "100 per cent premium," and also that the standard times which were developed are in no manner affected if a worker receives an increase in his base pay.

As indicated in the entry, *Time Standards*, the standard minutes (standard hours) are determined in such a way that a worker producing at a "normal incentive pace" actually can, without strain or hardship, produce 600 standard minutes in a 480-minute day. If the company is "on incentives" and pays for all the standard minutes he produces, he has every incentive to hit the "incentive pace" output. Normally, the system used will provide that the worker is not penalized if he produces *less* than 480 standard minutes of work in a 480-minute day. He gets his base pay, regardless—480 minutes worth of pay even if he produced only 400 minutes worth of work. However, here is where the supervisor comes in. Since he doesn't want his department's average to be low, he works with and encourages the slow worker to bring him up at least to standard output, if not to bonus production.

For the part of the day when employees are working on jobs not covered by the standards, they work at their regular "day rate," and they also get day rate for the time they must spend in waiting for work if there has been a delay or production-planning foul-up.

Group Plans. Incentive groups are established where the nature of the work is such that performance does not depend upon an individual, but rather on the team effort of a group, as in an assembly line, or in certain kinds of process work. In effect, their work is pooled, and any bonus earned is divided on an equitable basis.

The Company's Stake

How does the company stand to gain if it has to pay twice as much in direct labor for twice as much production? It gains in the better use of its facilities and equipment, in better absorption of factory overhead, in better "zip" on the part of its employees who feel they are "in business for themselves," and, very importantly, in the practical elimination of below-standard production. Studies have shown that the typical industrial employee on unmeasured day work produces only about 50 to 70 per cent of what carefully engineered performance standards would establish as a fair day's work. Thus the biggest gain is in essence the elimination of payment for work not produced.

The Supervisor's Role

With a direct financial incentive plan, the responsibility of the supervisor is increased, even though at first blush you might think that, since employees are in business for themselves, the system becomes automatic. Thus:

1. The supervisor must understand the plan thoroughly, and be able to explain the workings of it, and defend the standards arrived at. In discussions with employees leading to final setting of standards, he must exercise the skills of communication and persuasion.

2. The very fact that employees *are* in business for themselves means that the supervisor must see to it that there are no avoidable delays which would result in a monetary loss on the part of workers who for certain stretches of time will be on straight pay rather than incentives.

3. He has special training and coaching responsibilities to see that all members of the department are at least up to standard.

4. He also has added responsibilities with respect to accurate record keeping.

5. Finally, it is obvious that the supervisor has special responsibilities with respect to quality, since without proper supervision employees may tend to sacrifice good work for volume of output.

Related Entries   *Motivation; Time Standards—Standard Minute (Standard Hour).*

INFORMAL LEADERS

Every working group soon develops "informal leaders"— individuals who exercise a surprising influence on the members, quite aside from the formal organization. They are the ones who take an active part in moulding the attitude toward the supervisor, and toward management. They are the ones around whom others seem to cluster during the coffee break. . . . and they are the ones who seem to give the nod of acceptance required before a newcomer is "in." They settle disputes between employees and grievances against management on an informal basis before they reach the stage calling for official action.

Who are the informal leaders in your department? Try to elicit their aid in making newcomers feel at home, or in ironing out special problem situations that your judgment tells you had best be handled on an informal basis, or in running down and correcting false rumors. And don't forget that the informal leaders have their little vanities too. Show them that you recognize their special kind of influence. . . . go out of your way to ask their opinion about contemplated changes or special actions you plan to take. . . . keep them informed about matters affecting the department (and give them an occasional special privilege).

INSPECTION

The entry *Waste—1. Reducible Waste* lists as one of the four classes of reducible waste, "inspection to verify for quantity or dimension or quality characteristic." Inspection adds no value to a product—it is, as W. C. Zinck says in that entry, merely a "costly, constant reminder that sufficient quality has not yet been built into the product."

While a staff quality control department will be responsible for *quality analysis* and for determining tolerances and the statistical and other techniques needed to assure satisfactory end products, *quality assurance* itself is a line responsibility. Production workers, and not inspectors, are solely responsible for the quality of work. Obviously, anything that can be done to make workers themselves inspect for quality while they are doing their value-adding work will eliminate waste work done by separate inspectors. (This will be an example of "combining operations" discussed in *Methods Improvement* and *Work Simplification.*)

Note Here's a good example of do-it-yourself inspection, from operations at a U.S. Naval Air Station reported in *Navy Management Review*: A quality control officer was concerned because during weekly aircraft inspection, the pilots discovered only a fraction of the discrepancies that the full time quality control inspectors discovered during their monthly inspections. He decided to attach to the pilots' standard inspection form a list describing the most common discrepancies and how to find them, organizing the list so that each page dealt with a single portion of the airplane. The list called attention to easily overlooked items and hard-to-remember tolerances. . . .

Results became evident at once. The pilots became almost as good at inspecting as the professional inspectors. At first the number of discrepancies detected increased through such increased concentration, but because of better quality control, discrepancies eventually decreased. The "inspection time per discrepancy detected" dropped from twenty minutes to five.

Related Entries   *Methods Improvement—1. The Questioning Attitude; Methods Improvement—2. "Selling" the Need for Savings; Quality; Scrap Costs; Waste—1. Reducible Waste; Waste—2. Dramatizing Avoidable Waste; Work Simplification.*

INTEGRITY

Stress to your employees that personal integrity is not only a matter of honesty with company funds and property—it is a daily test of the way they use their time. It's a matter of being honest with minutes as well as property. . . . it means doing a fair day's work for a fair day's pay—keeping absence to a minimum, coming in on time, restricting personal telephone calls, and staying with a job as required, even after the stroke of quitting time.

This type of honesty is necessary, not only to do a good job, but for a feeling of self-respect. Both suffer if an employee doesn't accept personal responsibility for the proper use of his time.

Related Entry   *Fraud by Employees.*

"INTERNS" AND "CADETS"

Management "intern" programs (or "cadet" training or junior executive development programs) are in use in many large companies and in governmental career programs. Selection and overseeing of the program is usually centralized in a staff unit, which requires periodic progress reports about the interns. However, the supervisor obviously plays an important part while the intern or cadet is assigned to his department.

Management intern programs have been part of Federal government training since 1934. Here are some guidelines advanced by Warren B. Irons, Executive Director, U.S. Civil Service Commission, which will be useful in private companies as well as in government units.

1. The intern should always be placed in an active role, however small. He will not learn as an observer, and less from library research assignments.

2. Preference should be given to work assignments which take the intern away from his supervisor and unit in order to round out his experience and prepare him for promotion.

3. The work assigned should be sufficiently difficult to challenge the intern, broaden his knowledge, and improve his work habits. Emphasis should be placed on finding work experience which will take him away from technical activities into those where he will have to get things done through people. Activities which require self-direction and independence should be given to those who have the capacity to accept them.

4. Each work assignment should last long enough to give the intern a thorough knowledge of why and how the work is done. In general, the assignment should be for more than one month. (In the Federal service, few training assignments exceed four months.)

5. As far as possible, the work assignments should be made after the intern has explored all possibilities and identified those which will help him grow the most. (However, in many organizations, interns are rotated through departments in specified sets of duties.)

6. After each work assignment, the supervisor should

evaluate the intern's performance, and pass the evaluation on to the counselor or other central staff unit.

Here are the kinds of questions you should consider in your evaluation:

1. Give examples of how he has shown initiative.

2. What proposals or ideas has he given you? Has he seen ways to make improved operations? Has he found fault with existing operations without making suggestions for improvement? Has he accepted all present methods of operation without questioning them?

3. How well does he budget his time?

4. How well does he set goals for himself and others. What does he need to learn about obtaining data and analyzing them?

5. How well did he operate in your group? Did your subordinates accept him? Does he talk too much or too little? Can he stand personal criticism?

6. What things seem to annoy or irritate him? What does he do when he is annoyed? Can he stand frustrations? Can he release tensions in others?

7. How does he respond to new or unfamiliar problems? Is he cautious or bold? Can he come to a decision readily?

8. How did he react to you as a supervisor? How well does he accept the right of management to require certain actions of him? Does he need close supervision?

9. What are his major deficiencies in performance, training, or experience?

Related Entry *Promotions—2. Assessments in Depth.*

INTERVIEWING

See *Recruitment; Appraising Subordinates—2. Appraisal Interview.*

J

THE JITTERY EMPLOYEE

Many otherwise good employees become panicky when things begin going wrong, or when there is a pressure situation, or even simply when the boss happens to be passing by (and if he looks over the jittery employee's shoulder—!!!!). The "boss complex," as one executive puts it, "makes mice out of men, liars out of the honest, cowards out of the most courageous, and shifty-eyed morons out of straightforward intelligent citizens." An employee in that frame of mind forgets obvious answers to simple questions, cannot locate familiar objects, and explains mistakes that no one has even noticed.

"I found out a long time ago," said General Motors' Bill Knudsen (as quoted in Melvin Copeland's *Executives at Work*), "that if I yelled at a fellow, I'd scare him, and when he was scared, he'd lie to me. If you're going to be a boss, it's your business to help out the fellows who are actually doing the work."

Some Morals to Be Drawn

1. Don't judge too hastily that a worker is "dumb." Maybe he's suffering from boss complex and will straighten out with more experience on the job and with you.

2. Don't unwittingly add to jitters. Remember "Big Bill" Knudson. And remember that a girl in tears will

probably be worth nothing to your department for the rest of the day.

3. *Know your people!* Who are the Nervous Nellies? The fellows with the butterfly stomachs? What's the background of that new young employee?

Related Entry   *Emotional Reaction; Self-Confidence.*

JOB ANALYSIS AND EVALUATION

Most companies today will (at least for hourly-rated jobs) have some sort of systematic *job analysis* and *job evaluation* procedure. Where there is a union, the degree to which a company follows thorough and objective methods in analyzing and describing jobs and weighing them on a *comparative* basis will determine the degree to which it can conduct constructive discussions regarding fair rates of pay.

Job analysis and job evaluation will usually be administered by the personnel department. But the foreman and supervisor will play an important part—both in arriving at sound conclusions about jobs, and in selling management's evaluations to employees.

You should be conversant with the principles involved, even though the fine points will be left up to trained analysts and rating specialists. The kind of analysis involved will give you a better insight into your own departmental operations.

First of all, keep in mind that the analysts are bent on analyzing and rating jobs, and are not at the moment concerned with rating the *people* on the job. They want to determine what the job is, and what demands it makes upon a person who is to carry out the duties and responsibilities competently.

Their next step is to apply some sort of *quantitative measure,* or *point-evaluation* of the job, based on the job factors, so that all jobs can be viewed in proper relationship to one another, and so that jobs making comparable demands in terms of skill, physical exertion, working conditions, etc., will have the same number of evaluation points. (As used here, "job" means a collection of duties. Thus there may be only one job of welder in the plant, although there may be ten men on the payroll with that title.)

The final step is to agree upon the number of points per dollar, so that a wage rate can be applied to each job.

The Job Specification

The first step is the obtaining of detailed information about all jobs. Following are the important elements on which facts are gathered.

1. Job title, alternate titles, and identification by department.

2. Listing of principal duties, secondary duties, and working procedure.

3. Special equipment and machines used.

4. Special knowledge required, such as elementary shop mathematics, advanced shop mathematics, ability to read simple or complicated blueprints, etc.

5. Knowledge of special instruments required.

6. Previous experience required; length of time, with such experience, it should require to break in on the job, etc.

7. How closely the employee on the job would normally be supervised and also whether the same employee would supervise others.

8. Types of mistakes that could be made on the job, and their seriousness in terms of spoiled work, equipment damage, safety to others, etc.

9. Description of working conditions, as to hazards, unhealthy or unpleasant surroundings, etc.

10. Special physical requirements of the job, such as heavy lifting, severe eyestrain, etc.

Based on such information, a *Job Specification* can be drawn up, as shown in Exhibits J-1a and J-1b, Atlantic Refining Company, giving an overall description of the job. Exhibit J-1b gives further information in terms of five factors which are present in varying degree in all jobs.

Rating the Jobs

The next step is for the analyst to develop point values for all jobs, based on the common factors such as shown in the job specification. (It is at this stage that they must have the benefit of the supervisor's knowledge of the job, special conditions surrounding it, etc.)

Exhibit J-2 shows a set of factors, developed by the National Electrical Manufacturers' Association, and widely used in other industries as well as electrical. The exhibit gives weighting points for each factor (i.e., depending upon the judgment of the analyst, points for each factor are assigned up to the maximum given).

One method used by analysts is to do a very thorough job of weighting factors for about 12 "bench-mark" jobs in a plant, running from one requiring least skills, to one calling for the highest skills. Jobs are picked on which it is relatively easy to reach agreement on point assignments. Then all other jobs can be rated relatively quickly, by comparing them, factor by factor, with the bench-mark jobs. For example, on a job being rated, the factor "Physical Effort" might be just a bit higher than that factor for, say, Bench-mark Job No. 6, but "Working Conditions" may be "slotted" by noting that it is just a bit below that factor for Bench-mark Job No. 9.

Putting Jobs into Grades

After rating points have been agreed upon by supervisors, union representatives, and others, all jobs in a plant are usually placed in *grades*, based on the point-score ranges within which they fall. For example, using the NEMA factors, there would be ten grades: the highest, No. 1, could be a range of 360-381, with 21 point intervals for all grades, making the lowest, No. 10, 162-183. (Total range of points of all jobs in a plant could be divided up differently—the main thing is to get an agreed-upon set of grades.)

Translating Points into Money

The final step is to translate points into money. Rates presently paid for the bench-mark jobs will be used as a starter. The analysts will then make community and industry surveys to show what comparable jobs are being paid elsewhere. In a union situation, the rates paid for the various grades are then arrived at by negotiation.

It can be seen that once all jobs are properly classified, no new points need be assigned unless the duties change. Changes in pay will merely mean agreement by management as to the dollar value of points—and when this value is changed, all jobs will still bear a fair and proper relationship to one another.

EXHIBIT J-1a

HOURLY JOB SPECIFICATION.

DATE 7/1/64

CFN:bjg

DEPT. Phila. Refinery DIVISION Process LOCATION Lubricating Section
Lubricating Packaging Plant

DESCRIPTION OF DUTIES

Under general supervision of Filling Supervisor and work guidance of Leaderman, is engaged in performing various package unloading, assembly line, preparation, finishing and general handling duties in connection with all types of filling operation at Lubricating Packaging Plant or other locations where applicable.

Receives specific work assignments and instruction from Leaderman, works as part of package filling assembly line gang performing heavy duties (except actual filling of cans or other containers) involved in packaging motor oils and other lubricating and specialty oils at Lubricating Packaging Plant or other filling locations as applicable. As assigned, performs filling line operations such as the following:

1. Unloading empty cans, buckets, drums, cartons, etc., from box cars, trucks and/or trailers and transferring to filling machine locations or storage by chisel, roller, placing on conveyors or loading on skids, pallets or hand trucks, moving by hand jack, elevator, etc.

2. Removing cans from cartons or cases and feeding to filling machine can conveyor or stacking on hand truck; transferring empty cartons or cases to package location by conveyor or hand truck.

3. Operating carton packing machine in semi-automatic filling line and placing filled cartons on conveyor to gluing machine.

4. Receiving cans or buckets from manifold filling machine and sealing containers using plug wrench cap sealer, lid crimper, etc.; observing package condition, wiping off excess oil and occasionally rejecting leakers or other damaged container.

5. Labeling designated packages and cartons for any filling operation as instructed, using materials and equipment supplied by Leaderman, such as stencils, decals, silk screen, paper labels, etc.

6. Removing filled containers, cartons or cases from filling line and stacking on pallets; transferring pallets to storage locations or occasionally shipping assembly points, using lift trucks.

7. Performing various miscellaneous duties such as: wiping down conveyor or changeover from bucket to carton operation; cleaning and emptying glue pots on filling lines; etc.

APPROVED

NOV 19 1964

PLANT SALARY
SUB COMMITTEE

CLASS 55

DAY ☒ SHIFT ☐ ☐

SPECIFICATION NUMBER	PAYROLL TITLE	ALTERNATE TITLE
2-198	Filling Line Operator	

Courtesy Atlantic Refining Company

EXHIBIT J-1b

MENTAL EFFORT	SKILL	PHYSICAL EFFORT	RESPONSIBILITY	WORKING CONDITIONS
EDUCATIONAL REQUIREMENTS OR EQUIVALENT Grade 6.	**EXPERIENCE REQUIRED TO START ON JOB** None.	**ACTIVITY** Standing, walking, lifting, hauling, some climbing; operating lift truck, packing machines, etc.	**MEN** None.	**PLACE** Indoors and outdoors.
	PREVIOUS TIME TO ACQUIRE & WHERE None.		**MATERIAL** Careful handling of packages to prevent waste of oils and packaged material; efficient use of caps, seals and other supplies; accuracy of packing; some detection and removal of unsatisfactory packages	**SURROUNDINGS** Oily, gang work; noisy at times.
	KNOWLEDGE ACQUIRED ON JOB & TIME TO ACQUIRE 2 weeks to gain general knowledge of filling line procedures, equipment, containers, etc.	**SPECIAL PHYSICAL REQUIREMENTS** None.	**EQUIPMENT** Proper operation of lift trucks, packing machines and similar equipment	**HAZARDS** Moving machinery falls, vehicles; falling objects; strain and other workers.
			MARKETS None.	**HOURS** 7:30 - 4:00 PM.
			MONEY None.	
			METHODS Execution of established methods.	
			RECORDS None.	

SPECIAL REMARKS:

Filling Line Operator

99-5020-3 REVERSE

Courtesy Atlantic Refining Company

EXHIBIT J-2 *Maximum Points Assigned to Factors*
(*NEMA Point System*)

Skill Factors

1. *Education:* Trades training or knowledge required to do the job—obtained either by formal education or on other jobs. (70 points)

2. *Experience:* Minimum length of time normally required to attain quality and quantity performance under normal supervision. (Does not include trade or apprenticeship training rated under *Education.*) (110 points)

3. *Initiative and Ingenuity:* Independent action, use of judgment, the making of decisions, and amount of resourcefulness and planning required by the job. (70 points)

Effort

4. *Physical Demand:* Kind, amount, and frequency of physical effort required; work position in which the effort is applied. (50 points)

5. *Mental or Visual:* Amount of mental or visual fatigue sustained through the concentration and co-ordination of mind and eye. (Does not measure the "intellectual level" of the job.) (25 points)

Responsibility

6. *For Equipment or Process:* Responsibility for preventing damage to equipment or process. (Usually considers dollar value of possible damage) (25 points)

7. *For Material or Product:* Responsibility for preventing loss due to waste or spoilage. (Usually considers dollar possible value.) (25 points)

8. *Safety of Others:* Extent to which injuries can be caused. (25 points)

9. *Work of Others:* Responsibility for setting up and/or checking work of others, instructing, directing and maintaining flow of work. (25 points)

Job Conditions

10. *Working Conditions:* Surrounding conditions; presence of dust, fumes, moisture, vibration, oil, etc. (50 points)

11. *Unavoidable Hazards:* Hazards connected with job, after making allowance for all protective devices installed. (25 points)

JOB INTEREST
How to Stimulate It

In its *Supervisor's Handbook,* Trans World Airlines has some valuable points on building job interest. The teacher or trainer, it says, is presenting new information—and the novelty of this is in itself an interest-catcher and a boredom-chaser. But the longer the training or learning period, the less effective this factor is. It needs supplementation. Here is how you can build on the initial interest with which the learner starts:

1. *Show your own interest.* If you're bored, you'll bore the trainee. Odds are, you won't be especially interested in many cases. . . . it's old stuff to you. Focus your attention on the person you're teaching—not on the job. Is he nervous? Is he catching on, or are you going too fast for him? Once you start to think about him, you yourself will have a new problem—your trainee—and that means a more interesting experience for you.

2. *Encourage self-development.* Don't explain everything. If you tell him all there is to know, he has no room to show initiative. That's deadly for job interest. Give the learner a chance to explore, to come up with answers. Start him thinking on his own, instead of repeating things you are saying. This will give him personal satisfaction and keep his interest on the alert. His discoveries may be old stuff to you—but they are achievement for him, and encourage his further exploration.

3. *Let him try it himself.* Let him do things himself—otherwise you will frustrate the very interest he himself has built. Give him a chance to do things you have demonstrated, and in addition, give him a chance to do some "next steps" without your showing him. It's also

good to leave him on his own occasionally, but keep these factors in mind:

a. Before you let him spread his wings, know the worst that can happen. And don't blame him if it does.

b. Stay within easy reach. Tell him where he can find you or somebody else who can lend a hand if he needs it.

4. *Give him alternatives.* Interest is born from variety. Give him a chance to see what happens when other than the recommended method is used. Knowing the consequences of the wrong way will strengthen his interest in the right one. If he does all right, congratulations are in order.

5. *Leave room for his ideas on improvement.* You will keep his interest more alive if you can point out that the job leaves room for improvement, that you are looking for better ways of getting it done. Point out to the learner that you'd welcome any new ideas on how the work method can be improved.

Related Entries   *Communicating—1. Selling Ideas; Music for Employees; On-the-Job Training—1. J.I.T. Program; Suggestions—1. Tapping the "Latent Resources."*

L

LABOR LAWS

Labor relations can be a ticklish subject in any plant, and the supervisor very often is the man in the middle when charges of discrimination and other unfair labor practices are brought by employees or unions.

Federal labor-relations law makes it clear that the supervisor is a representative and agent of management, and what he says and does may very well prejudice management's case in a hearing before an official of the National Labor Relations Board. Accordingly, it is the responsibility of the supervisor to be aware of the features of labor relations legislation as it affects his responsibilities and comportment—especially the National Labor Relations Act, which makes it an unfair labor practice for a supervisor to question employees concerning their union membership, to interfere with their union activity, or to discipline them in a way which can be construed as retaliation for union activities.

Following are separate entries to consult: *Civil Rights; Mediation and Conciliation Services; Minimum Wage Laws; National Labor Relations Act; State Labor Laws; Workmen's Compensation.*

LABOR TURNOVER

See *Turnover.*

LATENESS

See *Tardiness*.

LAYOFFS

Layoffs always bring a train of human-relations problems for the supervisor. Union contract provisions or stated company policy on seniority may somewhat ease your personal burden of choice—but where the layoffs cut deep, you may have the problem of exercising exception provisions to keep a semblance of order and continuity in your department's operations. In recommending preference for one employee over another, you will have to be able to substantiate your position with tangible appraisal evidence—proof of superior performance, general competence, and the like, or negative factors of infractions of rules, or poor quality of work. Most important, there must be no shadow of implication that a decision went against a particular employee because of his union activities. (See *National Labor Relations Act*.)

Quite aside from such problems of choice, you will have definite responsibilities to all employees affected, as follows:

1. Be sure that the reasons for the layoff are fully explained to everyone in the department. Be sure to give official information as early as permissible, to alleviate uncertainty and to scotch rumors.

2. Explain in detail the workings of seniority provisions to everyone affected.

3. Be sure you understand recall provisions as related to seniority rights, and that you can give straight answers on the subject. If the layoff is to be indefinite, be sure not to give rise to false expectations of early recall.

4. Be sure that all in your department who are to be laid off receive from you or the Personnel Department complete information and instructions regarding the effect on their group insurance (conversion privileges, etc.), pension, hospitalization, etc. If they will be eligible for unemployment insurance benefits, see to it that they receive proper information and instructions about that.

5. Follow up on compliance with all requirements regarding return of company property, passes, keys, etc.

6. If the layoff is to be of indefinite duration, give all help possible regarding leads on other jobs.

Related Entries *Appraising Subordinates—3. "Best versus Poorest"; Discharging an Employee; Exit Interviews; National Labor Relations Act.*

THE LAZY WORKER

A lazy person is someone who is "disinclined to action or exertion." Of course, such disinclination may be due to fatigue or other physical reasons (see *Fatigue*). Leaving aside the possibility of a misassigned physically handicapped person (see *Handicapped Employees*), it would be a rare thing to find workload in industry in this country to be beyond normal physical abilities.

What we're concerned with here is the employee who seems to be just plain "lazy" in the ways we all recognize: Greatly unenthusiastic about any special chores; skillful at determining the precise minimum of effort of accomplishment that will permit him to "get by legally"; the world's leading non-volunteer; output inclined to be slipshod because he doesn't want to give that extra effort to be sure it's right. One trouble is that he may be a very likeable person, simply because he is so easygoing.

If you are going to keep such an employee in the department, here are some pointers from the Trans World Airlines' *Supervisor's Handbook*:

    1. Try to correct the situation by reassignment, more responsibility, putting color into his job.

    2. You can kid this fellow, appeal to his self-respect.

    3. Provide him with worthwhile goals; emphasize the opportunities of competition.

    4. Always give him direct, clear orders. Be tough about holding him to minor responsibilities—living up to them is his weak spot.

    5. Make him think. . . . ask his opinion.

    6. If he's better than average in intelligence, you may be able to turn his laziness to use by getting him to work on labor-saving ideas.

Related Entries *Job Interest—How to Stimulate It; Motivation.*

LEADERSHIP

To be a good leader, you have to make it your business to learn about people: why they act the way they do, what they will respond to, how to put them at ease, how to direct and criticize without antagonizing, how best to make a new employee a productive member of his work group. . . . Surveys among rank-and-file employees to find out what they consider important in a supervisor whom they would characterize as a good leader have elicited the following (try them on for size!):

1. That the supervisor know his job.

2. Courteous and consistent treatment.

3. That the supervisor see to it that they have the necessary tools, materials, and instructions to do a good job.

4. Fair play—no favoritism.

5. Opportunity to talk things over freely.

6. Understanding of the employee's problem.

7. Prompt handling of grievances.

8. Adequate representation of the employee's point of view to management.

9. Recognition for a job well done.

10. That the employee be looked upon as an individual.

Related Entries *Informal Leaders;* "*People Problems*"— 2. *Employee Types.*

LEARNING

Educators, psychologists, and others have devoted a great deal of experimentation and study to the subject of learning—ranging from observing the reflexes of animals, the behavior of rats learning their way out of mazes, speed of learning of students and industrial workers under controlled conditions, effect of practice, length of learning periods, and the like. As with all studies of behavior, the experiments are not always conclusive or even consistent in their results. However, certain broad principles have emerged on which there is general agreement today among psychologists and other social scientists, and these can provide valuable insights to the supervisor in all of his personnel work—whether on-the-job training, coaching, arrangement of group training programs. Thus:

1. *Motivation.* Rate and effectiveness of learning are tied in with motivation. No matter how good an instructor you are, you will not get satisfactory results with an indifferent employee. Motivation will differ as between older and young workers, men and women, married and unmarried, social and racial factors, and the like. The

good instructor draws upon his knowledge of these factors in appealing to the interests of those whom he is teaching. It comes back to the repeated admonition—know your people! (See *Personnel Audit* and *"People Problems"*— 2. *Employee Types*.)

2. Reinforcement. People learn best when they see some evidence of progress. This, of course, is simply a continuance of motivation. Psychologists term this "reinforcement"—the feeling that what they are doing is getting them part of or closer to the reward they are seeking. In some situations it may be possible to give tangible rewards, such as step increases in pay after certain satisfactorily concluded learning periods. In any event, the object is to *reinforce* a desired behavior pattern. This matter of encouragement and reinforcement is extremely important in the learning process, and has been found to be much more effective than criticism, punishment, or threat of punishment when mistakes are made.

3. Individual differences. The rate of learning varies considerably among different individuals, and learning does not take place at a uniform rate for the same individual. If you are concerned with training only one individual, you can adapt your instruction to meet his learning potential. If you are dealing with a group, you will have to adapt instruction speed to the rate of the slowest learner, unless you spend extra time with him individually. Often you can help meet this situation by providing the more capable ones in the group with more challenging exercises or practice work.

4. Meaningfulness. A "positive transfer" in learning (using the psychologists' term) takes place most readily when what is being learned has some meaningful relation to the employee's past experience, or to well-defined tangible goals. Therefore in teaching, avoid abstractions as far as possible—translate what you are teaching into "real" terms by showing practical relationships to the learner's previous experience and to the present job situation. For many types of jobs, a certain amount of theoretic instruction is called for. But the theory will be most meaningful if it is tied in with the learning-by-doing phase—and conversely, the learning by doing will be done much more intelligently if underlying theory is effectively tied into it.

5. *Learning by doing.* Learning speed increases when people become as totally involved in the process as possible—when they not only read about what they should know and do, but also hear an explanation, and see the job performed—and, best of all, when they get the "feel" of the job by actually doing it themselves. Therefore don't rely so heavily on films and other teaching aids as to short-cut learning by doing. (See *On-the-Job Training.*) Of course, this implies that there is someone there to watch for mistakes and prevent incorrect work patterns at the very start.

6. *Learning units.* Learning is improved when the learning units are small enough to be "digestible." This provides for the reinforcement mentioned above, making it possible to sense progress by consecutively mastering pieces of the whole. Units that are too large are discouraging in the first instance, and may be simply too unwieldy for ready remembering or for practical learning by doing. But conversely if the job is broken into pieces which are too small, they may appear like disjointed bits, difficult to fit into the whole process.

The size of the learning (teaching) units will obviously depend upon the task or programmed subject. The main criterion is the logical structure of each piece. It should be quite self-contained in itself, but furnish a part of a smooth, continuous sequence. You may have to encourage the learner to tackle what may seem to be a forbiddingly large segment, in the interest of long-run learning efficiency.

7. *Practice for specific skills.* Beyond doubt, practice is extremely important in the acquisition of skills. However, for most tasks repeated experiments have shown that short periods of practice interspersed with brief periods of rest result in more efficient learning than continuous practice. It is not possible to give any specific prescriptions, beyond saying that practice periods should be short, but not so short as to break up a task into artificial or meaningless units. Within reason, the longer the rest period, the more rapid the learning of the skill, but very long rest periods will bring diminishing returns. In general, it appears to be much more effective to have short practice periods interspersed with frequent short rest periods than to have long rest periods and long practice periods.

8. *Learning patterns—"learning curves."* Psychologists use the term "learning curve" to indicate the way the rate of learning changes with practice. Measures used include the number of mistakes made in repeated trials, or the speed of performance after days or weeks of practice.

In many experiences of skill acquisition, the learning curves will show level portions, or "plateaus," perhaps halfway to the time when the curve levels off at the attainment of maximum proficiency.

A hypothetical learning curve is shown in the accompaning exhibit, from *Personnel: The Human Problems of Management,* by George Strauss and Leonard Sayles. The authors point out that when an employee first begins to learn a new job or a new skill, he is likely to find

EXHIBIT L-1 *Typical Learning Pattern*

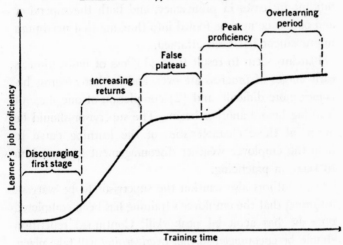

Hypothetical learning curve.

From *Personnel: The Human Problems of Management,* by George Strauss and Leonard Sayles. © 1960. By permission of Prentice-Hall, Inc., Englewood Cliffs, N.J.

himself clumsy or inept—"all thumbs." This can be discouraging, and during this stage he needs the supervisor's support and encouragement. The duration of this first stage depends on the complexity and newness of the new skill being learned—it could be part of a day or a few weeks.

After the first period, the typical learning rate is rapid.

This is the stage of increasing returns, in which small additional amounts of practice usually produce substantial increases in proficiency. The employee's confidence and satisfaction rise.

After more training time, a plateau is likely to develop. Now additional training time doesn't result in very significant increases in proficiency, and both the supervisor and employee may be fooled into thinking that maximum improvement has been attained.

Plateaus seem to result from (1) loss of motivation as early surges of progress are over, and further progress becomes more difficult, and (2) completion of one stage of learning before another begins. The supervisor should be aware of these characteristics of the learning curve to help the employee weather discouragement and get him to keep on practicing.

The authors also caution the supervisor to be wary of assuming that the employee's training has been completed once he has achieved peak skill. Continued repetition should be encouraged so that *overlearning* will take place. An experienced automobile driver, for example, can refrain from driving for years and still be able to drive when the occasion demands. This is largely the result of overlearning.

But in all of this remember Point 3, above—the learning curves of all employees are not the same. There will be differences due to specific aptitude, remembered previous experience as related to the skill learned, and motivation.

Related Entries   *"Learning Curve" in Estimating; On-the-Job Training—2. Job Breakdown and "Key Points"; The Slow Worker.*

"LEARNING CURVE" IN ESTIMATING

Every foreman or supervisor who has a voice in estimating time schedules and labor inputs on new jobs or projects should have some familiarity with the application of the learning curve concept to estimating, which has developed out of experience in the aircraft industry in World War II.

The theory of the learning curve (see *Learning*) is that a worker learns as he works, and becomes more and more proficient as he repeats an operation, so that the direct labor input per unit declines. Experience has shown that this holds, whether the industry is aircraft, metalworking, textile, or candy-making. The important new discovery was that the rate of improvement is regular enough to be predictable.

Studies in the aircraft industry, as quoted by Frank J. Andress in *Harvard Business Review*, showed that the same learning pattern appeared every time a new plane was put into production—while the starting inputs varied for each type of plane, the *rate* of improvement was the same: once production got going, the 4th unit required about 80 per cent as much direct labor as the 2nd, the 10th, 80 per cent as much as the 5th; the 200th, 80 per cent as much as the 100th, etc.—always a 20 per cent reduction between doubled quantities. It can be seen that eventually a plateau is reached where relatively little further improvement takes place.

In aircraft production, approximately 75 per cent of the total direct labor input is assembly; the balance is represented by machine work. In assembly, there is a relatively large scope for learning; in machine work the ability to reduce labor hours is restricted. In operations made up of approximately three-quarters machine time and one-quarter assembly time, the approximate rate of learning has been found to be 90 per cent rather than 80 per cent: the labor hours drop only 10 per cent between doubled quantities.

We bring up learning-curve theory here not to suggest precise percentage figures for you to use—but to add to your perspective in dealing with professional methods people, estimators, project managers, and the like. As Andress points out, the concept is obviously more useful in some companies than in others. Where major and minor design changes are frequent, or where new products are often introduced, or where manufacturing is characterized by short runs at well-separated intervals, operations are usually near the "top" of the learning curves, and the learning curve should be seriously considered in direct labor time forecasts. . . . The more an operation is made up of machine time, as already stated, the slower the reduction of labor time is likely to be. . . . The more the pressures of immediate production can be overcome, so that an operation can be planned in advance, particularly in methods analysis and tooling, the more predictable the rate of reduction in labor time will be, since changes in methods, tooling, etc., during a production run will make the learning curve "jerky."

Related Entry *Workload Forecasting.*

LETTER WRITING

Does your supervisory job call for a lot of correspondence? Or is your department in general one in which a lot of letter writing is done? If so, here are some hints on streamlining the work and time involved advocated by Hammermill Paper Company:

1. Get *all* necessary facts before dictating a reply. If information is needed from others in the department, see that they get it to you promptly. A good idea is to devise a simple form or printed slip for Request for Information, so you don't have to route the incoming letter around. Such routing invites lost correspondence and delays. *Don't* scribble requests on the incoming letter and route it around.

2. When you have the information assembled, analyze it and put it into the order of your presentation in framing the reply.

3. If there is a letter which has to be followed up if no reply is forthcoming, a good idea is to have the typist produce an extra carbon on a special color as a *Pending File Copy*. This can be filed under month and date without interfering with the regular filing.

4. Develop *form paragraphs* which the typist can use in different combinations for recurring types of correspondence. Give a lot of thought to phrasing these the first time around.

5. See where actual mimeographed or multilithed formletters will serve just as well as personally typed ones, without loss in public relations or customer goodwill. Perhaps even postcards can be used, saving time of addressing envelopes and inserting letters. Also, look into the possibility of window envelopes.

6. See that your department is following an intelligent procedure in marking files with a notation as to who has taken out certain correspondence. Simple forms are available or can be devised for this purpose.

7. See whether your filing system should include a

simple "Cross-File Record" form, calling attention to additional correspondence on the subject.

Related Entry *Correspondence Speedup—"Correspondex."*

LIFTING AND CARRYING

Your employees—especially youngsters on their first job—should be shown how to avoid injuries from lifting, carrying, reaching, twisting, pulling, and pushing.

They should be shown how to lift safely in accordance with rules advocated by The National Safety Council, by stooping down to grasp the object, keeping the back straight at about a 60-degree angle, and then lifting by use of leg muscles rather than bending down and putting all the strain on the muscles of the back and abdomen. "Remember," says Armco in its *Office Safety Manual*, "Your back is NOT equipped with a spring!"

Teach employees to take a firm, secure grip of the object and to ask for help if it appears to be too heavy for one person. Except in emergency situations, the maximum amount that a woman employee should be permitted to lift is 25 pounds, but check to see if there is even a lower limit set forth in your state's labor laws. On stairways, the limit should be 15 pounds. Tell your employees this: "You can judge whether an object is too heavy by testing it. With knees bent, try lifting a corner. If it feels too heavy, it is BETTER to: (a) get someone to help you; (b) split the load—make two packages, and make two trips; (c) get a hand truck. Material should be lifted, not dragged, from a pile."

When long material is carried, the front end should be kept higher than the rear to avoid injuring others. Material should be carried in such a way as to permit clear vision ahead.

Gloves or hand leathers should be used to protect hands, and shoes with metal toe box should be worn by those whose job calls for a lot of lifting and carrying.

Reaching too high, too far, or too quickly can cause serious strains, even though the load is not heavy. If it is necessary frequently to remove supplies, booklets, or light machines from a position higher than the employee's head, a small sturdy stool or stepladder should be available. But care should be used to see that these are tucked away when they are not in use.

Twisting the back pulls the muscles and may result in strains. Arrange the work so employees don't have to twist, particularly when lifting.

Housekeeping is important. Tripping hazards or objects on the floor can cause a person carrying a load to fall and be seriously injured.

Hernias may be caused, aggravated, or enlarged by lifting, carrying, or placing large heavy objects; by taking a position such that movement causes protective muscles to relax; by twisting, turning, or jerking. In simple terms, hernia means a hole or opening in the lining or inner walls holding our insides in their proper places that allows the intestines to come through. When a loop of the intestines is doubled up and caught in the ring at the canal's end, the blood supply is shut off. This is dangerous and may be compared with a serious attack of appendicitis. It may result in gangrene, which often ends in death.

Analyze the lifting or carrying jobs done by each of your workers. Taking each in turn, determine: What does he lift or carry? . . . . How much does it weigh? . . . . How far does he carry it? . . . . How often does he lift or carry it? . . . . Does he carry it up or down stairs or ramps? . . . . Is mechanical lifting equipment provided?

. . . . Should such equipment be provided? . . . . Are arrangements made for other workers to assist?

LIGHTING

Proper lighting can increase production and efficiency, decrease rejects, cut down on material waste, and reduce accidents and absenteeism.

Most supervisors will have no authority to make any improvements in the lighting available in their departments—but the chances are that if a supervisor can come up with some demonstration of a needed lighting improvement, something will be done about it.

Research has shown that different quantities of illumination are required to perform different tasks with the same efficiency. Exhibit L-2 gives an indication of the illumination requirements for typical plant and office operations. (It is only a small part of the complete table prepared for industry by the Illuminating Engineering Society.)

To measure lighting in your department you need only one piece of equipment—a footcandle meter which measures the quantity of light received at a given surface. If you don't have such a meter, certain common photographic exposure meters are satisfactory. Two different types can be used: (1) those that measure footcandles directly, and (2) those that provide conversion tables from which footcandle measurements can be determined. (Photographic exposure meter readings are reliable enough for this evaluation.)

Lay or hold the meter on the plane of various working surfaces such as a desk, drawing board, or the top of an assembly jig—whether it is horizontal, vertical, or at any angle. Record all footcandle readings on a dimensional layout of the area. Take these readings in all parts of your department.

Compare your readings with the figures shown in the table. (A complete, detailed table can be found in the IES Handbook.) Some of your readings may be higher than the recommended *minimums*—others may be lower.

In addition to quantity, don't overlook lighting *quality*. To utilize increased intensity of light, you must control shadows, glare, and contrasts. Sylvania Lighting Products Company suggests the checklist shown in Exhibit L-3. If you can honestly score YES on all or almost all of the questions, your lighting is probably good to excellent. If not, you have some idea about the condition of your present lighting compared to what it should be.

Related Entries *Working Conditions, and related entries there indicated.*

EXHIBIT L-2 *IES Recommended Illumination Levels*

Minimum on task at any time

Area	Footcandles
ASSEMBLY	
Rough, easy seeing	30
Rough, difficult seeing	50
Medium	100
Fine	500*
Extra-fine	1,000*
DRAFTING ROOMS (See Offices)	
INSPECTION	
Ordinary	50
Difficult	100
Highly difficult	200*
Very difficult	500*
Most difficult	1,000*

EXHIBIT L-2   *IES Recommended Illumination Levels (continued)*
Minimum on task at any time

Area	Footcandles
MACHINE SHOPS	
Rough bench and machine work	50
Medium bench and machine work, ordinary automatic machines, rough grinding, medium buffing and polishing	100
Fine bench and machine work, fine automatic machines, medium grinding, fine buffing and polishing	500*
Extrafine bench and machine work, grinding, fine work	1,000*
MATERIALS HANDLING	
Inside truck bodies and freight cars	10
Loading, trucking	20
Picking stock, classifying	30
Wrapping, packing, labeling	50
OFFICES:	
Reading high-contrast or well printed materials, tasks and areas not involving critical or prolonged seeing, such as conferring, interviewing, inactive files	30
Reading or transcribing handwriting in ink or medium pencil on good quality paper, intermittent filing	70
Regular office work, reading good reproductions, reading or transcribing handwriting in hard pencil or on poor paper, active filing, indexing references, mail sorting	100
Accounting, auditing, tabulating, bookkeeping, business machine operation, reading poor reproductions, rough layout, drafting	150
Cartography, designing, detailed drafting	200
PAINT SHOPS	
Dipping, sample spraying, firing	50
Rubbing, ordinary hand painting and finishing art, stencil and special spraying	50
Fine hand painting and finishing	100
Extra-fine hand painting and finishing (automobile bodies, piano cases, etc.)	300†

EXHIBIT **L-2** *IES Recommended Illumination Levels (continued)*
Minimum on task at any time

Area	Footcandles
STORAGE ROOMS OR WAREHOUSES	
Inactive	5
Active	
Rough bulky	10
Medium	20
Fine	50

* To assure these values at all times, higher initial levels should be provided as required by maintenance conditions. General illumination should not be less than 20 footcandles, and should constitute at least 1/10 of the total illumination level.

† Obtained with a combination of general lighting and specialized supplementary lighting. Care should be taken to keep within recommended brightness ratios. These seeing tasks generally involve the discrimination of fine detail for long periods of time and under conditions of poor contrast. To provide the required illumination, a combination of the general lighting indicated and specialized supplementary lighting is necessary. The design and installation of the combination system must not only provide a sufficient amount of light, but also the proper direction of light, diffusion, and eye protection. As far as possible it should eliminate reflected glare as well as objectionable shadows.

Courtesy Illuminating Engineering Society

LISTENING

In communication, there must be a receiving set as well as a sending set. Have you recently taken stock of your skill (or bad habits) as regards listening? Here are some points to check:

1. *Do you keep an open mind?* How readily do you entertain suggestions or differences of opinions from subordinates and associates? A man is not old until his mind has atrophied against new ideas. (See *Problem Solving— 2. The Open Mind.*)

EXHIBIT L-3 *Evaluate the Quality of Your Illumination*

	Yes	No
Has your lighting system been installed within the past ten years?	____	____
Are the lighting levels equal to or higher than the IES-recommended levels for the tasks being performed?	____	____
Are the variations in footcandle readings less than 30% within a specific area or department?	____	____
Are your lighting fixtures mounted in continuous rows?	____	____
Is the spacing between fixture rows no more than the height of the fixtures above the floor?	____	____
Do the fixtures in your industrial areas have 10% to 30% uplight to provide acceptable brightness ratios?	____	____
Are your ceilings walls and floors light in color for adequate reflectance?	____	____
Are your workers protected from direct glare by adequate shielding of the lamps?	____	____
For critical seeing tasks, is reflected glare minimized by proper shielding or fixture placement?	____	____
Do your workers comfortably perform all but the very highest precision work without supplementary lighting?	____	____
Have your fixtures been cleaned recently enough to maintain designed efficiency?	____	____
Have the lamps in your fixtures been changed within the past 5000-6000 hours (of their actual use) for optimum light output?	____	____
	TOTALS ____	____

Courtesy Sylvania Lighting Products Company.

2. Do you give subordinates a chance to talk freely?
This is especially important in periodic merit-rating interviews and in handling specific grievances. Here the effec-

tive supervisor will not show surprise or irritation at any remarks the subordinate may make. It's a good rule to pause occasionally in the course of your own remarks to give him a chance to make some of his own.

3. *Have you set up "feedback mechanisms"?* You can't run a department blindfolded. An effective supervisor will make full use of the key people and informal leaders in his department to give him prompt and reliable feedback on attitudes toward company and departmental policies, projected innovations, etc.

4. *Have you ever gauged your attention span?* Psychologists report that the average attention span while listening is extremely brief—sometimes as little as two or three seconds. After that the listener's mind wanders off on problems of his own. Do you frequently "come to" with a start, wondering to yourself, "What did he say??"

5. *What is your "bias factor"?* Most people don't listen objectively. They translate much of what they hear in terms of their prejudices, their mood, and their attitude toward the speaker.

6. *Do you ask questions when something doesn't come through?* Or are you concerned about giving the impression that you didn't catch on?

Notes Says Rev. George Heaton, writing in General Foods Corporation's *Manpower Management:* "Whenever you isolate an individual you violate his dignity. That's why I always say to supervisors, you need to wear a mouth gag and use a hearing aid. . . . The dignity of every individual requires that there will be someone who will listen. No man's dignity is improved if he is merely talked to. If he is not listened to, he feels affronted."

• In his book, *The Management Profession*, Louis A. Allen says: "The ability to listen is one of the basic personal skills every manager should master. When we are talking, we are probably repeating something we already know. When we listen, we may learn something new. Listening encourages other people to talk. It enables us to find out how they are reacting to our message and what they understand. The first requirement in successful listening is to learn to press both lips firmly together. If pauses ensue, relax. The build up in tension will encourage the other person to talk if we don't rush in with our words."

• Speaking before the Chicago Industrial Management Society, Dr. Norman B. Sigband, industrial consultant, emphasized that background, experiences, education, emotions, and feelings color word meanings. He gave this prescription for removing communications barriers:

1. Note the person's physical response, such as a look of enlightenment, slump in posture, tensing of the arm. Such involuntary reactions say "no" when the spoken reply is "yes" to your question as to whether he understands what you're saying.

2. Listen with understanding. . . . Often unspoken words are the real key to what is meant, and these can only be inferred from inflections of voice and from a knowledge of the speaker's ego, position, and inhibitions.

3. Put yourself in the other fellow's shoes when judging his opinion. You don't have to agree, but your understanding of his viewpoint is a positive step to working with him.

4. Do you see yourself as others see you? The knowledgeable, confident, friendly supervisor that you think yourself to be may look like an unsympathetic, self-centered incompetent to subordinates.

Related Entries   *Employee Counseling; Exit Interviews; Grievances—2. Handling Complaints; Problem Solving—2. The Open Mind; Suggestions—1. Tapping the "Latent Resources."*

LOAD CHARTS

The foreman or supervisor who has various machines or work stations in his department should have some means

of visual control over their loading, so that he can keep
an even distribution of work in his department. A simple
form such as the one in the following Exhibit L-4 will
help. It shows the load schedule on a unit of equipment—
a final assembly conveyor. Two types of products are indicated as called for by the two order numbers listed, as
well as the quantity called for, and the number of standard hours required per hundred for each product type.
This is translated into the cumulative standard hours
loading for the date shown. The conveyor capacity is 7.8
standard hours' worth of work for an eight-hour day. (See
Time Standards.)

According to the information filled in, the conveyor is
now loaded to a total of 6.8 standard hours. Therefore,
one standard hour is available for more loading. If more
than one standard hour' worth of work comes in, the foreman will have to schedule the work on another conveyor
if he wants to do it that day, or add it to the next day's
loading of this conveyor, or work this conveyor overtime.
Often different units of equipment can handle the same
type of product or part, but may have varying outputs for
it, so that the foreman has a list of preferred units for
each product type, as a further guide in loading.

The exhibit is from a continuous-manufacturing plant,
but the concept of loading charts is also applicable to job-
order production, where departments are organized according to process. The foreman or supervisor would have
to study the characteristics of material or product going
through his department and construct a form which would
enable him to determine loading in terms of scheduling
time. (If standard times on the various products that
pass through the department are not available, he would
have to make approximations based on products which

EXHIBIT L-4   *Final Assembly Conveyor Loading Chart*

LOADING DATE March 25, 1965
CAPACITY - 7.8 STANDARD HOURS

Order number	Product	Number of pieces	Standard hours per hundred	Standard hours per order	Cumulative standard hours
6125	B-241	200	1.2	2.4	2.4
7527	B-811	400	0.5	2.0	6.8

had previously gone through that were somewhat similar in nature.)

Related Entries   *Planning and Control Boards; Planning and Scheduling—1. Progress Charts; Planning and Scheduling— 2. "Critical Path" and Other Network Plans; Seasonal Peaks; Time Standards; Workload Forecasting.*

M

MAINTENANCE COSTS
Operating Departments

Surveys have shown that maintenance charges can in some industries run as high as 33 per cent of the cost of goods manufactured. While the actual maintenance is usually the responsibility of a separate department, *preventive* maintenance is a direct responsibility of the operating foreman and supervisor. Here are some things you can do to keep this entirely unproductive cost to a minimum:

1. If regular cost reports issued to you don't break out maintenance charges, look into the matter with the cost people, or try to get some spot figures, to see the significance of the problem in your department.

2. Develop a cooperative relationship with the Maintenance Department. . . . Be sure your people follow maintenance rules laid down. . . . Give proper notification for maintenance needs.

3. Be sure to stress proper "use without abuse" of all equipment to new employees. Be sure maintenance pointers as well as safety pointers are part of all written instructions and checklists on machine use.

4. Where applicable, draw up a schedule of regular cleaning of certain machines, with time allowed for it.

5. Draw up schedules for checking certain equipment, motors, etc., as required.

6. Enforce proper feeds, speeds, etc., and warm-ups if required on certain machines before loading. Guard against overloads.

7. Enforce proper care of tools, gages, etc. . . . and use of proper tools and gages. Analyze causes of tool breakage. . . . Make operators report tool damage.

8. Keep a record of delays due to equipment failure, and pinpoint and report to the Maintenance Department critical places where delays and breakdowns occur frequently.

9. Follow this example from the Buick Motor Division of General Motors Corporation *Supervisor's Guide*: Make a special list of equipment in your department which:

—will shut down integrated unit if it fails;

—is the only equipment available for its kind of job;

—must be continuously available;

—has a high value, calling for special care;

—operates in unusually severe surroundings.

10. Call for a report on condition of equipment at the end of each shift. In this way you can spot trouble before it occurs.

Note   Maintenance problems are by no means confined to the plant. A *Nation's Business* article reported that a large insurance company spends $10,000 a year just to keep its typewriters operating, and a Midwest manufacturer spends $2,600 a year to maintain only 100 dictating machines. . . . Are office workers reporting to you given proper indoctrination as to the care of their equipment? Even an experienced typist has to be checked out pretty thoroughly when she is given a new typewriter—and some of the electric models run into many hundreds of dollars. A typist who carelessly erases mistakes without moving the typewriter carriage to one side often inadvertently causes clogging grit to fall into the segment slots of her machine. Later she will complain about sticking type bars and put in a request for a service call.

Related Entries   *Housekeeping; The Maintenance Foreman— 1. General Planning; The Maintenance Foreman—2. Criteria for Urgency; The Maintenance Foreman—3. A Systematic Maintenance Program.*

THE MAINTENANCE FOREMAN

1. General Planning

Maintenance is usually the responsibility of a separate Maintenance Department. Supervisors of operating departments have the responsibility of seeing that their employees follow rules laid down for proper operation and care of equipment and other preventive maintenance measures. But now, while operating foremen and supervisors look over our shoulder, let's list a few practical pointers for the maintenance foreman himself:

1. Set up a work-order priority system for all jobs. (See *The Maintenance Foreman—2. Criteria for Urgency.*)

2. See to it that there is a craft-time breakdown on each work order prior to doing a job.

3. Try to have a full day's work planned ahead for each craftsman, at least a half working day ahead.

4. Set up a "master plan" for all large jobs, showing planned starting date, duration, expected completion date, by crafts. (See *Planning and Control Boards.*) Have the plan reviewed weekly by plant operating supervisors, plant engineers, and your key assistants.

5. Stick to schedules for routine inspections, servicing, and repairs.

Related Entries   *See listing under preceding entry.*

THE MAINTENANCE FOREMAN
2. Criteria for Urgency

The Buick Motor Division of General Motors Corporation has developed the following "Criteria for Urgency" to guide its maintenance foremen on the order in which maintenance should be done:

1. *Emergency work.* Consider any work "emergency work" when it involves a shutdown of equipment or when product quality is affected, hazardous conditions are present, or high values are jeopardized. This is work which cannot be postponed.

2. *Scheduled preventive work.* Next in order of urgency should be all work which is scheduled to be done to prevent the development of any emergency situation as listed above.

3. *Scheduled major repairs.* All scheduled and preplanned major repairs.

4. *Direct maintenance.* In this category are all repairs to operating or productive equipment, which are not of an emergency nature.

5. *Indirect maintenance.* This level includes modifications, specialty work, convenience items, testing work, minor construction, etc.

6. *General property maintenance.* This last item in your order of urgency should be any work on buildings or property other than operating or productive equipment.

Related Entries   *See listing under Maintenance Costs—Operating Departments.*

THE MAINTENANCE FOREMAN

3. A Systematic Maintenance Program

The seven-part approach to systematic maintenance developed by the Buick Motor Division of General Motors Corporation is widely applicable:

1. *Current Repair Work*
   a. *Every maintenance job request should be written.* This constitutes a contract to do the work and to purchase the parts and materials needed. . . . A written record assures that all supervisors involved, both production and repair, will know of all work which has been begun. . . . A request in writing will serve as an authoritative communication on what is required and the degree of urgency. In addition, it can contain any necessary special instructions, and will facilitate the Repair Department's planning of daily work. . . . Written records provide the basis for complete and accurate reports.
   b. *Job assignments to repairmen should also be written.* Such written assignments will form a basis for accurate job analysis. . . . Supervisors will know of the jobs being done, and the men doing them. . . . Instructions can be complete, and there will be less chance of misunderstanding, when the supervisor has taken the time to write the assignment. . . . Written assignments facilitate the accurate charging of time and materials. . . . A written assignment makes available to the repairman a form on which a report of the job can be made.
   c. *Every job should be reported.* Such reports form the basis for necessary records. . . . The repair supervisor will be kept more fully informed of all the things which are happening when a report is required on each job.

2. Preventive Maintenance

a. *Analyze completely one work center or facility at a time* and schedule whatever actions are required to keep it operating with a minimum of wear. . . . Items which are not economically sound should not be included.

b. *Perform the work as it comes due,* week by week, in accordance with the "criteria for urgency" approved for preventive maintenance. [See *The Maintenance Foreman—2. Criteria for Urgency.*]

c. *Re minor work:* Generally, as scheduled preventive work is performed, the need for other corrective work becomes apparent. Minor work that will not seriously tie up scheduled labor should be done on the spot.

d. *All newly discovered work* should be listed by the mechanic, and notation made as to which items were done "on-the-spot." The remaining work, then, is written on job assignment forms, and becomes part of the "current work" of the department.

3. Major Repairs

a. *Outline and estimate the job* as though you were a contractor arriving at true cost of material and labor in preparing to bid.

b. *Plan the job* as though you were awarded the contract and want to eliminate waste of time and material.

c. *Get set on the time-table and job limitations,* and work to those conditions so that on the "performance date" the manpower, materials, and arrangements will be all set.

d. *Keep actual material and labor costs* so that you can determine how you came out on the project.

4. Records and Reports

a. *Accurate and timely records and reports* are the basis for self improvement, and for informing others of progress. They should include such items as: description of work done. . . . cause of a failure. . . . what should have been done to prevent the necessary repair. . . . shift on which work was done. . . . amount of downtime due to the equipment failure. . . . cost of job, including material and labor. . . . stockroom record of all materials and parts used.

b. *Reports and analyses should include:* number of work orders per department, per month. . . . amount of downtime due to machine or equipment failure, monthly and cumulatively, by machine and department. . . . cost of materials and labor due to negligence. . . . list of jobs repeated, over and above normal expectations.

c. *The effectiveness* of maintenance and repair efforts can be determined by: number of "emergency" repairs compared with "routine" jobs each month. . . . number of man-hours each month on scheduled work, versus routine and emergency work. . . . specific cost records, e.g.: cost of hydraulic oils per production dollar during one time period with that of another similar period.

5. *Design and Methods*

a. *The maintenance factor* must be a prime consideration at the time of the design and/or selection of equipment.

b. *Equipment already in use* may be modified to improve maintenance factors.

c. *There should be free communication* between maintenance personnel and technical people. This exchange of information should include: parts lists, operating instructions, wiring diagrams, lubrication instructions, etc., sent to repair supervisors for their department files. . . . modifications made or desired by the Maintenance Department. . . . reports to technical departments of designs which have contributed to high maintenance costs.

d. *Standardization:* Efforts of technical and repair departments should be directed toward standardization, e.g.: of equipment components. . . . stockroom materials. . . . operating and control devices.

e. *Techniques, "tricks of the trade," "kinks and wrinkles,"* should be communicated to all concerned. . . . work organization, work sequence should be studied on every job. . . . special equipment and tools should be designed and utilized where they will measurably affect performance.

6. *Spare Parts and Supplies*

a. *Protect against shut-downs* by adequate stocks of parts in every factory and maintenance area.

b. *Storage:* Parts and supplies should be stored in an enclosed and locked area, arranged so that they can be obtained quickly when needed.

c. Have an *up-to-date information system* on stocks and supplies, and an annual inventory to determine what is on hand, and what should be disposed of as obsolete.

7. *Training*

a. *Members of supervision* may be trained through management training conferences, suppliers demonstration, and planned distribution of information, on such subjects as: philosophy of preventive maintenance. . . . preventive maintenance policies, practices, procedures, and systems. . . . current information on improvements, equipment, materials, and methods.

b. *Skilled trades personnel, including trainees and apprentices,* may be trained by departmental meetings, personal instruction, special group meetings, selected demonstrations, and planned distribution of bulletins and other media. Items covered will include: the objectives of preventive maintenance. . . . techniques and new developments. . . . trade instruction. . . . special instructions for the operation and maintenance of equipment. . . . procedures and systems to be followed.

Related Entries *See listing under Maintenance Costs—Operating Departments.*

MANNERS

Don't let departmental manners get out of hand. Develop a simple, short, clear code of social behavior, see that it is understood, and stick to it. This will cover such obvious things as loud talk, swearing, lack of ordinary courtesy, horseplay, even extremes of dress. This need not be any formal, published set of rules and regulations—but prompt admonition where there are flagrant breaches will let everyone know where you stand. "Like master, like man" is a good saying to remember. Slovenliness and poor decorum in your department will reflect on you more than on the direct offenders.

Related Entries *Discipline—1. Day-by-Day Discipline; Horseplay; Informal Leaders; Sex; Telephone Etiquette.*

MEDIATION AND CONCILIATION SERVICES

As part of his background information on collective bargaining and labor relations in general, the supervisor should know something about the outside agencies which may make their services available in settling a labor dispute in his company. The terms he will hear often are *mediation*, *conciliation*, and *arbitration*.

Mediation is a method for solving labor disputes where an outsider persuades parties to reach a *voluntary* agreement. *Conciliation* is simply another word for mediation, with negligible variations.

Arbitration differs from mediation in that the outsider has the power to make a binding decision. The parties have given him this authority to decide for them. The mediator has no such authority—he can only help the parties to decide for themselves, and they are free to reject his advice and aid. The foreman and supervisor may be very much involved in arbitration proceedings—therefore, see the entry, *Arbitration*.

Another important outside agency, of course, is the National Labor Relations Board. For information on this, see the entries on *Labor Laws*.

The neutral mediator can be any public or private individual who is acceptable to the disputing parties. If the parties are bargaining, he acts to avoid a deadlock. If a deadlock happens, he tries to restore negotiations. He tries to prevent complete breakdowns, and if one occurs, he does all he can to end it. For each of these phases, the consent of the parties involved must be obtained.

The mediator invites the principals to meet with him and discuss the issues. He seeks to determine the relative importance of the issues (after the parties have blown off steam), and then usually separates the parties and consults with them privately. Basically, the mediator strives to keep the parties talking and to explore each other's and the mediator's proposals.

Federal, state, and local governments have fostered mediation because they are concerned about possible breakdowns of economic services. In 1947, under the Taft-Hartley Act, the United States Conciliation Service was taken out of the U.S. Department of Labor, and given independent status under its present name—the Federal Mediation and Conciliation Service. Most states also provide some form of mediation service. Under the Taft-Hartley Act, a notice of proposed contract termination or modification must be given to the FMCS and existing state agencies 60 days before contract expiration. The FMCS usually intervenes if the dispute threatens a substantial interruption of interstate commerce. Some agencies intervene immediately, while others await a call from either side.

While the FMCS is the major Federal agency, with a staff of over 200 mediators reporting to a Director appointed by the President, there are other, specialized ones, such as the National Mediation Board under the Railway Labor Act, the Atomic Energy Labor Relations Panel, and the Missile Sites Labor Commission. The FMCS maintains close working relations with all other government mediation agencies.

Related Entry *Arbitration.*

THE MENTALLY DISTURBED WORKER

While the supervisor must be sensitive to emotional needs, and stand ready to listen to and help anyone in his department with an emotional problem (see *Employee Counseling*), he must be careful not to get over his depth in attempting to handle a situation involving a person who is mentally ill and should be referred to professional care.

If you notice the following symptoms, refer the individual to your company's medical department, or discuss with your own superior the proper sort of professional referral: The employee shows "psychotic" symptoms; that is, his behavior seems irrational and uncontrolled. The most obvious examples are people who hear voices, talk to themselves consistently, or insist that somebody is trying to "get them" when there is obviously no basis for such persecution fears, or who believe other things are happening which in reality are not. Others who should be referred include: people who speak of suicide or make suicidal attempts, those who threaten others with physical violence on trivial provocation, or who threaten forms of physical violence beyond all normal reactions, those who have a record of repeated offenses against the law or the company rules, those who are paralyzed into inactivity by their inability to make decisions, those who have constant physical symptoms or mannerisms that they cannot control.

The business of referring an emotionally disturbed patient for special treatment is not a simple procedure. It takes tact and understanding. Here is some advice offered by the National Institute of Mental Health:

"You can't go up to a man and say, 'Joe, the way you're acting around here, nobody can live with you. I think you need to see a psychiatrist. Better talk with the employee counselor about it.' Joe might punch you in the nose and tell you in no uncertain terms what he thinks of you—and you'd probably deserve it. He certainly would not be inclined to take your advice and, even if he did, he would approach treatment with a chip on his shoulder which would make it that much harder for the physician or psychiatrist to help him. Another thing—don't 'accuse' someone of having emotional problems; you don't 'accuse' someone of having a cold.

"The basis for making a good referral when a man needs help with emotional problems is the same as in setting the stage for a work situation under normal conditions—mutual respect and understanding. In looking for the best time or way to suggest that a person with serious problems seek treatment, try to put yourself in his shoes. . . . What would make you feel more comfortable if you were in his position? What would be most likely to convince you that your boss was really interested in you as a person, and that it might be a good idea to see a doctor? All this is much easier, of course, if you have already established a good personal relationship with the people working under you. You know them, they know you, you respect one another, they feel free to talk fairly openly with you about things that trouble them. Then when a problem seems to be one that the man can't find an answer for, you can suggest as tactfully as possible that he might want to talk to an expert who could give him help."

Related Entries *Emotional Reactions; Employee Counseling; Tension and Stress; The Worried Employee.*

THE MENTALLY *RESTORED* WORKER

The general attitude toward a person who has recovered from a "nervous breakdown," or even a more serious mental disorder, is much more enlightened today than it was even a few short years ago. Mental illness is looked upon as any other illness, and not a "disgrace."

Most companies will take back an employee who has been pronounced by qualified medical and psychiatric doctors to be ready to assume his place in society. . . . and some companies will take on new employees with full knowledge of such medical history. Therefore you, as a supervisor, may well find yourself in a position of having a mentally restored person made part of your department. Perhaps you are wondering how to treat him. The only ground rule, says the President's Committee on Employment of the Handicapped, is the Golden Rule. Here are some other *Do's* it offers:

Do consider him as an average human being, same as any other. If you eye him suspiciously, sort of as a creature from another planet, you're not helping in his effort to lead an average life.

Do trust him to keep hold of his emotions. He's probably less likely to fly off the handle than most.

Do help him put his mental illness behind him. He's been ill; he's been helped; a chapter has ended and a new chapter is about to begin. He is changing roles in the drama of his life—from "patient" to "worker." Encourage the new role.

Do give him his share of work. He'll know if you are trying to "baby" him, trying to protect him from more difficult assignments. Over-protection doesn't help him; it slows his comeback.

Do give him thorough orientation—where he is to work, timeclock, lockers, restroom, cafeteria or lunch area, drinking fountains, public transportation, clothes to wear, whom to report to, rates of pay, payroll deductions—as you would any new employee. If he has been in the hospital any length of time, orientation may take a bit longer than usual. Give him time.

Do keep in mind that you will know more about the mentally restored worker than about the average job applicant coming off the street. The mentally restored worker has been tested and probed and analyzed by any number of professionals. When they decide "this man is ready for work," you can depend on their judgment.

Do make him feel he's a member of the work-a-day team, not an outsider. He will respond to human warmth and kindness from his supervisors. Don't we all?

Do let him know you are there if he wants to talk to you about anything, including his former mental illness (which, after all, was a major experience for him). Your "permissive" attitude of sympathetic understanding will be helped by "developing big ears and a small mouth."

Do make note of his on-the-job strong points. When he turns out to be a satisfactory employee, pass the word along to other department heads.

Notes "Help wanted. Ten factory workers for private employment. Must have a history of mental illness to qualify." More than 100 replied to this ad by B&K Industries, Berkeley, California, toy manufacturer. Those employed weathered a screening by a psychiatrist and the firm's young co-owners. Results, as summed up by the owners: "You couldn't ask for a better work force. There are no accidents to report beyond a scratched ear lobe."

• *Who's normal?* "If you do a good enough screening job you may get people in your employ who are perfectly normal. But you will have screened out people who discover things like nylon."—Dr. Frederick Dershimer, formerly psychiatrist, E. I. du Pont de Nemours & Co.

THE MENTALLY *RETARDED* WORKER

In line with today's more enlightened attitude regarding problems of mental illness, which may be a temporary situation (see entry, *The Mentally Restored Worker*), and of mental retardation, which implies permanent handicap, many companies are cooperating in the placement of mentally retarded employees in job situations which they can handle. You may well be called upon to supervise such individuals.

Mental retardation, according to the U.S. Department of Health, Education, and Welfare's Vocational Rehabilitation Administration, is not a disease, or even an illness. Rather, it is a symptom and a name tag that indicate *limited ability to learn*, especially to learn things of the

kind taught in the average school. The retarded referred
to you for employment will have been trained and cer-
tified to hold jobs by a trained counselor in a state division of vocational rehabilitation. Remember that though
their intellectual capacity is below average, their total
beings are not retarded. Their other skills and aptitudes
make them valuable employees in the right jobs.

Of course, many jobs are beyond their abilities. As a
rule they are best in simple, repetitive, or short-cycle jobs
—like attending machines, running errands, doing manual
labor, performing simple hand operations—the very kind
of job you may be having trouble keeping filled with suitable and satisfied "normal" people. They know that they
are "different," although all of them may not know that
they are "retarded."

Because they have a narrower field of understanding,
they are less likely than you are to see the relation of one
thing to another, or to find a quick and easy way to solve
a problem. For example, if you can't find a screwdriver,
you'll use a dime on your cigarette lighter; the retarded
person won't figure this out so readily. On the other hand,
once he's learned a routine, he does it well and he sticks
to it, performing it in the same way over and over again.
He will often do this better than "normal" people would,
because his behavior is so guided by habit.

The President's Committee on Employment of the
Handicapped has offered the following *Do's* to keep in
mind in supervising such employees:

Do talk to him on a person-to-person level, as you would
to anyone else. Only, try to be more specific, more precise
and crystal clear—as if you were speaking to someone in
the upper levels of grade school. Don't "talk down" to
him as though he were a small tot. He's not.

Do speak in concrete terms, not abstractions. If, for example, you want him to put a tool away, show him exactly where "away" is.

Do demonstrate what you want him to do; don't just tell him.

Do show him where things are—time clock, lockers, restroom, cafeteria or lunch area, drinking fountain, supply room—the same as you would do for any new employee. Only DO take time, don't rush, and be sure he understands.

Do take extra care to explain about working hours, proper clothes on the job, his work station, whom he reports to, what his pay will be, where the bus or streetcar stops. It's doubly important for him to know these six points.

Do ask a question now and then to make sure he's keeping up with you. "Now show me your work station," or "Where does the bus stop?" or any kind of question that checks his understanding.

Do introduce him to his fellow employees and his supervisors. He may seem a bit withdrawn at first, but he'll warm up once he gets to know the people. He'll warm up faster if he can find one co-worker at first with whom he can feel free and easy; someone to answer questions and listen to problems.

Do let him know he's one of the work-a-day family. He may learn to mix with others at work, but tend to be by himself after work. After-hours friendships shouldn't be forced; he may be vocationally ready, but not quite socially ready.

Do be ready to give him a guiding hand should new situations and new problems arise which present problems of coping.

Do make note of his on-the-job strong points. When he turns out to be a good employee, pass the word on to other supervisors that it can be good business to hire qualified mentally retarded workers.

Notes Strong points that most mentally retarded men and women show on the job: They want to make good; they will work particularly hard to make good. . . . They want to stay put on the job; they're not anxious to job-hop. . . . Their attendance record usually is better than average. . . . They are willing workers, and will stay at routine tasks.

 • A Connecticut psychologist studied the records of employed mental retardates after they had been on the job 12 years, and found: Employers rated them just as high as the nonretarded on promptness, regularity, friendly relations with fellow workers, and steadfastness on the job. Their weekly earnings compared favorably with those of the nonretarded doing similar work, and the psychologist predicted that most would continue in their present jobs until they retire.

MERIT RATING

See *Appraising Subordinates.*

METHODS IMPROVEMENT
1. The Questioning Attitude

Here is how W. Clements Zinck, who has written and lectured extensively on foreman and supervisory development, lists the supervisor's role in methods improvement, in his entry on Work Simplification in *The Encyclopedia of Management*:

> The foreman's role is three-fold: (1) to be an alert observer, with eyes newly opened to waste; (2) to be a

cooperative assistant to full-time methods men, after being indoctrinated with the elementary principles of the industrial engineer's techniques of charting and analysis; and (3) to develop improved methods of his own.

Every supervisor should have a continuing, hard-headed insatiable, *questioning attitude*, which takes nothing for granted, approaching the improvement problem without any preconceived ideas. To be effective, however, the questions cannot be haphazard. They must be channeled toward four possible results, as follows:

1. *What can we eliminate?* This could be a process, a value-adding or non-value-adding operation, a delay or storage, or idle or inspection. To eliminate is to improve!

2. *What can we combine?* The use of known faster devices may be the answer. [Here the supervisor may draw upon experiences in entirely different operations: slide bins, gravity chutes, an automatic tool, etc.] If two operations can't be combined, it may be possible to combine a transportation with an operation.

3. *Should the sequence be changed?* Changes in sequence may eliminate or reduce non-value-adding operations, transportations, delays, storages, and inspections. Again, the use of known faster devices will often make this possible.

4. *What can we simplify?* The time to start to think about ways to simplify is when the processes and operations have been reduced as much as possible through elimination, combination, and/or change of sequence.

In this purposeful channeling, the six basic questions of Work Simplification are used over and over again: What? Why? Where? When? Who? How? The way in which these can be pinpointed to locate improvement possibilities is shown in Exhibit M-1.

Related Entries *Methods Improvement—2. "Selling" the Need for Savings; Motion Study; Problem Solving—1. A General Prescription; Suggestions—1. Tapping the "Latent Resources"; Suggestions—2. Helping Make the Company Suggestion System Work; Work Simplification.*

EXHIBIT M-1 *Six Basic Improvement Questions*

Key question	Idea kickers	Improvement possibilities
WHAT is done?	What is its purpose? Does it do what it is supposed to do?	Eliminate
WHY is it done?	Should it be done at all? Can as good a result be obtained without it? Is it an absolute must?	Eliminate
WHERE is it done?	Why is it done there? Why should it be done there? Where should it be done? Can it be done easier by changing the location of person or equipment?	Combine and/or change sequence
WHEN is it done?	Why is it done then? Is it done in right sequence? Can all or part of it be done at some other time?	Combine and/or change sequence
WHO does it?	Why does this person do it? Is the right person doing it? Is it logical to give it to someone else?	Combine and/or change sequence
HOW is it done?	Why should it be done this way? Can it be done better with different equipment or different layout? Is there any other way to do it?	Simplify

From the article, "Work Simplification," by W. C. Zinck, in *The Encyclopedia of Management*, edited by Carl Heyel, Reinhold, New York, 1963, p. 1055.

METHODS IMPROVEMENT

2. "Selling" the Need for Savings

How big is a "saving"? Everyone understands the importance of increasing sales. However, the contribution to net profit by reducing costs and eliminating non-profit expenses, though not as apparent on the surface, may be of equal or even greater value to the company.

This aspect of methods improvement is not always made sufficiently dramatic to employees—usually because not enough emphasis is given to the fact that each dollar of sales probably results in a relatively few pennies of net profit. Remember also that sales (unless they are some form of subscription) are individual transactions, and additional effort and expense will have to be incurred to secure future business from the same customer. On the other hand, savings brought about by reducing costs and eliminating unnecessary waste have a much more lasting effect.

Bring home to your employees the fact that, conservatively speaking, a fundamental improvement in methods can be expected to have a life of five years, after which time, possibly, changes in basic procedures or other developments will take the place of the original improvement.

On the above basis, even for a company with as high a ratio of profit as 10 per cent of sales, each annual $1,000 saving made possible by an improvement in operations (assuming the improvement will be effective for five years) corresponds to the increase in profits brought by a $50,000 sale.

If only a small unit of 30 employees is involved, with

an average pay of $5,000 a year, or a total of $150,000, an improvement in procedures resulting in a 10 per cent decrease in cost would represent a saving of $15,000 a year. This, again assuming a net profit of 10 per cent of sales and a five-year life for the improvement, would be the equivalent of obtaining a $750,000 order.

Related Entries *See listing under preceding entry.*

MINIMUM WAGE LAWS

Minimum wage laws help the employee, the employer, and the community by raising the purchasing power of the lowest-paid workers, improving working conditions, and protecting employers who pay a fair wage from unfair competition with other employers who would not voluntarily pay such a wage.

Note that minimum-wage laws do not determine the wage rate which an employer pays. He may lawfully decide what he will pay, as long as he does not pay less than the established minimum.

Federal Law

The *Fair Labor Standards Act*, in effect with amendments since 1938, establishes a minimum wage—applicable to employees of an enterprise engaged in or producing goods for interstate commerce, unless specifically exempt, —as of this writing, of $1.25 an hour. It provides for overtime pay of not less than 1½ times the employee's regular rate for hours over 40 a week. The Equal Pay Act of 1963 amended the Fair Labor Standards Act by prohibiting wage discrimination on the basis of sex, in establishments having employees subject to minimum wage requirements of the latter Act.

The Act does not limit the number of hours an adult employee may work in a day or in a week. It does not require payment for days or hours not worked, such as holidays, vacations, or sick leave, and it does not call for different rates of pay for work on Saturdays, Sundays, or holidays, as such.

Under this law, employees are divided into two groups:

1. *Exempt:* Those who work in executive, administrative, professional, or outside salesmen positions are exempt from both the minimum pay and overtime provisions. (The Act also specifies employees of certain retail, laundry, and drycleaning establishments, and small newspapers, and of certain types of hotels, motels, and other businesses doing more than half of their business within a state.) . . . Certain employees, as in transportation, delivery, processing industries, etc., are exempt from the overtime provisions but not the minimum wage.

2. *Non-exempt:* Those who are in all other positions are subject to the provisions of the law.

Administrative employees include supervisors and foremen . . . executive or administrative assistants who regularly and directly assist a proprietor or executive or administrative employee . . . staff employees who, under only general supervision, perform work along specialized or technical lines that requires special training, knowledge, or experience . . . employees who do all kinds of special assignments under only general supervision.

Piecework. For the employee on piecework, the regularly hour rate of pay is computed for each workweek by dividing the total piecework earnings by the total hours worked. For overtime, the worker is entitled to be paid, in addition to piecework earnings for the entire period, a sum equivalent to half the regular hourly rate multiplied by the number of hours worked in excess of the applicable maximum workweek.

Workweek. The workweek is a fixed and regularly recurring period of 168 hours—seven consecutive 24-hour periods. The workweek need not coincide with the calendar week.

State Laws

At this writing (1965) 33 states, the District of Columbia, and Puerto Rico have minimum wage laws. (The exceptions are Alabama, Delaware, Florida, Georgia, Indiana, Iowa, Maryland, Michigan, Mississippi, Missouri, Montana, Nebraska, South Carolina, Tennessee, Texas, Virginia, and West Virginia.)

In about half of the states with such legislation, the laws apply to both men and women. Originally, state minimum-wage laws applied to women and minors only, but since enactment of the Federal Fair Labor Standards Act in 1938, states have extended coverage of their laws increasingly to men.

In general, all industries and occupations, except domestic service and agriculture, are covered by state minimum-wage laws.

In covered states, the minimum rates are set either by law, or by wage boards which can recommend establishment of higher minimum-wage rates through wage orders. (Eight states and Puerto Rico use both methods.)

Wage orders generally are issued by the state labor commissioner, based on recommendations of industry or occupation wage boards, composed of representatives of workers, employers, and the public, and after a public hearing.

MISTAKES

No batter expects to make a home run every time at bat, and an occasional foul ball or even a strike-out happens to the best of them. So you are not expected to be perfect either, and you should not allow an occasional blooper, even a serious one, to deal your morale too serious a blow. . . . This is easy for someone else to tell you, of course. However, the more conscientious a person is, the more he is apt to fret over an avoidable something that went wrong. And some of us are more introspective than others—we bruise ourselves too easily. . . . When you've made a mistake, the best thing to do is to step back and get a good perspective. Here are some ways to handle the situation:

1. Always be ready to admit a mistake. (But you needn't go around advertising it!)

2. Don't brood—what's past is done.

3. What can be salvaged? Forget about yourself, analyze the problem objectively, and jot down a list of actions to take and people to contact.

4. What can you learn from this one? What danger signals can you set up to warn against recurrence? What personal deficiencies need constructive attack? (See *Notes.*)

So much for a mistake *you* made. . . . How about a foul ball by a subordinate? Before chewing him out, check the following points:

1. What can be salvaged? (See (3) above.)

2. Was it his fault or yours? (Remember the J.I.T. slogan in the entry, *On-the-Job Training*: "If the worker hasn't learned, the instructor hasn't taught!")

3. If it was his fault, count ten before talking to him about it. Hot tempers don't solve problems.

4. Don't beat a dead horse. Don't keep referring to the same mistake after it has once been discussed in an orderly fashion. (He probably feels worse about it than you do.)

5. Keep the long view. Don't let a recent critical incident obscure your long-range appraisal of the subordinate.

6. How can the experience best be used in further developing the subordinate? It is a good idea, where possible, to have the person who made the mistake rectify it.

7. How can the mistake best be used as a training pointer for others in the department?

Notes Remember that what you or your subordinate learn from a mistake or a failure is of no value until you convert it into action. . . . Now is the time to take steps to assure that this kind of mistake won't be repeated. . . . Start working on your plan of action without delay. . . . Failure need not be the end of the road if you make it your business to rebound.

• F. B. Whitlock, Chairman, Ortho Pharmaceutical Corporation, has this to say: "Mistake-making is part of the learning process. Unless the error will be costly to the project or company, don't stop a man from trying a method that you know won't work. The young manager has to be taught to make his own decisions and to realize that not all those he makes will be correct. Learning not to be rattled by one's fallibility is a step toward maturity."

• Eddie Arcaro, the leading money jockey, had 250 consecutive losers before riding his first winner. . . . Babe Ruth's record of 714 home runs will never be forgotten, but how many of us know that the Babe struck out 1,330 times, a record unapproached by any other player in the history of baseball?

Related Entries *Criticism—1. How to Dish It Out; Criticism —2. How to Take It; Emergencies—2. Post-Mortems; Self-Confidence; Self-Criticism.*

MODESTY

See *Note* on the entry, *Age—The Young Supervisor*.

MONEY
Responsibility for Handling Company Funds

If any of your employees have access to company funds in any form, be sure they know and follow the prescribed rules for handling and protecting money. (If your company does not spell this out in written instructions, then it's up to you to develop some instructions yourself.)

If an employee's job calls for him to make adjustments on bills, spend company money, or incur personal expenses for which he will be reimbursed, it is up to him to use good judgment and to see that the company gets value received for what is spent. Certification as to correctness of vouchers and bills should never be made without reasonable knowledge that the amounts are proper. Your supervisory approval should never be perfunctory. When money is owed to the company, as in refunds for transportation, it is the employee's duty to notify the proper person promptly.

Related Entry *Fraud by Employees.*

MONOTONOUS WORK

The reaction to boring and monotonous work is again an example of the wide differences between human beings, once more underscoring the need for the supervisor to *know his people*, and keep personal reactions in mind if he is to get the most out of them. Many workers will regard a job that requires only slight attention from them as boring, fatiguing, and undesirable. They want a challenge from their job. On the other hand, some workers like no-attention jobs, on which they can think of family activities (as in the case of married women) or just plain daydream.

There have been many articles and discussions by psychologists and other behavioral scientists as to whether extremely repetitive and monotonous work is harmful to workers—and, quite aside from that, as to whether productivity in general is adversely affected by it. The results of investigations as reported have actually not been conclusive one way or the other, and some authorities indeed feel that the "problem" has been overemphasized. Whether monotonous jobs are satisfactory or unsatisfactory seems to depend almost entirely on individual likes and dislikes. Only broad generalities seem to come out of the study reports, as follows:

1. On the whole, men seem less satisfied with monotonous work than women.

2. Single women seem less satisfied with monotonous work than married women.

3. Older men approaching retirement, and boys awaiting induction into the armed forces, seem most contented on monotonous jobs.

4. As might be expected, records indicate that among men and women, those who appear to be most ambitious are the first to quit or request to be transferred out of monotonous jobs.

5. Contrary to earlier widely held beliefs, careful studies do not seem to indicate a direct relationship between low intelligence and satisfaction with boring and repetitive work.

In addition to the above, there is, of course, a physical aspect to repetitive work. Fatigue can often be traced to boredom, with strain relieved not by rest, but by changing the nature of the task performed, as indicated in the entry, *Fatigue*.

In view of the foregoing, the supervisor's action must be governed by the type of people working for him, rather than by any abstract formula or prescription about repetitive operations. He may have no complaints about monotonous tasks, and no outward signs such as careless mistakes or accidents, whereas another supervisor, with exactly similar operations, may have sufficient complaints or output problems to warrant action. Here are ways to attack the problem:

1. If complaints or poor work concern operations over which the employee has no control as to tempo or interruptions or choice of alternate tasks, as in an assembly line or on a conveyor belt, you have no great freedom of action, except in greater care in *selection* and *assignment*. With a view to what has been said above as to individual likes and dislikes, check with the Personnel Department regarding your job specifications in this regard, and possible improvement in screening applicants. (What can you learn from the type of people in your department who seem to do monotonous jobs well, and don't complain about them?)

2. If the operations involve work done by individuals in batches, see whether the employees can be given more leeway as to their own pace, timing their own interruptions and rest breaks, and the like.

3. Can workers be assigned groups of tasks which must be done within a given period, but regarding which they can themselves chose which they will do first, which in the morning, which in the afternoon, etc.?

4. Are some tasks monotonous because a worker is "so-

cially isolated"? An employee who is completely absorbed in his work may feel little need to talk to others, but someone on a boring job may want to break the monotony by chitchat. The very fact that it *is* monotonous-type work would indicate that no important attention-diversion would be occasioned by conversation. (See *Talking*.)

5. Knowing your people, is it possible to effect an improvement by changing the make-up of individual groups doing monotonous work, so that they will have more in common?

6. Should you improve the rotation of work assignments, to have everyone satisfied that all are getting their fair share of the tiresome chores? Can some routine work be split up so that more people get smaller pieces of it?

7. How can you spark up interest in "drab" jobs? Do your employees know the end results of their work? (One foreman got permission to take a few of his workers on an inspection tour of the plant, to visit each department and find out how the sum of the parts made a whole. He then asked the slowest worker of this group to take another group around and point out interesting features in the same way. See other examples in the entry, *Waste* —2.) Can some form of friendly competition as to output scores be developed? (Note the point made in *Time Standards* about posting "standard minute performance" records of individual employees. Such scorekeeping gives zest to otherwise monotonous work, since workers want to rate high on the list. In this connection, note also the experience in athletics: Coaches will tell you that runners cannot make as good speed when running "against time" as when competing directly, neck and neck, with other runners.)

8. Can music be introduced? Is there anything wrong

with a radio in the department? Would it distract others?
Could it perhaps be turned on at certain specified hours?
(See *Music for Employees*.)

Note In a food processing plant, many of the jobs at the
packaging machines were extremely monotonous. To add
interest to their work, management used to shift the girl
machine tenders from one machine to another at frequent
intervals, often to a machine in an entirely different department. Since these shifts always occasioned interruptions to
production, the plant manager decided to look for another
means of making the work interesting. Individual records were
the answer: He prepared simple 8½ x 11 in. forms, showing
normal hourly outputs for different kinds of packages. These
were clamped on boards at each operator's station, and she
was requested to keep track of machine production and to
enter the hourly figures on the form. The normal figures
were set low enough to permit the girls to beat them if they
exercised reasonable care. The idea took hold immediately—
the girls became so interested in making good performance
records that they preferred not to be shifted to other machines. Jams occasioned by faulty boxes or incorrect insertions
dropped. "Their whole attitude changed as soon as they
were given a running account of what they, as individuals,
were accomplishing," reported the manager.

Related Entries *Fatigue; Job Interest—How to Stimulate It;
Motivation; Music for Employees; Rest Breaks; Talking.*

MOONLIGHTING

One of the contradictory developments of this day and
age of shorter working hours and increased leisure is the
phenomenon of "moonlighting." A lot of employees are
using their new-found leisure not for recreation, education, or cultural pursuits, but simply to get outside work
to add to the family income—perhaps to meet time-pay-
ments on the new car or television set.

What should be the supervisor's attitude? Is he entitled to *have* an attitude on what the employee does with his own time?

It would seem that the supervisor is certainly entitled to concern himself with anything that might affect the efficiency of his department. Here are some questions to consider:

1. *Is there a company policy?* If so, the supervisor has no choice but to enforce it. (In certain types of government employment, for example, part-time outside jobs are prohibited.)

2. *Is there a conflict of interest?* The supervisor is entitled to answers to specific questions as to the nature of the outside work, who the employer is, whether the company's "classified" information is likely to be used on the other job, etc. Is a direct competitor the employer?

3. *Is there a chance of interfering with the employee's regular work?* Will he be in a position where he may be reluctant to stay overtime or come in on a Saturday to help out in an emergency? (But how likely are such emergencies?) Will he have to think twice about scheduling some out-of-town trip?

4. *Is the employee overtaxing himself physically?* An employer has the right to expect a normally rested, alert employee to show up for work every day. Are there signs of fatigue?

5. *Is there any tangible evidence that the employee's productivity is lessened?* If not, and if there is no positive company policy on the subject, the supervisor may have difficulty in defending any objection to moonlighting simply because he's "agin" it.

6. *Is there a personal hardship situation?* If an employee has a problem at home requiring special measures to clear up a load of bills, to support a relative, etc., the supervisor may want to treat this as an exceptional case, and make allowances. Determine whether the situation is temporary, and for how long. If an exception is made, be sure the others in the department know enough of the situation (but don't reveal confidences) to understand your handling.

7. *Is the outside work likely to be a positive asset rather than a hindrance?* Some part-time work, such as conducting an evening course at a local college, in the case of a specialist, may contribute to his professional standing—and may also have some public-relations value to the company.

Note A *Fortune* study on moonlighting concluded with this observation: "On the management side, moonlighting arouses fears of lowered productivity. According to some executives, the double jobholder may be accident prone, may punch in late, and may have a high rate of absenteeism. There are no studies or statistics to verify or refute this allegation, but it is significant that, except for those who work on farms, moonlighters put in a shorter total week on both jobs than most workers did in one job thirty-five years ago."

MOTION STUDY

Motion study and time study in a plant or office will be undertaken by staff specialists, and the supervisor's role will usually be limited to one of understanding the objectives and basic techniques, answering questions by the specialists regarding operations in his department and volunteering information and suggestions to them regarding improvements, and finally answering questions and securing the necessary understanding and cooperation of his employees in the department. Some of the techniques of analysis used by the industrial engineers will also be applicable by the supervisor himself, as outlined in *Work Simplification.*

Before the engineers make motion studies of an operator, they will make a preliminary analysis to see what overall savings can first be made by eliminating or combining operations, changing the flow of work, improving machine utilization, etc. For these studies they will develop detailed *Process Charts, Man-and-Machine Charts,* and *Operation Charts,* such as those described in the entry, *Work Simplification.* In addition, they may develop *Activity Charts,* which list a breakdown of the process or series of operations, plotted against a time scale, and *Flow Diagrams,* which consist of flow lines on a plan drawing of a department or work area in which the activity takes place.

Where advanced practices are in use, the engineers may apply *micromotion analysis.* Motion pictures are made of the operation or activity studied. A special clock is placed in the picture to show the time on the film, or the camera is driven by an electric motor so that the time interval from one frame to the next is known. Using the resulting film, the motions for the hands, arms, or other body members are timed and analyzed for shortening, elimination, combination, changes in sequence, improved balance and rhythm, etc. In these analyses, elements of motions called *therbligs* are used, referring to the 18 elementary subdivisions. (Examples: "Search" —that part of the work cycle during which the hands or eyes are groping or feeling for the object; "Find Select"— which occurs at the end of the therblig "Search." The term *therblig* is the backwards spelling of Gilbreth

(Frank B.), the motion and time study pioneer who developed this measuring system.)

22 *Principles of Motion Economy*

The 22 principles of motion economy originally developed by Gilbreth may be profitably applied to all types of work situations. The supervisor can use them as a guide in taking a hard look at all operations in his department to see where improvements can be made in terms of more efficient operation or reduced fatigue:

1. The two hands should begin as well as complete their therbligs at the same instant.

2. The two hands should not be idle at the same instant except during rest periods.

3. Motions of the arms should be in opposite and symmetrical directions, instead of in the same direction, and should be made simultaneously.

4. Hand motions should be confined to the lowest classification with which it is possible to perform the work satisfactorily.

5. Momentum should be employed to assist the worker wherever possible, and it should be reduced to a minimum if it must be overcome by muscular effort.

6. Continuous curved motions are preferable to straight-line motions involving sudden and sharp changes in direction.

7. Ballistic (rhythmic) movements are faster, easier, and more accurate than restricted (fixation) or "controlled" movements.

8. Rhythm is essential to the smooth and automatic performance of an operation, and the work should be arranged to permit easy and natural rhythm wherever possible.

9. Definite and fixed stations should be provided for all tools and materials.

10. Tools, materials, and controls should be located around the work place and as close to the point of assembly or use as possible.

11. Gravity feed bins and containers should be used to deliver the material as close to the point of assembly or use as possible.

12. Drop deliveries should be used wherever possible.

13. Materials and tools should be located to permit the best sequence of therbligs.

14. Provisions should be made for adequate conditions for seeing.

15. The height of the work place and the chair should preferably be so arranged that alternate sitting and standing at work are easily possible.

16. A chair of the type and height to permit good posture should be provided for every worker.

17. The hands should be relieved of all work that can be performed more advantageously by the feet or other parts of the body.

18. Two or more tools should be combined wherever possible.

19. Tools and materials should be pre-positioned wherever possible.

20. Where each finger performs some specific movement, such as typewriting, the load should be distributed in accordance with the inherent capacities of the fingers.

21. Handles such as those used on cranks and large screw drivers should be designed to permit as much of the surface of the hand to come in contact with the handle as possible. This is particularly true when considerable force is exerted to use the handle. For light assembly

work, the screw-driver handle should be so shaped that it is smaller at the bottom than at the top.

22. Levers, crossbars, and handwheels should be located in such positions that the operator can manipulate them with the least change in body position and with the greatest mechanical advantage.

Related Entries *Fatigue; Work Simplification.*

MOTIVATION

Motivation is simply defined—it's whatever makes people move. And when we use the term "employee motivation," we usually mean whatever makes employees move in the direction desired by management.

As a manager of a department or unit, you want employees to move in the direction of high output, without accidents and abuse of equipment, producing good quality, and on the whole showing a willingness to accept changes made necessary by management objectives, and to rise to the occasion when emergencies or rush periods require special effort, overtime, inconvenience, and the like.

How do you motivate employees toward these ends? Psychologists will tell you that motivation is a state of tension caused by some unfulfilled need—and that the individual moves in such a way as to "restore equilibrium" by satisfying the need. The trouble is, people are complicated mechanisms, subject to all sorts of tension created by all sorts of needs, and these differ among individuals, and in the same individuals at different times. Psychologists talk about *physiological needs*, covering such basics as hunger, thirst, and sex; and about elementary *safety* needs which make them react against physical danger, the fear of the unknown, etc.; about *love needs or social needs:* the need for affection, for "belonging" to some group; *esteem needs:* the so-called "egotistic" needs for self-confidence, prestige, recognition; and finally, *self-fulfillment* needs, which become operative when the other needs have been largely met, and lead people to want to bring to fruition certain creative desires they have, to express themselves in painting, or music, or other fields.

Obviously, insights such as the above are of value, but the big question remains, how are you to apply them in a given business situation? The first and foremost thing for the supervisor to remember is that *there are no pat answers.* Enough has been said in this book about "people problems" to indicate that nothing having to do with people is simple. We know, of course, that we can fairly safely predict human reactions to certain actions: practically everyone will jump if you stick him with a pin. But how about less obvious situations? They may jump and wince *inside* when you stick them with a barbed remark or a sharp criticism—but to what extent, you may never know; and how this will reflect on their productivity even the psychologists now admit they don't know.

Knowledge of some of the most powerful motivators won't help the supervisors in most situations. Take *hunger:* Fringe benefits being what they are, together with unemployment insurance, relative ease for skilled workers to get jobs, union protection against arbitrary dismissal, etc., we find that in this country, at least, workers will hardly be motivated on the job by considerations of hunger. And except under threats of enemy attack, workers are hardly motivated by *physical fear*—

under any circumstances, a supervisor in his right mind
would hardly threaten an employee with physical violence—and you can hardly use the *sex motivation* in your
department (nay, you may more likely have to wonder
about curbing that stimulus in mixed groups!).

The "Climate" for Motivation

The problem boils down to the application of certain
general, basic prescriptions, regarding the general "climate" that is conducive to good employee motivation.
Some of these are given in the entry, *Leadership*, and
many, many, are evident in lines of action laid down in
other entries throughout this book. In various forms they
are emphasized in countless texts and courses on supervision. They were succinctly summarized at the start of
our participation in World War II in the four-step formula of the Job Relations Training (JRT) program of
the War Manpower Commission's Training Within Industry Section. The JRT steps, given under the head,
People Must Be Treated as Individuals, are:

1. *Let each worker know how he is getting along:* Figure
out what you expect of him. Point out ways to improve.
2. *Give credit when due:* Look for extra or unusual
performance. Tell him "while it's hot."
3. *Tell people in advance about changes that will
affect them:* Tell WHY if possible. Get them to accept
the change.
4. *Make best use of each person's ability:* Look for
ability not now being used. Never stand in a man's way.

To the above, many people who have been working,
teaching, and writing in the field of human relations in
industry—especially those advocating and conducting
work simplification programs—would add a fifth:

5. *Encourage employee participation:* Encourage suggestions. Where feasible, get workers' prior opinions on proposed changes. Give them as great a say as possible over their own work.

Getting Down to Specifics

Without detracting from the general soundness of the above prescriptions, some important provisos and qualifications are in order when it comes to putting them into practice. Thus:

1. *Know your people.* This goes far beyond the usual admonition to "treat people as individuals." Most writers mean by that to be alert to individual feelings, to remember an individual's human dignity, and the like. The point made here is that you must go beyond such platitudes, and really *know* the individuals in your group. Pointers on that are given in *"People Problems"*—2, and *Personnel Audit.* Study them carefully. The real motivators may well be below the surface.

2. *Qualify general prescriptions to meet individual cases.* If your personnel audit has led you to assess a certain employee as a bright, energetic chap, ambitious to go places, you should adjust the "motivators" accordingly. You can heap a lot of extra work on him. . . . you can go a long way in "putting him on his own." But if you have a "Nervous Nellie" who is apt to break up under stress, apply the appropriate motivators regarding her. Try not to give her rush jobs. . . . be especially careful in explaining change. . . . and patient in instructions. A teen-ager living at home will have different motivations from those of a man with six children and a mortgage, or a married woman helping with the family budget.

3. *Don't downgrade individual money incentives.*

There is impressive industrial experience on the side of positive results. But remember that money incentives must be *on top* of all of the other human-relations motivating factors, not a *substitute* for them.

4. Be realistic about employee participation. The pendulum in industry has definitely swung to a greater stress on *individual performance.* For the most effective operations, there will be carefully engineered performance standards (see *Time Standards*). The supervisor can not abandon his right and duty to manage, and must be careful about the extent to which employees can set their own pace.

5. Always welcome suggestions. (See *Suggestions* and *Suggestion Systems.*) This also holds in connection with the general advocacy of telling people about contemplated changes. Before you discuss changes with employees, find out to what extent changes may still be possible, so that you may know whether to encourage suggestions, or merely to explain established policy.

6. Be ready to discuss personal problems within reason. (See *Employee Counseling.*)

7. Finally, remember your responsibility as a "motivator changer." This is part of your continuing problem of training and development. (See *Development-Appraisal-Development.*)

Related Entries *Communicating—1. Selling Ideas; Incentive Wages; Job Interest—How to Stimulate It; Leadership; Methods Improvement—2. "Selling" the Need for Savings; Monotonous Work; Praise; Privileges; Punishment; Resistance to Change; Safety—3. Dramatization to Employees; Suggestions—1. Tapping the "Latent Resources"; Suggestions—2. Helping Make the Company Suggestion System Work; Waste —2. Dramatizing Avoidable Waste; Work Simplification.*

MUSIC FOR EMPLOYEES

There is ample evidence that the playing of the right kind of background music can have an important beneficial effect in plants and offices—especially where work is repetitive and tends to be monotonous.

Of course, the idea of music to stimulate workers is not new—records exist showing that apprentices sang at their work in European factories in the fifteenth century, and in our own history we have our cowboy songs and chants of railroad gangs and the singing on plantations and river packets. But in recent years there has been increased interest on the part of managements, and many companies and services exist (Muzak is a well recognized name) to "pipe" background music into work situations (and, of course, public areas such as hotels and restaurants) or to install systems where tapes or records can be played, or FM radio music received (with automatic devices to turn off the commercials).

An interesting recent innovation is the so-called Serenade system developed by Voicewriter Division of McGraw-Edison Company, for use in central typing departments. Here music is piped into the department and the girls hear it through their individual ear sets. Thus each transcriptionist listens to the dictation she is transcribing against a background of continuous, specially programmed, nonvocal music, over which she has complete control. She can lower or raise volume or turn it off completely to suit her mood. American-Standard and Equitable Life Assurance Societies are examples of companies using the Serenader system.

Through its counteraction of boredom, monotony, and other causes of worker tensions, music at work has been found to reduce errors, employee turnover, absenteeism and tardiness, and to increase production. Management literature is full of favorable reports, many of them citing beneficial results in specific, statistical terms, from such companies as General Petroleum Company, Union Tank Car Company, Eastern Airlines, Loft Candy Company, Lever Bros., and a host of others. Many others with such installations, while not citing quantitative evidence, report ample justification in terms of employee satisfaction alone. (According to Prof. Stephan Konz of the University of Illinois, as of 1962 some 20,000 companies, including nine of the 12 rated as "best managed," used background music.)

Even though at least one investigator (Prof. Richard S. Uhrbrock of Ohio University) contends that claims of statistically significant results of case studies publicized by manufacturers of music systems often do not bear too close scrutiny, the generally highly favorable reactions of companies of the calibre of those cited above are impressive indications that the matter is worth serious consideration.

Most supervisors obviously will not be in a position to arrange for services such as the above on their own initiative. However, if the chances of using music to good advantage exist in their departments, they may wish to make recommendations for demonstrations and cost estimates. Or at the very least they may wish to seek a ruling on the use of soft-pitched radio music or a record player in the department at stated times.

Here is a rundown of results that seem to emerge from objectively reported experience and controlled-study reports to date.

1. Controlled experiments have shown that music stim-

ulates increased output in workers doing simple, repetitive, and monotonous tasks. These are the sort of workers whose jobs demand less than their best, and who may tend to chatter aimlessly, complain, or daydream, and have a high quit rate.

2. However, not all workers like music. From one to ten per cent may be annoyed by it. Music can be a definite hindrance to a job that requires a high degree of concentration. (An average of about three per cent of companies using music drop it each year—but newcomers replace them at about three times that rate.)

3. Music is beneficial where the noise of office machines or plant equipment is likely to produce sound fatigue, and where nervous tension may be a factor. (It's a common misconception that music can be used only where the noise level is low.)

4. Some companies have reported that music may have increased accidents. Therefore caution is indicated where hazards exist.

5. Different types of music are best suited for different types of work, and more stimulating music may be best at high-fatigue periods, say at the end of the morning and before quitting time in the afternoon. This experience has given rise to the development of "functional work music"—a point to check with suppliers of equipment and systems.

6. Experience has demonstrated the value of silent periods, since continuous uninterrupted music may soon go unnoticed. Many companies now play work music on a 15-minutes-on, 15-minutes-off basis.

Related Entry *Monotonous Work.*

N

NATIONAL LABOR RELATIONS ACT

The principal Federal law governing labor relations is the National Labor Relations Act, originally passed in 1935, and popularly known as the Wagner Act. There have been a number of amendments since then, two important ones being the Labor-Management Relations Act of 1947, popularly known as the Taft-Hartley Act, and the Labor-Management Reporting and Disclosure Act of 1959, known as the Landrum-Griffin Act, or the Labor Reform Act. Basically, the Taft-Hartley Act guarantees workers the right of *refraining* from joining labor unions, and spells out unfair practices by unions in addition to the Wagner Act's listing of unfair labor practices by management. The Landrum-Griffin Act deals with the regulation of internal union affairs, and of management-labor reporting as a means of eliminating autocracy, racketeering, and dishonesty. Also, importantly, it provides that a state agency or state court may take jurisdiction where the National Labor Relations Board declines to exercise its powers. Its Title VII carries amendments to the Taft-Hartley Act which tighten restrictions on the unions' uses of secondary boycott, and on recognition and organizational picketing.

Provisions of the National Labor Relations Act of significance to supervisors follow:

Objectives and Administration

The Act guarantees the right of workers to organize and to bargain collectively with their employers and to select their bargaining representatives, or to refrain from all such activity.

Administration rests primarily with the National Labor Relations Board, composed by Presidential appointment, of five members with five-year terms, and the general counsel of the Board with a four-year term, also appointed by the President. Most of the day-to-day work of investigating and processing charges of unfair labor practices and handling representation proceedings is delegated to various NLRB regional offices located in major cities throughout the country.

The Board may conduct elections to determine whether or not employees wish to have a representative bargain for them, and it may conduct polls to determine whether employees who have been under a union-shop agreement want to revoke the authority of their bargaining agent to make agreements.

Employees Who Are Not Covered

The Act does not apply to employees in a business or industry where a labor dispute would not affect interstate commerce (although this is usually broadly interpreted). It also specifically excludes employees covered by the Railway Labor Act, and others such as agricultural workers, domestic servants, and government employees.

Supervisors are excluded. Whether or not a person is considered a supervisor is determined by his authority rather than his title. Here is what the Act says:

The term "supervisor" means any individual having authority, in the interest of the employer, to hire, transfer, suspend, lay off, recall, promote, discharge, assign, reward, or discipline other employees, or responsibility to direct them or to adjust their grievances, or effectively to recommend such action, if in connection with the foregoing the exercise of such authority is not of a merely routine or clerical nature, but requires the use of independent judgment.

Right to Strike

The right to strike is in general preserved, but the Board and courts have ruled that "sitdown" strikes are not protected because they involve unlawful seizure of property. The Board has also held that the law does not protect slowdowns by employees who remain on the job, or partial strikes such as refusal to work on certain days each week.

Unfair Practices of Employers

1. *To interfere with, restrain, or coerce employees.* Examples: Threatening employees with loss of jobs or benefits if they join a union. . . . Threatening to close down a plant if a union is organized. . . . Questioning employees about their union activities or membership in a way to tend to restrain or coerce them. . . . Spying on union gatherings.

2. *To dominate or interfere with the formation or administration of any labor organization* or contribute financial or other support to it.

3. *To discriminate in hiring or tenure of employment* or in any other way to encourage or discourage membership in any labor organization. (For example, demoting or discharging an employee because he urged fellow em-

ployees to join or organize a union, or refusing to reinstate an employee because he took part in a lawful strike). The law prohibits the closed shop where only an individual who already holds membership in a labor organization can be hired, or union-hall hiring, where only persons who have permits from the union may be hired. But the law permits a form of union shop, where employees may be required to join the union at the end of 30 days (or seven days in building and construction industries). However, an employer may not discharge an employee whose membership in the union is terminated for reasons *other* than nonpayment of uniform union dues or initiation fees. An employee may not be discharged for failure to pay fines or assessments or for otherwise being suspended or expelled from the union.

4. *To discriminate for participation in NLRS proceedings.*

5. *To refuse to bargain in good faith with the representatives chosen by the majority of the bargaining group.* For example, refusing to put an agreement with representatives in writing, or refusing to deal with representatives because the employees are out on strike.

6. *"Hot cargo" agreements.* Employers are forbidden to enter into agreements to cease handling another employer's products or to cease doing business with any other person, except under certain circumstances in the construction and apparel and clothing industries.

Unfair Labor Practices of Unions

1. *To restrain or coerce employees.* Examples: Mass picketing in such numbers as to bar nonstriking employees physically from entering the plant. . . . Force or

violence in connection with strikes. . . . Threats of bodily injury to nonstriking employees.

2. *To restrain or coerce an employer* in the selection of his representatives for collective bargaining.

3. *To cause or attempt to cause an employer to engage in discrimination against an employee* which tends to encourage or discourage union membership, for reasons other than nonpayment of uniform union dues or initiation fees under a union shop contract. This reinforces the outlawing of the closed shop.

4. *Refusal to bargain in good faith.* An example is the refusal to make a written contract of reasonable duration.

5. *Secondary boycotts and certain types of strikes and picketing.* This section also prohibits "hot cargo" contracts with certain limited exceptions. However, not prohibited is *publicity* other than picketing for the purpose of "truthfully advising the public, including consumers and members of a labor organization, that a product or products are produced by an employer with whom the labor organization has a primary dispute."

6. *Charging excessive or discriminatory initiation fees.*

7. *Featherbedding*—to cause or attempt to cause an employer to pay for services not performed or not to be performed.

8. *Recognition and organizational picketing* with certain specified exceptions are prohibited. "Informational" picketing and other publicity measures are permitted, as long as they are truthful, there is no physical coercion, and such picketing does not induce any individual employed by any other employer to refuse to pick up, deliver, or transport any goods or perform any service.

9. *Jurisdictional disputes.* Jurisdictional strikes and boycotts are prohibited. The Act provides special ma-

chinery for deciding disputes over assignment of work to a particular group of employees.

"Free Speech"

An important provision of the Taft-Hartley Act is that it gives employers a protected area of "free speech" in opposing unions. Explicitly permitted are "the expressing of any views, arguments, opinions, or the dissemination thereof, whether in written, printed, graphic, or visual form. . . . if such expression contains no threat of reprisal or force or promise of benefits."

Determining the Collective Bargaining Representative

The principle of majority rule is followed in determining the representation of a group. The representative may be an individual or a labor organization, but not a supervisor or a representative of an employer. Elections may be held by agreement between the employer and the labor organization or individual claiming to represent the employees. If the parties can't agree, the Board's regional director can order an election after a hearing.

Bargaining Units

In determining the unit appropriate for bargaining, whether it be industrial, craft, single plant, or multiplant employer, the Board considers such factors as similarity of skills, wages, hours, and other working conditions; any history of collective bargaining; the desires of employees; and history, extent, and type of organization in other plants of the same employer, or of other employers in the same industry.

Special pointers for supervisors. A supervisor, while acting within the scope of his general authority, is an agent of management, and therefore has to be careful at all times to deal with employees in a way which will not give rise to charges of discrimination because of union activities. In the majority of cases involving such discrimination charges, the employer's liability has been based upon acts and statements of supervisors. Following are points which the NLRB has indicated it will want to know when it conducts a hearing on an employee's charge of such discrimination. To emphasize that the foreman is looked upon as "the company" in dealings with employees, we have substituted the word *supervisor* for *the company* in the Board's list of points:

1. What reason did the supervisor give for taking action against the employee?

2. Did the supervisor take the same action against other employees for the same reason?

3. Was the employee given any warnings before the supervisor acted?

4. Did the supervisor know that the employee was active in union matters or was a union member?

5. What is the employee's record as to length of employment, efficiency ratings, wage increases, promotions, or words of praise from his supervisor?

6. What was the supervisor's attitude toward unions, and particularly this employee's union?

It can be seen from the above that the underlying themes in the Board's inquiries are *consistency* and *proof*. This underscores the importance not only of proper action on the part of the supervisor, but that he keep proper records of disciplinary measures taken against any employee.

Note Information may be obtained from the Division of Information, National Labor Relations Board, Washington,

D.C. 20570. From the Superintendent of Documents, Washington, D.C. 20402, you can get an easy-to-understand booklet, "Federal Labor Laws and Programs, a Layman's Guide," *Bulletin* 262, 55¢. For other background information, also written for the layman and not the lawyer, consult the entry, "Labor Relations Legislation," by Dr. Willard A. Lewis, in Heyel's *The Encyclopedia of Management*, published by Reinhold Publishing Corporation, New York.

Related Entries *Arbitration; Civil Rights; Discharging an Employee; Mediation and Conciliation Services; Minimum Wage Laws; State Labor Laws; Union Organization; Workmen's Compensation.*

THE NERVOUS EMPLOYEE

See *The Jittery Employee.*

NEW EMPLOYEES

How the new employee is "inducted" into the job can have a great deal to do with his general attitude, and the speed with which he gets to be a productive member of the team. Here are some pointers:

1. Be sure you're making use of whatever booklets or other materials for indoctrination are provided by the company.

2. If the new employee is a woman or girl, and the job is an industrial one, be sure to know how familiar she is with a shop environment, and stress safety and other factors accordingly.

3. Is it possible to designate an older worker as a special coach?

4. The following should be covered specifically—be sure this has been done, even if the Personnel Department is supposed to be responsible:

    a. Job name and classification.

    b. Wages or salary; how and when paid.

    c. Incentive system details.

    d. Hours.

    e. Increases, automatic or merit.

    f. Working conditions, washrooms, lockers, etc., also problem of getting to work—transportation, parking facilities, etc.

    g. Union agreement, if any.

    h. Employee benefits—group insurance, etc.

    i. Rules regarding sick leave, time off, regarding notification of absence or lateness, etc.

    j. Special training program to be followed.

    k. Where to report for work.

    l. Special information, such as safety devices or work clothing required.

5. New employees will generally want to know about the following:

    a. Who's who in the business? The name of the supervisor; names of other executives; company organization, its main divisions, etc.

    b. What is the business? Company products or service; highlights of company history.

    c. What is expected of employees? Elaboration of 4-d and 4-i, above: Rules for discharges; payoff and suspensions; rules for lateness and attendance; smoking regulations; fire rules; safety and accident-prevention rules; grievance procedure, whether in the union or not; passes.

    d. What benefits? Services available, location, and how to use: cafeteria, library, washrooms; cashing of checks; elaboration of 4-h—group insurance for life or health; profit sharing; hospitalization;

EXHIBIT N-1

How The Supervisor Helps The New Employe

ASSUME HIS RESPONSIBILITIES WITH THE COMPANY
MAKE THE BEST USE OF HIS ABILITIES
FEEL AT HOME IN HIS GROUP AND NEW SURROUNDINGS

PROSPECTIVE EMPLOYE

Employment Department assists operating departments in recruiting, screening and selecting applicants
Provides new employe with general information about Company and his job

Supervisor welcomes the employe and talks with him

Introduces him to:
- People he should know
- His work location
Lays ground work for favorable relationship with him

Gives him induction "Packet" material
Discusses general department and Company information
Points out key policies and practices
Considers his particular problems
Lets him know
(1) What job requires of him
(2) What he can expect from his job

Trains him on his job

Plans for his development
Gives him careful instruction
Shows him importance of his work

Arranges attendance at one-day induction program

Within Three Months

Discusses program before he attends
Reviews his experience and reactions after program

Keeps him posted on how he is getting along

Talks over progress and adjustment periodically
Plans his development

Discusses benefit plans with him

4th or 5th Month

Pay Roll sends insurance and retirement booklets to employe's home

Induets him as permanent employe

(PERMANENT EMPLOYE)

Supervisor reviews six months' experience
Recognizes him as a regular member of team
Discusses progress
Employment Department has follow-up placement interview with employe

Supervisor maintains frequent contacts with him
Follows up on job performance, personal adjustment and overall development
Helps him continue progress

   discounts on company products; stock purchase
   plans; credit union; social activities.

e. What information channels? Company paper or
   magazine; bulletin boards; public address system.

f. What chances ahead? Opportunities for training
   and promotion; transfers; merit rating; salary increases.

6. Review entry, *On-the-Job Training*.

The accompanying exhibit shows the new-employee induction program of the Detroit Edison Company. It can
largely be the sequence followed by any supervisor.

Related Entries *Civil Rights; Learning; On-the-Job Training;
Recruitment; References; Temporary Personnel.*

NEW IDEAS

See *Brainstorming.*

NO—NO—NO
How to Say No

In all of management (indeed, in all of life) the little
two-letter word "no" often becomes one of the most difficult to utter—and make stick. Yet failure to make it
come through "clear and loud" can lead to king-sized
difficulties later on. In other entries of this guide we have
stressed the need to be sure of all your facts in reprimands
and criticisms, to be mindful of morale in negative ap-
praisals and in all communications, and the like. These
are not meant to imply that you cannot or should not
take a firm stand in denying a request which in your eyes
has no justification. Here are some "no" rules:

1. Do a good job of listening. Give the other fellow

plenty of time to explain why he thinks he deserves a "yes." (See *Listening*.)

2. Don't put off a "no" that has no chance of becoming a "yes"—simply because it's unpleasant news. To say "I'll let you know" when you know now, is just begging the issue. Worse still is to say that and not come back with the answer at all.

3. Don't give a bald "no." You should have sound reasons. Explain them clearly.

4. See if it's possible to "integrate your conflict of views"—i.e., encourage him to suggest ways, if possible, in which the surrounding situation can be altered to make a partial "yes" possible. . . . or to make a full or partial "yes" possible at a future date.

5. If the matter is a serious one, you may be inclined to see what can be done under the special circumstances. But in no case leave any room for doubt that the answer is anything but "no" as far as your authority is concerned. Don't make rash promises.

6. If, under union or other rules, there is a formal mode of appeal open to the employee, point this out to him, but again make clear your position.

Related Entries *Back Talk; Company Policy—When You Disagree with It; Favoritism; Privileges; Self-Appraisal—2. What Is Your "P.Q."?; Smoking on the Job.*

O

OFFICE ACCIDENTS

So much emphasis in safety work is placed on hazards in production departments, that *office* hazards are frequently overlooked. Below is a checklist compiled by the National Office Management Association. If you haven't stressed office safety recently, it may pay you to have this run in the employee paper, if you have one, or posted on bulletin boards.

1. Pushing and crowding at entrance doorways, on stairs, on elevators.
2. High heels catching on stairs.
3. Fooling, running, and scuffling.
4. Walking fast around blind corners of aisles.
5. Walking into glass door panels.
6. Leaving loose objects on floors, causing people to fall, trip, or slip.
7. Leaving sharp objects on floors, chairs, and desks.
8. Lifting loads improperly, or lifting loads that are too heavy.
9. Leaving desk and file drawers, and safe, locker, and closet doors open.
10. Putting objects on shelves insecurely, or piling them too high.
11. Using chairs and boxes instead of a ladder.
12. Tipping chairs back too far.

13. Straining muscles and catching fingers when opening and closing windows.

14. Throwing objects out of windows.

15. Throwing burnt matches, cigarette and cigar butts, and broken glass into waste baskets.

16. Throwing clips or shooting them with rubber bands.

17. Not covering the points of pins when pinning papers together.

18. Putting papers on sharp-pointed bill files.

19. Carrying pens and pencils with points exposed— in hand or pocket; carrying pens and pencils in the mouth.

20. Keeping sharp objects scattered through desk drawers.

21. Using knives, scissors, and shears without due care.

22. Cutting fingers and lips on sharp edges of paper.

23. Putting fingers close to electric fans while they are in operation.

24. Stretching electric cords across aisles.

25. Reading correspondence while walking.

Related Entries *Office Machines and Safety; see also listing under Accidents—1. Reporting.*

OFFICE ARRANGEMENTS

Try your hand at a "puzzler" offered its readers by the *Navy Management Review*:

The technical reference branch whose office layout is shown in Exhibit O-1, page 245, is about to receive a new file, and is trying to decide where to put it. The file will fit in only the three places marked X, Y, and Z, and it appears that no one in the office will be satisfied unless the file is next to his desk.

Mr. B, the supervisor who occupies the corner cubicle, "couldn't care less" where it goes, since he will not use it. However, his employees have been raising such a fuss

EXHIBIT O-1

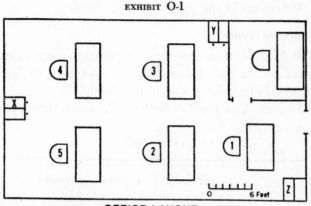

**OFFICE LAYOUT:
TECHNICAL REFERENCE BRANCH**

that he has decided to ask the Methods staff to help him. This much is known:

1. The office layout is optimally suited to work flow and should be left unchanged if at all possible.

2. All will use the file; it cannot be broken down into smaller units.

3. Desk 1 is occupied by Mrs. C. who will use the file 40 times a day. She is a pleasant woman, about 50, and has a picture of her husband, Admiral C, on her desk.

4. Miss A sits at desk 2. She is an attractive girl of 23 who will use the file only about 7 times a day while serving as secretary to Mr. B.

5. Mr. D sits at desk 3. He is bald, 40, and jolly. He will use the file an average of 11 times a day.

6. Desks 4 and 5 are occupied by Mr. E and Miss F

who are engaged. Miss F at desk 4 is the newest member of the office and will use the file 32 times a day while Mr. F, the next junior member, will use it 12 times a day. Both are 21.

Where would you put the file?

Answer to Puzzler

The Methods man constructed a "distance-usage index" based on the scale indicated in the floor plan, for each position. The index is shown in Exhibit O-2.

Position Y is the "mathematical" answer because it

EXHIBIT O-2

Desk #	Daily Usage	POSITION X		POSITION Y		POSITION Z	
		Round Trip in ft.	Total Distance/ Usage	Round Trip in ft.	Total Distance/ Usage	Round Trip in ft.	Total Distance/ Usage
1	40	62	2480	26	1040	18	720
2	7	40	280	34	238	44	308
3	11	40	440	20	220	50	550
4	32	14	448	44	1408	76	2432
5	12	14	168	58	696	70	840
		"X" INDEX #	3816	"Y" INDEX#	3602	"Z" INDEX#	4850

will mean less overall office effort. So the solution is Position Y. Correct?

Well. . . . maybe. Unfortunately, the index can only "solve" the problem in terms of the quantitative variables given—distance and usage. But how do you account for such variables as power, prestige, and personality? Though they affect most solutions in problems of this kind, they are still quite unmeasurable, and the supervisor must rely on good judgment as well as arithmetic in problems of this kind.

OFFICE ECONOMIES

Here is a little quiz on office efficiency, developed by Remington Rand Office Systems:

1. How much does it cost to keep a carbon copy on file for one year?
   A. 2¢——   B. 4¢——   C. 6½¢——

2. How much does it cost to dictate, type, and mail a business letter?
   A. 50¢——   B. $1.15——   C. $2.00——

3. If a $20,000 a year executive spends 3 minutes every hour just waiting for data, how much is his wasted time worth in a year?
   A. $250——   B. $700——   C. $1,000——

4. How much does it cost every year to create and maintain an ordinary four-drawer file?
   A. $105——   B. $350——   C. $500——

5. How many sheets of paper do most companies keep on file for each employee on the payroll?
   A. 240——   B. 1,254——   C. 2,000——

6. What percentage of money spent on paperwork is wasted?

A. 15%——   B. 35%——   C. 65%——

Chances are, according to Remington Rand, that unless your office has had a thorough systems overhaul, and is using the latest available time-saving equipment, the correct answers for your operations are *all* in choice C!

We don't advance the above figures as precise yardsticks, because Remington didn't document the statistics on which they are based. But they are worth passing along as an interesting brain-teaser, if for nothing else, although they're more than that. They draw attention to the fact that items on which too few supervisors have anything but a hazy idea of costs can add up to significant losses in efficiency.

Large offices, especially, are prone over the years to succumb to a "creeping laxness," and therefore it is worthwhile, every now and then, to review operations as a whole to see where economies are possible. The Veterans Administration recently drew up a checklist on the subject which can be applied to any office. "Over 80 per cent of our money goes for personal services," the VA reminded its department heads, and suggested specific action steps to keep down avoidable costs. Here are some highlights:

1. *Control who does what and where it is done.* Assure that the appropriate person takes action, attends the meetings, is asked to make the decisions, etc. . . . and that it's done in the right location. See to it that no employee is doing what should be done by another.

2. *Control of quality.* Accept only good and complete work. Cross-train employees to provide backing and to permit work continuity. Set up training plans that will develop the efficiency and capacity of individual em-

ployees. Utilize the probationary period as the test period it was intended to be. Utilize the per-step increases as they were intended, by withholding them from non-deserving employees.

3. *Control quantity.* Set realistic work standards and goals for each employee and each job. Check to see that production meets such reasonable standards. Eliminate overlapping procedures or consolidate them. [See *Methods Improvement* and *Work Simplification.*] Eliminate unneeded or seldom-used records or files unless you are required to keep them. Establish written procedures. This makes seldom-done tasks easier and assures effective performance. [See *Standard Operating Procedures.*] Eliminate use of written reports locally when a telephone call will do the job.

4. *Control time.* Consider cutting staff meetings by 30 per cent. Set an opening and closing time for all meetings, and adhere to them. [See *Business Conferences.*] Limit personal carriers and eliminate unnecessary trips around the Center. . . . most items will get there in plenty of time by regular messenger service. Know where your employees are and what they are doing.

5. *Control supplies and equipment.* Assure life of equipment through elimination of careless and improper use. [See *Office Machines and Safety.*] Use equipment only for designated purposes. Set controls on the use of office supplies, ward supplies, etc., where usage seems excessive. Review available standard items before ordering non-standard. Lay plans for the use of supplies so that needs may be met with a minimum of costly special orders. Turn in to the Supply Division items no longer needed in your program.

6. *Control utilities and general repairs.* Keep down the use of utilities—turn off unneeded lights, but not fluorescent lights which are going to be turned back on in less than an hour. Report leakage or dripping of water. Avoid using long-distance telephone when a teletype will do. . . . and avoid using teletype when a letter will do.

Monitor personal use of telephones. Cut down on upkeep costs by protecting wall coverings and painted surfaces.

Related Entries   *Correspondence Speedup—"Correspondex"; Letter Writing; Office Accidents; Office Arrangements; Office Machines and Safety; Office Work Measurement; Paperwork —Forms Control; Smoking on the Job; Telephone Etiquette; Temporary Personnel; Work Distribution.*

OFFICE MACHINES AND SAFETY

"Office equipment and supplies can be dangerous," says Armco Steel Corporation in its employee manual, *Office Safety.* Here are Armco's rules from its section, Office Machines, which may be worth posting in your department, with necessary modifications or additions:

1. Our offices have been made as electrically safe as possible and it is required that all office appliances be grounded. Adequate electrical outlets have been installed as far as possible; however, if additional outlets are required to avoid connecting more than two cords for each receptacle, report the condition to your supervisor for correction.

2. Use care in removing plugs. Yanking on the cord may break the insulation or loosen terminals. Grasp the plug itself, then pull.

3. Examine extension cords carefully and often for broken insulation, especially at the flex point at the plug. Report any possible defective cord to your supervisor and do not use it until it has been replaced or repaired.

4. Avoid touching a metal desk, chair, or other metal object with one hand while inserting a plug into an outlet with the other.

5. Never operate a machine until you have been trained to operate it safely.

6. Unauthorized "fixer-uppers" can cause double trouble.

7. Some machines have "OFF" and "ON" switches or buttons. Be sure the switch on such machines is turned "OFF" before plugging it into an electrical outlet. Be sure to shut off electrical machines or disconnect them before cleaning or adjusting them in any way.

8. Use only approved non-flammable cleaning fluids for cleaning machines, following the directions on the label. Do not use Carbon Tetrachloride. The fumes are harmful, even if inhaled in small quantities.

9. Place office machines as close as possible to the electrical outlets to avoid cluttering the walking area with long cords. Erect a barricade or "flag" the cord to warn co-workers of the hazard if it must be temporarily strung across the floor. Chairs may be used as a barricade, but should be properly tagged to prevent removal.

10. If a machine begins to smoke or spark or give off acrid odor, or if a trickle of leaking current is felt, don't try to find the trouble. Turn it off immediately, disconnect the plug, report it to your supervisor, and he will call the electrician. So no one will use the machine until it has been repaired, put a sign on it advising that it is out of order. (Note: The *one* exception to this rule is the Xerox copying machine which may give off smoke when the paper is jammed. Do *not* disconnect the plug in this case. Notify the person responsible for repair and maintenance of the Xerox machine, and do not operate until the paper has been removed by *authorized* personnel.)

11. Never operate a machine requiring a guard, from which the guard has been removed. Only authorized personnel may remove safety guards, and they are responsible for replacing them.

12. If you operate moving machinery, dress suitably for the job. Loose sleeves, long scarves and ties, rings and bracelets—even long hair—may create hazards which could result in serious injury.

Related Entries *Office Accidents; see also listing under Accidents—1. Reporting.*

OFFICE WORK MEASUREMENT

For improving office manpower or girlpower utilization, for making arrangements for smoother flow of work, etc., the professional systems and methods analysts will use the various techniques discussed under *Work Measurement* entries, and your part as a supervisor, as there stated, will be to offer maximum cooperation and to "sell" the need for measurement to your employees.

An additional measurement technique which can be effective in the office, and which you may want to use yourself, quite aside from any formal study conducted by staff personnel, is that of *Employee Reporting*.

Under this approach, employees themselves keep records of their current input and output of work. It is simple and inexpensive. Each employee reports the distribution of his time in terms of work items which are defined for him. These records are quite objective and meaningful (if the supervisor has done a proper job of explaining) and will contain enough detail to make adjustments possible for any special and distorting factors that occurred during the current period of work.

You can prepare a simple tally form for use over some period of time, perhaps two weeks, over which you feel you will gather significant data. For example, you may have a clerical staff working on certain types of records (various kinds of claims, say, in an insurance company), filing, general typing, report-assembling, etc. You can give all of these work elements an identifying number, together with a number for "idle time" (the record can state why idle), or "filler jobs" (to be done during slack periods—the employee can write in what particular job). A simple mimeographed tally sheet can be prepared, which shows along one side the time of day (perhaps to the nearest quarter hour) and the employee can be asked to jot down the identifying number for the tasks on which he or she worked for every time period. Or a form encompassing a whole week can be prepared, as shown in Exhibit O-3, page 254.

Note: Even though you explained the purpose of the study, it's a good idea to distribute a mimeographed statement repeating the explanation when you hand out the form.

Related Entry *Office Economies.*

THE OLDER WORKER

Every supervisor knows the value of mature, seasoned employees. They provide stability to the working force, guidance to newcomers and younger employees, and experience and judgment as an aid in his own decision making. In general, American industry provides rewards, promotion, increased responsibility, and job security for long service. However, when it comes to hiring an "older" worker (and in many quarters this is interpreted as anyone over 40 years of age) supervisors and others in management are prone to do an "about face." They equate youth with imagination, drive, and aggressiveness—and link older workers with inflexibility and lack of dynamic energy. . . . These are points made by the National Association of Manufacturers in its 1963 publication, "The Productive Years—Ages 45–65."

By the end of the present decade, the U.S. labor force is expected to increase by 13.5 million, and of this increase, almost 12 million will be either under 25, or over 45. The NAM feels that our economy will have to rely

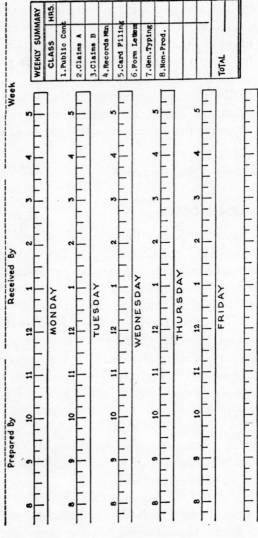

EXHIBIT O-3

WEEKLY EMPLOYEE REPORT OF DISTRIBUTION OF TIME

Prepared By   Received By   Week

MONDAY

TUESDAY

WEDNESDAY

THURSDAY

FRIDAY

SATURDAY & OVERTIME

WEEKLY SUMMARY	
CLASS	HRS.
1. Public Cont.	
2. Claims A	
3. Claims B	
4. Records Mtn	
5. Card Filing	
6. Form Letter	
7. Gen. Typing	
8. Non-Prod.	
TOTAL	

From "Work Measurement in the Office" by Anita P. Loeber, in *The Encyclopedia of Management*.

254

on the older workers as it has never done before, and is anxious to explode "myths" which it feels have grown up about employing them. Its findings, based on results of surveys of management experience with older workers, will give valuable insight to the supervisor who has older workers in his present employ, or has occasion to interview applicants of mature years for job openings.

Some Myths

Myth No. 1: "I have schedules to keep. I can't take a chance on an older worker; he's liable to be absent too often." *NAM answer:* Numerous studies of workers' absence show the opposite to be true: as a group, older workers can be expected to be absent fewer times each year than their younger counterparts.

Myth No. 2: "I'm afraid for the safety of an older worker. He's more accident-prone." *NAM answer:* False. All the available research shows the older worker to be generally more safety-conscious, actually less accident prone.

Myth No. 3: "I have to keep production at a high level. I wonder if an older worker can keep up with the rest." *NAM answer:* If there is any difference in the rate of production of an older worker, it does not show until after 55. Even then it is an *individual* factor. Some older workers outproduce the younger ones.

Myth No. 4: "Too many older workers are set in their ways." *NAM answer:* Some older workers *are* inclined to be inflexible; so are some younger workers. The important consideration is the individual's outlook—his "functional age."

Some Valid Factors

Physical strength. With the power-operated equipment in use today, physical strength is less important than it has been in the past. But older workers are not well suited to jobs where the chief considerations are great physical strength or continued exertion.

Speed of learning and memory. The NAM reports that older workers may not be as adept at rote memory, nor may seem to learn a skill as quickly as younger workers— but once having learned the skill they will perform with great accuracy. Reports by the U.S. Department of Labor quote psychologists as saying that an older worker learns differently but as well as the younger—"his experience enables him to select, to value, to conserve, and his background enables him to grasp principles."

Work speed. When speed is the chief asset for a job, the older worker is at a disadvantage. He may suffer from the pressure and tension involved.

. . . and Some Plusses

Ability to stay with a job. Surveys by the NAM and the U.S. Chamber of Commerce show less turnover among older workers.

Quality and accuracy. If a mature worker's speed is not as great as his younger counterpart's, it can be expected that the quality of his performance will be superior.

More time on the job. A Bureau of Labor Statistics survey showed that workers over 45 were absent an average of only three days per hundred, compared to an average of six days per hundred for workers under twenty.

Better safety record. An older worker will take fewer risks than others. Company records, confirmed by insurance company accident surveys, show that older workers have less than the average number of disabling injuries, although their recovery time is greater.

Less supervision required. Once the older worker masters the job, he can be expected to work well on his own, with minimal supervision.

Emotional balance. As a rule, an older worker lends an emotional balance to a working atmosphere. He is a settled member of the community, more willing to accept situations as they are, and more interested in the progress of the company for which he works.

Employer Costs

U.S. Department of Labor studies show that ultimate costs will not be substantially greater under most current pension plans, if older workers are hired. Pension plans relate benefits to length of service or to levels of current or future earnings—or to both. Since newly hired older workers will have shorter service before retirement, the benefit payments will be correspondingly smaller. Workmen's compensation rates will not be affected, since these are based on accident experience of a company, not on employee age.

Note In a 1963 *Wall Street Journal* story, International Shoe Company's Hartford, Ill., tannery was reported as hiring no one under 45. "We find older workers are of better quality," said Vice President R. H. Richards. "They've got more interest in what they're doing". . . . A recent report by the Connecticut General Life Insurance Company on turnover among women employees showed that of women hired during the preceding ten years, in the 30- to 40-year age bracket, only one in three was still on the job; of those hired in the 40- to 50-year bracket, the number was one in two; of those hired in the 50- to 65-year bracket, not one had left.

ON-THE-JOB TRAINING
1. The J.I.T. Program

During World War II, the Training-Within-Industry Program of the War Manpower Commission developed a four-step formula for on-the-job training by supervisors, known as J.I.T. (Job-Instruction Training). It has become a classic, and is still the basis for this type of instruction throughout industry in this country and abroad. Here it is:

How to Instruct

1. *Prepare the Worker*
   Put him at ease.
   State the job and find out what he already knows about it.
   Get him interested in learning the job.
   Place him in correct position.

2. *Present the Operation*
   Tell, show, and illustrate one important step at a time.
   Stress each *key point*.
   Instruct clearly, completely, and patiently, but no more than he can master.

3. *Try-out Performance*
   Have him do the job—correct errors.
   Have him explain each key point to you as he does the job again.
   Make sure he understands.
   Continue until YOU know HE knows.

4. *Follow Up*
   Put him on his own. *Designate to whom he can go for help.*
   Check frequently. Encourage questions.
   Taper off extra coaching and close follow-up.

Always remember: IF THE WORKER HASN'T LEARNED, THE INSTRUCTOR HASN'T TAUGHT!

Note Here are some pointers for putting the formula to work:

Preparation: Develop a timetable on how much skill you expect him to have, how soon. Break the job into key steps (see separate entry, *On-the-Job Training—2: Job Breakdown and "Key Points"*). Have everything ready—the right tools, equipment, and materials. Have the work place properly arranged, just as the worker will be expected to keep it.

Putting the learner at ease: A nervous, "jumpy" worker can't concentrate. Put him at ease by a friendly attitude. Don't rush him. Make him feel that you want to be sincerely helpful. Calmness on your part will make the learner feel calm.

Try-out performance: As soon as possible, let him do the simple parts of the job. Choose the part or parts which you are sure he will do correctly, to give him confidence. Help him do the whole job. (The first time through, have him go slowly.) As he goes through the job, always have him tell you what the next step is to be, and have him tell you the key points as he comes to them. Be sure every move he makes will meet safe-practices requirements. Encourage him as much as possible, but keep him aimed at a high standard. "Pretty good" is not going to be good enough for you. Carefully consider the time to interfere if he makes minor mistakes. Of course, if a mistake is being made which can result in injury to him or damage to the equipment, you must interfere before harm is done. Get the new man to see the *cause* of the mistake, and give him some constructive advice on how to get rid of that cause.

Related Entries *See succeeding two entries and listing under Development of Subordinates—1. Development-Appraisal-Development.*

ON-THE-JOB TRAINING
2. Job Breakdown and "Key Points"

The points about teaching a job given in the preceding *On-the-Job Training* entry cannot be applied without first making a complete and detailed breakdown of the job to be taught. A breakdown of this sort is shown in Exhibit O-4, page 261, taken from an analysis of a skilled job in a paper bag manufacturing plant.

Don't make the mistake of thinking you can teach a job properly without first breaking it down on paper. No matter how well a person knows a job, he can't repeat his instruction twice and cover exactly the same things in the same sequence unless he has organized it by breaking it down on paper. Doing that will not only produce a better trainee, but can save you an appreciable amount of training time.

As to "key points"—a large portion of every job is easy to learn, and can be mastered by almost anyone in a few hours or a few days. But it is the 5 or 10 per cent that constitutes the "hard" or "tricky" parts. These require time to learn and represent the real skill that is necessary.

A "key point" is whatever is the "key" to the right doing of a job step. It may mean: "knack," "trick," "feel," "savvy," "safety precaution," "special timing," "bit of special information." It does *not* mean every conceivable thing that is to be watched or that may go wrong.

Key points are the *important, commonsense* things that make or break an operation. Knowing what they are and how to pick them out quickly and easily is perhaps the most important single thing in on-the-job instruction. Here are some examples of key points:

1. *Feel.* When putting a micrometer on a piece of stock, the key point is "how tight"—a matter of "feel." It can be imparted only by actual demonstration.

2. *Knack.* When riveting, an important point is to know when to remove the pneumatic riveter. The "key" to this point is to *listen* to the riveting. The sound will change when the pieces are solidly together.

3. *Timing and placing of heat.* When welding, there are among others two main key points: (a) apply the flame *ahead* of the weld, and (b) get the metal to the

EXHIBIT O-4

JOB BREAKDOWN

Adjusters, Square and Flat

1. IMPRINT

Job Instruction A. Change imprint block and imprint

Important Steps	"Key Points"
1. Loosen two cap screws on frame	1. Cap screws located on brackets on impression roll shaft 2. Enough for assembly to slide
2. Pull back assembly	1. Enough to clear blocks
3. Loosen set screw on left hand collar	1. Enough to clear shaft
4. Slide collar on shaft or remove cap screws and remove imprint	1. Slide until pins disengage block
5. Loosen binding screw on side of clamp	1. To release imprint
6. Remove imprint and numbers (when used)	
7. Insert new imprint and tighten binding screw	
8. Lower ink roll if using larger block	1. Loosen cap screw on bracket
9. Replace block	1. Reverse procedure for removing block

right heat. These are a matter of observing the color and behavior of the metal.

4. *Hazard.* When using a knife, a key point is to "cut away from you." When lifting a load with an overhead crane, a key point is to pull the chains or cables taut, then hesitate for a moment to check the hitches, before lifting the load.

5. *Special motion.* When catching hot rods rushing out of rolling mills, the key point is to swing the flowing rod quickly in an arc away from you before inserting the end in the next set of rolls.

6. *Special information.* On some kinds of electric wiring the key point is to attach the identified negative wire to the tinned screw, and the positive wire to the brass screw.

7. *Knack of judging sound.* In mines, the strength and safety of the roof is determined by tapping the roof rock with a steel bar. The "sound" as the bar strikes the roof tells the story. Judging the sound is the "key point."

Note In breaking down a job for instruction, always list principal steps *first,* then pick out the key points. Be careful that the breakdown is complete as to *steps* and *key points,* but not wordy.

Related Entries *See preceding and succeeding entries, and listing under Development of Subordinates—1. Development-Appraisal-Development.*

ON-THE-JOB TRAINING
3. Program and Timetable

If you are going to develop an organized on-the-job training program, it's a good idea to list all of the important jobs in the department that a man has to learn to qualify for a specific job title, and to set up a time allotment for the instruction.

Exhibit O-5 is an example of such an outline in a paper bag manufacturing plant. There are nine "families" of jobs. Breakdowns similar to the one illustrated in *On-the-Job Training—2. Job Breakdown and "Key Points"* were prepared for all the jobs indicated by letters.

ADJUSTER TRAINING PROGRAM

Square and Flat

(½ Day)   1. Imprint
          (a) Change imprint block and imprint.
          (b) Adjust ink roll and impression roll to imprint.
          (c) Check ink fountain—Change speed (Grocers).

(½ Day)   2. Install Former
          (a) Remove former, check condition, and replace.
          (b) Center and align.
          (c) Set tuck plates and guides (on squares) and partially set draw-roll.

(3 Days) 3. Shaping Up Tube to Size
          (a) Place and align roll of paper.
          (b) Draw paper over machine and partially adjust draw rolls.
          (c) Change cut-off knife and check condition.
          (d) Change and adjust gears.
          (e) Adjust breaker and pinch bars, and adjust impression roll on specials.

(2 Days) 4. Adjustment of Bottoming Rolls
          (a) Move head to proper position.
          (b) Set cylinders.

(2 Days) 5. Complete Making of Bag
          (a) Adjust paste bar.
          (b) Check second pinch, speed, and draw rolls.

(2 Days) 6. Adjustment and Care of Carrier
          (a) Align drums and rolls, and check press roll.
          (b) Put on carrier felts and adjust.
          (c) Gears, drive and speed.

(1 Day)   7. Catch Box and Kicker
          (a) Adjustment and care.

(3 Days) 8. Duplex Bags
          (a) Duplex pads.
          (b) Adjustments.

(2 Days) 9. Compensator Adjustment
          (a) Line up sprocket.
          (b) Change compensator gear.
          (c) Turn on power and set print.

(16 Days)

(Incidentally, the department head worked the entire program out as a co-operative project of the key adjusters.) The time estimates given are not for "green" employees, but for men being upgraded from related work.

Timetables such as this are helpful on simple jobs also. Exhibit O-6 shows a program and timetable for a secretarial-clerical job. Here it was assumed that basic skills such as typing, shorthand, etc., were acquired prior to hiring.

Related Entries *See preceding two entries, and listing under Development of Subordinates—1. Development-Appraisal-Development.*

THE OPEN MIND

See *Problem Solving—2. The Open Mind.*

ORDERS AND INSTRUCTIONS
1. Transmission and Reception

Despite all our electronic marvels, the biggest problem of communications is still with us—the direct day-to-day talking between one individual and another, or one individual and a group. Faulty transmission and reception of spoken and written communications is at the root of most mistakes, most grievances, most delays, and snarl-ups. . . . Here are some check questions to keep asking yourself about your own communications techniques— both written and oral.

1. *Is anybody listening?* In important messages, do your opening statements arouse interest and attention? (This is important with "captive" audiences and direct subordinates as well as those whose passing attention

Job Title: Secretary   Dept.: Sales   Date: 11/12/62

Basic responsibility	Key points and essential information	Set aside this much time for explanation
1. *Dictation:* review the different techniques used, such as shorthand, dictaphone.	Familiarize with operation of equipment, when necessary.	1 hour
2. *Typing:* review the different types of work involved; correspondence, rough drafts of reports, memos, stencils, etc.	Indicate different types of stationery and materials used; indicate number of carbons commonly desired.	1 hour
3. *Appointments:* indicate clearly hours and times when appointments can be made. Suggest that reminders are appreciated.	Show and explain appointment calendar, receiving callers.	½ hour
4. *Telephone:* explain policy on telephone calls, and how phone messages should be received.	Show forms for records kept on long distance calls; explain long distance dialing procedures.	½ hour
5. *Filing:* Explain file system used and show location of various types of materials, i.e., reports, correspondence, budget and cost data, etc.	Provide key to files where required.	1 hour
6. *Supplies:* show the supply cabinet, explain requisition procedures, introduce to Supply Center Clerk.	Emphasize importance of economy here.	¼ hour
7. *Mail system:* explain mailing procedures, where stamps are purchased, how often delivered and picked up.	Request that all mail may be opened except personal or confidential.	¼ hour

EXHIBIT O-6 (continued)

Job Title: Secretary   Dept.: Sales   Date: 11/12/62

Basic responsibility	Key points and essential information	Set aside this much time for explanation
8. *Travel reservations:* explain where air, rail reservations are made. Discuss making hotel and motel reservations, setting up itineraries.	Mention type of accommodations usually desired, billing procedures and how to make up Expense sheets.	¾ hour
9. *Weekly & monthly reports:* as they occur for the first time, explain format of periodic reports. Indicate sources of data, how assembled and prepared.	Indicate number of copies required, when required, distribution list.	½ hour each

Clerical Guide, courtesy New York State School of Industrial and Labor Relations, Cornell University, *Bulletin 52, Employee Training in Small Business Organizations.*

must be captured by advertising copy-writers.). . . . Don't present objectives simply as good things to do, but stress why, from the employee's and the department's point of view, it is good to do them. There is hardly a management policy, decision, or act that cannot be presented with "openers" showing its direct benefit to employees. (See *Communicating—1. Selling Ideas.*)

2. *Do you tell enough?* Where an order involves changes in the customs or routines of employees, it's important to get across the "why." Adequate information not only assures a more cooperative compliance, it also scotches rumors and ungrounded fears.

3. *Do you tell soon enough?* Keep surprises down! As a supervisor, you don't like a request (order) calling

for something to be done "yesterday," or suddenly upsetting established routines. The same reaction is inevitable down the line.

4. *Do you tell often enough?* This means steering the right course between oversupervision and insufficient follow-up. You've got to know the people you're talking to. With a green worker, you've got to keep telling until *you* and *he* know that he knows.

5. *Are you explicit enough?* Be absolutely clear on the limitations of individual discretion in the carrying out of an assignment. The broadest possible latitude makes for the most spontaneous team (see *Oversupervision*), but where for good reason complete adherence to your specifications is essential, that stipulation should be definitely understood.

6. *Are you speaking the right language?* Be sure your vocabulary, illustrative examples, statistics, charts, graphs, etc., are suitable for the "receivers." Remember the educational level and cultural background of the group you want to get through to. (See *Briefings and Presentations*.)

7. *What about your tone?* How you say something is just as important as *what* you say. Does it hurt to preface a command or instruction with the little word *please*? Are you consciously *selling* your ideas to employees? (See *Note*, below, also *Communicating—1. Selling*, and *Note to Age—The Young Supervisor*.)

8. *Are all bases covered?* Was everybody there when you told about those schedule changes? . . . . Who should have received a carbon of that last memo you sent? . . . . Was everyone who attended that meeting told about the final action?

9. *How about the "action close"?* Every important

message deserves an "action close"—don't let your message dangle without a clear indication of just what you want him, her, them, to do, and when.

Note Don't give too many orders at once. . . . Should something be confirmed in writing? . . . Should receipt of the message be acknowledged? . . . Don't issue mutually contradictory orders—and if this is done inadvertently, clear the situation up fast, and don't be afraid to take the onus for the change if the confusion originated with you. *"Accentuate the positive!"*: By reshuffling a few phrases and rephrasing a few words, the safety man in a railway yard cut careless accidents in half. He simply put the usual safety slogans into more personal and positive terms. Samples: "Remove your gloves when operating this machine" to *"Save your fingers— and your income—*by removing your gloves when operating this machine." . . . "Wear goggles at this grinder" to *"Eyes aren't replaceable; goggles are.* Please use both at this machine." . . . "Pick up those tools" to *"Scattered tools cause accidents.* Pick up your tools and save your conscience."

Related Entries *See succeeding entry; also: Back Talk; Communicating—1. Selling Ideas; Criticism—1. How to Dish It Out; Discipline—1. Day-by-Day Discipline; The Jittery Employee; NO—NO—NO—How to Say No; Oversupervision; Praise; Reprimands; Resistance to Change; The Sensitive Worker; The Slow Worker; The Stubborn Worker; The Timid Worker.*

ORDERS AND INSTRUCTIONS
2. Types of Instructions

Here is how American Airlines spelled out the various types of orders and instructions in its *Basics of Supervision Conference Manual*:

1. DIRECT ORDER
   Use: In cases of emergency; to maintain strict control;

for immediate action. *Example*: "Mary, Flight 405 was canceled. Call the passengers right away."

2. REQUEST
   Use: In normal situations; when some discretion is permitted. *Example*: "Bill, would you prepare the budget for the next period?"

3. SUGGESTION
   Use: When only a suggestion is sufficient to get the job done, as: to stimulate initiative, to direct fully competent people; to direct people who readily accept responsibility. *Example*: "It would be helpful to re-arrange the office to utilize space more effectively."

4. CALL FOR VOLUNTEERS
   Use: To assign a task you cannot require the worker to perform when beyond the call of duty; in situations involving danger or abnormal conditions. *Example*: "Airfreight has requested our help in getting out their peak workload. Who is willing to work with them Saturday and Sunday?"

Note: None of the above types could be used to the exclusion of the others. It would be unwise to make a demand upon an employee when a mere hint will result in the job being done. . . . The key to giving instructions is to know your personnel: know their capabilities, their experience levels, their attitudes, and their need for guidance.

Related Entries   *See listing under preceding entry.*

ORGANIZATION

1. AMA's "Ten Commandments"

The "Ten Commandments of Good Organization" issued by the American Management Association are prefaced by the statement, "If you are a manager, no matter how great or small your responsibility, it is your job to create and develop voluntary cooperation among the people you supervise." Here are AMA's ten commandments:

1. Definite and clear-cut responsibilities should be assigned to each executive, manager, supervisor, and foreman.

2. Responsibilities should always be coupled with corresponding authority.

3. No change should be made in the scope of responsibility of a position without a definite understanding to that effect on the part of all persons concerned.

4. No executive or employee, occupying a single position in the organization, should be subject to definite orders from more than one source.

5. Orders should never be given to subordinates over the head of a responsible executive. Rather than this, the executive in question should be supplanted.

6. Criticisms of subordinates should be made privately. In no case should a subordinate be criticized in the presence of executives or employees of equal or lower rank.

7. No dispute or difference between executives or employees as to authority or responsibility should be considered too trivial for prompt and careful adjudication.

8. Promotions, wage changes, and disciplinary action should always be approved by the executive immediately superior to the one directly responsible.

9. No executive or employee should be assistant to and at the same time a critic of the person he is assistant to.

10. Any executive whose work is subject to regular inspection should, whenever practicable, be given the assistance and facilities necessary to enable him to maintain an independent check of the quality of his work.

Related Entries *See succeeding entry; also: After-Hours Relations with Subordinates; Appraising Subordinates—3. "Best versus Poorest"; Committees; Delegation; Exit Interviews; Informal Leaders; Job Analysis and Evaluation; Layoffs; Oversupervision; "People Problems"—2. Employee Types; New*

ORGANIZATION

2. Continuity through "Runners-Up"

The entry, *Personnel Audit*, stresses the need for analyzing the personnel situation in a department, both from the point of view of really *knowing* the people in it, and of anticipating retirements, promotions, training and development needs, and the like.

Here we stress the need for tentative plans to fill the gaps created by anticipated vacancies. Knowing where the vacancies will occur, do you also have specific persons in mind for a "promotion chain" to cover the positions as they open up? A single promotion may well create the need for a whole succession of promotions. Ideally, this would require the filling of only the lowest job in the chain—although in real life, things rarely work out with such nice precision.

Try putting down on paper the chain reaction as you want it to take place, if anticipated retirements, transfers out, and promotions out take place as scheduled. However, use this mainly for your own guidance, and for possible discussion with your own superior or the Personnel Department. Unless some move is imminent, it will undoubtedly be wiser not to make promises of promotions, or even to indicate tentative plans to someone whom you have scheduled to move up. The reason for this is clear:

You should preserve for yourself the maximum freedom of action. Retirements may not come when expected, death or unexpected promotion out may create an opening sooner than you anticipated, company expansion or contraction plans may change your whole scheme. For example, you may have a man in mind for a move at some future time. If the need to fill the position for which you had slotted him comes sooner than you had expected, the man may not be ready for the position (even though he himself may think he is!) Or an "heir apparent" may become impatient because the anticipated vacancy is to come several years later than you and he had counted on.

However, without specific commitments, you may be in a position to groom "runners-up" for all key positions in your department. In some cases, "assistants-to" positions may be in order, which of itself is a tacit indication of a line of succession, with, however, no hard-and-fast commitments and no timetabling. Or, you may see to it that certain people get an opportunity to acquire experience suited to specific higher positions—making them unofficial "runners-up." Incidentally, the same person might be considered a runner-up for more than one position.

Related Entries   *See listing under preceding entry.*

OVERHEAD

In the manufacturing end of a company, there are three broad classifications of costs: (1) *direct labor*—the labor cost of workers directly engaged in producing the products; (2) *direct material* going into the product; and (3) all other costs, which are classified as *factory overhead* (sometimes called *factory burden*).

Factory overhead includes indirect labor, such as materials handlers, maintenance men, inspectors, time-study men, etc.; salaries of supervision (including all management salaries from assistant supervisor to the head of the plant); tools and supplies; cost of having a place to work—rent (or taxes and building depreciation), light, heat, power; and other items which the accountant must charge against the operation as a whole—depreciation costs of machinery, cost of spoilage and salvaging returned goods, cost of fringe benefits to labor, wastage of direct supplies, etc.

The foreman or supervisor has no trouble in visualizing the direct labor and direct material costs, and the portion of them for which he is accountable. But overhead is something else again—much of it is not direct and visible, and much of it is not at all under his control. The average supervisor need not be concerned with mastering all of the cost-accounting theories, assumptions, and practices used by the cost accountants in determining total and unit costs—but he is so important in the total cost picture that he should be conversant with certain fundamentals, so that he can do a better job. Companies differ in the detail and refinement with which they compute, analyze, and allocate costs; but the following points are fundamental:

Some overhead costs are *fixed* for all practical purposes, no matter what the volume of output of the plant is— such as rent or taxes on the property, fixed supervisory and executive salaries (for example, within very wide ranges of volume, you would still have the same core of managers, heads of important departments, foremen, etc.);

and depreciation charges against the plant's equipment. Over these the supervisor in an operating department has no control—but he must remember that in the last analysis they have to be allocated into the products turned out.

Some costs *vary* with the volume of work done: If your department is busy, it uses more power (which in some plants is directly metered to a department, in others is allocated by some method, perhaps according to the number of employees, or class of equipment used, or ratios established historically, etc.). If you turn out more work, you use more general supplies, and draw upon more services of maintenance personnel; and for higher activity you may make greater use of janitorial services. For higher output, more supervision may be required, in the form of assistant foremen; and the plant as a whole may have to have heavier-staffed methods or industrial engineering departments, the cost of which may be prorated to your department.

Before the beginning of the year (which may be a "calendar" year or a "fiscal" year—the latter meaning twelve months beginning at some other time than January 1), the cost analyst obtains historical data from accounting, information from the sales department as to expected volume, and other information from plant management, industrial engineering departments, and from the foremen themselves. He will then to the best of his ability compute all of the variable overhead costs for the production level anticipated for the forthcoming year. To that figure he adds the amount of fixed charges, and comes up with a total, which can then be distributed to the products to arrive at costs of factory overhead going into a unit product. (To do this, the analyst also gets estimates from the sales department as to the "product mix" anticipated, as well as expected total sales.) It can be seen that the constant part of the burden cost gets distributed over more and more products as volume increases, which is why unit costs go down if larger volumes are expected. (See Exhibits O-7 and O-8.)

Many important management decisions hinge on accurate determination of overhead allowances, and on close living within those allowances—the price to be charged for products, cost of inventory, profit estimates, need for modernization, etc. That is why the foreman should realize his highly important two-fold responsibility:

(1) He must give accurate information and estimates to the cost engineers and others involved concerning his needs for supplies, services, indirect labor, maintenance needs, perhaps the need for an assistant foreman, etc.

(2) He must attempt to *live within* the estimates established. All of the higher management decisions will be thrown off if he permits a greater overhead or burden cost in his department than the one set by the cost analysts in their standards. (See *Cost Control.*)

Overhead costs are usually expressed in terms of some common denominator, usually as so many dollars per dollar of direct labor, or per hour of direct labor. For some departments, the overhead may be expressed in terms of so many dollars per machine hour.

If standard hours (or standard minutes) are used in the plant (see *Time Standards*), the cost engineer can compute standard factory overhead dollars per standard hour (standard minute), since he can convert the budgeted products to be produced into budgeted direct-labor hours. He can then arrive at a standard overhead cost per product, based on the number of standard hours of direct labor it represents. This is convenient, if a company is making many different products.

Two terms which the foreman may hear are "over-absorbed" and "under-absorbed" overhead. A somewhat simplified explanation is as follows: The total computed plant overhead is distributed over a budgeted amount of production expressed in direct labor hours and/or machine hours for the year, broken down by months. Then if a

EXHIBIT O-7   *Total Overhead Related to Volume*

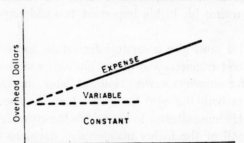

Variable portions of overhead are superimposed upon portions which remain fixed over wide ranges of volume.

department works more than a budgeted number of direct labor or machine hours in a month, or if its people turn out more units per hour than the standard rate at which overhead was charged into the units produced, the department is "over-absorbing" overhead. Conversely, if it works less than a budgeted number of direct labor or machine hours, or if its people are turning out fewer units per hour than budgeted, it is "under-absorbing" overhead.

Many plants operate on a flexible budgeting system (see

Budgeting). This simply means that the cost analyst produces overhead estimates (budgets) based on varying levels of activity, making for a more refined basis of reports to the foremen and department heads, on which "variances," or departures from budget, are computed and must be explained. Here again the foreman has an important responsibility in helping the cost engineers and

EXHIBIT O-8 *Overhead Per Unit Related to Volume*

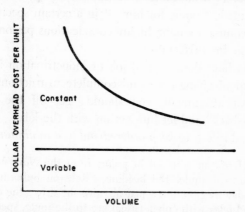

As the constant portion of overhead is distributed over more and more units produced, the overhead cost per unit goes down.

methods-department representatives arrive at a sound estimate of needs based on different levels of activity. He is then expected to meet the overhead charges for the particular level on which he operated during the period.

Related Entries *Budgets;* "*Cost Consciousness*" *in Employees; Cost Control; Incentive Wages; Inspection; Maintenance Costs—Operating Departments; Methods Improvement— 1. The Questioning Attitude; Methods Improvement—2. "Selling" the Need for Savings; Overtime; Scrap Costs; Seasonal Peaks; Standard Costs; Time Standards—Standard Min-*

ute (Standard Hour); Waste—1. *Reducible* Waste; Waste—
2. *Dramatizing Avoidable* Waste; *Work Simplification.*

OVERSUPERVISION

Do you *oversupervise?* This is a common failing on the
part of a man who has been promoted to a supervisory
position because he was the best man on the line or in
the field, or who came to a supervisory position after
having made a name for himself in a certain specialty. It
is also common among highly conscientious persons with
a passion for perfection.

If you have done a good job of indoctrination in general, and of giving clear and complete instructions on a
particular assignment, you should "get off the subordinate's back" and let him get on with the job.

A good rule is to *keep order-giving to a minimum.*

Note Here's an editorial in point, from the *Navy Management Review,* under the heading, "Rely on Subordinates":
"Every day we step into a taxicab, give the driver the destination, and relax with only a casual eye to the route, speed, and
methods of driving. None of us would think of questioning
the driver's driving ability or his knowledge of traffic regulations, or of asking him to check with us for approval to change
lanes, turn a corner, start, stop, slow down, or make any other
driving decision. We assume that as a licensed taxi driver he
knows his job and will get us to our destination. Only in the
unusual case will he ask for a decision on such things as a
change in route.

"Our subordinates are no different. They are qualified,
capable adults who know how to go about their jobs. They
must know where we want to go and our guiding policies,
just as the taxi driver must know our destination. But we can
trust them to do their jobs properly without constant checking
and clearance of every minor decision. Further, the subordi-

nate whose abilities are respected by his superior will do a far better job than one who is continually being checked.

"Treat your subordinates as you do your cab driver!"

Related Entry *Delegation*.

OVERTIME

Every supervisor knows that he must be sensitive about his overtime record. As a rule, overtime is looked upon as the unusual and undesired condition.

But is "no overtime ever" a good target? Obviously, good supervision will strive to keep down unnecessary overhead. But too many departments, especially office operations, are run on a strict eight-hour-day basis. Without vigilance, there will be a tendency to man for a workload that is closer to peak than to average.

There is another aspect to overtime—the fairness with which the supervisor apportions overtime when, by virtue of time-and-a-half, or even doubletime, it becomes a sought-after plum. Unless there are intervening factors, the overtime should be rotated on a strictly impartial basis among those qualified to do the work. But if a rush job would benefit from the special skill of a certain employee, the requirements of the job come first.

The other side of the coin, of course, is overtime which is not paid for, and is an extra chore for the employee concerned. Not only must the supervisor be impartial in the distribution of this extra workload—he must also be as considerate as possible in regard to advance notice. Much overtime cannot be anticipated, but the chances are that well over half of it can be planned sufficiently far ahead of time to prevent undue hardships to those asked to stay over.

Cost Aspects

Even if your departmental manning is streamlined, with no "fat," don't take our remarks above opposing the idea of "no overtime ever," as a way to explain away frequent overtime charges. You are still responsible for keeping them to a minimum. Here are some reminders:

1. Can more careful planning avoid the overtime situation? Are you keeping any sort of load charts or planning boards? (See *Load Charts; Planning and Scheduling.*)

2. Are you too easy-going in agreeing to special rush jobs. (See entry under that head.)

3. Can you avoid overtime by part-time people, either (a) drafted from another department, or (b) engaged from a temporary-help company. (Regarding (b), see *Temporary Personnel.*)

4. Are you realistic in agreeing to deadlines?

5. Is there anything you can do about seasonal peaks? (See entry under that head.)

6. Where you must schedule overtime, are you planning properly for the best utilization of the expensive premium time? For example:

    a. Did you check stock, to see that parts, materials, and supplies will be available?

    b. Will the machines or special equipment you plan to use be available for the work?

    c. Must any special arrangements regarding heat, lights, notification of guards, etc., be made?

    d. If your company or governmental department has a rule of compensating for overtime by later time off, how will this affect your choice of individuals—are you building up a "time debt" which will cause even a greater bind later on?

Related Entries *Deadlines; Planning and Scheduling—2. "Critical Path" and Other Network Plans; Minimum Wage Laws; Rush Jobs; Seasonal Peaks; Temporary Personnel; Workload Forecasting.*

PAPERWORK
Forms Control

Paperwork continues to be a bigger and bigger headache. . . . it seems that no matter what business you are in, a mountain of paper has to be produced for every pound of end-product or every completed service.

Regardless of the size or nature or specific business of your department, the important thing is to exercise some sort of control over the production of paperwork *before* the fact. This will not only eliminate unnecessary paperwork, it will also prevent the expensive job of supporting a huge family of papers far beyond what is actually needed, and will also save the expense of a "crash" program later on to reduce the volume of paper in your files.

One obvious place to begin is in the production and control of forms that you request for your work, or that you may design or procure for other departments.

It is realized that not all supervisors or department heads have a large voice in the initiation of forms, although many of them do. But all supervisors can keep an eye open regarding suggestions as to forms use (as we'll point out in the *notes* to this entry.) Therefore you should be interested in the following quick and easy method of checking the efficiency and economy of any form—*new or old*—before placing a print order for it. We are indebted to Hammermill Paper Company for it:

Necessity

1. Has the entire system been checked—would a written procedure for the use of this form help put it into more efficient operation?

2. Are all copies of the form or report necessary?

3. Have the actual users of this form been consulted for suggested improvements, additional requirements, and possible eliminations?

4. Can the data furnished by this form be combined with some other form, or can some other form be eliminated or consolidated with it?

5. Has everyone responsible for the form or the form system approved it?

Purpose

6. If the form is to be sent from one person to another, are proper spaces for "to" and "from" provided?

7. Will routing or handling instructions printed on each copy be helpful?

8. Should this form be consecutively numbered, or have a place for inserting a number?

9. If this is an outside-contact form, should it be designed to be mailed in a window envelope?

10. If this form is to take information from, or pass information to, another form, do both have the same sequence of items?

11. Have you taken into consideration the number of forms which will be used in a given time (4 to 12 months) —the possibility of changes, and how long the form will probably remain in use?

Size and Arrangement

12. Is the size right for filing, attention value, ample room for information, and susceptible of cut without waste?

13. Is all the recurring information being printed, so that only variable items need to be filled in?

14. Has space been provided for a signature?

15. Is spacing correct for handwriting or typewriting? (Hammermill will provide a Form Layout Sheet that will help you check items like this.)

16. Are the most important items, which should be seen first, prominently placed? (Near the top, if practicable?)

Wording

17. Does the form, by title and arrangement, clearly indicate its purpose?

18. Is there a proper space for the date?

19. Is the form identified by company, agency, or institution name or code number to aid in reordering?

20. If this is a revised form, can it be distinguished from the previous form?

Paper and Printing (Specifications)

21. Should the form be on colored paper to speed up writing, distribution, sorting and filing; to designate departments or branch offices; to indicate days, months, or years; to identify rush handling?

22. Have you specified paper which will be thoroughly satisfactory, economical enough for form use, consistent in performance, and surely available for later re-orders?

23. Is the proper weight of paper used for original and each carbon copy? (Bond substances 13, 16, and 20.

Ledger substances 24, 28, and 32. Mimeo-bond substances 16 and 20. Spirit and gelatin duplicator substance 16 and 20.)

24. Are detailed specifications complete? (Paper, type, ink, rules, punch, perforate, score, fold, gather, pad, car-bon sheet, stitch, etc.)

25. Can other forms, printed on the same paper as this one, be ordered now to reduce the production costs?

26. Have requirements been estimated correctly, and is the quantity to be ordered most economical? (Consider probability of revision and rate of use.)

Notes The major paper mills all make available a great many advisory services in printing and duplicating. Typical are the customer services of Champion Papers, Inc., Hamilton, Ohio, and West Virginia Pulp and Paper Co., New York, both of whom have printing specialists available on call anywhere in the country, and the Form Designing Kit distributed by Hammermill Paper Co., Erie, Pa., which gives information on paper and printing as well as on forms design.

• *You don't have to be head of a forms-design or systems and procedures department* in order to make economies in forms usage. Here's an example from the Navy: Each day for two years Fighter Squadron One-Twenty-One, U.S. Naval Air Station, Miramar, Calif., submitted a four-page daily aircraft status sheet to the C.O. and Operations Officer via the Maintenance Office. One man was required to come in two hours early each day to compile the data, which included engine serial numbers, "time since" check, aircraft availability, aircraft deficiencies and reason for grounding, and aircraft in an overhaul status. One morning the report was delayed because of an emergency situation. During the furor raised about this, the Assistant Maintenance Officer questioned the need for such a complex report in the first place. A few 'phone calls showed that the mass of information served no useful purpose, and that only a simple status report was really needed. He redesigned the report to a single page containing only the number of aircraft available for flight, and those aboard in repair status. The new report took only 15 minutes to compile, as against well over an hour for the old one!

Related Entries *Correspondence Speedup—"Correspondex"; Office Economies; Letter Writing.*

PEAK LOADS
See *Seasonal Peaks.*

"PEOPLE PROBLEMS"
1. Pointers from the "J" Programs

During World War II, the Training-Within-Industry Program of the War Manpower Commission developed its famous "J" programs: Job Instruction Training (J.I.T.); Job Relations Training (J.R.T.); and Job Methods Training (J.M.T.).

For J.I.T. and J.M.T. see, respectively, the three entries under *On-the-Job Training,* and the two under *Methods Improvement.* Here we give TWI's succinct four-step formula on human relations—*How to Handle a Job Relations Problem:*

1. GET THE FACTS
   Review the record.
   Find out what rules and plant customs apply.
   Talk with individuals concerned.
   Get opinions and feelings.
   Be sure to have the whole story.
2. WEIGH AND DECIDE
   Fit the facts together.
   Consider their bearing on each other.
   What possible actions are there?
   Check practices and policies.
   Consider objective, and effect on individual, group, and production.
   Don't jump at conclusions.

3. TAKE ACTION

Are you going to handle this yourself?

Do you need help in handling?

Should you refer this to your superior?

Watch the timing of your action.

Don't pass the buck.

4. CHECK RESULTS

How soon will you follow up?

How often will you need to check?

Watch for changes in output, attitude, and relation-ships.

Did your action help production?

Related Entries *See succeeding entry; also: Altercations; Criticism—1. How to Dish It Out; Discipline—1. Day-by-Day Discipline; Discipline—2. Handling Critical Incidents; Emotional Reactions; Employee Counseling; Favoritism; Friction; Grievances—1. When the Employee Goes Over Your Head; Grievances—2. Handling Complaints; Horseplay; Leadership; Listening; Manners; Personnel Audit; Prejudices; Privileges; Problem Employees; Reprimands; Rumors; Sex; Smoking on the Job; Tension and Stress; Women and Girls—1. ("God Bless 'Em").*

"PEOPLE PROBLEMS"

2. Employee Types

In a way, people are like patent medicines—you have to know how to take them. This volume, as we stated in our opening pages, is largely concerned with the many aspects of working with and through people. Here we want to say something about how to deal with different *types* of employees, and to bring together a list of the specific entries you should consult on them.

For our introductory comments, we can do no better than to quote from the section "How to Handle Different

Types of Employees" in Trans World Airlines' *Supervisor's Handbook*. Six of our separate entries are drawn from this section of the handbook. Here is how TWA introduces the subject:

> We tend to group people into types, like: slow, timid, stubborn, careless, sensitive, bold, lazy. But the timid man often becomes bold in a given situation; the lazy man springs into a burst of activity from time to time. At best, such classifications give you the man's batting average—they don't tell you exactly what he will do when he comes up to the plate. That's what makes the ball game.

How should a supervisor guide his own relations with the various types in his work group? How should he approach each one? What should he guard against?

The first rule, says psychology, is to be tolerant and understanding. Try to avoid giving any impression that you have contempt for a man because he's timid, for example.

As a supervisor, it's not your job to turn the timid into the bold, the lamb into the lion, even if it could be done. A trained psychiatrist would hesitate to do that. You can only take the personality for granted. You study character not to change it but to use it at the highest peak of efficiency and to extract from it the greatest degree of cooperation.

As you turn to the entries covering the specific types we list below, you will find it most helpful to keep a particular person in mind. It may be a good idea to list, alongside the heading, the initials of a certain person or persons who fit in that particular slot. For example: *The Sensitive Worker* (L.K.). Keep that person in mind as you read along—*and notice too, that he or she does not fall entirely into any one group*.

Here are the types (or temporary conditions) on which
you will find extended entries on other pages:

Related Entries *As above; see also listing under preceding
entry.*

PERSONNEL AUDIT

How much do you really know about the people working for you? Are you so "production oriented" that you lose sight of the people problems which may be the critical factor in your department's output?

No supervisor has so many people reporting directly to him that he cannot make it his business to find out with respect to each individual the significant facts about family background, racial origin, special personal obligations, ambitions, and drive—all of which will have a definite bearing on the way that particular human being will interact with others in his group.

Without appearing to pry, you can get such knowledge over a period of time by a sympathetic interest in his off-the-job activities, by a question dropped now and then, by non-business conversations at company social gatherings and get-togethers.

Periodically—perhaps at budget time when you are planning ahead—it will pay you to make up a "personnel audit" of your department. Thus:

1. Who is facing retirement? Are there any special personnel adjustment problems?

2. Who for reasons of age or health will soon have to be assigned to less demanding tasks?

3. Which of the girls will be getting married in the coming year? Are they going to leave the department?

4. How about pregnancies among some of the married girls. Are these girls coming back after the big event?

5. Do you have any "problem employees"? What have you done about them during the past year? What measures should be taken in the coming months? (See *Problem Employees*.)

6. Are there any probable promotions or transfers out of the department in the coming year? How are you providing for replacements?

7. What will be the people-needs in known expansion moves?

8. Who should get special attention from you in a continuing development program? Are you scheduling definite time for personnel appraisal? How are the young, new employees getting along? (See *Development of Subordinates—1. Development-Appraisal-Development.*)

Related Entries *Appraising Subordinates—3. "Best versus Poorest"; Development of Subordinates—1. Development-Appraisal-Development; Organization—2. Continuity through "Runners-Up"; Promotions—1. Assessing Your People's Potential for Growth; Promotions—2. Assessments in Depth; Training—1. An Audit of Needs; Understudy.*

PHYSICAL HANDICAPS
See *Handicapped Employees*

PLANNING
Use of Checklists

One of the most effective devices to insure proper planning of work and smooth departmental operation is a checklist to be sure that no essential detail is being overlooked. Below is a planning checklist taken from Thompson Ramo Wooldridge's *Supervisors' Manual.* See how many of these ideas can be adapted to your own operations, and draw up a tailor-made one for yourself: (*Note:* In the titles used below, the supervisor of an operation at TRW reports to a foreman, who has numerous supervisors under him).

1. Contact the supervisor of the previous shift. Find out what work is being performed in the department. Learn how long jobs will run, and what problems require special attention.

2. Supervisors of grinding and machining should inquire regarding bottlenecks, machinery down for repairs, jobs running out, new jobs to be run, revised schedules, special problems, etc.

3. Check your working force for absenteeism and get the maximum number of operations started. Assign work as necessary, and make sure all workers have a job to do.

4. If additional manpower is needed, you may, depending on circumstances, elect one of the following:

   a. Reassign workers within your own unit.
   b. Obtain additional help from another supervisor within the department.
   c. Request the foreman to secure additional help from another department within the division.
   d. Request the foreman to requisition additional workers from the Employment Department.

5. If you are overstaffed, immediately call this to the attention of your foreman who will take such action as is necessary.

6. Make sure the worker has proper equipment, supplies, materials, tools, checking scales, gages, micrometers, or indicators to do the job according to standards.

7. Check the job to make sure it meets standard requirements. This may be done by checking the job against the sketch, blueprint, routing, and job card.

Planning Production

1. Decide how long the present job will run.

2. Learn what job will follow the one that is being finished. Determine whether it has been run in your group before. If the job has been run previously:

   a. What difficulties did you have?
   b. Which employees did the work, and are they still available for your use?
   c. What other workers can do the job?

    d. Does the job offer training opportunities?

  3. If the job has not been run previously:

    a. What problems or features are involved regarding tolerances or limits, finish, nature of material, volume of work, supplies, or standards?

    b. What machine or other equipment is to be used?

    c. What tooling is necessary?

    d. What are the job conditions to be considered, i.e., oil, cutting compounds or coolants, heat, dust, lifting, etc.?

    e. Is the present operator qualified for the job, or is it necessary to start training at once?

Prepare Well in Advance for the Next Job

1. To avoid delay, you should have the necessary equipment, materials, or tools ready well in advance of the time to start the new job.

2. Supervisors of grinding and machining will also check the sketch, blueprint, or routing—and be sure the required gages are available and in good condition.

Assign the Job and See That It Gets Started Properly

1. Be sure the job meets specifications.

2. In production groups, the check for quality should be made when the setup is completed and a few pieces are run. Get the supervisor's and the inspector's okay on the job card before the operator takes over on a production basis. Keep the approved job card on the machine while the job is running.

Follow through on the Work Being Done during the Course of the Shift

1. Give special attention to special jobs or inexperienced workers. Check jobs to make sure standards and schedules are being met.

2. Supervisors of grinding and machining will analyze causes of below standard work, such as improper setup, wrong speed or feed, etc., and correct bad situation.

Pass Job Information on to the Succeeding Foreman and Supervisor

1. Let them know what work is being performed, how long it will run, and what problems will require special attention.

2. Supervisors of grinding and machining should pass on information regarding bottlenecks, machinery down for repairs, jobs running out, revised schedules, special problems.

3. Assist the succeeding supervisor and foreman in getting the next shift started.

Related Entries   *Emergencies—1. Avoid and Prepare; Follow-up: Planning and Control Boards; Planning and Scheduling—1. Progress Charts; Workload Forecasting.*

PLANNING AND CONTROL BOARDS

Simple planning boards are often a great help in controlling production in a department. They can be set up to show at a glance the progress of work that has been scheduled, what is behind schedule, and the load of work ahead. (The well-known Gantt Chart is described in *Planning and Scheduling—1. Progress Charts.*)

Various types of control boards are on the market, e.g., one which consists of moving various colored pegs into holes along horizontal lines, marked off for days (or other time periods), pulling along horizontal strings to form a Gantt-type chart, or one utilizing movable magnetic bars and symbols which cling to their background. You may perhaps find these more complicated than they are worth —and that it is more effective to construct a simple home-made board. For example:

Each work station in a department can be represented by three horizontal sets of hooks. The first set represents *work in progress;* the second set represents work that has been sent to the work station and is *awaiting operation;* the third set represents work scheduled for the department but *not yet sent* to a work station. As work progresses through the department, the work order forms or job tickets, or special tickets expressly for the board, are moved up on the hooks in order, or changes are made to give rush orders priority. Pigeonholes or compartments can be added to hold supplementary instruction forms and papers. Instead of hooks, of course, slots or pockets can be used for insertion of tickets.

An interesting variation developed at the Harrison Division of Worthington Corporation, as reported in *Navy Management Review,* is shown in Exhibit P-1, page 297. Horizontal and vertical pockets hold groups of tickets. The vertical scale represents days (or any other time unit), and the horizontal scale, in the same time units, represents lead time required for the projects represented by the cards.

A ticket is prepared for every work order coming into the department. Count down on the vertical scale from desired finish date, a number of days equal to the lead time. This will put you on the horizontal line representing starting date. Move over to the right the number of days equal to the lead time, and put the ticket in that pocket. (Obviously, this date has to be "today's" date or later. You can't start earlier than today.)

Now have a set of index bars made, as shown—a hollow double triangle, with a horizontal bar and two slanting bars, sloping upwards and downwards so that they reach a height, at the right-hand edge, equal to the total number

EXHIBIT P-1

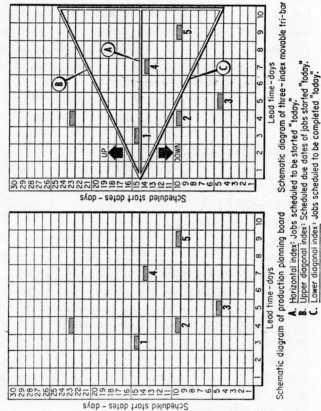

Schematic diagram of production planning board

Lead time – days

Scheduled start dates – days

Schematic diagram of three-index movable tri-bar

Lead time – days

Scheduled start dates – days

A. Horizontal index: Jobs scheduled to be started "today."
B. Upper diagonal index: Scheduled due dates of jobs started "today."
C. Lower diagonal index: Jobs scheduled to be completed "today."

296

of days marked off on the lower scale. (If the scales are the same, these will obviously be 45-degree lines.)

You can get a quick picture at any time by moving the horizontal bar to "today." Any tickets *below* the downward slanting line are late—they should have been finished and removed. Any ticket on today's line is scheduled to start today and is due on the date represented by the upward sloping line which is crossed vertically above the ticket. For example, the job represented by ticket No. 4 is due on the 21st. (Due date on any ticket can be determined similarly by positioning the horizontal bar on it.)

Related Entries *See preceding and succeeding entries; also: Deadlines; Follow-up; "Learning Curve" in Estimating; Rush Jobs; Seasonal Peaks.*

PLANNING AND SCHEDULING

1. Progress Charts

A progress chart will be a big help in checking and reporting the progress of work on a particular job or order. The best type of progress chart for manufacturing (as distinguished from research and other special projects, where there is a great deal of activity interrelationships— for which see *Planning and Scheduling—2. "Critical Path" and Other Network Plans*) is the Gantt Chart, illustrated in Exhibit P-2, on page 298. It charts cumulative work done against time and against schedules.

The figures in the upper left-hand corners of the time periods (in our illustration, five-day weeks) are amounts scheduled for that particular period. Figures in the upper right-hand corners show the cumulative schedule. As work is finished, a bar is drawn in each period, showing work completed for that period. A heavier bar at the bottom shows the cumulative amount finished. (For week 8-4, in the exhibit, 20 per cent more work was done than was scheduled for that week, represented by the double light line.)

In the exhibit, "today" is the end of Week 8-4. A vertical chain or weighted string suspended from hooks at the top of a Gantt wall chart can readily be moved to today's date to show status at any time.

EXHIBIT P-2

GANTT CHART, PRODUCTION CONTROL

WEEK ENDING 7-14				WEEK ENDING 7-21				WEEK ENDING 7-28				WEEK ENDING 8-4				WEEK ENDING 8-11			
100				125			225	150			375	150			525	150			675

The relationship of the solid heavy bar to "today's" vertical line is significant—if it is to the right, you are ahead of schedule; if to the left, you are behind. The ratio of the length of a bar in a period to the total space for that period is significant. For example, in Week 7-21, only 100 of the scheduled 125 pieces were produced. As of "today's" date, you are behind on the cumulative, even though during Week 8-4 a big step toward catching up had been made, since, as stated, more work was done in that period than originally scheduled for it.

Related Entries *See listing under preceding entry.*

PLANNING AND SCHEDULING
2. "Critical Path" and Other Network Plans

Foremen and supervisors play an important part in the newer "network" or "arrow diagram" plans for the planning, scheduling, and control of complex projects—large, non-repetitive projects in research and development, construction, new-product development, major retooling programs, maintenance, and similar activities far removed from the Pentagon's far-flung projects which gave them their dramatic impetus just a few years ago. You will hear these referred to as "Critical Path Scheduling," "Critical Path Method (CPM)," or "PERT" (Program Evaluation and Review Technique)." The electronic computer has made it possible to apply the techniques to large, complex networks which otherwise would be far too cumbersome to handle.

The plans and diagrams will be developed by project planners and others, rather than by the supervisor (but, of course, there is nothing in the concept to prevent the supervisor using the techniques for special projects in his own department). Where the supervisor comes in, as will be shown, is in adding his estimates for his own part of a complex project, to enable the project planners to determine the "critical path" of a sequence of operations which dictates how long and costly a project will be unless that path is shortened.

These plans embody an "arrow diagram" or network, as illustrated in Exhibit P-3, page 300, showing sequence and time interrelationships (and in some cases, also cost interrelationships.)

In CPM, as in PERT, *events* are shown by circles in the network, as illustrated in the exhibit, and *activities* are designated by arrows leading from one event to its successor event or events. An event represents the time and resources required to progress from one event to the next.

In CPM (Critical Path Method), after the arrow diagram is established, two time and cost estimates are applied to each activity and referred to as *normal* and *crash*. With the normal estimate, the primary consideration is

EXHIBIT P-3   *CPM Schedule/Cost Network Plan*

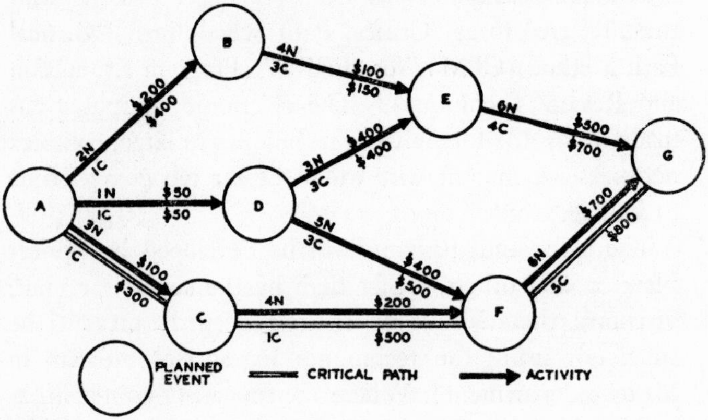

minimum *cost*, and the time associated with it. Normal time is considered to be maximum time: a speedup would presumably be accomplished only by more outlay for labor, overtime, etc. Costs associated with normal times are assumed to be minimum cost. *It is obvious that the supervisor plays a highly important part in the development of these estimates.* The central planners and their computers are no better than the sum total of supervisor estimates.

The crash estimate for a job is defined as the absolute minimum time and cost associated with it. In the exhibit, "N" designates normal, "C" designates crash, and the digit before each represents a time unit, such as days, or weeks. The *critical path* is that sequence of activities as indicated by the double-ruled sequence which will require the greatest normal time to accomplish. *Unless this is shortened, the total project cannot be shortened.* (The arrows are not drawn to any scale, and their lengths have no significance.)

Initially the planner (or his computer) analyzes the normal times of each activity on the critical path and computes a maximum time schedule. Then the activity in the critical path is selected which offers the smallest cost increase in relation to time decrease, after which a new schedule is computed, with the selected activity "crashed." (This may produce a new critical path, if the crashed time represents a substantial reduction.) The planner (computer) continues to "buy time" along the latest critical path as cheaply as possible. The last computation is based on "total crash" assumption, and is the most expensive. A summary can be tabulated, listing all the schedules computed, time durations, and necessary costs. Time slippages that can be tolerated in any activity without affecting the completion date of any other activity, or of the total project, are also computed (termed "float," or "slack").

Both CPM and PERT are based on the same network principle. The project manager using PERT expresses his timing uncertainty in a range of "optimistic," "pessimistic," and "most likely," from which a statistical determination of the "expected time" is made. Again, it must be stressed that the planners will depend heavily on individual supervisors for the "optimistic," "pessimistic," and "most likely" estimates.

Note For concise but quite complete descriptions of these techniques, consult *The Encyclopedia of Management* (edited by Carl Heyel, published by Reinhold Publishing Corporation, 1963), under the headings "Integrated Project Management"; "Critical Path (CPM)"; and "PERT (Program Evaluation and Review Technique)." A recent comprehensive book on PERT is *Schedule, Cost, and Profit Control with PERT,* by Robert W. Miller, published by McGraw-Hill Book Company, 1963. (The description above follows the treatment in *The Encyclopedia of Management.*)

Related Entries *See listing under Planning and Control Boards.*

POLICY FORMULATION

Most supervisors will not be directly concerned with policy *formulation* for their companies, although their role will, of course, be vital in many phases of policy *execution.* However, as your responsibilities begin to embrace a large department or a group of units and sections, it will be increasingly necessary for you to think about departmental policies, to bring consistency into actions taken over wide periods of time. And, of course, most supervisors, no matter what the size of their departments, will from time to time be asked for their opinions on specific phases of a broad problem, or will in other ways play a part in policy established at a higher level. Accordingly, it will pay to review here some of the theory behind policy formulation, since the theory can be applied to the formulation of operating policies at any level as well as to top-level, broad administrative policies:

First, let's think through to a basic definition, beginning with the distinction between a "policy" and a "rule" or "regulation."

A "policy" is a statement of fundamental principles which serves as a long-term guide for action.

A "rule" or "regulation" is a specific guide for conduct which is based on, or consistent with, underlying policy.

Thus policies can be likened to a bill of rights, or Federal law, setting forth fundamental principles and relationships which are changed only after the most careful deliberation. Rules and regulations are like local laws and ordinances, based on the underlying bill of rights or basic "law of the land."

In this broad sense, then, the use of policy statements as a management tool provides:

1. A "compass setting" for long-term direction of an enterprise or important part thereof. They help define broad objectives and directions.

2. Consistency of action throughout the organization. This makes possible efficiency in decentralization: broad policies can be stated, within which local managements can act with a high degree of freedom.

3. Consistency of action over a period of time. This is, of course, tied up with No. 1.

4. A framework for the construction of manuals of procedures which can be used as a reference source for particular action, and for training. (See *Standard Operating Procedures*.)

5. Clarification of organization. By indicating responsibilities and authorities, statements of policy avoid procedural confusion.

We can now develop our definition more precisely:

A *"policy"* is a statement of fundamental principles which serves as a guide for future action—and should usually include a statement of objectives, and indicate how the policy is to be carried out.

Sound policies are not made in a vacuum. They involve ascertaining facts, and the careful weighing of data and opinion. Often an appreciable amount of research is called for, on a number of related topics and subproblems, before a policy can be formulated intelligently.

There are five points to be considered in the formulation of a clearcut policy statement, whether operating or administrative:

1. State the underlying need.

2. Break the major question raised by the proposed policy into the required subquestions.

3. Conduct the necessary research to establish needed facts.

4. Consider the problem of implementation.

5. Formulate the statement.

The five points are not only important in themselves, but their sequence is also important, Step 1 logically leading to Step 2, and so on.

Regarding Step 1: Think in explicit terms about objectives, and possible alternatives.

Regarding Step 2: What are the profit-and-loss effects of the proposed policy? Can the company (department) afford the move at this time? What has been the experience of others under similar situations? Has this situation arisen before—and if so, how was it handled. What embarrassing contingencies might arise if the policy is adopted?

Rank the subquestions in sequence of importance and

sequence of attack (the two rankings need not necessarily be the same).

Regarding Step 3: On important policy problems, the subproblems requiring research will themselves require clarification of objective, perhaps further breaking down into component problems, assignment of responsibility for conducting the research, etc. (See *Problem Solving*.)

Regarding Step 4: When you issue a policy statement, put yourself in the shoes of those who will have to carry it out, and see that they are covered in an explanatory statement when you get to Step 5. Thus, what approvals are necessary in implementing the policy? What helps from staff or service departments are available? What broad limits of authority are contemplated by the policy? What outside helps can be used? What time limits are involved? What sort of check-ups will be made? Etc., etc.

Regarding Step 5: The following prescription is suggested, against which every policy statement should be checked. The ingredients will be needed in varying degrees, depending upon the nature of the policy:

a. Give an opening sentence or brief paragraph as to the "why" of the policy.

b. Keep the statement of general policy distinct from the detailed procedural rules and regulations for carrying it out.

c. Try to separate the independent parts of the policy.

d. Indicate broadly how the policy is to be implemented, with necessary approvals. *If helps are available, say so.*

e. Be as brief as clarity permits.

Related Entries *Communicating—2. Answering the "Unanswerable"; Company Policy—When You Disagree with It; Standard Operating Procedures.*

POLICY MANUALS
See *Standard Operating Procedures.*

POOREST VERSUS BEST EMPLOYEES
See *Appraising Subordinates—3. "Best versus Poorest."*

PRAISE

A successful advertising and sales executive made the letters "P.F." one of his chief slogans. P.F. stands for *Praise Fearlessly!* This executive was always ready to praise those under him when praise was deserved. He believed that the man who is afraid to give recognition to associates or people under his supervision fears that someone may advance at his expense, and is suffering from an inferiority complex.

Note Could the following scenario, with minor changes, have been taken from your department? J. David Hauser describes it in *What People Want from Business:*

A visitor in a plant engages in a conversation with a minor executive in a marking department—

"Does a marker ever know the result of her work?"

"Well, no. Not exactly. She just does it and it's usually O.K."

"What standards have you set for 'O.K.' or better work?"

"It has to be done right and fast enough to keep up."

"How fast is that?"

"Oh, it varies with the volume of work."

"I see. And how do employees know how they stand?"

"Well, if they don't hear from me, they know it's all right."

Related Entry *Motivation.*

PREGNANCY
See *Women and Girls—2. Special Physiological Problems.*

PREJUDICES

We all have prejudices—prejudgings. . . . We wouldn't be human if we didn't. They are the results of our religion, our upbringing, shattering experiences and tragedies that we may have lived through, and what we absorbed at our mother's knee or over our father's knee. In your dealings with people, the trick is to recognize that you have prejudices, and to be on guard lest they influence your actions —and to recognize that others have them, and to govern yourself accordingly.

As to your own: It will be a good idea to take time out sometime to draw up a list of possible prejudices you may have about people. Since nobody will see the list, you can be brutally frank. Try some "Am I's" or "Do I's": Am I affected by certain kinds of features, dress, and voice? Am I too ready to jump to conclusions about somebody simply on the strength of a fixed idea I might have as to his or her "type"? Do I have strong feelings about a person's religion or race? Am I "against" college graduates? Noncollege graduates? Am I suspicious of people of a certain nationality, or political persuasion? Am I resentful of women as bosses (because they're women)?

The intent here is not to "go into psychoanalysis" to find out the long-buried roots of your emotional reactions. The simple act of recognizing prejudices will go a long way—you can then lean over backwards with respect to them in interviewing people, in criticizing them, in appraising them, and in weighing their suggestions.

As to prejudices in others: Hear again, the step of recognition will be the first long one toward constructive comportment. Since prejudices are rooted in emotions, you can't do much on the rational level. Learn to accept them as factors in the other fellow's make-up, and do your best not to rub against them. Often a wise supervisor can create situations where a growth of *understanding* will overcome or lessen prejudice—a technique quite different from an attempt at arguing a person out of a fixed persuasion. Pairing two workers of different race or religion on a job where, both absorbed in the same end result, their mutual working together will lead to tolerance and understanding is one way. Your sense of timing, the urgency of the job to be done, the make-up of the individuals, possible dangers if friction develops, all must be considered. All of this underscores a point made in other entries: *Know Your People!*

Related Entries   *Civil Rights; National Labor Relations Act.*

PREVENTIVE MAINTENANCE
See *The Maintenance Foreman—3. A Systematic Maintenance Program.*

PRIVILEGES

With all of the stress on the supervisor's need to be fair at all times, is there an excuse for special privileges in the department? Yes—provided they are of two kinds:

1. *If they are earned*—and if everyone has a chance to qualify for them. For example, seniority may dictate who gets company parking lot privileges, or preferred positions in it. It is conceivable that paid time-off rewards may be given for perfect accident records over a given period, or for hundred per cent quality performance. Special privileges can be a valuable incentive.

2. *If there are special circumstances—which everyone*

is made to understand. Somebody may have illness in family, or a crippled parent to take care of, and the like— and may be given the privilege of leaving early, or leaving early and coming in slightly early. Keep vigilance over these situations. Make it clear that none is to be construed as a precedent—and follow up to see that nobody abuses a privilege by continuing it when the original need for it has ended.

Related Entry *Motivation.*

PROBLEM EMPLOYEES

In every large department there are always a relatively few employees who seem to have most of the troubles— who get into most of the scrapes, have most of the absenteeisms, cause most of the snafus. These are the "problem employees." But don't dismiss them with that tag, which is misleading. Problem employees aren't a separate race of people who are born that way. Something is causing their difficulties, and it's up to you as a supervisor to look beneath the surface and get at the *why's.* For example:

1. *Is there a physical reason?* Is constant fatigue or be-low-par health causing carelessness and accidents? What do recent absenteeisms indicate?

2. *Is there a personal problem?* The foreman isn't expected to pry into the personal lives of his employees, but the good supervisor does make it his business to know his employees and their backgrounds. His general attitude should be sympathetic enough to invite discussion. If he knows the facts of a case, he can take proper measures regarding work assignments, provisions for occasional early leaving, and the like. (See *Employee Counseling.*)

3. *Is there a suspicion of alcoholism?* (See *The Alcoholic Employee.*)

4. *Is there a training lack?* Is some special on-the-job training called for? (See the three entries under *On-the-Job Training.*) How about coaching? (See *Coaching.*) Is there an older employee in the department who can help you develop this person?

5. *Is there a problem of friction within the department, or non-acceptance by the group?* Is this an employee who, perhaps because of origin, or race, or religion, just doesn't seem to be included by the others in their informal get-togethers, their coffee breaks, their outside activities? If so, can you go out of your way to demonstrate your own tendency to "include him in" in friendly conversations, to show marks of appreciation, etc.

6. *Is this employee just plain nervous?* (See *The Jittery Employee.*)

Related Entries   *See listing under "People Problems"—2. Employee Types.*

PROBLEM SOLVING
1. A General Prescription

As a supervisor you are continually confronted with the need to analyze specific departmental problems and to come up with proposed lines of action. Or you may be assigned a piece of a larger division-wide or company-wide problem by your superior, and asked to help him draw up recommendations.

While all problems are different, there is a single, uniform, orderly *mode of attack* which will greatly increase your effectiveness, no matter what the particular problem is. This is set forth in the following six-step procedure for the systematic solution of problems. In applying it, keep this overall motto in mind: *In all of the steps, get the* FACTS. . . . *face the facts.* . . . *interpret the facts.* . . . get OPINIONS. . . . place opinions in *their proper perspective.*

1. *Determine the objective(s) and state the problem.* It will help to put this in writing, to be sure you have thought the basic problem through. State the problem in broad terms, to be sure that you are not spending all of your time on only a piece of a more general situation (unless, of course, you have been assigned a specific piece).

2. *Break the main problem into independent pieces, and clarify the sequence of attack.* Distinguish between priority in importance, and priority in actual attack. Assign overall responsibilities and authorities if others are helping you in the necessary research and solution recommendations.

3. *Make a breakdown of questions on which working data are needed.* Here, decide whether there are sources of preliminary data which can be obtained relatively quickly and inexpensively. Often such preliminary information will strongly indicate whether or not a line of action is "in the cards" without going further in the undertaking.

4. *Devise a formula for solving the problem.* Of course, no general recipe can be given here. Once the essential data are at hand, together with a full awareness of the limitations of the data, devising the formula becomes a matter of interpretation and plain hard thinking. Keep "people problems" in mind—the "one best way" for one type of organization, under one set of conditions, may not work with other people under other circumstances of tensions, morale, background, etc. Iron out as many kinks

ahead of time as possible, by preparatory discussions at the operating level. If possible, arrange for pilot studies or preliminary tryouts.

5. *Organize for action.* Set up *realistic* timetables. Fix specific responsibilities and authorities. *Prepare the ground* by word passed along through proper channels, and by meetings for explanations and instructions, where necessary. Provide check sheets wherever they can assure proper and uniform action, based on consultations at the operating level.

6. *Arrange for effective follow-through.* Determine upon periodic reports. Make periodic check-ups. Determine upon proper "danger signals" for continuing operations, to prevent recurrence of the original problem, or to prevent costly variances if an entirely new situation is being handled.

Related Entries *See succeeding entry; also: Follow-up; Methods Improvement—1. The Questioning Attitude; Planning and Scheduling—2. "Critical Path" and Other Network Techniques; Waste—1. Reducible Waste; Work Simplification.*

PROBLEM SOLVING

2. The Open Mind

Persons with rigidly fixed preconceived ideas never shine brilliantly in creative thinking, or in coming up with bold new solutions when all the old ways of doing something don't seem to be getting the department or the special projects anywhere.

A slate which is all cluttered up with previous writings cannot be the vehicle for original expression. Therefore if you want to be in a position to cope with unexpected situations, or, even more important, if you want to be able to *imagine* unexpected situations, you must be able to erase from your mind any preconceived notions you may have had about how such-and-such a situation was always met before, or how your father or grandfather used to cope with a given set of circumstances.

Mind you, this doesn't imply that a person should come to a problem absolutely innocent of ideas as to how similar problems were attacked before, or how the XYZ Corporation usually handles a matter of that kind. The point to be emphasized here is that the man with an open mind is willing to hold *in abeyance* (not *discard*) any conclusions previously arrived at. The ideal, thus, is a seasoned man with an *open* mind, not a young tyro with an *unused* mind which may in effect be a blank slate upon which anyone may write anything—true or false.

Notes "If we've been doing something the same way for a year, we say, it's time to examine it and see if there isn't a better way. If we're still doing it the same way after two years, we say the same thing in a louder voice. If we're still doing it after three years, we scream. There's an endless pursuit of excellence in this company. Why? Because we like to feel good."

—Don Cook, President, American Power Company.

• In his *Techniques of Administration,* Prof. Erwin H. Schell says, "The most serious error in administration is the *initial error.* At the beginning of your thinking, you may define your problem incompletely; omit some vital but inconspicuous element. This mistake will cure your later thinking. Few people are entirely free from prejudices or preconceptions, almost everyone has a mental blind spot that causes him to underestimate or overlook. . . . Elihu Root said: *'The greatest curse of thought is preconception.'* "

Related Entries   *See listing under preceding entry.*

PROCEDURE MANUALS

See *Standard Operating Procedures.*

PROGRAMMED INSTRUCTION

"Programmed instruction" is a recent major innovation in teaching technique which a supervisor may use to advantage in training others, or in his own self-improvement. Its most important advantage is that it is "learner centered." It is tailor-made to the needs of the individual learner by careful testing, during program development, among groups representative of the target audience. With such specially constructed programs, the learner can set his own pace, since he learns without a teacher and without having to gear his speed to the pace of a group.

In more elaborate applications, programmed instruction makes use of so-called "teaching machines," and may even be tied in with an electronic computer which poses questions and supplies answers, determining succeeding questions from the answers given. But by far the most widespread employment of the concept requires only specially constructed textbooks in which answers to questions are temporarily masked from the reader's view, or makes use of simple devices which present portions of text together with relevant questions and responses in a programmed sequence.

Programmed instruction material—which may be a course in algebra, or methods-improvement techniques, or programming and operation of a computer—is organized into a *program* of carefully written, brief, logical steps. Each step gives the learner a new piece of information, and may also repeat information given in previous steps. Then it poses a question that calls for a *response* from the learner.

Each step, in programmed-instruction jargon, is called a *frame*, and in addition to giving information, the frame asks a question and provides space for the learner to write down his answer. The text in the frame may refer the reader to a page or *panel* in a supplementary textbook or manual, or to other material.

Programmed-instruction texts keep the answer from the reader until he either turns the page as directed, or slides a masking device with a "window" in it along the page (see Exhibit P-4, page 317). The window is the size of the frame, and when it opens up a new frame, it reveals at the same time the correct response to the question posed by the preceding frame. This immediately tells the trainee whether he is right or wrong. Success enhances learning; and if he is wrong, the error is so small that he can usually find out quickly why he made it. (Contrast this with a classroom, where a trainee may have misconceptions, but can't clear them up until he has a chance to ask questions—and the chance may not come. And in classroom tests, the graded paper often does not tell why a wrong answer is wrong.)

Programs using a masking device which reveals one frame after another going down a page are said to be "vertically structured." Some texts are "horizontally structured," and require no special gadget. Instead, for a given set of pages, the reader proceeds horizontally by reading frame No. 1 at the top of page 1, frame No. 2 at the top of page 3, frame No. 3 at the top of page 5, and so on for the given number of pages, after which he goes back to page 1 again, and reads, say, frame No. 6, which appears second from the top of page 1, then frame No. 7, which appears second from the top of page 3, and so on. The advantage claimed for the vertical type is that it is less confusing and, more importantly, that by obscuring *everything else* on the page, the masking forces the learner to concentrate on the frame without distraction.

A text programmed sequentially as above, whether vertical or horizontal, is said to be a *linear* program. In a *branching* program, sometimes called a *scrambled* program, the learner reads a frame and is then tested by questions which provide for a multiple-choice response. The next frame he reads is determined by his answer. If correct, he moves on to more advanced material, but if incorrect, the next piece of information is designed to clear up his misunderstanding. The multiple-choice method tends to be more complex and possibly confusing in use. In general, the linear programs have been found to be best for straight instruction, and the branching programs perhaps better suited for more advanced management training in decision making.

To be effective, programs must be constructed with great care, and this is usually a job requiring special training. A program is not simply a presentation of questions and answers or open-ended statements to be completed. The writer must have a thorough knowledge of the subject

Template for Cutting a "Window" for Exhibit P-4

26. Ed Rickert, supervisor of a linotype crew on a newspaper, is observing his employees. What symbols would he use for these activities? 1) An operator sorts the material he will typeset. 2) The operator typesets the material. 3) The operator carries the set type to a table.	
1) ○ 2) ◉ 3) ⟶	1) 2) 3)

27. Inspection is a check or measurement to ensure the quality or quantity of a product. It involves counting, weighing, or checking the product. The symbol used for inspection is ☐. Which situation would be marked as ☐?				
| | | X	BOTH	A	B	NEITHER

28. Moving something from one operation to another, such as carrying a finished product to storage, is referred to as:	transportation. ⟶			
X | | |	BOTH	A	B	NEITHER

29. Which of these is referred to by the symbol ☐?	counting, checking, or weighing a product to ensure its quality or quantity			
X | | |	BOTH	A	B	NEITHER

30. A typical flow process chart is given in Panel 3.1. The first step in the preparation of the chart is to identify what is to be studied. 1) Under what heading does this appear on the chart? 2) What is being studied?	
1) Process 2) Packing 100 valves (Part #1782) from tote box to shipping carton	1) 2)

Illustrated here is a representative set of frames from *PRIME IV—Methods Improvement for the Supervisor*, published by the American Management Association. (You will recognize here references to the subject matter covered in our entry, *Work Simplification*.) AMA's format uses a plastic flap, or mask, with a clear window in it of the shape shown on p. 316. (In the PRIME book, the pages are 8½ by 11 in.) To get an idea of how programmed instruction works, cut a matter, and be able to organize it into small, discrete steps in exactly the right sequence, with clear definitions and new terms introduced at just the right time, and with each response adding to the understanding of the new material given in the frame. As stated, professional programmers test their programs on carefully selected persons as they develop them, to be sure that they are getting their ideas across. A finished program may vary from a relatively few to several thousand frames.

Note A number of companies have come on the market with various kinds of teaching machines, ranging from a simple mechanical desk model to complex electronic and mechanical units, displaying information on television-like screens. Some machines present their programs on sheets or rolls of paper, while others use some form of film. On some, the learner writes in his response, on others he presses a button to indicate his choice of answers. Following 1954, when the present great interest in programmed instruction was triggered by investigations into learning processes reported upon by Dr. Burrus F. Skinner, Director of the Psychological Laboratories at Harvard, there was a brief wave of excitement about machines and gadgets of all sort—many of which, however, were hardly more than mechanical page turners.

Programmed instruction has now settled down to a more sober technique, to be used along with other training methods. Leading publishing companies produce programmed-instruction texts on a wide variety of subjects, and many consulting groups and others are active in developing programs for a fee. The Center for Programmed Learning for Business at the University of Michigan is active in continuing research. The American Management Association has been a

---

window in a sheet of paper, to the exact size of the template shown on page 316. Then slide the mask down the PRIME page, and you will see how one frame at a time is opened up, and how the correct response to a frame is disclosed when the succeeding frame is opened up.

leader in developing programmed instruction courses of the linear type, under the name PRIME (Programmed Instruction for Management Education). The accompanying exhibit is a representative page from "PRIME IV—Methods Improvement for the Supervisor," reproduced here through the courtesy of Dr. Rose Clavering, Manager, AMA Programmed Instruction Projects.

Related Entries *See listing under Development of Subordinates—1. Development-Appraisal-Development.*

PROMOTIONS

1. Assessing Your People's Potential for Growth

Helping people grow is one of the best ways to grow yourself, to make yourself available for a bigger job. The supervisor who is "going places" will always be concerned about what he can do to improve the *promotability of the people working for him*—at least those who exhibit any spark of "ambition-plus" (the "plus" being willingness to work instead of mere wistful desire to get a better job). In-depth discussions of accountability, objectives, and performance, as discussed in *Development of Subordinates —1. Development-Appraisal-Development*, should enable you to answer the following questions about every man and woman reporting directly to you:

1. How good is this employee on his present job? Is there a good job-man-match? If he is not ready at present, how near, in terms of probable years of development, is he to full-fledged senior status in his job grade?

2. What are his best areas in terms of performance results?

3. What are his correctible weak points? What immediate line of action is indicated for their correction, (a) by you? (b) by the employee himself?

4. Are any inherent limitations indicated, in terms of basic intelligence or education, which cannot be overcome? Any ingrained attitudes which place a ceiling on his performance in his present job?

5. Is there an age, health, or other physical condition which makes transfer or change of duties advisable? Inadvisable?

6. Does the employee's present position permit the best use of his capabilities? Is he ready for a bigger or different job? How can you help him, directly or by encouragement, to focus his aim and prepare for examination or other qualification tests? What special training programs should he be taking advantage of?

7. If his present position uses his capabilities reasonably well, is there still room for personal growth within the job?

Related Entries   *See succeeding two entries; also, Appraising Subordinates (three entries); Personnel Audit.*

PROMOTIONS

2. Assessments in Depth

Promoting a person is serious business. By this act you are placing your bet on an employee as someone who is ready to move higher. If you promote somebody too soon, you can do him more harm than passing him by the first time. The latter mistake is much easier to correct than the first!

The business becomes more serious when a really big step in a person's career is involved—when, say, you are recommending one of your key people for an important vacancy outside of your department, or when you are asked by higher management to help make a choice from a number of candidates for a particularly important assignment, or when you are rendering an opinion about a "cadet" or "internee" who has been on a tour of duty in your department, and you are asked whether he is ready for bigger things.

Appraisal for potential on a bigger job is still one of the most difficult arts of management. Trial-by-error is costly, and there are no quick-and-easy tests which a personnel department can apply to spot the winners and screen out the losers. By far the biggest responsibility will always fall on the employee's immediate superior—the one who presumably has been watching his progress and measuring results. Accordingly, for an important personnel judgment of this sort, you should take enough time to make a thorough analysis of the employee involved. This calls for the long view—you should not be unduly influenced against him because of some recent blooper, nor, conversely, overswayed in his favor because of a recent scout's-merit-badge achievement.

To justify your recommendation, you should be able to answer a series of searching questions about the employee's performance while he was under your direction. A set of such questions is given below. They obviously cover an employee holding a fairly responsible position—and, in larger departments, may concern someone who is himself a supervisor. Note that the questions can't be handled with quick answers. They are "panoramic" in scope, covering the whole span of your contact with him:

1. How would you comment on this employee relative to his showing special interest in his work—in the form of staying late or coming in at odd hours on special jobs,

of his own accord; of volunteering ideas and suggestions; and appearing to want to learn as much as possible about aspects of the business with which he comes in contact?

2. Would you say that he is ready to express his own viewpoints to his superiors in staff meetings, when the occasion warrants? . . . . Having "said his piece," can he be counted upon to fall into line if some policy or procedure is adopted contrary to his own point of view?

3. With further reference to his participation in staff meetings, can you cite instances when, after a discussion of a more or less confidential or delicate nature, he was not as careful as he should have been in talking with others later about what took place?

4. Does he show evidence of being conscious of the cost-implications of his actions? Can you cite instances when he failed to follow through promptly on approved procedures for cost reduction?

5. Can you cite any instances during, say, the past year when this employee was in your opinion responsible for any serious mistake of judgment on any work assignment, or for any serious incorrect action?

6. Conversely, were there outstanding instances of his "using his head" in an emergency or unusual situation?

7. Have you had any direct evidence, over the past year or so, of any difficulty he has had in getting along with those under his direct supervision?. . . . With anyone in an administrative position?. . . . With subordinates of others?. . . . With persons of his own level?

8. How would you rate this employee on conscientious observance of expected working hours? Extremely reliable _____ Reliable _____ Frequently absent or tardy _____ Undependable _____?

9. Does he see to it that work assignments are carried out *on time?* Can you cite specific instances when he was responsible for undue delays? . . . Does he turn in necessary reports on time, properly completed?

10. From your own personal experience with this employee, would you say he is ready to admit responsibility for mistakes he has made? Or is he likely to try to "alibi" his way out of a situation that reflects on him?

11. If this employee is someone who has other employees reporting to him, can you cite instances over the past year when he—

a. Did not properly transmit general management directives or your own specific instructions to subordinates?

b. Created a problem by failing to transmit necessary information from a staff representative, or line administrative or operating personnel?

c. Failed to keep you properly informed on down-the-line developments of interest in the conduct of your department?

12. Were there any instances, over approximately the past year, when he sacrificed quality to meet a quota, or because he apparently did not exert the required effort to assure good workmanship?

13. Can you point to any specific bottleneck situations for which he was primarily responsible? In this connection, if he has subordinates reporting to him, do such bottleneck situations point to poor delegation of work?

14. Would this employee be qualified to be your own understudy? To be qualified to take over your duties, what, if anything, does he need in the way of (a) more experience; (b) additional technical training or schooling; or (c) other personal development?

Note three characteristics about the above questions:

First, they seem to lean heavily toward a discussion of *negative* aspects of the employee's performance—mistakes in judgment . . . . poor cost performance . . . . failure to get along with people . . . . bottlenecks . . . . etc.

Second, they call for citation of *specific instances* of performance and behavior.

The intent is the same in both cases: to get away from generalized, favorable recommendations. Focusing on things that could cause trouble in the bigger job is the soundest possible procedure—and demanding chapter and verse will guard against off-hand, superficial, and unfair criticisms.

Third, you will note that except for the last question, nothing is said about the technical aspects of the job. Technical proficiency for the employee's present job assignment is assumed, based on prior selection procedures. What you are now looking for are *management aptitudes* required if the man is to go up the ladder, and for this his technical proficiency on the present job will have no decisive bearing. In any event, you are passing upon his performance while under your direction. Objective tests can easily be made by others of any technical demands of the higher job in question.

A sound summation can be made from the careful replies to the fourteen questions. You can judge whether he is now ready, or practically so, for certain specified positions; or if not now ready, what his potentials are, and how long it might take him to become qualified. Most important of all, the questions will enable you to pinpoint the specific areas in which he must be strengthened.

Related Entries *See succeeding entry and listing under preceding entry.*

PROMOTIONS

3. The Employees Passed Over

Every promotion will inevitably leave from one to as many as ten disappointments in its wake. For every winner, there will be a number of also-rans. The supervisory problem here is to see that those who were passed by remain effective members of the working team. You won't be successful in all cases—but you can do a lot to minimize your own losses. Here are preventive measures to take.

1. Plan ahead for promotions. Always have an up-to-date "audit" of vacancies you expect, and when and how you plan to fill them. (See *Organization—2. Continuity through Runners-Up* and *Personnel Audit.*)

2. Plan ahead for the also-rans. Thus in addition to listing runners-up, try listing for each important vacancy those who you think will consider themselves qualified.

3. When a promotion looms ahead, review once again the position specifications and your listing of candidates. Have there been changes in job requirements or in personal development of candidates which alter the previous picture?

4. With respect to the aspirants who will be disappointed, make a list of strong and weak points as related to the position to be filled. Think of all the positive, constructive things that can be said about each—and make a realistic assessment of other promotional opportunities that still remain for each (in other departments as well as your own), and what you consider to be the area in which he needs further experience or development in order to qualify.

5. What job enlargement possibilities are there for the

unsuccessful aspirants in the jobs they are presently holding?

6. As soon as a final decision on the promotion has been made—who and when—schedule a private discussion with all who can reasonably consider themselves to be in the running. Start with the successful candidate. Go through the whole list as soon as possible—the same day if that can be done—so that there is a minimum period of "cliff-hanging."

7. The interviews are important both to the employees' morale and your own departmental efficiency. Therefore they are worth devoting sufficient time to them. Don't make any of the interviews hurried or perfunctory.

8. Conduct the interview with the same care and consideration applied to the yearly appraisal interview discussed in *Appraising Subordinates—2. Appraisal Interview.* Open by saying that, as he undoubtedly knows, such-and-such a job is to be filled. Then say you know that there are a number of good people in the department obviously worth considering for the promotion—such as himself —and you want to be sure he understands all of the factors going into the decision. Then get into a discussion of the requirements of the position—not as a lecture on your part, but rather drawing him out to discuss the requirements as he sees them. If there are certain qualifications which the employee does not have, intersperse comments and enlarge upon these job specifications, and see if you can lead him to recognize gaps or thin areas in his own background whose importance he had not realized—or had not wanted to face. . . . Tell him who has been chosen, and reasons for the choice. Then turn the discussion to positive points to the employee's own future, and what-

ever plans for personal development, whatever opportunities exist in the relatively near future.

9. In closing the interview, express appreciation for the employee's services to the department, and stress the confidential nature of your disclosure of the choice made, pending formal announcement on your part. He can, of course, discuss any aspect he cares to with his own superior (if the employee does not report directly to you), who has of course been informed of the decision, and with the successful candidate who has by now also received prior information.

10. In a large department, a memorandum from you to all personnel may be in order, announcing the appointment and indicating any related changes in mode of reporting and in duties which may be involved.

Related Entries *See listing under Promotions—1. Assessing Your People's Potential for Growth.*

PUBLIC SPEAKING
When the Supervisor Has to Make a Speech

Anyone with leadership responsibility should be able to speak effectively in public. He may never have to make a speech on his present job, but if he advances into more responsible positions he may find himself called upon to speak before various-sized groups at trade association or management-society gatherings. Or he may become active in community affairs (which many corporations encourage in their executives). And, of course, he may have occasion to address employee groups, or say something at a company-sponsored dinner or other gathering.

There are only four requirements to be a capable speaker, according to the newsletter *Assignments in Man-*

agement: (1) know your subject; (2) know how to give information on it in sharp, clear language; (3) know how to cover key points in logical order; (4) have the *wish* to give an effective talk. Many knowledgeable people fail as speakers, says AIM, because they won't take the trouble to make the effort. Here are AIM's pointers:

Preparing the Speech

Jot down an outline of your subject. For example, an outline of a supervisor's talk on *Grievance Handling* might look like this:

1. Definition of a grievance as given in the union contract.

2. Steps of the grievance procedure.

3. Importance of handling a grievance promptly.

4. Importance of consistency and precedent in grievance handling.

5. Value of good two-way communications in grievance handling.

6. How a sound grievance procedure improves employee relations.

Since the supervisor already knows his subject, all he has to do is note the six main headings on separate 3- x 5-in. cards, and under each of them enter short sentences describing related topics he may wish to discuss. After two or three dry runs to familiarize himself with his outline cards, he should be able to give a hard-hitting talk.

Some Questions about Delivery

Here are two questions most frequently asked:

1. *Should I write my talk in full before I give it?* AIM's answer: *It depends on you.* Some speakers prefer to

use cards which outline their main ideas. Others feel more comfortable if they have the text before them. Use the method that gives you the greatest feeling of confidence.

2. *Should I write my speech and then memorize it?* AIM's answer: *No!* However, it's wise to read your text over and over again until you're familiar with it. Then you can read your talk without being too obvious about it. Actually, you're using the written text as another man uses reference cards.

Pointers for Effectiveness

1. Don't worry about being nervous—many experienced speakers confess to stage fright. Moreover, you usually do a better job if you run a little bit scared.

2. Don't bury your nose in your manuscript. Look at the people who are listening, so that you can sense their reaction.

3. Don't be a speed merchant. Make sure your words are clearly understandable.

4. Put expression into your voice. A monotone can put a listener to sleep.

5. Be yourself, and don't apologize for your shortcomings as a speaker. You were asked to talk because you have something to say, not because you are an orator.

6. Watch your humor. Make sure it's appropriate and doesn't offend anyone in your audience. Don't add jokes because you think this is expected of a speaker.

7. Move quickly to win audience attention. If your opening remarks grab the listener's attention like a newspaper headline, he's more likely to listen to details.

8. Use examples to drive home points. People will re-

member facts that have been underlined by a pertinent anecdote.

9. Be natural in your gestures.

10. Talk to all of your listeners. Never select a particular individual and address your remarks to him. Don't fix your eyes on a picture on the wall or some object in the back of the room.

11. Don't wear out your welcome. A good vaudeville performer tries to "leave them laughing" or wanting more. A good speaker quits while his audience is still with him.

Related Entries   *Briefings and Presentations; Communicating —1. Selling Ideas; Visual and Audio Aids.*

PUNISHMENT

We are all familiar with punishment or the threat of punishment as used in the upbringing of children, and also accept it without question as society's means of keeping public order. And, of course, military discipline is strongly based on punishment.

We don't often think of punishment as a supervisory tool, because we associate it with some form of physical action, incarceration, etc. Actually, however, punishment is often implied in management actions: Dismissal, for example, has been characterized as the "capital punishment" in the business world. Graduated downward from that are all sorts of punitive devices—withheld promotions or privileges, no salary increase, demotion, transfers to a company's particular "Siberia," etc. We don't subject a departmental offender to a cat-o'-nine-tails flogging or put him in the stocks—but punishment in its less corporeal forms must definitely be considered in our discussion of management principles and techniques.

Based on experiments in behavior, psychologists have come up with some interesting conclusions on the effectiveness of punishment that should provide valuable insights to anyone in a position of authority:

In psychological language, punishment is the "application of an undesirable stimulus in order to change a certain kind of behavior."

Repeated controlled experiments with animals and people tend to show that the effect of punishment as a behavior-control device (as contrasted, for example, with other tactics such as praise, tangible rewards, etc.) is much less effective than one might suppose. Its effectiveness is largely dependent upon the degree to which the punished behavior is motivated, and the degree to which those punished have available alternate lines of behavior satisfactory to them. Punishment does tend to reduce the undesirable (to the punisher) behavior, especially at first, but it apparently cannot *eliminate* the response. As a matter of fact, after a time, the old response tends to be resumed in the same degree as noted in those who were not punished! In general, studies reported by investigators indicate that:

1. Responses can be eliminated by mild punishment if they are not highly motivated.

2. Highly motivated responses can be eliminated by mild punishment if they are not the only responses that can satisfy some drive. Here the effect of punishment is usually to make behavior more variable—animals and people will try to find other ways to satisfy their drives when punished for some particular response. (Query for the supervisor—are the alternative responses any less undesirable to you than the one you are trying to eliminate?)

3. The effects of punishment are not always simple or

predictable, and as a frustration may lead to disturbances of behavior.

In his book, *Introduction to Psychology*, Dr. Clifford T. Morgan points out that there are two circumstances in which punishment, or the threat of punishment, usually proves effective in controlling human behavior:

1. Mild punishment may be used as a cue to information about what should or should not be done. If there are desirable alternatives for a person, the threat of punishment about what not to do can be helpful.

2. The threat of punishment also serves well in our society to eliminate undesirable behavior (in the area of public order). Actual punishment for infractions often does not seem effective—if one can judge by the number of "repeaters" in prison—but in most instances, the threat of punishment serves its purpose well without having harmful effects.

The net effect of what we know about punishment, concludes Dr. Morgan, is to lead us to be cautious about its use. It should be used discerningly, with an eye to its possible undesirable consequences.

Related Entries   *Favoritism; Motivation; Prejudices.*

Q

QUALITY

"The best way to reduce or eliminate defects in the final product is to eliminate the original causes," says the Thompson Products *Supervisors' Manual.* "One thing is certain—maintenance of quality is the job of everyone. . . . To disregard quality standards means that eventually costs are adversely affected. The individual employee's attitude will largely reflect the attitude of supervision. You can build up the proper attitude by impressing the employee with the various losses caused by defective work." Here are some quality pointers the manual stresses:

Employee Attitudes

1. *Monetary losses.* Make the employees aware of the approximate cost of raw materials. . . . Stress the cost of preceding operations. Point out that the product increases in value in direct proportion to the operations performed on it. . . . Cite the cost of handling by the service department, and of purchasing, rescheduling, trucking, inspection, etc. . . . Let them know that overhead is often 200% or more of the direct cost of an item, and that cost of salvage or repairs sometimes exceeds the actual cost of an item.

2. *Damage to the employee's and the department's reputation and work record.* "Quality of work" is al-

ways an important item considered when making a promotion. . . . Job security must be earned by producing good quality of work at lowest possible cost. Such work assures a large and stabilized volume of business, creating more and steady work for employees.

3. *Damage to customer good will.* Stress that distrust by the customer of the quality of a product can have serious consequences. . . . A defective product can result in a dissatisfied buyer who may refuse to buy in the future. Poor quality and delayed shipments can spoil a good reputation that was built up over a long period of years. . . . For non-productive or maintenance groups, the "customer" is the manufacturing division. Defective workmanship by them will cause additional delays which affect customer schedules.

Corrective Action

1. *Have employee assume personal responsibility for checking his own work.* Specify the exact intervals at which the employee should check his own work, and instruct him to report conditions that make quality work difficult. . . . Make production workers realize that they, and not the inspector, are solely responsible for the quality of work.

2. *Analyze defective work.* Determine what the defect is, and its cause. Determine who is involved. Explain the circumstances to the person(s) involved. Make sure the reasons for the defective work are understood. . . . Have your facts straight; dates, number of pieces, scrapped parts or inferior work, part numbers, exactly what happened, etc.

3. *Handle indifference, carelessness, or negligence.* *Warn* against repetition. Check quality of work closely

until you are satisfied the employee is capable of working under normal supervision. . . . *Reprimand* in accordance with company policy. A company that pays high wages is entitled to superior people. . . . *Write a "personnel memo"* explaining the action taken. The memo should cover the type of, and the reasons for, the defective work, the number of pieces or value of the item, date of occurrence, and disposition. The worker's reaction should also be noted. . . . Be sure the employee reads the memo. If he does not sign it, write, "Read—did not sign" on the bottom of the memo. Give the union steward an opportunity to sign the memo also. It becomes part of the employee's record.

Note "I never see my boss," said a workman one day. "Do you know how I stand with that fellow?" To this his listener replied that only the day before he had heard his boss mention the fact that he would hate to lose the man, because he was one of the best grinders on the job.

"Well, I had just about made up my mind to quit. I've been working up there for a year and a half, and no one yet has told me whether I was doing well or doing poorly. I don't know whether I'm worth anything to this outfit or not. I'd just about decided I wasn't. I'd made up my mind that I would slip backward if I stayed here much longer."

When this situation was called to the foreman's attention, his comment was, "Gee, what's the matter with these fellows anyway? Are they soft? Do you have to nurse them all the time? He is supposed to do good work, isn't he? And, if he does, he gets paid for it, doesn't he?"

How practical was this foreman? If commended, the man would certainly continue to produce a good-quality job, knowing that what he did was appreciated by the boss. On the other hand, there was a chance that the man was about to leave, indicating that credit for a job well done, to which he was entitled now and then, was the difference between interest and lack of interest in the job. (From T. A. Armstrong's chapter on "Quality Control and Waste Reduction," in *The Foreman's Handbook*.)

Related Entries   *The Careless Worker; Inspection; Statistical Quality Control.*

R

"RATIO DELAY"

See *Work Measurement—2. Work Sampling, or "Ratio Delay."*

RECRUITMENT

The chances are that your Personnel Department will do the initial screening of applicants for positions in your department, based on specifications of the job to be filled (as to this, see *Job Analysis and Evaluation*), and will take care of whatever initial tests are given, review of suitability from the point of view of education, prior employment, general impressions, etc. However, as a supervisor you will undoubtedly interview the finalists before a choice is made. Here are some good interview points taken from the United Shoe Machinery Corporation's Mears Division *Manual of Personnel Policies and Procedures.* (Details such as completion of medical questionnaire, of course, will depend upon company procedure.):

1. Honesty and courtesy must be applied throughout the interview, since the applicant's impression of you and of the Company will play an important part in his eventual decision.

2. If the applicant is obviously *not* qualified for the job, tell him so in a tactful manner. Never keep him in suspense unnecessarily. Remember that an applicant's

welfare, and the welfare of those dependent upon him, is directly related to his employment decision.

3. If an applicant is a contender for the job, he should be advised accordingly. However, if the situation warrants, he should be told that other applications are being considered, and that he will be advised at the earliest practicable date.

4. If the results of the interview are generally favorable, review the starting and future wage rate (and incentives and piece work rates if applicable), and general fringe benefit program.

5. Have the applicant, if a definite contender for the job, complete the medical questionnaire form and attach it to the Application for Employment form for later review.

6. Inform the applicant that you intend to check his references, and check Application Form for Employment to be sure there are at least two personal references in addition to previous employers. [See *References*.]

7. If the applicant is employed at the time of his application, check to see whether he has given permission to contact his *present* employer. If he feels that such a contact would endanger his present position, assure him that the company will *not* make such a contact *until* he is in the Company's employ, at which time the employer would be contacted to verify his personnel record.

* * *

Here are some additional pointers:

8. See that you get, sufficiently ahead of time, all the necessary papers from Personnel: application blank, results of any tests, and comments of the Personnel Department Interviewer.

9. Be specific regarding hours, working conditions, training given, learning time, etc. Don't oversell or misrepresent the job—it's far better to get all of the

applicant's negative reactions before he is hired, rather than after.

10. If the applicant's attitude is favorable (and your impressions of him are favorable), switch your role from that of an explainer to that of a questioner. From here on in, do as little of the talking as possible, merely posing questions that will reveal significant information respecting his attitudes and qualifications. Questions might go something like this:

—Do you think you would like this job?

—What do you think you would like about it?

—Is it similar to work you have done before? With what tools?

—What did you like most about your former jobs? What did you dislike about them?

—Did you like your foreman? Why—or why not?

—Why did you leave? And why did you apply here?

To the above you might add a few questions on which you know the desirable answers, as:

—How frequently did you usually check the quality of your work?

—When your machine produced poor work, what did you usually do?

—What would you use this tool for? (a plug, gauge or socket wrench, etc.)

11. By keeping your ear open for little slips of the tongue, observing reactions to each question, and noting the accuracy and consistency of responses, you should be able to size the applicant up reasonably well. . . . You should be able to sense his likes and dislikes. . . . whether he is self-confident or not. . . . whether he appears calm or nervous and high-strung. . . . whether he seems friendly and shows a sense of humor. If the job requires a craftsman, ask a few questions to find out whether he knows his job or not.

Related Entries *Civil Rights; References.*

REFERENCES

Getting References

How good are references? Recall the last few references you wrote for people leaving your employ, and consider them from the point of view of a prospective new employer. Of course, you told the truth, but—. You're probably a little more frank over the telephone than in a letter. You tell friends and people you trust more than you tell strangers. If this is generally true, the telephone is a better source of reference than a letter, and references from a source where there is a permanent contact are probably better than those from a less frequently used source.

Here are some prescriptions about references given in the United Shoe Machinery Corporation's Mears Division *Manual of Personnel Policies and Procedures:*

1. Verify dates of employment.
2. Verify wages or salary.
3. Verify position held.
4. Verify reasons for changing jobs.
5. Obtain opinions of the applicant's strong points.
6. Obtain opinions of the applicant's weak points.
7. Check attendance record (punctuality, absenteeism, dependability, etc.)
8. Investigate the applicant's general conduct (be alert for a record of drunkenness, violence, destruction of property, fighting, insubordination, gambling, stealing, etc.)
9. If information obtained reflects the possibility of a criminal record, the local Police Department should be contacted for further information.
10. Verify whether or not former employers would rehire the applicant. Obtain reasons for a negative response.

11. Prepare brief notes of data received through reference inquiry, and attach to Application for Employment form for future reference.

Giving References

In giving references, no one, of course, wants to kick a man when he's down. But you do the man no good, and you may do yourself harm, if you give the impression of high competence, industry, etc., when the opposite is the case. A judicious qualification will usually tell enough between the lines, and still preserve you from making a directly damaging remark. "He still requires a fair amount of supervision," or "He'll be the first to admit that in such and such an area he needs lots of experience," are words to the wise that should suffice.

No matter how unpleasant the circumstances leading up to a dismissal were, you should have a calm and friendly "exit interview" with the person. (See *Exit Interviews*.) At that time, you can make clear the extent to which you're prepared to go in recommendations and references.

Related Entries   *Recruitment; Exit Interviews.*

REPRIMANDS

The work situation is not a pink tea party, and every supervisor worth his salt will have occasion to "get somebody told." Here are some excellent "key points in reprimanding" from the Thompson Products *Supervisors' Manual:*

1. *Keep cool—don't blow up.* Remember you are ineffective when you're angry. Walk away and cool off

if you are "too hot." . . . The purpose of a reprimand is to prevent a recurrence of the fault or error.

2. *Be sure the reprimand is deserved.* Have your facts straight: Dates, part numbers, and exactly what happened must be accurate.

3. *Reprimand in private.* Don't argue with the employee on the floor. In your office, away from the others, there is no compulsion to show off in front of the group.

4. *Get him to relax and "cool down."* You can't convince an angry man of anything.

5. *Talk straight.* State the causes of the reprimand in positive terms. . . . Talk facts, leave personalities out of the discussion.

6. *Show the man how to improve.* After you reprimand a man, don't leave him with his ego and self-respect all shot to pieces. Try to give him a lift—something on which to rebuild his good opinion of himself when you leave him.

Where There Are Unions

Your company's union contract may spell out detailed sequential disciplinary steps to be taken in various classes of violations, distinguishing between major violations, which can result in stated types of penalties up to and including discharge, and minor ones which call for various gradations of reprimand, e.g., oral, written, and time-off.

You should of course thoroughly acquaint yourself with contract provisions, and carefully follow directions for records, notification of shop stewards, presence of shop stewards during discussion leading to written reprimands, etc. The Jos. Schlitz Brewing Company's supervisory handbook spells out procedures in this area in great detail. Because union contracts differ, we shall not quote them here in extension. However, it will be helpful to give the substance of certain basic principles set forth which are unquestionably applicable, no matter what your specific contract provisions are:

By far the most disciplinary problems fall in the reprimand category. These are the type of plant rule violations for which time off or discharge would not be appropriate for the first or second offense, but for which time off and eventual discharge would occur if they were repeated frequently.

Always remember that the objective of a reprimand is not to *penalize* employees, but rather to *correct* violations of plant rules, instructions, and working habits. Examples are failure to follow job instructions, careless work, inattention to duties, habitual tardiness, smoking except in designated places, etc.

For such violations, the supervisor should notify the employee orally, and he should caution him that repeated violations will lead to the written reprimand.

Remember that the supervisor, as the company's management representative, is responsible for upholding his actions during any formal grievance procedures and arbitration preparation. On reprimand violations, it is often difficult to determine whether one day, two days, one week, or two weeks is correct for the third reprimand. Many variable facts must be taken into consideration, such as the employee's length of service, previous work record, previous disciplinary record, and, most important, what amount and type of discipline is most appropriate to attain the major objective, which is the correction of the employee's poor work habits. Here are some fundamental questions to ask:

1. Has the employee by his acts and attitude seriously damaged our confidence in him?

2. Is there a reasonable possibility that he will correct his poor habits?

3. What effect will the disciplinary action—either too harsh or too lenient—have on other employees?

Related Entries *Back Talk; Criticism—1. How to Dish It Out; Discipline—1. Day-by-Day Discipline; Favoritism; The Jittery Employee; Mistakes; Prejudices; Punishment; The Sensitive Worker.*

RESISTANCE TO CHANGE

Resistance to change is an instinctive reaction—we all manifest it to some degree, from the chairman of the board on down. Unless you take it into consideration in planning any change or improvement, you will find all sorts of stubborn obstacles in your path. Here are some practical check points assembled by Dr. H. Wilson of Marquette University on things to do to keep the resistance to a minimum:

1. Inform people well in advance of all changes that will affect them. Get them thinking and talking about the change. Give them all the facts they seek and need.

2. Explain the reasons for the changes. Emphasize how the company, department, and person himself will benefit from the contemplated change. *Sell* your changes.

3. Get the person's participation and involvement as soon as possible. Let him help you solve the problem and work out the details. (People have a stake in what they help create.)

4. Plan for the logical consequences that accompany changes. Anticipate and allay the threats to individual security. Plan also for possible pitfalls in the execution of change.

5. Time your changes carefully. Make changes slowly and gradually—never abruptly and suddenly. (Always know what you are going to do but carefully weigh the timing as to when you are going to do it.)

6. Expect additional problems you haven't anticipated in your planning. Follow up carefully to take care of any threats to the person whether they be real or imagined.

7. Make certain that all persons concerned have adequate outlets for their complaints, gripes, and grievances. Invite them, seek them out, get them to come to you. Be approachable.

8. Have a trial period to precede a careful re-examination to be participated in by all persons concerned.

9. Be patient—change in people is difficult, and takes a great deal of time!

Related Entries *Communicating—1. Selling Ideas; Methods Improvement—1. The Questioning Attitude; Methods Improvement—2. "Selling" the Need for Savings; Prejudices; The Stubborn Worker.*

REST BREAKS

The desirability of breaks in the morning and afternoon is now pretty generally recognized, and most organizations allow them. Many union contracts stipulate them, and in many large governmental offices they are formalized by ordinance or regulation. However, the following remark by a plant superintendent provides valuable perspective:

"I believe that when workers think they want a rest, nine times out of ten what they really need is a few moments' change in activity. In our plant, for example, the routine of some of our girls requires that they get up at certain intervals and walk to their next job. The interruption is very brief. A methods engineer wanted to change this arrangement, so that the girls could keep right on working where they were, but I vetoed the idea. I'm convinced that this change between jobs takes the place of a rest. If the girls didn't have this interruption, we'd have to provide a rest period for them in any event."

Related Entries *Fatigue; Monotonous Work; Music for Employees; Talking; Women and Girls—2. Special Physiological Problems.*

RULES AND REGULATIONS

See *Discipline—1. Day-by-Day Discipline; Policy Formulation; Standard Operating Procedures.*

RUMORS

Can rumors be controlled? Not very well, because once a story gets buzzing around, people's minds work like individual editions of newspapers. They remember and pass along the original story in headline type, and attempts to straighten out distortions react like small print on page eighteen.

One trouble, of course, is that there's usually just enough truth in the story going the rounds to make it sound credible. So the company is going to put in a central computer. This will mean great increase in efficiency. So this will mean layoffs . . . and firings . . . and before you know it a whole division is going to be shut down. Or somebody saw an item in a newspaper about a "merger overture" from the XYZ Corporation. So we're going to be merged and all operations, says the rumor mill, will be consolidated in Amarillo, Texas. Too bad you just bought that house, Joe! Truth is, the XYZ Corporation had just made an announcement about the types of businesses they were looking for in their expansion and acquisition program. Sure, they were interested in getting into the manufacture of widgets—but they hadn't approached *your* Widget Manufacturing Corporation (which, incidentally, is doing all right on its own, thank you).

Obviously this is a matter of communications. Any rumor coming to you as a supervisor should stop with you *as a rumor.* You should either have the straight story, or take steps to get whatever information is available. Here are some workable rules drawn up by Studebaker-Packard Corporation for its supervisors:

1. *Contact higher levels of supervision* if you don't feel you have the full story. Find out just what details can be made public. Discuss with the next line of management below you, and with your fellow managers, the best approach to take.

2. *Call in your key men.* Talk things over with them, find out their reactions, and see that they pass the right word along.

3. *Get all your people together and explain the situation.* If the news means that some are going to be hurt, be sure that everybody understands why the decision was necessary.

4. *Be reassuring as far as you can, but don't sugarcoat.* People can take bad news, if you give it to them straight.

5. *Never pass the buck.* If there are questions you can't answer accurately, don't guess, or give the questioner the brush-off. Promise to get the information, and keep your word.

Related Entries   *Communicating: Answering the "Unanswerable"; Informal Leaders.*

RUSH JOBS

"Surprise is the enemy of good management," and sudden rush jobs are among the nastiest surprises of all for any supervisor. Some departments and executives for whom the supervisor must turn out work or provide services are notorious saddle-burrs in this respect—for them, almost everything is "rush" or "urgent," and they make orderly planning difficult. The supervisor has to develop a diplomatic way of tempering some of their requests. On the other hand, the supervisor has to provide a certain amount of flexibility, because the business can't be run for his own department's convenience. Here are some tactics:

1. Be sure your intradepartmental planning permits you a maximum leeway. Don't let yourself open to criticism that you can't handle emergencies because you are lacking in good internal scheduling, versatility of employees, loading of equipment, etc.

2. As a general, overall policy, try to maintain the departmental "image" as one of readiness to cooperate. If (as frequently happens) the rush request is from Sales, to accommodate a valued customer, remember that in the last analysis "we all work for Sales." But—

3. Don't "rob Peter to pay Paul." That is, don't agree too readily to turn schedules inside out for Mr. A if that will cause disruptions to the work for Mr. B. Point out to A what's been accepted for B, and see if A and B can't get together to authorize the necessary changes without putting yourself in the middle.

4. Know your costs—and develop some cost figures if

they are not readily available through normal accounting channels. Be prepared to point out to a "Rush" requester what the cost factors in overtime, special machine set-ups, part-time help, etc. are. (Frequently a requester will change his mind when he finds out what the extra dollars are.) If the problem becomes acute, check with your superior or with Accounting on the possibility of charging the requester for rush-job dislocations.

5. Keep a record of rush requests for a month (or for any meaningful period), and then see if you can arrange a meeting on the subject to see if agreement can be reached for more orderly handling of work. You will probably have to work through your superior on this, or through the production control department.

6. *Turn the mirror on yourself!* Are you or your people imposing "Rush" requests on others because of laxity in your own planning?. . . . Are you aware of the cost factor of rush requests?. . . . Think of possible consequences before you decide to "bulldoze" a request through. True, you may get your way, but will the repercussions of disruptions to others boomerang on you later, causing far more trouble than the delay you're seeking to avoid? And remember, the person you bruise today may be the one whose co-operation you need tomorrow!

Note "Many labels have been used to coax, urge, and demand a meeting of deadlines, such as 'Rush,' 'Expedite,' 'Urgent,' and even 'Help!', writes Merritt H. Steger in *Navy Management Review*. Often 'Urgent' labels, printed and distributed to offices in large quantities, are used so indiscriminately as to be meaningless. . . . All of us should re-examine the use of these labels to insure that they are used selectively and properly. . . . It should be assumed that routine matters will be handled in an orderly and timely fashion without having to label them 'Urgent.' Such labels should be reserved for those matters that are truly urgent. The person fixing the deadline should be one who knows the relative importance and urgency of the matter. This person should examine the facts and set a reasonable and realistic deadline in the first instance."

Related Entries *Deadlines; Overtime; Planning and Control Boards; Planning and Scheduling—1. Progress Charts; Seasonal Peaks; Workload Forecasting.*

S

SAFETY

1. Safety ABC's

Safety is not as simple as ABC—but these fundamentals by H. E. Carroll* are vital. They were drawn up for plant management—simply substitute "department" for "plant" and see how many of the letters of this alphabet apply to you, or how many you can adopt:

Aim for a new safety record. Set your sights higher and keep your eye on your safety goal of fewer accidents and lower insurance costs.

Buy safety equipment and clothing. Money invested in safety will pay handsome dividends in better morale and fewer lost-time accidents.

Create a feeling of pride in safe work. See that your safe workers get plenty of recognition, and make it clear that horseplay isn't appreciated—by anybody.

Develop a better safety program. Any training program can be improved with new methods, fresh approaches, imagination, and variety. If it's static, revitalize it.

Elaborate on the safety theme until all are safety-conscious. Enthusiasm is contagious, spreads fast.

Fire accident-prone employees. *Check the records* of new applicants, and reject accident-prone people.

Get assistance from insurance companies. They know what to look for, which methods are most effective.

Hold regular safety meetings. They stimulate ideas, men get more safety-conscious as meeting time nears.

* Reproduced by permission from *Factory*, April, 1962.

Investigate *all* accidents, completely and carefully—not only to find and eliminate causes, but to prove constant interest and to build safety awareness.

Join and be active in safety organizations. Ideas picked up from other firms, even unrelated industries, can often be modified and adopted.

Keep your safety program in high gear. Emphasizing safety after accidents is fine, but emphasis at other times—when interest is lower—is much more important. *Control* accidents, don't just react to them.

Lay out work areas to reflect safety considerations. Weigh equipment location, material handling routes, and color coding to highlight potential hazards.

Mail safety booklets to your employees' homes. Families are vitally interested, can be a big help. *Home* injuries, too, put employees out of action.

Name key managers as well as employees to the safety committee, and rotate membership. This builds employee involvement, boosts the stature of the program, and leads to more and better ideas.

Overcome inertia to safety at *all* levels. Indifference and careless habits tend to build up if there has been a long interval since the last serious accident.

Praise your safe workers in public. Present safety awards with plently of showmanship, publicize safety records in local newspapers.

Question accident statistics to spot developing patterns. Certain work areas, age groups, or hours may be producing most of the accidents. Keep a record of *non-injury* accidents, too. For one thing, the next man may not be as lucky. For another, non-injury accidents can be very costly.

Report all safety activities, both to top management and to the workers. Regular *safety* reports are far more effective than occasional *accident* reports.

Stress safety everywhere, not just in meetings. Use pay-envelope inserts, signs, bulletin boards. Mail safety news and publicity to local newspapers, hold safety contests. One goal should be to *make safety a habit*.

Train *all* employees in safety. There is a safe way and a dangerous way to handle any work assignment, and one is as easy to learn as the other.

Utilize all safety literature, films, and posters available. One bad accident would dwarf their cost. And *use* this material—don't store it until someone gets hurt.

Visit other firms, and examine their safety programs. You can often pick up a multitude of ideas. Swap some of your own, and ask questions.

Welcome all safety suggestions. Specialists have no monopoly on ideas. And give recognition (rewards, if possible) to encourage ideas.

X-mark all accident areas. These act as a constant reminder not only of hazards but of safety. They're cheap, effective, and always on the job.

Yoke competition to your safety bandwagon. Pit departments against each other, and keep score on large colorful charts. Group pressure is a strong ally.

Zealously guard your plant's safety record, and try constantly to improve it. This isn't the concern of some committee, remember. Safety is everybody's business —every day.

Related Entries *See listing under Accidents—1. Reporting.*

SAFETY

2. Be Your Own Safety Engineer

Your plant may have a Safety Engineer whose job it is to police all operations continuously for hazard elimination. And it may have a methods department, with professionals constantly studying operations for possible improvement. But there are many commonsense suggestions the foreman or supervisor can make to safeguard operations, since the professionals cannot hope to get down into all possible details of your department's work.

Be a "safety engineer" one day a week. Walk through

your department (and don't let any business interfere with this practice) and look at everything through the eyes of a safety engineer. Try not to think of yourself as the supervisor of that particular department—you're now an outside safety inspector. It's surprising how many unsafe items you'll catch that way—operations and hazards you've been looking at every day in the week without really noticing them. . . . and don't think this applies only to plant operation. (See *Office Accidents*.)

William R. Mullee, a work simplification pioneer, has suggested the following things to look for and think about:

1. Study the motion path when considering the ways to safeguard an operation. If you don't, you're likely to install guards or prescribe safety methods that interfere with the natural motions required on the job. Result: As soon as your back is turned the operator removes the safety device or goes back to unsafe methods in order not to cut down on his output.

2. Remember that the hand is the poorest holding device. For example, a drill-press operator holds a piece fast to the table with the left hand and brings down the drill with the right. Halfway through, the drill binds and whirls the metal piece around, causing a nasty finger injury. Prescription: a fixed jig or vise to clamp the work —not only for safety, but to free the left hand to move pieces.

3. Confine motions to the normal working area.

4. Try to save on "get ready." For example, putting on goggles is "get ready." Taking them off is "clean up." Both can be saved by transparent guards at the work.

5. Minimize all handling as much as possible. For example, jigs and fixtures are often tapped for air ejection, to keep operators' fingers out of trouble.

Related Entries *See preceding entry, and also listing under Accidents—1. Reporting.*

SAFETY

3. Dramatization to Employees

Important safety lessons can be driven home by means of dramatizations, stunts, and the like which do no harm and which help make ideas stick. Certain gags and stunts, says The National Safety Council, have histories as old as the safety business—but they are always fresh when tried for the first time in a new location. For example:

A foreman in a machining department secured a glass eye from the safety department and carried it around in his pocket, producing it with appropriate comments whenever he discussed eye protection with his men.

Another supervisor had scheduled a safety meeting for the people in his department. Shortly before the session was to open, and after the crowd had gathered, he picked up a poster and a small nail, obviously with the intention of putting the poster where the crowd could see it. He held up the nail, and then seemed to fumble around for a hammer. Apparently not finding one, he impatiently reached for a pair of goggles (heavy duty) and proceeded to hammer the nail with the lens of the goggles. He played it deadpan, giving the impression that no one should be surprised that goggles could "take it."

For dramatizing eye protection, the "blindfold test" is a trusted device, with a good deal of emotional impact. Several volunteers are blindfolded and then told to light a cigarette, eat a meal, or do something else to show the price one may pay for indifference to eye safety.

If the protection in question is hard hats, a hat or two can be given to the cause: The men can be gathered around a compression testing machine or some other pressure or impact device which shows how much punishment a hard hat will take. You can add interest by offering prize money for the closest guess as to how much resistance strength a hat will have.

Note The foregoing are from The National Safety Council's *Supervisor's Safety Manual.* Maybe you can develop your own bag of tricks. You don't have to be original: A good idea, sound in principle and easy to apply, is just as good at Plant X as it has proven to be at Plant Z.

Related Entries *See preceding two entries, and also listing under Accidents—1. Reporting.*

SAFETY
4. Safety and Hand Tools

The National Safety Council reports that on a national basis, hand tools are the source of about 6 per cent of all disabling injuries. The disabilities include loss of eyes or vision from flying chips and tools, tendons cut by knives and axes, bones broken by slipping or defective wrenches, and infections from puncture wounds. In one study of steel particles in the eye, 80 per cent were found to be from the mushroomed edges of cold chisels, drills, or hammers.

You don't have to wait for these injuries to happen in your department. For a good job of prevention, NSC cites four *basic* practices, and states that failure to follow them accounts for most hand and portable power tool accidents. Here they are—be sure your employees are aware of them and heed them:

1. *Use the right tool for the job.* Don't use a file for a pry, a wrench for a hammer, or a pair of pliers instead of a wrench.

2. *Keep tools in good condition.* Don't use a chisel with

mushroomed heads, dull saws, hammers with cracked handles, or broken electric plugs.

3. *Use tools in the right way.* Don't apply screw drivers to objects held in the hand. Don't pull knives toward the body. Don't strike two hardened steel tools together. Be sure to ground electrical equipment.

4. *Keep tools in a safe place.* Don't leave tools on shelves, ladders, or overhead places. Don't carry knives and other sharp tools in the pockets. Don't lay chisels and other edged tools loosely in tool boxes, on benches, or elsewhere.

Note   NSC recommends that supervisors encourage their men to conduct a round-table discussion occasionally on the use of hand tools. Ideas can be shared and workers will often pick up valuable pointers from each other about tool use techniques. . . . The supervisor should have each of the workmen discuss his reasons for having purchased special hand tools of his own. Often the supervisor can get valuable information in this way on how a job can be done more safely and efficiently. The workman's contribution may be important enough to cause the company to standardize on the tool.

Related Entries   *See preceding three entries, and also listing under Accidents—1. Reporting.*

SAFETY

5. Safety for the Physically Handicapped Worker

The specific safety practice in supervising physically impaired workers should be to provide assistance for each individual who moves slowly, in the event of an emergency, by having two or three nearby responsible employees assigned to help him.

According to recommendations of the Accident Prevention Department of the Association of Casualty and Surety Companies, additional safety regulations or equipment, other than those regularly used, are generally not needed *when the physically impaired worker has been placed at the properly selected job.* Proper placement means that the impaired worker is no longer handicapped with respect to the job, and can match his fellow workers in productivity.

Avoid depending on recommending engineering changes to maintain the safety of an impaired worker on the job. If the job has been engineered for safety according to standards satisfactory for able-bodied workers and is still not satisfactory for an impaired person, it would be better to transfer him to a more suitable position. Every effort should be made to fit the man to the job, not the job to the man.

Related Entries *Handicapped Employees; also preceding four entries and listing under Accidents—1. Reporting.*

SCRAP COSTS

If your department is plagued by excessive scrap costs, you can effect improvement by making all operators acutely aware of them, and by setting a definite goal for improvement. First, get a weekly cost-of-scrap report, recording all scrap found the previous week. It should list the operator by name, number of part scrapped, number of pieces, cost of each part scrapped, and the total scrap for each operator and for the department as a whole.

Then, to make operators see how they are contributing to the continuing problem, make an operators' scrap chart. This should be a bar chart with names listed vertically. Scrap is posted cumulatively by weeks, by projecting a red line drawn to scale to represent the value of scrap for which each operator is responsible. Set your cost scale so that the lines for high-scrap operators will go off the chart before ten weeks have passed. You can post operators' hours on the same chart. Every ten weeks, compute operators' ratios (their scrap cost divided by their hours). Then start off on a new chart, with names listed in order of ratios, the ones with the lowest ratios at the top, and the highest at the bottom.

Campaigns of this sort will show up unsatisfactory conditions, such as improper equipment, poorly ground tools, etc. Analysis will show where most of the scrap is coming from, and suggest clues for correction.

Note Often the operator sees no reason for what he feels are extreme tolerances—a whim of the engineering or inspection department, as far as he is concerned. In one case this was corrected by means of a meeting between the employees of a machining department and those of an assembly department. The foreman of the machining department had the assemblers tear down and build up a complete electric fan, one of the products on which parts rejects were exceptionally high. The assemblers pointed out to the machine workers the parts they made, and the necessity for the tolerances specified. The result was a realistic appreciation of the necessity for the tolerances; fewer complaints from assembly-department employees who had been criticizing the machining section for not sending up standard parts; more production, because the assemblers did not have to waste time sorting out unusable parts before assembly.

Related Entries *Inspection; Job Interest—How to Stimulate It; Quality; Statistical Quality Control; Waste—2. Dramatizing Avoidable Waste.*

SEASONAL PEAKS

Most operations have seasonal peaks. Often these are due to the nature of the business, and their reflection in the workload of a given department is beyond the supervisor's control. However, there are often steps that can be taken within a given department to ease their dislocations. Thus:

1. First of all, and obviously, are known peaks properly taken into account in all planning, scheduling, vacation plans, etc.?

2. Peaks imply mountains—but often there are little ups and downs within a department that can be leveled out. What chores can be staggered?

3. Are there any questions you can raise with your own superior, or with other departments, re the need for the spacing of certain repetitive work? (Many public utilities now bill once every two months instead of once a month, and many utilities and department stores stagger their billing throughout the month. . . . All changes such as these must have originated by somebody asking a simple question, *Why?*)

4. Have you looked into the possibility of temporary transfers of employees in and out of your department, or between units within the department?

5. What about possible economies through the use of outside temporary help services?

Related Entries *Overtime; Planning and Control Boards; Planning and Scheduling—1. Progress Charts; Planning and Scheduling—2. "Critical Path" and Other Network Plans; Temporary Personnel; Work Distribution; Workload Forecasting.*

SELF-APPRAISAL

1. The "Management-Eye-View" of Your Planning Ability

How does higher management judge your planning ability? The following appraisal questions were developed by the present author in his book, *Management for Modern Supervisors*, published by the American Management Association. Try them on for size!

1. Can he give ready and definite answers to questions about the over-all output capacities of the facilities and people under his command?

2. Does he have a practical grasp of the probable cost effects of production step-ups? Of stoppages?

3. How thorough is he in sizing up the people under him? Do spot checks or discussions of specific incidents bear out his judgments? Is there any evidence of favoritism in his appraisal of subordinates?

4. When his opinion is sought by staff planning groups, does he give an honest and fair estimate of the time, equipment, and men required for a particular order or project?

5. Does he show evidence of trying to keep abreast of equipment developments pertinent to his operations? Does he take an interest in trade shows and technical-society meetings in his vicinity, and does he show familiarity with any of the magazines that cover his type of operations?

6. What has been his record in recent emergency situations?

7. Are there frequent crises in his department?

8. Is the overtime record of his department out of line? Does he plan ahead for expected fluctuations in workload?

9. Are there complaints about bottlenecks in his department? What does a spot check of backlog show about items held up, number and age of unprocessed documents, job orders behind schedule, etc.?

10. Can he show blocked-out work allocations and schedules for the most effective use of manpower and equipment time? Has he worked out definite deadlines by which designated phases of projects are supposed to be completed?

11. Does he keep up-to-date, complete, and accurate records of work scheduled and in progress in his department?

12. Does he have control points and measures by which he can take readings at intervals?

13. Has he trained enough people for adequate performance to permit normal functioning when there are unexpected absences? Does he have an automatic system for reviewing any absentee's work to pick up matters which may require prompt handling?

14. Does he have a plan for removing unusual problems from the regular flow of work and singling them out for his immediate attention or for some pre-arranged special procedure?

15. How has he organized to take care of his own absences from the job?

Related Entries   See succeeding entry; also, *Executive Ability; Self-Criticism; Self-Improvement—1. The Job Ahead.*

SELF-APPRAISAL
2. What Is Your "P.Q."?

What is your "P.Q."—your *Predictability Quotient?* How well can your employees predict your actions and reactions? Can your employees count on you to be consistent? Here are some self-check questions by the Personnel Division of the San Fernando, California, Veterans Administration Hospital:

1. Do you back your employees up when they are right?

2. Do you congratulate them for initiative in one case and then admonish them for not clearing with you in the next case?

3. Are you consistent in the kinds of decisions they are allowed to make?

4. Do you take them into your confidence enough so that they are familiar with your thinking?

5. Do they know what you want them to do in emergencies in your absence?

6. Are you always sympathetic to their problems—or only when you're not busy?

All of us can remember saying to ourselves, "Joe could have made the decision on this—why didn't he?" Maybe right at this point we should have asked ourselves if Joe could be sure that we wanted him to make this decision. On the other hand, what would we have done if Joe had made the decision—but the wrong one? The way we handle that situation would make a lot of difference to Joe the next time he finds himself in the same situation.

Related Entries   *See listing under preceding entry.*

SELF-CONFIDENCE

This entry is about the *lack* of self-confidence, since the supervisor or higher executive who has it doesn't have to read about it. . . . Lack of self-confidence is a common problem of anyone newly appointed to substantially larger responsibilities. Such a person may be overwhelmed by the magnitude of his new job, and may consider himself inadequate. The usual situation is that he was promoted because of outstanding accomplishments in a particular field, and now finds himself forced to deal with many problems with which he is totally unfamiliar. He may even have inherited a number of key people who as a group have immeasurably greater background.

The problem may be compounded in the case of an able man without a college education, who has risen from a relatively low economic level and now finds himself in the company of people who have advantages of family and background he himself never enjoyed.

There is only one answer to lack of self-confidence, and that is *success*. But the saving feature is that a large, dramatic triumph is not what is called for. Of tremendous value in bolstering self-esteem is a string of *small successes* —and these are usually within the man's power to achieve.

The odds are all in his favor. His fears in 99 cases out of 100 are groundless, since he wouldn't have been promoted in the first place if he hadn't shown every sign to astute superiors of being amply adequate.

If you are in such shoes, the answer is to face the issue squarely, and ask yourself, "What am I afraid of, and why?" The chances are that facing up to this question will show the absurdity of your fear. Or, if there are some tangible obstacles, the effort of analysis will encourage you to think logically and calmly about what you can do to help the situation.

Then say to yourself, "What can I do to bring about some small successes?" List the problems that are plaguing you, in the order of increasing severity, and tackle the *easiest* one *first*. While you're working on it, forget about the others. If possible, clear your desk of all papers except those pertaining to the matter at hand. The ones that you've now put in the desk drawer can wait, or can be kept cooking over a low flame, until you've completed this one.

Note If you've gone through an experience like this, you should be the more ready to lend a helping hand to someone whom you've promoted, or who has been promoted into your department. Give him some special, close coaching for a few weeks and see if you can't help him get a taste of success. . . . and then back off to let him go it alone.

Related Entries *Mistakes; Tension and Stress.*

SELF-CRITICISM

"Never sell yourself short". . . . "Don't knock yourself—there are too many others ready to do that for you."

The above are good pep-talk confidence builders, but a good supervisor will be well advised not to take them too literally. Self-criticism may well forestall justifiable criticism from the outside. Here's a good procedure:

Draw up a list of all of the things that could possibly be pointed out in your department as not being first-rate performance. Then go to work on them.

Related Entries *See listing under Self-Appraisal—1. The "Management-Eye-View" of Your Planning Ability.*

SELF-IMPROVEMENT

1. The Job Ahead

Are you ready for the job ahead? What *is* the job ahead? Have you ever sat down and mapped out the avenues of progression reasonably available to you in your company?

Specific directions will, of course, vary with the nature and size of the company, with the age of the supervisor asking these questions, the age and competence of the present incumbents of the jobs ahead, the realism with which he places possibilities next to his own qualifications and willingness to make the necessary sacrifices . . . and a host of others.

A good way to start is to turn the mirror on yourself: Try stepping back, and, in the third person as though you were not in your own shoes at all, answer *about yourself* the sets of assessment questions given in the two entries, *Promotions—1. Assessing Your People's Potential for Growth* and *Promotions—2. Assessments in Depth.*

How much do you actually know about the job or jobs you are bucking for? One of these may be your own superior's job—when he goes up or retires out. Sit down and put on paper the *tough kinds of decisions* he has to make. What kind of knowledge and seasoning does it take to come out on the right side of most of them? Do you match up?

What do you know about the headaches in the jobs that looks so alluring to you? (The grass is always greener, etc.) Are you willing to take them?

Is there an educational barrier? Don't accept the existence of one too readily—not with all of the opportunities open in this country. (Consider, for example, correspondence schools as discussed in the succeeding entry.)

In considering training programs or outside educational courses open to you, pay special attention to the following point: Are you putting too much emphasis on courses of a *technical* nature, as opposed to training in administrative techniques—especially those having to do with human-relations problems? Remember that as you go up the ladder, this kind of knowledge will be more and more important to you—and it may be the very area where your background is thinnest.

What experience within the company would best serve your progression plans? The years are going by fast—should you make inquiries about the possibilities of transfer? Would the long-run advantages make it worth while to take a cut in present income to get the necessary experience? Should you consider a change of companies?

Who is available in the company to whom you can talk about your plans and ambitions? Your own superior? Somebody in Personnel?

Who is your competition? What do they have that you don't have? What do *you* have that they don't have?

Finally—what about certain personal considerations? Would the job you are hoping for take you away from home a good part of the time? How would that affect your family life?. . . . Or would it mean that you would have to move? How would your wife feel about that?. . . . Are different kinds of social contacts and obligations involved? Are you and your wife ready for them—or would you even want them?

Related Entries   *Executive Ability; Promotions—1. Assessing Your People's Potential for Growth; Promotions—2. Assessments in Depth (for "turning the mirror on yourself"); Self-Appraisal—1. The "Management-Eye-View" of your Planning Ability; Self-Improvement—2. Correspondence Schools.*

SELF-IMPROVEMENT
2. Correspondence Schools

In your plans about your own further development, and in discussions of self-development you may have from time to time with your employees who come to you for advice on the subject, you should know something about correspondence schools, or "home study schools," as they are often called. They have been an important part of industrial and business training programs since 1900, and today over 8,000 business and industrial firms, unions, and professional organizations make use of them. Correspondence courses are available in such diverse subjects as mechanics, accounting, engineering, law, management, etc. In most states, but not all, the schools are subject to license and regulation by the State Education Department.

The National Home Study Council, Washington, D.C., accredits home-study schools. It makes a distinction between schools which merely provide educational and lesson material for self-study, without instructor, counseling, and examination services, and complete, well-rounded correspondence instruction. For accreditation, it defines correspondence schools as those "which provide lesson materials prepared in sequential and logical order for study. On completion of each lesson, the student returns the assigned work to the school for correction, grading, comment, and subject-matter guidance by qualified instructors." The instructor immediately returns the corrected lessons to the student, thereby establishing a student-instructor relationship. After courses have been completed, vocational counseling and continuing information are furnished as long as the student requests help.

In its 1964–1965 *Directory of Accredited Private Home Study Schools*, NHSC lists 65 schools. However, it is a voluntary agency, and the fact that a school is not accredited by it does not necessarily imply below-standard quality.

Maybe your company encourages employees to enroll in study programs by making partial or total tuition reimbursement. Check into this, and be sure your employees know what opportunities in this regard are available to them.

Correspondence courses today will run from about $75 to several hundred dollars (1965), depending upon subject matter, number of assignments, whether kits are included, and the like. High-school equivalency programs, for example, usually cost $200 to $250 and take 2½ to 3 years. See what your personnel department can tell you about home-study schools, or check with your state department of education, or one of the accrediting institutions mentioned below.

Here are some important pointers for you or anyone in your department:

1. Investigate the merits of the school you are considering.

2. Are you equipped to assimilate the course? Do you have the experience and background to profit from it? (Don't sign up for a course over your head.)

3. Do you have enough stick-to-it-iveness to complete the course?

4. Act upon facts, not impulses. Take time to consider. Make decisions based on information, not emotion. Don't buy a sales talk—buy an education!

5. Don't sign any contract unless you intend and expect to keep it. You can't break the contract any time you want to, or just because you have fallen behind in your study or because it is difficult.

Note National Home Study Council, 1601 18th St., N.W., Washington, D.C., will send you its list and give additional information. National University Extension Association, University of Minneapolis, Minneapolis, Minnesota, publishes a "Guide to Correspondence Study in Colleges and Universities." Among the well-known, long-established correspondence schools from which additional information may be sought are: Alexander Hamilton Institute, 235 E. 42nd St., New York; American School, Drexel Ave. at 58th St., Chicago; Dun & Bradstreet, Inc., Business Education Div., 1290 Ave. of the Americas, New York; LaSalle Extension University, 417 S. Dearborn St., Chicago; National Technical Schools, 4000 S. Figueroa St., Los Angeles.

Related Entries *See listing under preceding entry.*

SENIORITY

Seniority plays a dominant part in layoffs (even where there is no union contract covering the point), promotions, special privileges, and the like. While contracts usually provide that seniority shall be the main factor in determining such matters as layoffs and recall, rather than the *only* factor, seniority will in such cases usually be quite strictly applied. This is another reason for the supervisor's maintaining adequate records with respect to breaches of discipline, failure to follow job instructions, and the like if he expects to be able to make a departure from seniority provisions stick. Obviously the supervisor should be fully conversant with the seniority provisions of any union contract applying in his department, and of stated company policy where union contracts do not govern. Following are common ways in which seniority may be specified:

1. *Company-wide seniority.* The length of time an employee has worked for the company, no matter in what department or capacity. (Check what the provisions are with respect to leaves of absence.)

2. *Department seniority.* The length of time an employee has worked in a particular department.

3. *Job seniority.* The length of time an employee has held a specific job within a department.

Under agreements or policies specifying seniority, "bumping" of a person of lesser seniority by a person of higher seniority who has had to be laid off, but who can qualify for the job held by the one with lesser seniority can occur more frequently under (1), above than under (2), and more frequently under (2) than under (3). A sizeable layoff could occasion a large number of chain-reaction shiftings, involving problems of record-keeping and departmental dislocations. The supervisor will not as a rule have a great voice in determining which of the above types of seniority shall prevail—but he obviously must be able to analyze the effect of the provisions under anticipated situations, in order to plan his own operations when upheavals develop, and to explain the changes to his own people, and advise individuals as to their rights and most advantageous moves.

Related Entry *Layoffs.*

THE SENSITIVE WORKER

We are all "touchy" about certain things. But we call a man or woman a "sensitive worker" when we really mean that they are oversensitive. They are quick to catch the painful implications—even in remarks that are not intended to slight or insult them. Here are pointers given in the Trans World Airlines *Supervisor's Handbook* for handling such employees:

1. Your attitude is important, and should never be condescending. Be soft-spoken with such a worker.

2. Try especially not to issue direct orders to him (her). Instead, phrase your instructions as requests and suggestions. For instance: "How about taking this down to the store-room?"

3. Watch the group's reaction to him and be ready to repair the damage they do in rubbing him the wrong way. He's hard to hold on the team.

4. Take time with his grievances. He will magnify any sign of unfairness, and will frequently appeal decisions.

5. Don't kid him—he can't take it. Even casual teasing by you or others may seem brutal to him.

6. Reprimands should be light.

7. Be sympathetic toward his problems.

8. Remember that the sensitive worker's suggestions are often very good. He responds well to praise and is probably good on detail.

Related Entries   *The Jittery Employee; The Timid Worker; Women and Girls—1.* ("God Bless 'Em").

SEX

Sex is wonderful, and no home should be without it. But efficiency demands that sex be removed from the working area. In a chapter discussing special problems of supervising women in *The Foreman's Handbook,* Dr. Lydia G. Giberson has this to say: "Flirtation and familiarity in mixed groups cannot be tolerated, and even respectable courtship cannot be indulged in on company time. Even mild exhibitionism should be repressed immediately. An absolute ban must be placed on alcohol."

If the subject is not covered in the material supplied all new employees by your company, and if problems of the sort here discussed exist in your department, it will be a good idea to draw up a minimum code of social behavior, with the aid of some of your older, "steady," people, men and women, and have them mimeographed or posted as departmental rules. The women themselves will help enforce it.

Dr. Giberson adds some words about the supervisor and department head's own conduct: Familiarity with women employees is likely to be a costly affair for the male supervisor. He should maintain at all times the dignity of his authority. As a supervisor, this is your retreat from and protection against loose emotion. If you are the only male present, you inevitably will become the focal point of a great deal of feeling. You can be friendly, helpful, and cordial. But you can't be familiar and still keep control of your group. You should use your authority quietly, and as a last resort, but the authority must be definite, clear, and sharp.

Related Entries   *Discipline—1. Day-by-Day Discipline; Manners; Women and Girls—1. ("God Bless 'Em").*

THE SLOW WORKER

Trans World Airlines *Supervisor's Handbook* provides suggestions for handling the slow worker. Slowness, it points out, may be due to one of two prime reasons: The worker may be very thoughtful and deliberate; or he may simply be slow-thinking and dull. A supervisor should have no difficulty in deciding which is which, and should govern himself accordingly. Here are TWA's eleven pointers:

1. Be patient, with *both* types.
2. Give the slow worker more time between instructions and the carrying out of orders. It takes him (her) longer to adjust. So let him know as soon as possible what he is expected to do. Avoid giving him several assignments at the same time.
3. Talk slowly when addressing him, especially when you're giving instructions. Watch his facial reactions and listen carefully to his comments to determine whether you ought to repeat your instructions or expand on them.
4. Be very careful how you handle the complaints and grievances of the *deliberate* man. He has given thought to the matter. Don't give him a hasty decision. The same goes regarding his suggestions.
5. There is something about the deliberate man that encourages respect for his opinions. When you want to

get something across to your group, make a special effort to get his agreement.

6. With the *dull* man, be careful to show consideration. Show respect for his opinions and suggestions—he reaches them painfully and clings to them. Let him down easily.

7. A dull man can be very sensitive to implications that he's backward. Watch that.

8. Make your orders, instructions, and explanations simple and clear for the dull man. Use many examples.

9. Always check whether the dull man understands; keep a sharp eye on him when he begins something new.

10. Give the dull man a second opportunity before warning or reprimanding him.

11. When the slow or deliberate man does a job at noticeably better than his normal speed, he is making a special effort. In his case this calls for a word of praise.

SMOKING ON THE JOB

Where there are "No Smoking" signs, the duty of the supervisor is clear—smoking cannot be tolerated, and there can be no exceptions, even for himself. Your employees should be made to understand (this will be true in practically all cases) that there are fire insurance requirements to be met—even where there may be no obvious fire hazards involving industrial processes or materials. And, of course, smoking may be prohibited for reasons pertaining to product contamination. Where smoking is prohibited, there are usually rest rooms and other designated areas where smoking is permitted. The rules pertaining to them should be strictly enforced.

A more vexing supervisory problem may develop where conscious discrimination is decreed. For example, in many offices, stenographers, secretaries, female clerical workers, and other rank-and-file women workers are not permitted to smoke at their work stations, although all male workers, and women executives and professional workers may be puffing away. Spot checks indicate that bans such as these have been relaxed in many companies in recent years— but where management insists upon it, the supervisor has no choice but to comply. "Rules is rules." He should be concerned about two points: (1) to enforce the rule uniformly throughout the department; and (2) not to be swayed by the argument that "Such and Such Department permits it." Because another supervisor flouts a rule is no reason for him to follow suit. The point may be one to bring to management's attention for possible reconsideration of policy—but until there *is* a policy change, the answer is still No.

Note *Straws in the wind*—The Travelers Insurance Companies reports that there is now no policy against its employees smoking on the job. Of the company's 22,000 employees in 93 cities, approximately 15,000 are women. While Travelers concedes that at one time it was considered improper for women to smoke on the job, the company's attitude toward smoking changed during and as a result of World War II, when it became quite acceptable for women not only to work outside the home but also to smoke on the job (fire rules permitting). . . . Kelly Girl Service, Inc., a nationwide supplier of temporary office help, reports that it has never had any problems relating to its 80,000 women employees and smoking. During their indoctrination, Kelly Girls are advised to follow the policy of the individual company to which they are assigned. Says Vice-President Norman B. Jackson, "I know of no instance in which a Kelly Girl was requested not to smoke while she worked."

Related Entries *Fire Prevention; NO—NO—NO—How to Say No.*

STAFF MEETINGS

Many of the pointers that are given under *Busines Conferences* will serve to improve the effectiveness of routine staff meetings. In your job you may not have occasion to conduct many meetings that should be dignified by the term "conferences," but you probably do have numerous staff meetings. Every now and then it is worth while to take stock to see whether they're costing more in time than they are worth. Thus:

1. How many staff meetings and conferences do you call, as a rule, during the course of a month?

2. Have you ever made a formal evaluation of your meetings. Are more needed, or fewer?

3. What do your key people think of the way these meetings are being used as a management tool?

4. Are conferences and committees standing in the way of decisive action?

5. Even if the meetings under review pass the test of being worth while, how many of them should be attended by you? Can you leave many of them shortly after they are under way?

6. Are you insisting upon succinct minutes of meetings, indicating action called for in specific terms—when, where, how, by whom?

Related Entries   *Business Conferences; Follow-up.*

STAFF UNITS
How to Work with Them Effectively

Line and *staff* are two terms which are often used in ways that are loose and unclear. Attempts have been made in some organizations to dispense with them, and thus "operating" is often substituted for "line," and "auxiliary" and "service" are common substitutes for "staff." Effective co-operation with staff units is a prime supervisory responsibility, so let's look at the accepted meanings in terms of work done and authority exercised:

A *line* or *operating* organization unit is one that is actually doing the work that represents the *primary mission* of the larger organization unit of which it is a part. *Examples:* an assembly department in the manufacturing division; a selling branch in the sales division.

A *staff* or *service* organization unit is any unit which is helping the line do its work, or making it possible for the line to do its work, but is not actually engaged in the work itself. *Examples:* a purchasing unit, a time-study unit, a payroll-preparation unit, an in-service training unit.

When is it line and when is it staff? Misunderstandings arise from failure to realize that whether something is "line" (or "operating") or "staff" (or "service") depends upon whose shoes you are in when you're looking at the operation. Thus, the total organization headed up by a controller renders service to all of the other organization units in the entire company. Those other units therefore look upon his organization unit as staff or service. The controller, however, looking at his own operations, can consider the various units within his organization carrying out his primary mission as operating units as far as he is concerned. He may, however, within his organization, set up staff units (perhaps an economist to advise him, or a special analyst devoted solely to improving procedures in his own department).

Organizational relations and lines of authority. It is often said that a member of a staff unit cannot tell a manager or a member of a line unit to do anything—he can only inform or suggest or advise, or offer his specific services. This is largely true, but there are exceptions. For example, a safety engineer may be empowered to shut down a line activity, as could a quality inspector. Similarly, it is often said that a line manager cannot issue direct orders to a staff or service man. This is an oversimplification, as indicated under (6), below. Following are seven distinct types of line and staff relationships. Think about the staff units you deal with, and decide upon the classifications into which they fall:

1. *Advisory.* The staff unit is one that offers advisory help only—you may or not avail yourself of it. You may request it, but the staff unit cannot foist itself upon you. But the staff unit may *volunteer suggestions* on the basis of observations it has made, even though uninvited.

2. *Services requested.* This relationship is similar to (1) above, but involves services rather than advice or suggestions. The relationship of the staff personnel is similar to that of an outside contractor's personnel. Their boss is their own staff unit head.

3. *Staff services rendered to an organization unit as part of fulfilling the unit's mission, supplied on a programmed basis.* For example, there may be certain periodic specialized technical services rendered by a headquarters engineering unit, to customers served regularly by a customers' service department working out of a branch plant. There should be no question about lines of direct supervision—the boss of the specialists or technicians is the head of the central staff unit who is responsible for the quality of their service and their mode of operating. . . . The head of the customers' service department cannot attempt to supervise the specialists, but he can communicate directly with the head of the staff unit if he questions the

quality of their work, adherence to schedules, etc. At the same time, the head of the staff unit cannot dictate the degree of utilization of the services, since this is stipulated by an overall program previously authorized at a higher level.

4. *Auxiliary services necessary to operations routinely supplied.* Accounting and procurement are examples. The "supplying" organization has the right to insist that the operating organization follow officially specified rules having to do with reporting, requisitions, or other information necessary to rendering the service. If procedures are not complied with, personnel of the service unit (after normal courtesies in the form of requests to the operating personnel) have the right to insist to the operating supervisor that corrective action be taken. Personnel of the "using" organization unit can communciate directly with the "supplying" unit to request service or information about service, as long as specified initiating or confirming paperwork is executed.

5. *"Functional relationship" between a central staff unit and personnel in a counterpart staff unit attached to an operating organization.* Examples are a central quality control department which operates through a quality control department at each plant; and a central personnel department which operates through a personnel department at each plant. On organization charts, a "dotted line relationship" is shown between such central staff units and the counterpart units in the operating organization. A solid line goes up from the operating organization's staff unit through the operating chain of command, and its ultimate boss is the head of the operating organization. However, the *central staff unit* has responsibility for the professional conduct of the work, and its personnel can

EXHIBIT S-1 Seven Basic Line-Staff Relationships Compared

No.	Type	Relationship of staff-unit employees to head of operating unit	Relationship of head of operating unit to staff unit and members of staff unit working in his department	Relationship of staff-unit employees to employees of operating unit
1	Advisory	May only volunteer suggestions . . . but may not necessarily have to wait to be invited.	May or may not have to avail himself of suggestions.	Do not give or receive instructions.
2	Service as requested	Similar to (1) but involves services, and the staff unit must be invited into the department.	Same as toward any outside contractor. The "boss" of the staff personnel is their own staff unit head.	Through operating unit's supervisors issue such requests as required to make service effective.
3	Staff services supplied on a programmed basis	Somewhat stronger than (2). Services are rendered on a programmed basis approved by higher authority, and cannot be refused by operating unit head.	The "boss" of the staff personnel is the staff unit head. Operating unit head must work through head of staff unit if dissatisfied with mode of operation.	Same as (2).
4	Auxiliary services routinely supplied	Services are a routine part of operations, not on an "invited" or specially programmed basis.	Same as (3).	Staff-service personnel can insist on regular procedures being followed. Routine communications flow directly between staff and operating personnel except in cases of sharp disagreement.

5	Central staff and counterpart staff unit in operating department	Advisory and suggestive only . . . but does not have to wait to be invited.	May or may not have to avail himself of advice and suggestions of central staff unit. Through his own chain of command, head of operating unit is "boss" of the staff unit in his department.	"Functional" relationship between central unit and employees of the staff unit in operating department . . . on matters of professional standards, mode of operation, etc., "suggestions" from the central unit have strong force and are to be disregarded only under special circumstances and with approval of head of operating unit.
6	Personnel assigned to operating unit by staff unit	Assigned personnel are under administrative command of head of operating unit as to deployment on job, discipline, hours of work, etc., but their "boss" is the head of the staff unit.	In administrative command of the assigned personnel . . . Head of staff unit may, with notice to head of operating unit, withdraw them from the job if he can supply replacements.	Relationships are those of any employees under direct supervision of head of operating unit. They carry on their own activities and work through normal channels within department.
7	A staff unit which is part of an operating organization	Supply information and advise and recommend . . . Decisions are made by operating head, and he issues instructions to operating personnel.	Direct relationship, through chain of command.	Same as (6). Staff personnel do not issue direct instructions to operating personnel except under unusual circumstances (e.g., a safety man or quality inspector shutting down an operation where emergency does not permit normal working through channels.)

make suggestions for improvement. They do not give direct orders to the counterpart professional people in the operating organization's staff unit. If they have strong feelings about the way something is or is not being done, they can make strong suggestions to the head of the operating organization's staff unit, and, failing action, can only proceed higher in the operating chain of command.

6. *Relationship between a department head and personnel assigned to him by another unit.* Specialized personnel are often assigned to an operating unit by a staff unit which is responsible for their training and the quality of their professional work. They are considered as being permanently attached to their "home" *staff* unit, and their assignment may be of relatively long duration. But they are under the "administrative command" of the head of the operating unit, and for accounting purposes may be on the operating unit's payroll (the bookkeeping is not important in this connection). They are under the "professional command" of the head of their staff unit. The latter is their boss, since (a) he is the one who can deploy them from one location to another, with proper notification and as long as he supplies equivalent personnel to the using unit; (b) he determines their merit rating and makes recommendations for promotion or pay increases; and (c) he is responsible for their continued professional development. "Administrative command" means that the head of the operating unit can deploy them on the job—where and when they shall work—has the power of approval regarding personal time off and the like, and in general can direct them to follow his personnel rules. "Professional command" means that the staff unit head, and not the operating unit head, lays down the procedures and sets the standards with respect to their professional work. An

example is a special project team composed of research and engineering personnel assigned to a unit for the duration of a specific project.

7. *Relationship between an operating executive and an advisory or control staff person or unit reporting to him; and relationship between the latter and other personnel in the organization under the operating executive.* The staff man or unit only supplies information, and advises and recommends. The operating executive is the one who must make the decisions and take action. The staff unit can act only in the name of that executive—it cannot tell other employees what they must or must not do.

Note Exhibit S-1, pages 380–381 gives a bird's-eye-view of the seven basic line-staff relationships here described. (For a fuller discussion of this important subject, see the special report by the present author, published by Assignments in Management, Chester, Pa., 1964: *How to Achieve Effective Line-Staff Teamwork.*)

Related Entries *Organization: AMA's "Ten Commandments"; Technicians and Specialists.*

STANDARD COSTS

Many manufacturing plants operate on a *standard cost* system, and supervisors have the responsibility of "meeting standards." They should therefore know something about the cost-accounting theory behind the standards.

Standard costs are normally prepared a minimum of a year ahead, and provide a basis against which actual costs can be compared—usually by means of monthly reports. *Deviations,* or *variances* from standards furnish a ready measure of the efficiency of a department's operations. (In this connection, see *Budgets.*) Standard costs make it possible to assign costs properly and consistently to inventories of finished goods and of work-in-process, and to set prices realistically.

The most general practice is to establish standard costs on the basis of what is attainable under ordinary conditions of control, although some systems are in use which base the costs on *ideal* efficiencies of men and equipment. In the latter case there will almost always be variances in the undesired direction, the size of the variances expressing the approach of performance to "ideal." The closeness of the standards to "ideal" expresses the "tightness" of the standards.

Material usage is computed from the physical quantities required for products or parts being produced, based on engineering drawings, on quantities and weights of materials specified, etc.—with allowances, based on past experience, for wastage and spoilage to determine standard "yield."

Cost of the materials is based on prices paid for quantities budgeted for the year.

Direct labor usage and cost are usually based on motion and time studies or predetermined motion times (see *Time Standards*).

It is not difficult to see how standard costs such as the above can be determined for specific products, parts, and components. What is usually more difficult for operating people to understand about the accountant's computations is just how *overhead* costs find their way into *unit* costs.

The kinds of things (such as variable expenses, fixed costs, etc.) going into overhead or "burden" are discussed in the entry, *Overhead*. Briefly, it may be stated here that some charges like taxes and depreciation of equipment go on, regardless of how many items are produced, while others, like the amount of power consumed, incidental supplies used, and indirect labor such as material handling, will vary according to the volume of production. What is generally done is to determine the total amount of these costs for the amount of direct labor hours budgeted for the year in question. These costs are then prorated over budgeted standard direct labor hours. In this way, the proper amount of overhead can be charged into a product or part, depending upon the number of standard direct labor hours required to produce it. (In some departments, overhead may first be distributed over *machine hours*, and then find its way into unit costs by computations based on output per machine hour.)

We are purposely not here going into certain cost-accounting refinements involved: for example, the basis upon which certain overhead services such as the methods department or others may be prorated to a given department, and whether the standard unit costs are to reflect the *expected* overhead for the *expected* activity as expressed in direct labor hours, or whether overhead that would be incurred at *capacity* production is to be distributed over the direct labor hours that would be used in *capacity* production. These are accounting refinements which will depend upon the type of costing system in use at a particular plant.

The main thing for the foreman or supervisor is that he understands the principles involved, and then, most important, that he reaches an understanding with the cost analysts as to what kinds of variances from standard he can be held accountable for. For example, a production foreman will have no control over the volume of sales obtained by the sales department—and therefore cannot be held accountable for an off-capacity variance due to unexpected low-volume operations. However, where a flexible budget system is in use, as discussed in the entry, *Budgets*, the standards against which the foreman's performance are measured are specifically set up for different volumes of production—so that the variances which he will have to explain are variances under his own control. Such budgets may be used in conjunction with standard overhead accounting.

Here are some common types of variances mentioned in cost reports, with an indication of items which might be chargeable against a supervisor of an operating department:

1. *Material price variance.* Difference between actual and standard material cost because prices actually paid differed from the standard prices which had been estimated at the beginning of the year. The operating foreman normally does not do his own purchasing, and so would not have control over this variance.

2. *Material usage variance.* Difference between actual and standard material cost because actual quantities consumed differed from standard quantities allowed. Unless there was a change in specifications, this would be something the supervisor would have to explain.

3. *Labor rate variance.* Difference between actual and standard labor cost, because actual labor rate differed from standard labor rate. The supervisor would not ordinarily be responsible for this. He would, however, be responsible for rate variance arising from improperly using a high-rated man for a job calling for a low-rated man.

4. *Labor usage variance.* Difference between actual and standard labor cost because actual labor hours needed to produce the output differed from standard hours allowed. The supervisor would have to explain this. (*Note:*

As explained in *Time Standards*, output will usually be expressed in terms of "standard hours' worth of work" or "standard minutes' worth of work" produced in a given number of "clock hours.")

5. *Overhead budget variance.* Difference between the overhead charges incurred in a department and the budgeted overhead for the standard hours of output produced. The budgeted amount may be based on a standard flexible budget. (*Note*: Accounting systems differ in detail in their calculations of overhead variances. Some, for example, determine budgeted overhead on the basis of direct labor hours used, rather than on standard hours' worth of work actually turned out by those labor hours. They then introduce another variance, called *Overhead Efficiency Variance*, to account for the above- or below-standard efficiency in terms of time required to turn out the work. This becomes a subtle point in accountancy, but the supervisor should take the trouble to find out from the proper staff specialist exactly what is meant by the terms used to measure his overhead performance.)

6. *Overhead capacity variance.* Difference between actual and standard overhead costs, usually incurred because the hours the facilities were used during the month reported upon were above or below the normal hours upon which the standards were based. In essence, the intent is to have a measure which might draw attention to low-capacity usage entirely beyond the supervisor's control, and properly chargeable to general management, or to the sales department, for failure to do enough business to keep the facilities busy. Here again, accounting systems differ, and the supervisor should make it his business to know just what the basis of measurement is.

Related Entries *Budgets; Cost Control; Incentive Wages; Overhead; Time Standards—Standard Minute (Standard Hour); Work Measurement—Time Study.*

STANDARD OPERATING PROCEDURES

You are fortunate if your company has a well organized policy and procedures manual. If it has, be sure to keep your copy up to date and accessible to everyone in your department who may have to refer to it. It will be a good idea to fix in one person the responsibility for "policing" the manual—seeing to it that new sheets are entered when received, that issued corrections are made, and that all concerned are made aware of new policy and procedure statements and changes in existing ones.

If your company or division does *not* have a good system of "SOP," you will be well advised to set one up for your department on your own, if your department does any significant amount of paperwork. Once you set up the machinery for procedure statements, it will be relatively easy to keep it up to date. Here is how to go about it.

1. Set it up in loose-leaf form, so that changes can be made readily.

2. Have it *sectionalized* into a basic set of categories, identified by Roman numerals. Give a lot of care to setting up the right categories, because the flexibility of the manual for reference and upkeep will depend upon them. Think about the major kinds of activities your department is engaged in, and then set up the sections accordingly. Exhibit S-2, page 392, shows a possible listing, but yours will probably be different.

3. Check your categories before "jelling" them by asking a number of your key people to name some important

activities on which they think there should be a clear statement of policy and a written set of instructions. If you don't have a ready category or "pigeonhole" for *every* one of these, you have to add one or more to your list. While our exhibit shows "Miscellaneous," there should be very few that have to go there. Too many in "Miscellaneous" means you've done a sloppy job of categorization.

4. Don't try to develop a comprehensive manual all at once, covering every conceivable procedure with which people in your department are concerned. Instead, once you have set up your categories, or sections, write up procedures "where the shoe pinches most"—where you have had troubles and mix-ups, or where most confusion would arise if the person doing a particular phase of the department's work should be absent.

5. Parcel out the work of preparing draft statements of procedure among as many key personnel as possible.

6. Set up a *coding system* for the write-ups that will go into each section, and for later insertion of corrected or new pages. This can be done easily as follows:

    a. Provide for *General Statements* on any given subject, and for *Detailed Statements*. (These are described below.)

    b. In the upper right-hand corner of every General Statement, identify the statement by a Roman numeral for Section, then the letter "G," and then an Arabic numeral for the number of the specific statement, together with issue date and page number. Thus:

Section IV, G-1

Jan. 20, 1964

Page 1

Each statement will, of course, have a title, as:

DEPARTMENTAL BUDGET PREPARATION

or

JOB ORDERS AND WORK ORDERS

Number the General Statements consecutively, as issued. A table of contents, as described below, will make possible ready look-up, even though the statements are assembled in the book serially, and not alphabetically.

c. The Detailed Statements are filed consecutively behind the General Statement to which they apply. In the upper right-hand corner of each page, identify them as follows:

> Section IV, Ref. G-1
> Statement D-1
> January 25, 1965
> Page 1

d. There may of course be more than one Detailed Statement for a particular General Statement. These would be numbered consecutively—e.g., Ref. G-1, Statement D-2; Ref. G-1, Statement D-3; etc.

e. It is important to identify each sheet, since in later revisions you will want to specify precisely which sheet is to be removed and replaced by a new sheet.

7. *General Statements* should not go into great detail on the handling of all forms, etc. They should fix basic responsibilities and types of authorizations and initiating actions required. In general, they should give a brief description of the activity. . . . indicate the organization units chiefly involved. . . . describe in general how the activity is carried out. . . . who initiates the action . . . type of paperwork involved (without going into details). . . . etc. Certain General Statements will cover broad matters

of department policy, and will not conform rigidly to the pattern here indicated.

8. *Detailed Statements* give whatever specific information is required to instruct your personnel on how an activity described in a General Statement is carried out. They are written as step-by-step procedures, and as a rule go into details as to forms used, special authorization required, distribution and filing of the forms, etc.

9. A *Forms Reference List* should follow the last statement in each subject-section of the manual. This should list the forms prescribed in all of the preceding detailed statements in that particular section, together with form numbers.

10. A complete *Form File* should be maintained in your department by a designated person, with subject-file folders corresponding to the sections of your manual. Each folder should have a list of the forms mentioned in that section's procedures, with identification numbers of the statements which refer to the forms. The folder should also have a specimen of every form mentioned, or, if not, a notation as to one of the other subject-file folders where the specimen may be found.

11. A *Form Master Card Index* (alphabetic) should also be maintained. This is filed by name of form, and gives the form name, number, and the subject-file under which a specimen may be located. The main function of this index is to insure that when form eliminations, changes, or consolidations are made, all affected Detailed Statements may be checked for conformance.

12. Your loose-leaf procedures manual should have a *Table of Contents* with all of the Roman-numeral section headings, as in Exhibit S-2, page 392. Under each heading, list those statements by name and code number

for which you have drawn up statements. You can simply add in, consecutively, any additional table-of-contents entry whenever you have a new statement for the manual.

EXHIBIT S-2   *Policy and Procedures—Sections*

I	GENERAL INFORMATION—Company and Department
II	ORGANIZATION
III	PERSONNEL ADMINISTRATION
IV	EMPLOYEE BENEFITS
V	BUDGET
VI	PROCUREMENT
VII	STORES CONTROL OF MATERIALS, SUPPLIES, AND EQUIPMENT
VIII	ACCOUNTING CONTROLS
IX	EQUIPMENT REPAIRS
X	SPECIAL SERVICES
XI	SAFETY
XII	SECURITY
XIII	EMERGENCIES
XIV	SYSTEMS AND PROCEDURES CONTROL
XXX	MISCELLANEOUS

The above is a possible set of categories for a policy and procedures manual in a large department. Specific headings should be tailor-made for your own department. "Miscellaneous" has been given number XXX and spaced apart, to allow for addition of other categories as time goes on.

Related Entry   *Paperwork—Forms Control.*

STANDARDS

See *Standard Costs; Time Standards.*

STATE LABOR LAWS

Although the Federal government and the courts have construed "activities affecting interstate commerce" quite broadly, there are a great many concerns engaged in purely intrastate employment. Labor relations in such companies are governed by state labor legislation. It is important for the supervisor to note this, because the Taft-Hartley Act of 1947 (see *National Labor Relations Act*) leaves the permissible form of union security agreement between employers and labor unions to the law of the state concerned.

The supervisor should check with his personnel department to be sure he is aware of any special state labor laws affecting his work. In addition to state labor relations acts and state anti-injunction acts, there are laws restricting picketing, fair employment practice statutes, union regulation laws, pension and welfare plan disclosure laws, laws restricting wage assignments, mediation, arbitration, labor dispute settlement statutes, and so-called "right to work" laws. The last-named type of state law prohibits, as a condition of employment, membership in a labor union. More than 18 states have legislated such enactments which declared closed shops, union shops, and other types of union security, in varying degrees, to be unlawful.

Related Entries *See listing under National Labor Relations Act.*

STATISTICAL QUALITY CONTROL

Statistical quality control is a set of techniques used in manufacturing to prevent waste and rework by catching out-of-line conditions *before* they become serious. It is based on sampling and the laws of probability. By charting critical measurements of successive samples of lots of pieces or parts being produced, the SQC engineer can tell whether departures from ideal dimensions are significant and are forecasting out-of-tolerance production if necessary changes in tools, or other adjustments, are not made.

The mathematical proof of the technique, and the precise fixing of the "upper and lower control limits" on charts, within which readings must fall if the process is under control (discussed below) are up to the staff specialists. However, it will be easy for a supervisor to see the reasonableness behind the charts if a program is adopted by his company, without himself having to get into the higher mathematics. It is up to him then to see that employees watch the charts as they would their speedometer if they caught a glimpse of a motorcycle cop in the rear-vision mirror.

"100 Per Cent" Inspection

Offhand, you would think that "100 per cent" inspection is the best guarantee possible of assuring that only good parts or pieces are passed. Not so. Engineers have found that 100 per cent inspection is by no means insurance that all defects will be found. Quite apart from the expense, it is a poor way of guaranteeing that all pieces passed will meet specifications. Even though all pieces are looked at, operator fatigue will permit below-standard items to get through—as will such factors as interruptions and distractions, the type of gaging being done, working conditions in general, the frame of mind of the operator, and the like. And as more and more pieces of the same kind are inspected, the monotony can cause drowsiness and carelessness, which then cause bad ones to get by.

Statistical Sampling

On the other hand, it has been found that inspection of *samples*, if done with calculated risks based on probability theory, actually provides more assurance than inspection of every single piece.

Today your employees are quite used to sampling "polls" —like those published before elections, based on questioning a relatively small but carefully selected sample of voters; and the famous "ratings" of TV and radio shows, where telephone queries of only a small number of viewers or listeners is used as the statistical base for calculating how many sets across the country watched a program like "Gunsmoke" or listened to a radio quiz show at any particular time.

You can explain the scientific basis of statistical quality control in the same way: In the production of machine-made parts, for example, there are always a very great many small chance factors at work to cause departures from specifications. Thus there may be small chance variations in the diameter and hardness of the stock, in the play of gears and tools of the machine making them, etc. These small chance factors affect each piece separately, but departures in one direction tend to cancel out departures in the other. The resultant variation which can be expected in all the pieces forms a definite pattern, which the SQC engineer can determine. The important thing to remember is that for any particular manufacturing process, its own pattern will be repeated over and over again, as long as nothing other than the chance causes of variations is affecting the results. (The *non*-chance causes which the charts are designed to show up are such things as wear of a tool, an incorrect adjustment by the operator, etc.) As long as the pattern remains unchanged, there is assurance that no new or "assignable" cause of variation has affected the process.

When careful sampling shows that the pattern is repeated over and over again within the tolerance limits established for the item being produced, the process as a whole is said to be "in control." Departures from the pattern is a sure sign that something is wrong, and the cause must be tracked down and eliminated.

Control is effected through periodic inspection of very small-sized samples, sometimes as few as 4 or 5 pieces, obtained in a continuing sampling process. Based on about 25 such samples, the SQC engineer establishes the "central tendency" and the "control limits" of the process.

Two sets of measures are shown on the commonly used charts: *Average* (the familiar arithmetic average) of the sample readings, and *Range* (the difference between the highest and lowest reading) in each sample. By means of tables and computations, the SQC engineer establishes upper and lower control limits for the averages, designated "UCL" and "LCL." The control limits for the range will be "URL" and zero.

Exhibit S-3 shows a typical SQC chart. You will find that when operators have been shown the significance of control charts and have gained some experience with them, they welcome them as aids. Here is how one girl put it: "When I understood that the idea was to keep between the control lines on the chart, it was easy for me to sense all of the things I did when the points come between the lines, and then keep feeling my way back and forth whenever the results come too near the control lines."

Related Entries *See listing under Quality Control.*

STRESS

See *Tension and Stress.*

EXHIBIT S-3 *What a Quality Control Chart Looks Like*

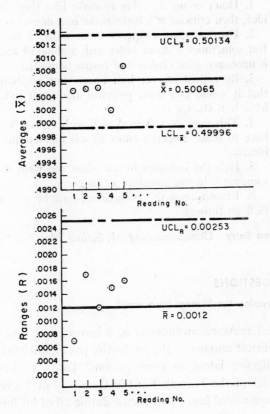

$\overline{X}$, R CONTROL CHART

THE STUBBORN WORKER

The stubborn worker is the man or woman whose first inclination to anything that smacks of change is to say no.

The Trans World Airlines *Supervisor's Handbook* offers these supervisory pointers:

1. Don't argue. . . . Try to make him think it's his idea, then criticize it a little, make him defend it.

2. Use the request-type of order most of the time. But sometimes a direct order with a show of authority is necessary. [See *Orders and Instructions—2.*]

3. Be consistent—let him know your position, and that it would take some powerful arguments indeed to have him change it.

4. This man doesn't work well with others. You will have to make a special effort to sell him on the team idea.

5. He's the last man to use when you want to have someone help you introduce a change.

6. Emphasize goals, competition; once he gets started he'll go through.

Related Entry   *Communicating—1. Selling Ideas.*

SUGGESTIONS

1. Tapping the "Latent Resources"

"Great as American industry is, it leaves largely untapped its greatest resources—the productive power, initiative, and intelligence latent in every person." James F. Lincoln, founder of the Lincoln Electric Company of Cleveland, has hammered home that theme during all of his business life.

The value of employee suggestions has been amply demonstrated in industry—in an especially dramatic way during World War II. Arousing an interest in improvement in every worker is at the heart of every successful work simplification program. (See *Work Simplification.*)

Even if your company does not have a formal suggestion system, replete with forms for entering suggestions, committees of judges, schedules of awards, etc., it behooves you to keep alert for and encourage suggestions. Even the lowest-paid employee may have a good idea for bettering a method in his department that everyone has overlooked, or may question something that everyone has been taking for granted. What are *you* doing to tap the "latent resources"? (Or are you guilty of erecting barriers to them?) Here are some points to take up with yourself:

1. Do you have a positive plan for encouraging suggestions? A good idea is to encourage *why* questions on the part of everyone in the department. Keep everyone questioning the reason for every system and procedure— especially the time-honored ones.

2. Do you give credit where credit is due? When you have occasion to tell your own superior about some constructive suggestion that someone in your department has made, try to do so within the hearing of the person who made the original suggestion, if at all possible.

3. Do you kill off the bum ones too fast? Don't be curt and unappreciative when an employee makes a suggestion that is obviously impractical. Show him you're glad he's thinking, and let him see why his idea won't work at this particular time.

4. Do you try to change the bum ones into good ones? Have you thought of the value of trying, somehow, to use some adaptation of a subordinate's suggestion, mainly to encourage him? . . . To avoid the reputation of never welcoming a suggestion, it is always worth while to consider how an idea *can* be used, rather than why it *cannot.*

Note You violate the dignity of the individual when you talk big—for example, on the importance of reducing costs— and then don't give him a chance to answer the basic questions about how you can reduce cost, says the Rev. George Heaton, writing in *Manpower Management*, a publication of General Foods Corporation. "I think of one corporation," he says, "where they've been doing a lot of big talk about fins for jet airplane motors—each one costing $50 apiece, made out of titanium. Yet only 47 per cent of each day's production was accepted, and 53 per cent was rejected! The records of that company will tell you that when the big talk was changed, and the dignity of individuals was exalted, and groups of people were gathered together by their foremen and given a chance to talk about how they could improve the quality and cut down the waste, the acceptance rate rose to 89 per cent. Made on the same machines, out of the same material!"

Related Entries   *See succeeding entry; also, Listening; Methods Improvement—2. "Selling" the Need for Savings; Problem Solving—2. The Open Mind.*

SUGGESTIONS

2. Helping Make the Company Suggestion System Work

If your company has a suggestion-and-awards program, you as a supervisor should play a vital role in it. Following are the ways in which you can give most effective cooperation:

1. You will undoubtedly be asked for an opinion on any suggestion affecting your department's work. Don't be stingy about giving time to investigate it thoroughly, even though it may necessitate reference to blueprints and records, or personal observation of equipment involved, to get all the facts.

2. Encourage suggestions by a willingness to discuss an employee's ideas, and to help in the final filling out of forms, etc. His write-up should answer the following ques-

tions: WHY should the change be made? . . . . WHAT must be done to make the change? . . . . WHERE will it apply—department, or local, or company-wide? . . . . WHEN should the change be made?

3. Employees should be prepared to write up their suggestions on their own time, but they should be discouraged from spending any considerable amount of money developing an idea. If the idea is accepted, the company will follow through on development.

4. Unless you have proper clearance and in other ways are fully in control of the situation, employees must be advised not to attempt experiments or changes of any kind on company equipment to demonstrate or prove a suggestion—or for any other reason.

5. Don't be concerned about somebody other than yourself getting a lot of credit. Employees who get deserved recognition always reflect credit on their supervisors.

6. If two employees discuss the same kind of idea preparatory to submitting a formal suggestion, consider proposing to them that they make a joint entry. But before such an agreement is reached, don't tip the hand of one to the other.

7. Be sure anyone in your department who receives an award, or even only an "honorable mention," gets full publicity in the department—with information about it on the departmental bulletin board, and a reference to it in any departmental meeting held shortly after the event. See to it that an account gets into the company magazine if there is one.

Note Suggestion programs in major corporations each year net $20 million in additional earnings for a half million employees, based on an average award of just under $40, according to an evaluation published by Humble Oil & Refining Company. In some cases, the payoff to suggesters reaches remarkable heights. Humble paid $15,000 to a refinery man for a suggestion that lowered the cost of manufacturing certain lubricating oils while improving their quality. Elsewhere in industry, awards for a single suggestion have gone as high as $72,000.

Related Entries *See listing under preceding entry.*

SUPERVISORY TRAINING CONFERENCES

Following World War II, the so-called "conference method" was widely employed as the major technique in supervisory training programs. While still widely used, the more recent trend, however, has been to make it only one of many techniques, such as straight lectures and presentations employing a wide variety of audio and visual aids, "role playing," in which situations are acted out and then followed by group discussion, programmed instruction, employing special texts or teaching devices, case studies in which actual situations are reviewed, and the like.

The supervisor will not, as a rule, have occasion to use the conference method in the development of subordinates unless he happens to head a large department employing subordinate supervisory personnel. However, it will be worthwhile to review the technique briefly here, since this will perhaps make him participate more effectively if he is enrolled as a member of such a training group, quite aside from the possibility of his having to conduct a training conference himself.

Most training conferences are of the so-called "guided discussion" type. Here the instructor, or rather "conference leader," knows in advance what points he wants to drive home. These points are seemingly arrived at more or less spontaneously by the group. In fact, however, the leader usually follows a carefully pre-planned outline provided to him by the course developers. The outline indicates how he is to open the discussion, the kinds of questions he is to throw out for consideration by the group, how to stimulate discussion, etc. Audio-visual aids are usually not used, beyond a blackboard and chalk for jotting down important points as they are developed by the group.

The accompanying exhibits from the Long Island Lighting Company's *Customer Relations Conference Leader's Guide* will give you a good idea of the technique. They are the opening pages of the leader's instructions for a conference session on LILCO's Customer Relations Policy. (As a matter of interest, read in this connection *Policy Formulation.*)

In a controlled conference of this sort, the leader is not supposed to express his own ideas, or to lecture, or to act as an instructor. By means of leading questions, he is supposed to get the group to arrive at the desired conclusion. Usually all conceivable kinds of answers to be expected by group members are given in the leader's manual, with instructions on how to handle them.

There are, of course, limitations to the method. It is primarily suited to eliciting conclusions from a group whose background and seasoning are expected to supply them with the knowledge required for the answers sought. The conference method will not be successful if the topic under discussion is not related closely to the work, interests, and experience of the group.

The advantages are that the *combined experience* of the group can add significantly to the knowledge of each

EXHIBIT S-4

CONFERENCE LEADER'S GUIDE

○   This first session we are going to talk about Policy,
primarily LILCO's Customer Relations Policy. Before we do,
I think we should define <u>Policy</u>.

WHAT IS POLICY?

> Let the group discuss this thoroughly. Write their
> definitions on the board. The list should contain some of
> the following:
>
> 1. A course adopted and then followed.
> 2. A guide to thought and action.
> 3. A common aim or goal.
> 4. A guide to behavior or operations.
> 5. A statement of a business organization's principles
>   and beliefs.
> 6. Framework in which a company operates.
> 7. Backbone of a company--why it's in business.
>
> Exhaust all definitions before proceeding.

○ DO ANY OF YOU DISAGREE WITH ANY OF THE DEFINITIONS
ON THE BOARD? WHY?

> Try to get group agreement on definitions. Cross out
> words or add them if necessary.

    All these definitions give us a good idea of what policy
is. I always like to think of policy as a compass. A compass
is a useful instrument that gives us direction. Regardless
of the weather or the time of day we can make progress in
getting to where we are going if we are guided by the compass.
It is still only an instrument though. We have to be able to
read it and use it. The same is true of policy.

○   A policy too is a useful instrument. It is not just a
fine pronouncement in words that is denied by behavior. It
is not just a lot of propaganda. If it is, then it really

Courtesy Long Island Lighting Company.

. . . that people tend to learn more when they play an
active part in the learning process . . . and that they will
be more apt to accept decisions and conclusions which
they themselves helped develop or crystallize.

isn't a policy. In other words, we have to treat our customers
the way our Customer Relations Policy says we should or it
isn't really our policy.

CAN ANY OF YOU GIVE ME AN EXAMPLE OF THE POLICY OF
AN ORGANIZATION, ANY ORGANIZATION?

If no suitable example is offered ask:

WHAT IS THE POLICY OF THE NEW YORK TIMES?

Write on board: All the news that's fit to print.

It's really a slogan, but it's a policy too.

WOULD THIS STATEMENT BE OF ANY HELP TO YOU IF YOU
WERE THE TIMES CORRESPONDENT IN ROME OR LONDON?

The answer should be yes. It would help you decide
what was printable or not. But you would still have
to judge and decide.

In other words, when a company puts out a policy for its
employees, it is showing its confidence in the employee's
judgment. The policy gives the employee some leeway to use
his initiative and do what he thinks best.

IS THERE A DIFFERENCE BETWEEN A POLICY AND A RULE?

IF THERE IS, WHAT IS THE DIFFERENCE?

Allow a discussion. These are some of the conclusions
you might reach:

Yes, there is a difference between a policy and a rule.

A policy allows for discretion of application.

A rule is designed to control behavior more rigidly
and is used exactly the same way every time.

A policy requires you to use your own judgment.

A rule leaves you no decision.

To a supervisor who is a part of a conference training
group, the best advice that can be given is—*participate!*
The more you yourself put into the conference, the more
you will get out of it.

Related Entries *Many of the points on "Preparation and Technique" in the entry, Business Conferences, will prove useful in a training conference, in stimulating the right kind of discussion. See also the listing of related entries under Development of Subordinates—1. Development-Appraisal-Development.*

T

TAFT-HARTLEY ACT

The *Taft-Hartley Act* is the popular name for the *Labor-Management Relations Act* of 1947, which in turn is an amendment to the *National Labor Relations Act* of 1935, popularly known as the *Wagner Act*. For details, see *National Labor Relations Act*.

TALKING

A company with large-scale assembly operations found that group efficiency was increased when it permitted talking. According to the superintendent:

> Our experience has been that where there are good relations between management and employees, the workers will themselves control talking when they feel that it is interfering with results.
>
> The very fact that we permit talking helps build up proper relations—it eliminates resentment about a rule which many would think unreasonable. As a matter of fact, in operations where we did forbid talking except where the work required it, we found that the work generally seemed to require almost continuous conversation!

Note In a textile mill, girls who were engaged in strictly automatic work were formerly placed all facing one way, so that each girl saw only the backs of the girls in front of her. To discourage talking, management had even put small partitions between adjacent operators. After a period of heavy turnover, the supervisor regrouped the girls into a sort of round-table arrangement, and talking was not discouraged. Output improved and turnover was reduced to a normal figure.

Related Entries   *Job Interest—How to Stimulate It; Monotonous Work; Music for Employees.*

TARDINESS

You can't tolerate habitual tardiness—even on the part of your best performers, since they set an example for the others. But there are actions that can be taken that are constructive rather than the negative ones of docking from pay or reprimand. For example:

1. Make habitual late-comers realize their shortcoming by means of good-humored "wisecracks" instead of criticism.

2. On occasion, single out for special praise or other recognition an employee who was never late over an extended period.

3. If you have a number of departments under your supervision, try a competition based on attendance records.

4. Distribute a copy of the company's rules on lateness to everyone, with a memorandum reminding all of the importance of proper hours, without singling out any individual or individuals.

5. If an otherwise good employee is habitually late, try to find out if there is some special personal situation on which some help by you can be forthcoming. . . . Sometimes, because of invalidism at home, or other factors, an exception may be in order, allowing a certain employee to come in later and leave earlier than the others. Of

course, the rest of the department must be made aware of the reasons—or enough of the reasons—to scotch any charge of favoritism.

Related Entries *Car Pools; Discipline—1. Day-by-Day Discipline; Early Leavers; Favoritism; Privileges; Reprimands.*

TECHNICIANS AND SPECIALISTS

The use of or cooperation with technical specialists is becoming an increasing part of executive technique in industry and government. The problem appears in two forms: (1) Where an operation being supervised is large, the operating head may have technical specialists working for him. (2) The head of a smaller department may not have specialists on his staff, but will usually have to deal with and cooperate with staff specialists not under his direct control or with professionals called in as consultants—as will, of course, the heads of larger departments also, in addition to their own experts.

The main supervisory problems break down as follows:

Where the Executive Supervisor Has Staff Specialists Reporting to Him

1. *How to use specialists effectively without becoming overly dependent upon them.* You should never abandon to your own specialists your executive prerogative—the decision for action should be up to you, after they have rendered advice. As one executive put it, "The expert should be on tap, not on top." At the same time, don't resent the professional authority of the subordinate in his own specialty. If you do, you'll run the risk of making embarrassing errors.

2. *How to keep your eye on the big picture without*

becoming bogged down in the details of the specialists.
This is a danger incurred by too great a concern over the
point made above. . . . The only formula is to determine
for each kind of operation the general information you
need in order to judge whether the purposes of your group
are being achieved, and in order to justify opposing certain
recommendations of the specialists.

3. *Learn enough about the make-up of your specialists*
to be on guard on two counts: (a) Do they have a tendency to conform to your decisions by a desire not to
oppose you, even though they may have misgivings based
on technical knowledge? (b) Are they too prone to force
their own point of view by falling back upon their expert-
ness—"take what I say on faith"?

Where Specialists Do Not
Report to the Supervisor

Here you, the supervisor, must develop in yourself an
attitude of *active* and not *passive* cooperation. The outside specialist and you both have one objective—to
further the work of the company as a whole. How can
you and your people help? For example:

a. What information should be volunteered? (Staff
   people and consultants cannot be expected to be so
   familiar with your department's work as to ask all
   the necessary questions.)
b. Do all of your people involved know just what the
   objectives of the specialist are—what his project is
   all about? Have you made it your business to know
   enough about his work to be able to explain his purposes to your employees?

    c. What helps on chores can your people give the specialist to expedite his work?

    d. What sort of performance tryouts can you suggest to the specialist, to find out bugs ahead of time?

    e. What follow-up helps can you give to implement the professional recommendations?

Related Entries *Delegation; Staff Units—How to Work with Them Effectively.*

TELEPHONE ETIQUETTE

When one of your employees is on the 'phone with a customer or a member of the public, he or she *is* the company! Emphasize this point to any of your employees whose duties include telephone contacts. Quite aside from good public and customer relations, good telephone habits will increase departmental efficiency. Here are some pointers advocated by the Bell System companies. (Maybe you should post them on your departmental bulletin board!):

    1. *Distinctness . . . Pleasantness.* Clear, distinct speech is a business asset. A customer isn't encouraged to do business with you if he has to strain to understand what you're saying. Your lips should be half an inch from the telephone mouthpiece and should be used freely to form your words. . . . A pleasant, friendly voice on the telephone makes friends for you and your company.

    2. *When making a call.* Greet the caller pleasantly. . . . Ask if it is convenient to talk. . . . Try to visualize the person. Speak TO the person at the other end, not AT the telephone. . . . Be attentive. . . . Use the customer's name. (There's no sweeter music to a person than the

sound of his own name!). . . . Say "thank you" and "you're welcome". . . . Apologize for errors or delays. . . . Take time to be helpful. (It's better to spend seconds *keeping* a customer happy than months *regaining* his good will.)

3. When receiving a call. Answer promptly, at the first ring if possible. . . . Identify yourself. (Your company may have a policy on this. A good practice is to say, "This is Jones," or "Order Department—Miss Johnson." Avoid the time-wasting, out-of-date "hello". . . . If you make a promise to call back for information requested, *keep the promise* as promptly as possible. . . . Let the caller hang up first. Wait for the caller's good-bye. . . . And if you're going out, don't forget to leave word. If you can be reached, leave word on that, and when you'll be back.

4. When answering calls for others. Emphasize names. For example, "Mr. Jones' desk, Miss Smith speaking." . . . Be helpful. If you know, tell the caller when Mr. Jones will be back, or whether he can be reached somewhere else. . . . Be tactful. Some customers may be offended by a blunt, "Who's calling?" This implies that perhaps Mr. Jones is in but just isn't being "available" to the caller. It's more effective to ask, "May I tell him who's calling?" or suggest, "If you'll give me your name and 'phone number, I'll ask Mr. Jones to call you when he returns". . . . Leave clear messages: Who called, at what time, what it was about if you know, and 'phone number if the caller left it.

5. When you must transfer a call. Explain *why* the call is being transferred. . . . Be sure the caller is willing to be transferred. Some would rather call back than wait. . . . Be sure to give your operator enough information to complete the transfer without having to ask the caller to repeat his story. . . . Wait for your operator to acknowledge your request, then hang up gently.

TELLING

See *Orders and Instructions* (two entries).

TEMPORARY PERSONNEL
How to Use Them Effectively

Do you need one-and-a-half secretaries? . . . . Or two and two-thirds key-punch operators for a week? . . . . Or three crews of girls around the clock to get out a special mailing? . . . . Or fill-ins for vacationers?

These are the sort of peak and emergency situations that play hob with the best kind of personnel planning—especially if you are limited by budget restrictions, and additions to regular staff are out of the question. (And even if you *could* hire, what would you do with the new help when the peak needs are over?

Services available from temporary help contractors may be the answer. They are as near to you as your telephone, and as easy to turn on and off as a water faucet.

The big question is how to be sure you are using temporary help most effectively. Here are nine pointers from Elmer L. Winter, President of Manpower, Inc., a firm that supplies over 37 million man-hours of temporary service a year in this country and abroad:

1. *Precondition your regular employees.* Explain why you are calling in the "temporaries." Make sure they understand that this is a special situation, and that the temporaries are in no way competing with anyone on the job. Stress the need to give the temporaries all the help

possible, particularly in the first few days of the assignment.

2. Preplan the work. Make an outline of what the temporary employee is to do before she is to start. If you are not going to be on the scene when the temporary arrives, be sure that you have left word with somebody else to greet her, explain the work to her, and get her started.

3. Ready-up equipment and supplies ahead of time. Don't have the temporary worker wait around while others try to locate papers, erasers, typewriter, etc. (Remember, the "taxi-meter" is clicking!)

4. Introduce her properly to the people with whom she will have contact.

5. Explain office rules and location of facilities. The temporary worker will feel more at ease if she's told about office routines. . . . where rest rooms are. . . . lunch and "break" periods. . . . etc.

6. Give complete instructions. Take extra pains to explain the work. Remember she is not familiar with your operations. Make sure she learns the letter styles and forms desired by executives and departments for whom she will work. Have sample letters for her. If you have a manual outlining your procedures, make it available. Same thing for a job description for a permanent employee whose work she is temporarily taking over, if available.

7. Ask a regular employee to serve as a working companion. The newcomer should have somebody definite to look to for information when problems arise, and to introduce her to whatever luncheon group usually eats together—or if there isn't any, to go to lunch with her the first day.

8. Be sure she knows who supervises her job. Make

this relationship clear to the temporary worker and to her immediate supervisor.

9. *Be sure she has a signed slip before leaving.* Designate someone in the department to sign the temporary worker's time slip so that she doesn't have to leave the job without one—and as a result have to wait for her pay.

Note There are temporary help contractors in most cities (see your Yellow Pages). The time to select a firm is when you don't have an emergency or panic situation. Before deciding upon one, check into how long it has been in business, whether it uses adequate testing in its own hiring, and its general reputation for service and quality of personnel supplied. Be sure to check the insurance coverage it provides—personal and general liability, blanket bonds, etc. Ask for a certificate showing that it has proper and full coverage. If possible, check whether it has a reputation for paying its employees promptly, since disgruntled temporary workers are no bargain.

TENSION AND STRESS

Nobody can escape stress. But, as a Metropolitan Life Insurance Company booklet on the subject points out, there are varying degrees and different forms of stress—mental, emotional, physical—all having some impact, sometimes good, sometimes harmful, upon health.

Any "attack" on the body can cause stress. The attack might be an invasion of disease germs or it might be an injury, or even an emotional crisis. A sudden injury sets off an "alarm reaction" within the body. The nervous system sends out an SOS and the body gets ready to handle the emergency. The tiny pituitary gland, located under the brain, dispatches a "chemical messenger," a special hormone, which signals the adrenal glands, situated just above the kidneys. These glands, in turn, send out other hormones which help balance the body's chemistry so that disease can be resisted or an injury healed without disturbing the working order of the rest of the system.

Normal emotional stress is useful in many ways. You may get "steamed up" over an important or interesting job, and as a result, be able to handle the work more effectively. Pleasurable emotions involving stress and tension can be exhilarating. You may get excited and tense while watching a football game. This type of tension can pep you up, and the letdown that follows is healthy relaxation. As the Metropolitan booklet points out, we can't and wouldn't want to live like vegetables, without feeling.

The emotional stress that gets you down is the kind that makes it difficult or nearly impossible to relax. Intense and persistent anger, fear, frustration, or worry, which you may bottle up inside yourself, can threaten health. It is this undue emotional stress which leads to trouble. That's why it's important to *tune down* if you get too keyed up, *handle* your emotional tensions, and *know and accept* physical and emotional limitations. This is of course easier said than done, but here are Metropolitan's pointers on the subject:

1. *Balance work with play.* Schedule time for recreation. An interesting hobby can be relaxing as well as constructive. On the other hand, work can occasionally be a kind of cure for emotional situations that are hard to bear—like the death of a loved one, a divorce, or a broken engagement.

2. *Loaf a little.* While too much inactivity breeds boredom and may even *cause* stress, a few minutes a day

of doing nothing may help you to tackle your work with renewed enthusiasm.

3. *Put off until tomorrow.* You have to learn to let some things go. When a work load seems overwhelming, remember that you can do only one task at a time. Concentrate on the particular job at hand and then go on to the next one without worrying about everything that has to be done.

4. *Work off tensions.* When you're upset or angry, you can try to blow off steam or work off feelings with physical exercise.

5. *Talk out troubles.* It helps to "get it off your chest" sometimes by confiding worries to a sympathetic friend. Often another person can help you to get your feelings into focus and to see your problems in a new light.

6. *Learn to accept.* Learn to accept what you cannot change.

7. *Get away from it all.* When you feel that you are going around in circles with a problem or worry, try to divert yourself. There's no harm in leaving a painful situation long enough to catch your breath and regain the composure you need to come back and face the problem. When possible, a brief trip, a change of scene, can give you new perspective.

8. *Have regular checkups.* It's important to go to your doctor or clinic for periodic checkups. Just as the mind affects the body's working order, physical conditions will affect your outlook on life. If you keep yourself physically fit you'll have more zest for living and be able to take stress and handle tensions more easily.

Note Writing in *Dun's Review and Modern Industry* on "The Truth About Executive Stress," Dr. Mortimer R. Feinberg, an associate professor of psychology at the Baruch School, City College of New York, covered many of the above points, and gave some additional ones worth repeating here: *Face up to tension.* Fear, or avoidance of it, can be more destructive than the tension itself. . . . *Never cheat on* *sleep*. Sleep requirements vary from three or four to 12 hours a night, but all of us need some. Working late or carrying home a load of troubles can be an invitation to sleeplessness. . . . *Learn to recognize "tension triggers."* For some people, the warning signs may be an increase in smoking; for others, too many luncheon cocktails; for still others, two or three nights of disturbed sleep. You should know what the signals are in your own case. When you spot them, make a conscious effort to relax by changing the nature of your activity, selecting something that you can complete satisfactorily to obtain a sense of achievement. Says Dr. Feinberg: "Jobs aren't tense—people are!"

Related Entry *Emotional Reactions.*

TIME STANDARDS
Standard Minute (Standard Hour)

Every supervisor of industrial operations should have an understanding of work measurement and the setting of engineered performance standards. They are the backbone of scientific control of operations, and even if his present company does not make use of them, the supervisor may well run into them if he takes a job in some other company.

Where engineered performance standards are in force, the company will be using them for standard costs that form the basis of pricing, inventory control, and production planning in general. They will also form the yardsticks of output against which the supervisor can judge the performance of the workers in his department, and may well be the basis of an individual wage incentive system, and the means by which management judges the work of the department as a whole.

The supervisor's role is important. While he himself

will not be making the work measurements and setting the final standards, he will be cooperating with the staff specialists who do. More importantly, he will have to explain the workings of the system to his employees, and "sell" them on the fairness of it.

The use of standard times in wage incentive systems is explained in the entry, *Incentive Wages*, and their use in setting standard costs is discussed in the entry, *Standard Costs*. Here let's concentrate on what is meant by "standard times" or "time standards."

A widely used unit of measure is the *standard minute*. (Systems of the same type here described may use the hour, and a percentage subdivision of the hour, as a basis for calculations, and these are then called "standard hour," or "unit hour" systems. However, the arithmetic, with suitable conversion factors, works out the same as with the standard minute system.)

The standard minute system makes it possible to separate the question of how much money shall be paid a worker (which can then be made the subject of separate wage negotiations with unions or employee groups) from the factual determination of just what constitutes a *fair day's work*. By stopwatch measurements or by "predetermined times," (see *Work Measurement—1. Time Study*) the timestudy man arrives at the standard amount of time which should be taken to produce a certain piece, perform a certain operation, or the like. It can be seen that for all operations thus studied, all work can be expressed in terms of "standard minutes of production" instead of in terms of pieces or pounds or other measures. The common denominator, time, then measures the employee's output, no matter what he is producing— machined parts, assembled units, typed invoices, or even services such as sweeping a certain number of square feet of floor space. Therefore a "standard minute" should be thought of not as a unit of time, but as the amount of work which an employee is expected to do, as a minimum, in one minute by the clock.

It can be seen that whether or not there is an incentive or "piecework" plan, the number of "standard minutes' worth of work" produced by an employee in, say, 480 minutes (an eight-hour day) is a good measure of whether he is turning out work at a standard rate. If he turns out 460 standard minutes' worth of work, he is under par. If he turns out 500 standard minutes' worth of work, he is over par. Of course, the worker must be convinced that the timestudy man did a good job of measurement, and that the amount of work to be done in a standard minute is a fair task.

Obviously, no one can work steadily all day long without any interruptions for unavoidable delays, or to go to the washroom, or without some rest or slackening off of speed due to fatigue. Therefore when industrial engineers and timestudy people set the times based on their measurements, they add certain percentages to their stopwatch time, usually around 15 per cent, for such factors. (Where there are severe working conditions, the allowance may be more.)

Another thing the timestudy man has to take into consideration is the worker whose output he is measuring. The man he happens to be timing may be an exceptionally quick worker, or a noticeably slow one, or he may be deliberately "soldiering" by working more slowly than he usually does, in the hope that the timestudy man will then come up with a "loose" standard.

The timestudy man gets around this by adding a "rating

factor" to his measured times (or subtracting it, as the case may be). This is based on his judgment (derived from experience in studying many kinds of jobs done by all sorts of workers) of the pace at which a normally qualified employee would be working on that particular job. And he does not set his time from one reading—he will average a number of readings on the same operator and operation.

In a well engineered installation, *standard data* are compiled by grouping and analyzing many time studies on many jobs, to provide reliable time measures of specific elements which, in varying combinations, go into many different jobs. Consistency in ratings by different time-study men is also obtained by the use of training films on performance rating, developed by the Society for Advancement of Management and others.

Exhibit T-1, page 423 shows the derivation of a standard minute. You will note that with all of the allowances mentioned above, the analyst arrives at what is designated as "incentive time" (the second bar from the bottom) rather than the final standard minute. We shall come to that presently—but first let's see what has happened:

The operator here made one piece in 1.20 minutes. However, he is a fast worker and did the job in less time than the average normally experienced operator would take, in the judgment of the timestudy man. Accordingly, a grading factor of 1⁄6 has been applied, adjusting the time to 1.40 minutes for "adjusted timestudy time." (If the observed worker had been slower than average, the grading factor would have worked in the opposite direction.) The timestudy man then added an allowance for delays: personal time, fatigue, and unavoidable delays. These together were lumped into an allowance of 15 per cent, adding another 0.21 minutes. This takes in the necessary operations which are bound to occur during the day, but not regularly—for example, the time for a machinist to grind a drill or change a cutting angle, or for a bench assembler to move a new supply of components into position.

After the delay allowances have been added, the total is called the optimum, or *incentive time*, because the operator is assumed to be working at "incentive pace." This is the pace which the experienced timestudy man and industrial engineer determine that the man can keep up on the average all day long (remember, we have already added in for fatigue, etc.). But if he were paid so-and-so-much per minute, based on his regular hourly pay, and turned out work at that rate, all day, he would be working at high efficiency all day long and getting only his regular pay. Accordingly, the concept of adding a "bonus allowance" is applied. This bonus can vary according to the policy of any particular company, but is usually 25 per cent. In other words, management says, "Our standard *incentive time* for this piece is 1.60 minutes. But we will pay a bonus of 25 per cent—we will pay you not for 1.60 minutes, but for 2.00 minutes for each piece you turn out —that is, each piece is considered 2.00 "standard minutes' worth of work."

Thus if the man works steadily all day long, not at incentive pace, but at the standard, he turns out a piece every two minutes, or 240 pieces. He is paid for 480 minutes at his regular rate, and so earns no bonus. However, if he works at the *incentive pace* for 480 minutes, he turns out 300 pieces, which is 600 standard minutes'

EXHIBIT T-1 *Derivation of a Standard Minute*

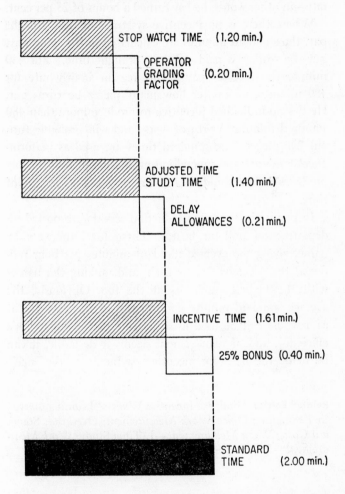

STOP WATCH TIME (1.20 min.)

OPERATOR GRADING FACTOR (0.20 min.)

ADJUSTED TIME STUDY TIME (1.40 min.)

DELAY ALLOWANCES (0.21 min.)

INCENTIVE TIME (1.61 min.)

25% BONUS (0.40 min.)

STANDARD TIME (2.00 min.)

worth of work. He is paid for 600 minutes at his regular rate—in other words, he has earned a bonus of 25 per cent.

Where there is no incentive system, but only straight pay, the standard minutes are calculated in the same way, but the worker is paid only on "straight time." For 480 minutes he receives pay at his regular hourly rate for 480 minutes, no matter how many pieces he turns out. He has no individual incentive to produce more than 480 standard minutes' worth of work, and will probably turn out 240 pieces. The standard times are used as performance standards, and supervision must see to it that nobody produces below standard for any appreciable length of time.

In many plants, daily production reports are posted on departmental bulletin boards. These list employees by name, giving the average standard minutes per hour produced the previous day by each, and ranking the names with the highest producers at the top. Obviously, the average standard minute performance of the department as a whole can be used as a measure of the supervisor's efficiency, and, if management deems it desirable, it can be made the basis for incentive payments to the supervisor.

Related Entries   *Budgets; Incentive Wages; "Learning Curve" in Estimating; Office Work Measurement; Overhead; Standard Costs; Work Measurement—1. Time Study; Work Measurement—2. Work Sampling, or "Ratio Delay."*

TIME STUDY

See *Time Standards; Work Measurement—1. Time Study; Incentive Wages.*

TIME WASTERS

A supervisor will rarely be called upon to assume responsibility for a detailed, scientific time study of workers or flow of operations in his department. However, one of his big supervisory jobs is to be ever alert to the way time is being used in the department as a whole, and where it appears to be wasted. Here is a brief checklist of the most common causes of wasted time:

1. Idle time caused by poor planning or supervision.
2. Waiting because of lack of supplies or facilities.
3. Delays caused by poor control over materials and supplies received—needed items cannot be found.
4. Too much handling and transporting.
5. Double checking instead of proper care in the first instance.
6. Manual operations that should obviously be performed by machines.
7. Chronic departmental bottlenecks.
8. Failures to ask the *why* questions—unnecessary work and useless functions.

Related Entries *Methods Improvement—1. The Questioning Attitude; Office Economies; Waste—1. Reducible Waste; Work Simplification.*

THE TIMID WORKER

It is easy to reduce a timid worker to complete ineffectiveness. But handled right, this kind of employee can be made to contribute usefully. The following pointers are from the Trans World Airlines *Supervisor's Handbook:*

1. It takes considerable encouragement to bring out his (her) suggestions and to get him to speak up on complaints.

2. Don't be overbearing; keep an eye on the group to see how they get along with him.

3. Approach him with calmness.

4. Keep in mind that timid persons may have an habitual feeling of insecurity. Make an effort to find out what work situations alarm such people most.

5. When you give instructions, be sure you're understood. The timid worker is often too shy to ask you to repeat.

6. Give him a hand as he starts new work, and step out of the picture only when you feel he's gotten up steam.

7. Emphasize the team idea: Always speak of "we" and "us." Remember he's slow to get to know people; check his knowledge of how others fit into the team.

8. Don't assign tasks requiring a lot of initiative and the making of decisions. If he must make decisions, expect him to lean heavily on you.

9. Be sure to praise him, particularly for overcoming difficulties himself and for using initative. These require real effort on his part.

Related Entries *The Jittery Employee; The Sensitive Employee.*

TRAINING

1. An Audit of Needs

The supervisor's training job is never done. He must orient and indoctrinate new employees; supervise on-the-job training for the inexperienced or for introducing new methods; coach key people in a long-range development program; see to it that seasoned employees adopt suggested new ways of doing parts of their job and bend their efforts to coming up with ideas for their own improvement; and continuously get across effective human-relations procedures.

While most companies make available helps for the supervisor in his orientation and training work, and many conduct apprenticeship and other types of training, the supervisor must always look upon these as adjuncts and supplementary services. Training will always remain a direct, prime responsibility of his job. (See *New Employees*; *On-the-Job Training*.)

Skills and experience change as people grow and develop. In addition, employee turnover changes a department's personnel resources. It will therefore be a good idea for you to make a periodic "personnel-development audit" of your operations. Who are your best people? Should you help to promote some of them out of your department, even at some temporary inconvenience to yourself? Which ones requires further training? What are you doing to develop them? Who are the idea spark plugs? Who needs constant prodding? Who are consistently high-standard producers? Is anyone "accident-prone"?

Checklist of Training Methods

Which of the following methods should you institute or, if presently used, intensify?

1. Organized on-the-job training. (See *On-the-Job Training*.)

2. Apprenticeship programs. (See *Apprenticeship Programs*.)

3. Special coaching of individuals. (See *Coaching*.)

4. Programmed Instruction. (See *Programmed Instruction*.)

5. Job Rotation. Can assignments be rotated more ef-

fectively within your department? Check with the Personnel Department regarding possible brief assignments of promising individuals to other departments.

6. Organized group programs. (See *Training—2. Group Training.*)

7. Observation in other departments. (Note comments in *Monotonous Work* regarding sparking interest in "drab" jobs.)

8. Encouragement to undertake home study. (See *Self-Improvement—2. Correspondence Schools.*)

9. Outside personnel-development activities: organized visits to other plants and companies; representation at professional and trade association meetings. (Check management policy regarding expenses.)

10. Special experience program for an understudy.

11. Supervisory training conferences. (See *Supervisory Training Conferences.*)

Training Timetable

A helpful tool is the simple "Training Timetable" shown in the accompanying illustration, used by the Department of the Army in its *Supervisor's Guide to Job Instruction.* This chart, properly prepared, gives an overall picture of the state of readiness of each member of the workforce, and what instruction is needed. From this you can plan the training needed to bring each worker to a satisfactory performance level. Mark it as follows: Cross if the employee doesn't need to do it; check if he can do it properly; minus sign if he does it but needs help; date at which needed training will start.

Related Entries   *See succeeding two entries, and also the listing under Development of Subordinates—1. Development-Appraisal-Development.*

EXHIBIT T-2

TRAINING TIME TABLE

SUPERVISOR __CLYDE T. JONES__

DIVISION __MAINTENANCE__

BRANCH __SHOPS__

SECTION ____

UNIT ____

DATE __FEB. 1, 1965__

OPERATIONS PERFORMED IN UNIT

NAMES	FILING	CUTTING	FORMING	BENDING	TRIMMING	DRILLING	PUNCHING	FITTING	ASSEMBLING & DISASSEMBLING	INSPECTING	NOTES (Special cases, Additional dates, Off-the-job training, etc.)
James Peters	X	✓	X	X	X	X	X	X	✓	✓	
Murray Thomas	X	✓	✓	✓	✓	✓	✓	X	X	X	
Nicholas Johnson	✓	✓	✓	✓	5-13	✓	✓	✓	✓	✓	
Paul Manager	✓	✓	6-3	✓	✓	X	X	✓	✓	✓	
Thomas Dennis	✓	✓	✓	✓	5-13	✓	✓	✓	X	X	
Jack Finkelstein	✓	✓	✓	✓	✓	✓	✓	X	X	X	
Kenneth Altemose	X	✓	6-3	✓	✓	✓	✓	X	6-17	6-17	
Donald Temple	✓	✓	✓	✓	5-20	✓	X	✓	✓	✓	
William Clark	X	✓	X	✓	✓	✓	✓	✓	✓	✓	
Jackson Hinners	X	✓	6-3	✓	✓	✓	✓	✓	✓	✓	
Abraham Cockrill	X	✓	✓	✓	✓	X	✓	✓	✓	✓	
Mark DePaul	✓	X	✓	✓	5-20	✓	✓	✓	✓	✓	
Archibald Harrel	✓	X	✓	✓	✓	✓	X	X	6-17	6-17	

TRAINING

2. Group Training

If you are going to undertake a group training program in your department, it will be well to keep in mind the following basic principles:

1. *The trainees should start from a common level of understanding.* Don't have such a wide difference in levels of current work, education, and background as to make the more advanced lose interest if the start is geared to the lowest level.

2. *The group should be sold on the goal.* Make clear to them the general and specific goals set up for the course. Give them a picture of the entire program.

3. *The place and conduct of the course should help the learning process.* There should be a properly lighted and ventilated meeting room, with reasonably comfortable seats. If training aids are used, they should be of good calibre, in good working order. (See *Visual and Audio Aids.*) Start and finish the meetings on time. Keep them friendly but businesslike.

4. *Have a qualified instructor.* He must be able to command the respect of the group.

5. *The trainees should feel that they are making progress.* The supervisor should show that he is personally interested in the program. Where justified, give a word of praise to the instructor, and have him transmit your expression of satisfaction to the group.

6. *Provide for as much member-participation as possible.* Adult education gains greatly from interchanges of experiences and opinions.

7. *Provide for individual recognition.* There should be some sort of certificate of completion or "diploma" at

the completion of a training course. This should preferably be signed by a high-ranking executive.

Related Entries *See preceding and succeeding entries, and also the listing under Development of Subordinates—1. Development-Appraisal-Development.*

TRAINING
3. How to Evaluate It

How can a company, a division, and a specific department be sure that they are getting tangible results from their training work? All training costs money, and should be evaluated continuously. Exhibit T-3, page 432, is a good guide for such continuing evaluation. It was incorporated by the New York State School of Industrial and Labor Relations, Cornell University, in its *Bulletin 52*, "Employee Training in Small Business Organizations." This appraisal guide proceeds from the individual-job level, to the departmental level, and finally to the organizational-policy level. You can use it in two ways: (1) as a guide in evaluating your own effectiveness in departmental training; and (2) as an indication of how higher management *judges you* as a trainer.

Related Entries *See preceding two entries, and also the listing under Development of Subordinates—1. Development-Appraisal-Development.*

TURNOVER

Labor turnover has to do with the rate at which a company (or division or department) must replace employees because its people leave either by voluntary quit or by discharge. Usually it is considered a reflection upon a

EXHIBIT T-3   Guide for Continuing Evaluation of Training Effectiveness

Immediate	Intermediate	Long-range
1. Was the time necessary to reach minimum standards of performance less than without training? Was it "on schedule?" 2. Was training adapted to trainee's starting level of skill? 3. Did employee demonstrate an interest and understanding of total job for which he was trained?	1. a) Has trained employee performance shown improvement over the minimum standards established by training? How much? b) Has experience revealed any important omissions or errors in the conduct of training? Was something important overlooked? 2. Have any motivational problems arisen with individual trainees? 3. Has trainee demonstrated a continuing interest in his job?	1. Are trained skills maintained? How? At what level? 2. Are rewards for effective learning on the job apparent to trainees? 3. Do trained employees make job-related suggestions for improvement? Are these recognized?

432

	Department level: Focus on training	Organizational level: Focus on training policy
	1. In what ways has training made tangible contributions to improving departmental work performance? 2. Have supervisors recognized training as an important responsibility? 3. Has training contributed to improved relationships and functioning among departments?	1. Are there different levels of turnover or absenteeism between trained and untrained employees? 2. Is training capacity considered as future plans are made? 3. Has the impact of training required modification of existing personnel policies, such as recruitment, employment, etc.?
1. How have departmental wage and/or material costs been affected by training? Are records of trainee performance maintained? Are they used as a basis for improvement? 2. Has training produced any operational problems within and between departments? Have these been solved? At what cost? 3. Is there evidence that trainees are effective members of work groups in the department?	1. Did the predetermined analysis of training needs prove adequate? 2. Are problems confronting trainers discussed? Are effective trainers recognized or rewarded in any way? 3. Has training contributed to improved cooperation and coordination of work processes between departments?	
1. Are day-to-day training efforts focussed upon the jobs and individuals needing it most? 2. How has responsibility for training affected the time and effort which supervisors (trainers) require for other job demands? 3. Did trainer consider need to integrate training with on-going department operations?	1. How much time is spent by supervision on training? Too little? Too much? 2. Are training activities consistent with other operating and personnel practices? 3. What is the general calibre of supervisory training ability?	

company or a unit of a company if turnover is high—for if it is due to "quits," it would appear that people aren't happy on the job; if it is due to discharge, it would appear that something must be amiss in a company's selection and/or training procedures, if it can't find or develop workers that it wishes to keep in its employ. That managements as a rule want to hold on to their employees is indicated by rewards offered for long service—many pay increases are given largely on the basis of the calendar rather than indisputable merit . . . and pension plans, stock purchase plans, longer vacations for long-service employees, and the like all have as their central motivating force the desire to keep the turnover rate low. An obvious reason is the cost of training new employees, disruptions caused by quits and discharges, the normal reaction of increased loyalty to the company as time goes on, and the like. However, as indicated below, there are two sides to the coin—and there are situations where a higher rate of turnover might be desirable.

Technically, the turnover measure is expressed as the percentage of average workforce over a period of time (say a year, or a month—the period must be specified or readily understood for the figure to have meaning) represented by replacements. It can be seen that if the labor force remains constant over the period, you would get the same percentage by dividing the number who *leave* ("withdrawals") by the average workforce, as by dividing the number who are *hired* ("accessions") by the average workforce, since those who leave are exactly matched by those who are hired. However, if the average workforce changes, the arithmetic isn't that simple. In that case, the measure is accepted to be the percentage obtained by dividing the accessions *or* withdrawals, *whichever is smaller*, by the average workforce. A labor turnover figure expressed on a monthly basis would be multiplied by 12 to get the turnover on a yearly basis. Thus a company (or department) which has a turnover of 2 per cent per month has a 24 per cent turnover per year.

It is not unusual to find turnover rates of 25 to 50 per cent per year in manufacturing companies. However, this doesn't mean that 25 to 50 per cent of all of the company's employees will have been replaced a year later—since there may be extremely high turnover in a few jobs or departments, some parts of its operations may be highly seasonal or unpredictably fluctuating, etc. For the company as a whole the rate reflects the *average* situation. (Breakdown of the turnover rate into components such as voluntary-quit rate, discharge-for-cause rate, etc., may be made for purposes of analysis.)

It can be seen that the mathematical expression of turnover rate can be a meaningful index of stability of employment for the country as a whole, or for specific industries and companies. Accordingly, the Bureau of Labor Statistics of the U. S. Department of Labor publishes turnover figures on industries and industry groups.

A certain amount of turnover is healthy, since an organization will be strengthened by bringing in new talent—and since a company with a large number of employees may want to maintain a certain average age of its workforce. (Think of the fighting ability of a large army if it lost no men over a long peace-time period through resignations or deaths by natural causes, and took in no new recruits either. It could start out as a young and vibrant military force, and twenty years later, while still of the same numerical strength, be a collection of paunchy middle-aged men!) Most companies you are familiar with have greatly increased in size of total workforce over a period of ten or fifteen years—hence they can maintain (through proper recruiting) a relatively low average age of employees despite a very low turnover rate.

In some situations a temporary high turnover rate may be advantageous—as when a company is automating or otherwise improving its operations so as to require many fewer workers. If management through such measures will, over the course of a year, effectively increase output per worker by 20 per cent, it would expect to require only 5/6 of its present labor force, since each man would be producing 6/5 as much as before. If it has an annual turnover rate of about 1/6, or 16.7 per cent, it would, mathematically speaking, not have to discharge anybody. It simply would not hire for a year. (In real life, of course, things don't work out that smoothly, since quit rates are not uniform throughout all departments, and since, indeed, an average increase in output of 20 per cent does not mean uniformly an increase of exactly 20 per cent by everybody. Also, of course, automation or other improvement measures may require a significant number of new skills.)

Assuming that in general you want to reduce your turnover rate, or maintain it at an existing low level, no specifics need be given in this entry, since this entire manual, oriented as it is to "people problems," has as its objective the development of the supervisory skills which make for a productive, high-morale working force. The prescription then boils down to—*Read all the other entries!*

Related Entries   *Discharging an Employee; Exit Interviews; Job Interest—How to Stimulate It; Motivation; New Employees; Recruitment; Working Conditions.*

U

UNDERSTUDY

Other entries discuss training as a supervisor's responsibility. But there is one aspect of training and development which bounces back especially hard on the supervisor—the development of an understudy.

Often supervisors, and, indeed, higher executives all the way up to the top, can't bring themselves to train an understudy because they can't seem to face the fact that there will ever be a day when someone else will be doing their job. They have an abiding sense of insecurity which leads them to guard their job jealously, for fear that if they do train somebody to take over, that particular somebody will push them out long before they are ready to go. They will never, of course, put this reason into words, or even admit it to themselves. There is always some other reason—too busy to take the time. . . . no one really qualified to take over the responsibilities. . . . no rush—will definitely get around to that a bit later. . . . would upset the morale of the department to designate a "crown prince". . . . and so on.

Such an attitude can boomerang heavily upon any executive. One of the first things his own superior will ask himself if the question of promoting him or transferring him advantageously comes up, is "Who's going to handle his job?" If the supervisor can't point to somebody he has been training as his stand-in, it may turn out that he is "too valuable where he is" ever to go higher!

How are you handling this situation? Who in your department is best qualified by experience and potential to handle things in your absence?

If there is no official "assistant to" position under yours, can you handle the matter informally? You do not have to designate somebody definitely as your "successor," but you can let the rest of the department know whom you are holding responsible during your vacation and other absences.

Are there several likely candidates in the department? Can you try them out by giving them special responsibilities for pieces of your job at certain times? Can a healthy sort of competition be developed to bring up the logical successor by natural evolution?

What specific guides have you set up regarding handling matters in your absence? Are there checklists and write-ups for important procedures?

Can you begin "peeling off" some of the more routine parts of your job for handling by an understudy?

If there is a definitely known date for your own permanent departure—scheduled promotion, transfer, retirement, etc.—have you mapped out an orderly progression of activities for the take-over man, as an orderly program for him to follow during the intervening time?

Related Entries *Delegation; Organization—2. Continuity through "Runners-ups."*

UNION ORGANIZATION

Figures of the Bureau of Labor Statistics show that membership in unions of all types—international, national,

locals affiliated with nationals, and single-company unions
—totals over 17 million in this country. After more than
a two-fold increase during 1937–44, union membership
reached a peak of around 17.5 million in 1956, with a
gradual decline since then. Membership losses over the
long run are for the most part due to employment decline in particular industries, and some of this has undoubtedly been due to automation.

The basic unit in organized labor is the local union,
whose members are from a particular locality, plant, or
company. Most locals are charted by national and international unions covering a particular industry, trade,
or craft. More than 80 per cent of the membership of
national and international unions headquartered in the
United States are in unions affiliated with AFL-CIO
(American Federation of Labor, now joined with the
Congress of Industrial Organizations).

The president, secretary, and other officers of locals are
usually unsalaried. Shop stewards and business agents
provide continuing guidance of members. Stewards typi-
cally collect dues and handle grievances, carrying on their
union activities while they are regularly employed. Some
union contracts provide for payment by the company
for stipulated time spent on such union work. Business
agents generally devote their full time to union work, and
are paid by the union.

Union Recognition

A wide range of "union security" or union recognition
is provided for in labor contracts. Here are the types and
terms commonly encountered, from weakest to strongest:

1. *Open shop.* In the open shop, each employee is
dealt with separately, without collective bargaining.

2. *Preferential shop*. Management recognizes the union, and grants union members preference when new employees are hired, and may give added security to union members on layoffs. Non-union employees can be hired, and they need not join the union to get the job.

3. *Union shop*. Here no discrimination is made between union and non-union members in recruitment. However, new employees are given a certain period during which to join the union. If they do not join in that time, the union may seek and obtain their dismissal. But employees need not be discharged if they have sought to join the union and have been denied membership.

4. *Agency shop*. Employees must pay union dues or their equivalent but need not actually become members.

5. *Closed shop*. In a "closed shop," only union members may be employed, and all employees must maintain union membership during their employment. The Taft-Hartley Act expressly prohibits the closed shop, although in practice in some industries, for example construction and shipping, employers and government officials have countenanced what amounts to the closed shop, for better protection to workers where employment is of short duration. In addition to the above union-security features of a labor agreement, there may be provisions for check-off and maintenance of membership. *Check-off* is the collection of union dues through payroll deduction. *Maintenance-of-membership* requires employees who are union members at the time a contract is signed to remain members for the term of the contract, or else be subject to discharge.

Related Entries *See National Labor Relations Act.*

V

VISUAL AND AUDIO AIDS

A picture, the old saying goes, is worth 10,000 words. Since most department heads are bound to have to make a presentation at one time or another—at an employee training session, before an executive committee, or for a public talk—you should be prepared to do the best possible job. The following pointers, supplemented by some source references and precautionary points—are from a publication, "How to Plan for, How to Conduct, How to Follow-through on the Effective Meeting," prepared by the Training Section of Automatic Retailers of America, Inc.:

1. *Select your visual and audio-visual equipment with care,* whether you're renting or buying it. (Your local "Yellow Pages" probably have an entry under "Visual and Aural Education Equipment" or a similar classification.) Browse around at suppliers, and see the latest devices.

2. *Be sure you know how to operate the equipment.* The suppliers will give you all the time you need to learn how to thread a projector, how to reel and unreel the film, how to back up and rerun points of interest, etc. (Caution: After they show you, be sure to follow the "performance try-out" specified in our entry, *On-the-Job Training.* This will keep you from being all thumbs at your meeting.)

3. *Check before each meeting* to be sure that there is sufficient chalk for blackboards and pads for easels, and that projectors and sound equipment are functioning properly.

4. *A prime rule for visuals:* Don't expose the visual until you want the audience's attention drawn to it, and as soon as you have finished with it, cover it. Don't let it become a distraction.

5. *Easel and paper pad.* A portable easel with pad or blackboard is minimum equipment for almost any type of meeting. Advantages of the easel and pad over the blackboard are (1) they're much cleaner—don't chalk your hands or clothing; (2) they eliminate the need for erasing—simply flip over and start the new sheet; (3) you can go back to something you discussed earlier, and you also have a permanent record of what you showed at the meeting. A portable, lightweight, collapsible aluminum easel weighs about 18 pounds and costs (in 1965) about $50. You can get one at almost any visual education equipment and supply house.

6. *The paper-strip take-down presentation.* This is a variation of the easel and pad. Key words or sentences are printed on a pad sheet that is then taped firmly to the easel. Next, paper strips are taped lightly over each word or sentence. You uncover them one by one as you go through your presentation. This technique prevents your audience from reading ahead by focusing attention precisely where you want it.

7. *Flannel board.* This has tremendous flexibility, and gives a fine touch of professionalism. The board itself is made of a piece of flannel stretched over a flat surface. Words, sentences, pictures, and graphs are then prepared on paper or cardboard, cut to size, and backed with flannel. For your presentation, the flannel board is suspended in an almost vertical position. When you place the cutouts against it, they will adhere flat. Commercially manufactured flannel boards cost about $75 (1965) without the stand. Look for flannel boards and flannel backing at the shops where you buy easels and paper pads.

8. *Movies and slides.* Silent and sound motion picture films, film strips with accompanying narration, and slides are excellent visual aids. Because they involve buying or renting a projector (and, of course, a certain amount of fussing at the meeting itself) they are not used as frequently as they might be. But the sound motion picture is certainly one of the most effective training and expository devices. Numerous excellent films are available on almost any industrial subject or management practice you can name. Many of these can be obtained by merely paying the postage from and back to the source. Others are available for a low rental fee.

Here are some sources which have been in the business for a long time, to whom you can write for catalogs and other information. (You can secure other contacts through your Yellow Pages.):

McGraw-Hill Book Company, Text Film Division, 330 West 42nd Street, New York, N.Y. 10036

Modern Talking Picture Service, Inc., 3 East 54th St., New York, N.Y.

Sterling Movies USA Inc., 375 Park Avenue, New York, N.Y.

Your local college or university should also have some good leads for you.

9. *Get the most from a film* by following these important steps:

a. *Preview the film.* Descriptions won't tell you enough. Preview it in its entirety.

b. *Introduce the film.* Briefly review the film and alert your audience to its key points.

c. *Project the film properly.* If you are not experienced at operating a projector, get someone who is. Avoid projection fumbling—this detracts from the presentation. (Fumblers have not been unknown to burn up a reel of film.)

At 1965 prices, a 16-mm. sound projector will cost from $500 up, and can be procured at all visual aids houses. Rentals will be from $15 up for a 24-hour period. You can also rent screens. (Incidentally, a good screen is an important factor in good results.)

Silent projectors, while cheaper, may be a poor investment, because most training films today have sound tracks. The few which do not can still be shown with a sound projector, but not vice versa. Using a silent projector for a sound film will ruin its sound track.

Film slides, and 35-mm. film strips with recorded narration, can both be projected by the same projector if you get one that has the proper adaptor. If you decide to invest in this type of projector, make certain that it can be used for both slides and strips.

Any good photographer can make slides for you. Custom-made slides have made the success of thousands of meetings. A strip and slide projector costs approximately $140 (1965). You can expect to pay $225 or more for a projector *and* a record player.

10. *Overhead and opaque projectors.* The overhead projector projects only transparencies. Recent improvements in reproduction techniques have made the production of transparencies a quick and inexpensive function of almost any company's duplicating department. With a grease pencil you can write or draw on the transparency while it is being projected, a feature which may be very helpful in getting across a point. Another advantage is that it can be used in a darkened room. Again as of 1965, models are available for approximately $225. With opaque projectors you can project anything—printed or hand-written pages, diagrams, etc. Disadvantages are that it must be used in a darkened room, and is quite noisy. Models at this writing are available for about $300.

11. *Remember that the purpose of a meeting is to communicate effectively.* Calculate the expense of meetings—both direct and indirect expenses. You may decide that money spent on equipment that will increase the effectiveness of your meetings for the next ten years is a wise investment.

Related Entries *See listing under Briefings and Presentations.*

W

WAGE AND HOUR LAW

See *Minimum Wage Laws*.

WAGNER ACT

The *Wagner Act* is the popular name for the *National Labor Relations Act* of 1935, which, with the *Taft-Hartley Act* of 1947 amending it, and other amendments, is the principal Federal law governing labor relations. See *National Labor Relations Act*.

WASTE

1. Reducible Waste

Functional departments, such as product designing, production engineering, machine and tool designing, and industrial engineering are established by management to strive continuously for the "better product at a lower cost." Full-time specialists in these departments will do the major part to lower costs by reducing waste—that is their job. However, as W. Clements Zinck points out in *Dynamic Work Simplification*, management will profit by the many minor and even major improvements suggested by non-professional personnel when they are made conscious of the extent and cost of *reducible wastes*. An important part of every supervisor's job is to instill such awareness in the minds of all employees. Zinck establishes four types of reducible waste:

1. *Transportation of a subject by any means, any distance, in any situation.* Transportation will be seen in many forms: e.g., the movement of a tote pan of parts from a storage area to a work area; the walking of a man from one work area to another; the body movement of a man to get his hands in position to do work; the movement of a hand to grasp or release or manipulate a tool; the travel of a part on a conveyor. (The reason a transportation is made is to move material to or nearer to the position where it will be worked on, or for a man to move himself to a position to do work, or to move the hand to a position to do work. But whatever the reason, *transportation adds no value to the product.*)

2. *Delay-Storage-Idle of the object in any situation.* Examples are the momentary hesitation of a hand in an intricate assembly, a hand idle for lack of something for it to do, a man waiting for the machine to finish the cut, a machine idle while it is being set up, a piece of material waiting in a tote pan for its turn to be worked on, a tank of chemical waiting to be treated, a major assembly in a stores bin waiting to be scheduled for the final assembly operation.

3. *Inspection to verify for quantity or dimension or quality characteristic.* Examples are the checking of single dimension of a part, the checking of the color of a batch of fabric, the inspection of the contour of a tooth of a gear, the checking of a number of close dimensions on a delicate and expensive part, the verification of a calculation, the efficiency performance run of a large generator. A thorough investigation of why an inspection is

necessary is bound to uncover opportunities for improvement, *because every inspection is the costly, constant reminder that sufficient quality has not yet been built into the product.*

4. Failure to use known faster devices. Just where in all the handling can slide-grasp bins, gravity feed chutes, peg-boards, and the like be used? Where can a holding hand be relieved by a foot treadle or an air chuck? How can time be saved by the use of a device found helpful on another job?

Related Entries   *See succeeding entry; also: "Cost Consciousness" in Employees; Methods Improvement—1. The Questioning Attitude; Methods Improvement—2. "Selling" the Need for Savings; Quality; Scrap Costs; Suggestions—1. Tapping the "Latent Resources"; Time Wasters; Work Simplification.*

WASTE

2. Dramatizing Avoidable Waste

How can you dramatize avoidable waste? Here are some ideas you may be able to adapt:

Translate waste into real-life terms. A railroad president had the following list published in the employee magazine, and posted on bulletin boards, under the heading, "When you waste materials, you are really throwing away what the company's transportation has earned."

Item	Equivalent Tons of Average Freight Moved One Mile
One switch point	2,872
One angle bar	121
One crosstie	117

Item	Equivalent Tons of Average Freight Moved One Mile
One switch stand	2,703
One staybolt	56
One boiler tube	364
One hammer	65
One gallon of oil	57
One gallon of paint	243
One oilcan	73
One pail	39
One marker lamp	893
One pencil	1
One typewriter	10,114
One file box	54
One typewriter ribbon	28
One track shovel	114
One coal scoop	118

Accentuate the negative. To dramatize waste to all employees, an automobile plant stationed bright-red "pork barrels" in every department. Large labels pasted on the barrels read, "Put in anything you find mislaid which has any value. WATCH THIS BARREL FILL UP!"

As the barrels filled, a record was made of the total value of the contents, and the figure was posted prominently.

Accentuate the positive. Has everyone in your department—especially the new employees—been given a good awareness of the *end results* of his work? Maybe a girl soldering contacts all day long doesn't really know the importance of her particular operation. . . . Does the typist know how high up the executive ladder the report she's working on will go—and what can be involved as a result of slipshod work?. . . . How familiar are your people with the special problems in the departments receiving their output? Would some in-plant "tours" be in order?

Related Entries *See listing under preceding entry.*

WOMEN AND GIRLS

1. ("God Bless 'Em")

What special differences between men and women workers should the supervisor keep in mind? Obviously there are important physical and physiological factors to consider if there are women and girls in the department (see separate entry following this one). Here are some pointers on the less tangible factors:

1. As to *intelligence*, psychologists are agreed that there are no discernible differences between men and women. Tests have shown that women differ from each other far more than they differ from men. (Don't make the mistake of considering lack of experience or unfamiliarity with technical terminology as lack of intelligence.)

2. As to *emotions*, there are certainly observable differences in reactions. "Women are not more emotional than men," says Dr. Harry Levinson, an industrial psychologist and expert in mental health (writing in the IBM publication *Think*). "It is, however, more culturally acceptable for women to *show* their emotions than it is for men to do so. This is an advantage, not a disadvantage, to supervisors. A supervisor has ready evidence in a woman's tears that something has gone wrong. If he will learn not to be afraid of the open expression of feeling, he can put it to constructive use."

3. Supervisors should recognize that women's attitudes

will tend to be more *personal* than men's. Therefore their need for praise and encouragement tends to exceed that of men. In giving job instructions, the supervisor should be especially patient, and be ever ready to show appreciation for satisfactory progress. However, he will be well advised to sidestep and refuse every invitation to place the supervisory function on a man-to-woman basis, and should keep the distance of his authority.

4. Women have a special need for *sociability and companionship*, and where possible women should be allowed to talk while working on their jobs. (See *Talking*.)

5. You can expect a woman to react emotionally to *criticism*. Therefore, as regards women employees, give double emphasis to the points made in *Criticism—1. How to Dish It Out.*

Note If there are women and girls in your department, here are some simple things to think about: Stress cleanliness, especially of sanitary facilities. . . . Have a large mirror in the washroom. . . . If you do not supply individual lockers, be sure to have a place at each girl's station where she can keep her purse. . . . Try to provide a room where the girls can go to eat their lunch, if they bring lunches. Equip such a room with a radio and, if possible, a television set, and try to have some comfortable reading chairs and a supply of periodicals. . . . For industrial operations, have management, if possible, furnish uniforms or at least smocks.

Related Entries *See succeeding two entries; also Sex.*

WOMEN AND GIRLS
2. Special Physiological Problems

The physiological problems of women in business are associated with childbearing—i.e., menstruation, pregnancy, and menopause, or "change of life." However, experience has shown that with commonsense working conditions (no heavy lifting, pulling, or carrying; suitably designed chairs; tensions on controls and footlevers properly adjusted) these physiological factors play little part in a woman's ability to work—except, of course, for limitations during pregnancy.

Menstrual periods as a rule involve no lessening of a woman's working ability, although some women experience distress and pain. Any department employing women should have access to special facilities with cots or beds. A short rest period and simple medication are all that is usually necessary.

Menopause, which may cause temporary disability in women over 49, is not the problem it used to be, thanks to medical treatment and minor surgery which medical science can now provide. Thousands of women go through this period without any appreciable change in their state of health. As a matter of fact, many women have found that upon completion of the menopause they have a new sense of well-being, with more endurance and fewer minor illnesses than before.

As to *pregnancy,* the exact time a woman should leave the job before childbirth will vary with the type of work and the individual. Don't substitute your judgment for the advice of the company physician or the woman's own doctor. (Experience has shown that where a company has set up a rigid policy of termination of employment upon pregnancy, women will tend to conceal pregnancy during the first three months, the very period when there is the greatest danger of miscarriage.) Obviously, pregnant women should be transferred from especially strenuous work, and from areas where toxic materials or other conditions create hazards.

Momentary faintness is not unusual even among healthy women, and is usually not serious. Medical people caution supervisors against being too ready to suspect malingering when women workers complain of faintness. Ten minutes' rest and a cup of tea or coffee in the rest room will usually work wonders. In general, frequent rest periods increase women workers' efficiency.

Related Entries *See preceding and succeeding entries; also Sex.*

WOMEN AND GIRLS
3. Safety and Women Workers

1. Slacks have generally been found to be the most satisfactory garments for women. They automatically remove the hazards of loose, flowing garments. A reasonable uniformity of style, material, and color also offsets a possible distracting effect upon male employees.

2. Hairnets or lightweight caps are absolutely necessary on machine work. In such work, also, the wearing of jewelry on fingers and wrists or around the neck must be prohibited.

3. The habit of stuffing handkerchiefs up the sleeve of a dress should be discouraged, and the use of vanity cases restricted to the dressing room, if women work at machines.

4. Proper footwear may present a problem, since safety shoes are not considered ultra chic. Work shoes with reinforced metal toe box are available for feminine wear —but in any event, women should be required to wear shoes that enclose the foot completely, and low heels are

essential. Proper shoes will reduce fatigue as well as afford better protection.

5. Chairs with approved posture support should be provided where women are seated while working.

6. Frequent rest periods should be provided.

7. Attractive lockers and rest rooms should be provided where the women can change comfortably from street to work clothes and back again.

8. A supervisor as a rule does not have too great a voice in modifying machine design. However, there are many things he can do to make the work safer and less fatiguing: Wooden platforms for short women will bring control within easier reach, and extensions of levers will reduce the effort required to move them. . . . Safety guards may have to be readjusted. . . . Illumination sources may have to be lowered. . . . Wastage and debris can be kept cleared away. . . . Electrical switches and wiring can be locked or tightly covered.

9. There is always danger from momentary faintness or dizziness. Lay stress on having the women be alert to detecting fatigue in themselves and others.

10. *All* of the heavier lifting and handling should be performed by men.

11. Be especially careful in your indoctrination of new women employees: If the job is around machinery, be sure you know just how much familiarity the newcomer has with an industrial environment. Be sure she gets special pointers on fatigue, personal hygiene, safety, machine operation, and the like. What help can you get in such indoctrination from the older women in the department?

Related Entries   *See preceding two entries; also Sex.*

WORK DISTRIBUTION

Every now and then it is a good idea to make some spot checks in your department, with a special view to effecting the most even flow of work. Get answers to these questions:

1. *What activities take the most time?* In preparation for this analysis you may, in office operations, want to have employees keep a tally of work done over a given period, as described in *Office Work Measurement*. Or you may want to tighten up procedures for maintenance workers, analysts, and other special-assignment people as regards turning in accurate time records showing specific job orders or project numbers. (See *The Maintenance Foreman—3. A Systematic Maintenance Program.*) Even high-level (prima donna?) research scientists and other professional workers can be asked to keep simple daily records, perhaps to the nearest quarter hour, of time spent, identified by projects.

2. *Is there misdirected effort?* Does analysis show a lot of time spent on relatively unimportant activities? Time wasted by one person may be small, but it adds up when many people are lax—and a hold-up by one may contribute to delays by others.

3. *Are skills used properly?* Are high-priced men doing chores others should do?

4. *Are there too many unrelated tasks?* Unrelated tasks may mean waste motion. Maybe new groupings are in order.

5. *Are some tasks spread too thin?* Tied in with No. 4—can one person do more pieces of a given operation?

6. *Are workloads distributed evenly?* Is there too

much work for one employee and not enough for another?

Related Entries *Bottlenecks; Employee Efficiency; Office Work Measurement; Rush Jobs; Work Measurement—2. Work Sampling, or "Ratio Delay."*

WORK MEASUREMENT

1. Time Study

Work measurement (time study) is defined as "a collection of techniques used to determine the time required by a qualified and well trained person working at a normal pace to do a specific job." Time-study men from the methods department will normally do the actual measurement of operations in the supervisor's department, and the responsibility of the supervisor himself will be to cooperate with them, explain to his employees what they are doing, and make the necessary arrangements for the observation by the staff men of the work of specific operators.

The uses to which the time studies are put are the development of standard costs and the establishment of engineered performance standards. In many plants the latter will be used as the basis for incentive wage payments, in which case the supervisor will be especially concerned with understanding the techniques and results. (See *Time Standards.*)

A time study is made to determine the time required to perform a job at a "normal pace." It is conducted by timing the job through several performances, or *cycles.* A stopwatch is generally used, except where *predetermined times* are used, as discussed below. The job is broken down into logical segments of a cycle which have easily distinguished beginnings and endings. The segments are not too short for practical timing, but short enough to be compared with similar segments or elements in other jobs, and to be used in constructing *standard data* from which times on other operations can be computed. As explained in *Time Standards*, the observed data are adjusted by *rating factors* to conform to the observer's concept of the "normal pace" at which the operator should be working. In addition, allowances are added to provide for recovery from fatigue, allow for unavoidable delays, and make provisions for getting a drink, going to the washroom, etc. The result, if expressed in minutes, is the *standard minutes* for the operation to be performed, or if expressed in hours, the *standard hours*. (For most operations this is a small fraction of an hour.) The time-study engineers will usually precede the time study by a study to improve the operation.

Various systems of *predetermined times,* all similar in principle, have been developed from extensive measurement data. The names of systems which the supervisor will most frequently hear are Motion Time Analysis (MTA), Work Factor, Methods Time Measurement (MTM), Basic Motion Times (BMT), and Dimensional Motion Times (DMT). By summing up times established for minute elements of motions, an analyst arrives at the time for an operation. He can do this by studying a description of the operation, without having to clock the motions of the worker performing the job.

The method is especially useful where an operation has not yet been started, and an estimate of time is required. Employees may at first be inclined to doubt that an analyst can arrive at a fair time standard from predetermined data, but very high accuracy has been demonstrated.

Of the systems mentioned, MTM is probably used as much as all the others put together. Typical basic MTM motion elements are Reach, Grasp, and Release. Combinations of these motions alone account for probably 50 per cent of the work that people do. The time values are given in Time Measurement Units, "TMU's," where one TMU = 1/100,000 of an hour, or 0.0006 minutes, or 0.036 seconds. Thus a second is equivalent to about 28 TMU's. Tables for other principal elements cover Move, Turn and Apply Pressure, Disengage, and Eye and Body Motions.

In recent years, somewhat simpler variations of the predetermined time plans have come into rather wide use, where the refined motions are lumped into fewer and somewhat coarser units. These appear under such names as Master Standard Data (MSD), Universal Standard Data (USD), and General Purpose Data (GPD).

Related Entries *See succeeding entry; also, Incentive Wages; Office Work Measurement; Standard Costs; Time Standards.*

WORK MEASUREMENT
2. Work Sampling, or "Ratio Delay"

To do the right job of assisting the methods and time-study people in your company's methods and systems department, you should have a general knowledge of what the various techniques of work measurement are, and the kinds of results achieved with them. One of the techniques used is "Work Sampling," also called "Ratio Delay." This is a form of work measurement which (at least for a lot of applications, and without all the statistical refinements used by the professionals) can be used by the supervisor himself, if he wants to get a "fix" on a certain type of operation. It is discussed here—for other techniques, see *Work Measurement—1. Time Study, Time Standards* and *Office Work Measurement*.

Work Sampling (Ratio Delay) is a random sampling method of accumulating information about the activities of workers and the utilization of machines. In this technique, facts are gathered inexpensively and with a high degree of accuracy about an operation, a process, or any other activity, for the purpose of improving manpower utilization.

The ratios of delays and defined elements of work to total process time are obtained by random observation. An observer visits a machine or other work location a certain number of times a day—maybe ten. Note that this does *not* mean exactly once every 48 minutes in an 8-hour day, since that would not be *random* sampling. His visits follow no set pattern. The observer records the element of the job being studied which is being performed at the time of the visit. For example, a machine operation may have been separated, for purposes of the study, into four basic elements as far as the worker's activity is concerned: *Setup; Machine Operation; Delay for Maintenance;* and *Delay for Cause.* The theory is that if sufficient observations are taken at random, the *percentage occurrence* of each of the four elements based on total number of observations will give a good indication of the percentage of time the four elements are occurring throughout the working day or week.

Obviously, the more observations that are taken, the more confident you can be of the results. The analyst uses statistical tables to determine, for a given percentage of occurrence of an element, how many observations he would need for, say, a degree of accuracy within a magin of 1%, or 5%, or 10% of certainty. ("Certainty" can of course never be achieved—you simply come closer to it by taking more and more observations.) The observer would, for example, need 1,600 observations to be "within 10% of accuracy" for an element that occurs 20% of the time. Two observers might each take 50 observations a day, for a period of 16 days, to achieve this.

In selling the validity of this method to your employees, you can use a pair of dice as an illustration. There is one way to make a "two." Two ways to make a "three." Three ways to make a "four." Four ways for "five," five ways for "six," six ways for "seven," five for "eight," four for "nine," three for "ten," two for "eleven," and one for "twelve." Your workers will see the reasonableness of the assertion that if you throw the dice for hundreds of times, the various combinations will distribute themselves in the above proportion. This will also make them see the reasonableness of saying that you can draw similar kinds of conclusions about their continuing operations by taking a whole lot of random samples. (*Note*: We have assumed that your dice were not loaded.)

Related Entries *See listing under preceding entry.*

WORK SIMPLIFICATION

Work Simplification is a way of getting something done, step by step, breaking a problem down into simple segments. As defined by W. Clements Zinck in his text, *Dynamic Work Simplification*, it is "an organized, commonsense attack upon the way in which work is done now, with a view of doing it better. It makes use of the techniques of *Methods Improvement* [see two entries under that head] but it goes beyond a series of techniques. Work Simplification 'stretches the mind' by introducing and solidifying the concept of what useful work is. It changes habits of thinking about what must be considered waste work."

The heart of a Work Simplification program is the recognition by management of the foreman and supervisor as a vital part of the methods improvement team, and through them tapping the enthusiasm of everyone to suggest ways to improve methods and reduce costs. The basic premise of Work Simplification underscored by Zinck is that *once a person really sees how a job is done, asks why it is done that way, and attacks the job with the desire to improve the present method, possibilities for improvement will inevitably occur to him.*

Another premise of Work Simplification is that any work that does not *add value* to material, does not *plan or calculate*, does not *give or receive essential information*, is *reducible waste*. There are four types of reducible waste: (1) transportation; (2) delay-storage-idle; (3) inspection; and (4) failure to use known faster devices. (See *Waste—1. Reducible Waste.*)

By concentrating attention on the elimination of waste wherever it occurs, you can help management achieve a very substantial total of "little" savings which the professional methods men in staff departments will not have time to unearth. Especially on short-run jobs, as Zinck points out, waste will keep on going unnoticed. . . . the way the jobs were set up in the first place to get them done somehow will be the way they will be done until you take the initiative to make improvements. (But this does not mean that numerous large-scale savings may not be made. Company Work Simplification programs have been known to result in individual improvements representing first-year savings of $10,000 and more.) The "hard-headed, insatiable" *questioning attitude* needed by the supervisor for such a program is discussed in the methods-improvement entry referred to above. Briefly, you should constantly ask: (1) *What can we eliminate?* (2) *What can we combine?* (3) *Should the sequence be changed?* (4) *What can we simplify?*

The Written Record

A vital part of a Work Simplification program is the analysis of work by means of a written record made by the supervisor of just how a particular job or process is done. The mere making of such a record will of itself generate ideas for improvement.

The written record is made by means of simple charting techniques, with each element of work marked with its own symbol. Such charting shows in clear relief the wastes that constantly occur when a man uses his hands; when material is processed, operation by operation, part by part, to the completed product. The Work Simplification definition and symbol for each element in a written record are shown in Exhibit W-1, page 466. (Some programs use ⇨ for transportation, and add a symbol **D** for delay.)

(1) *The Process Analysis* records in chronological sequence all the elements of work in the series of operations in a process whose purpose is to change a subject in any of its physical or chemical characteristics, or to disassemble it from another object. A *single subject* is followed. (A Process Analysis could follow a *man* as well

as a part. When a man walks, it is "transportation"—he is "transporting" himself.) Whether the *transportation* is made with a container or holder or is moved part by part, there is always a "pick-up" waste operation before and a "place" waste operation after the transportation operation.

A part cannot begin a *delay* or *storage* until it or its container is placed in some particular spot to wait until it is needed again. It cannot end a delay or storage until it or its container is picked up. So there is always a "place" before a delay and a "pick-up" after a delay.

An *inspection* is almost always made part by part. There is always a "delay" before and after an inspection.

It is good to shade in the symbol for a value-adding operation. This makes the few value-adding operations stand out starkly. There is always a "delay" before and after a value-adding operation.

Forms are usually provided for convenience of charting. A portion of a Process Analysis is shown in Exhibit W-2, page 467. While terse, it records *all* the information of a process as you see it. After you improve the process, the new chart will almost always show a dramatic reduction in operations, distance moved, and time. A chart will show that the small amounts of *value-adding* work stand out, in Zinck's words, as "tiny islands in a huge sea of waste."

(2) *The Man-Machine Analysis* comes into play after you have satisfied yourself that an operation must be performed. ("Why must it be done at all?") The operation studied will be either "machine-controlled" or "man-controlled." In a Man-Machine Analysis the transportation includes the body motion of the man. This is because the subjects of the analysis are the man *and* the machine. It is the transportation of the man, by him-

self, that is the waste transportation here. As shown in Exhibit W-3, page 468, each element of the man and each element of the machine are recorded separately, with the machine elements placed in proper time sequence with the man elements.

(3) *The Operation Analysis* is the observation of the operator himself, and concerns the use the man makes of his hands and the assistance rendered to the hands by other members of the body, such as use of a foot to push a pedal. Note that the Process Analysis didn't look inside any of the value-adding operations, and that the Man-Machine Analysis was a broad, overall look at the man's activity. The Operation Analysis, to give complete coverage to all phases of work, centers in detail on the right- and left-hand activities of the operation.

An *operation* occurs when a hand is changing material in any of its characteristics or is assembling or disassembling one object from another; or when a hand is used to prepare material, machine, tools, jigs, fixtures, holders, or appliances; or to dispose of the material after the value-adding work. A *transportation* occurs when an empty hand is moved to be in position to be used effectively, or is moved to a position to become idle, or when it is transporting something. Here *inches count,* because of the sheer number of hand movements. *Idle-hold* occurs when the hand is idle, or is merely holding something. See Exhibit W-4, page 469.

Motion Study

After all major wastes under prevailing conditions have been eliminated, you are ready to study the operator in detail. You will want to be sure that he is using his hands properly and that all his actions are performed with minimum fatigue and waste motions. Here you must apply the principles of motion economy. Work Simplification programs drill supervisors in the basics of motion economy without going into the refinements of micromotion study and other techniques of the industrial engineer (see *Motion Study*). Motion economy is the last technique to employ, since obviously it would be difficult to get a worker to cooperate by changing his usual way of doing something if he himself sees all sorts of glaring opportunities for making substantial improvements in planning, handling, and flow of work. His attitude would understandably be, "Why pick on me?" Moreover, you would be red-faced if you went to a lot of trouble to improve a particular operation only to have it eliminated when purposeful thought is applied to the process as a whole!

Note *Dynamic Work Simplification*, by W. Clements Zinck, published by Reinhold, New York, 1962, covers in clear detail the application of Work Simplification by the foreman on his production job. Note that Work Simplification is not limited to manufacturing operations. It is being applied in offices, in retailing, and even in the medical profession, in streamlining surgical techniques. The discussion above follows Mr. Zinck's briefing of the concepts presented in his book, in his article on Work Simplification in *The Encyclopedia of Management*, also published by Reinhold. The brief factual presentation here cannot convey the almost religious fervor with which those who become "converted" to Work Simplification techniques engage in a war on waste. Their slogan, made famous by Allan H. Mogenson who first put the techniques and philosophy together into a unified program some 30 years ago, is *"Ship a better product or perform a better service at a lower price and at the right time!"* To that end they seek to harness the enthusiasm of everyone in a department to "question everything about everything" and come up with suggestions for improvement.

Related Entries   *"Brainstorming"; Methods Improvement—1. The Questioning Attitude; Methods Improvement—2. "Selling" the Need for Savings; Motion Study; Resistance to Change; Suggestions—1. Tapping the "Latent Resources"; Suggestions—2. Helping Make the Company Suggestion System Work; Waste—1. Reducible Waste; Waste—2. Dramatizing Avoidable Waste; Work Measurement—1. Time Study; Work Measurement—2. Work Sampling, or "Ratio Delay."*

EXHIBIT **W-1**   *Work Simplification Definitions and Symbols*

○ *Operation:* An *operation* occurs when the subject is changed in any of its physical or chemical characteristics, or is assembled with or disassembled from another object, or is arranged or prepared for another operation, transportation, delay or storage, or inspection. An operation occurs when information is given or received, or when planning or calculating is done.

o *Transportation:* A *transportation* occurs when the subject is moved from one place to another.

▽ *Delay-Storage-Idle:* A *delay* occurs when the subject is prevented by any condition from having the next operation performed on it, or the next planned operation does not require immediate performance. A *storage* occurs when the subject is kept and protected against unauthorized removal. *Idle* is the delay of a man or a machine; that is, when the subject remains in one place awaiting further action.

□ *Inspection:* An *inspection* occurs when the subject is verified for quality or quantity, or checked in any of its specified physical or chemical characteristics; that is, when the subject is checked or verified, but not changed.

WORKING CONDITIONS

1. How good are the seeing conditions in your department? Have you ever checked (or asked for a check to be made) to ascertain how the actual foot-candle levels in

EXHIBIT W-2 Process Analysis

ELEMENT NO.	DESCRIPTION — GIVE ALL DETAILS. ALL YOU WILL KNOW ABOUT THE PROCESS FOR YOUR IMPROVEMENT ANALYSIS ARE THE FACTS YOU RECORD HERE WHILE ACTUALLY OBSERVING THE PROCESS	SYMBOL	DISTANCE In Feet	TIME In Minutes	NOTES - DATA - SKETCHES Things To Check For IMPORTANT POSSIBILITIES / WHY IS IT DONE?
1	Regular Pork Trimmings (140%) in truck in Cooler No. 21, where it had been placed in storage by trucker during hog cut operation	▽			Tub 28 X 57 X 23 deep Capacity 1000 lb. approx. Why not taken directly to cooler No. 9?
2	Truck grasped by grinder and grinder-helper from Dept. 15 - Sausage.	○			
3	Truck pushed to grinder in meat preparation room of Sausage Department. Two men needed on account of the unevenness of the floors and weight of truck.	◁	375		Grinder secures pork when needed. Two tubs are ground ahead of the frankfurter emulsion grinding operation.
4	Truck released by grinder and helper in position at grinder work area.	○			Will not a tub each of Regular and Jowl Trimmings do just as well, and grind as needed?
5'	Till forked into grinder.	▽			Grinder head has 3/16" grid, Grinder is Buffalo 78B, John E. Smith's Sons Co.
6	Pork Trimmings forked from truck and tossed into bowl of grinder by grinder. Jowl Pork Trimmings forked simultaneously into the bowl by grinder helper. The two pork trimmings are thus mixed by the grinding operation. The ground fresh pork falls directly into a truck, and it is leveled in the tub as needed. The truck is turned end for end when about two-thirds full.	●		9	Grinder bowl is a bit too high—making the forking a bit awkward. Can machine be lowered with little cost? Why not chop directly into tubs?
7	Till trucks of regular pork and jowl trimmings have been all ground, and grinder and helper are ready to move it.	▽			The grinder cannot grind the two pork items as fast as the two men can fork them into the bowl — hence there is IDLE TIME in this man-machine combination
8	Truck of ground fresh pork grasped by the two men.	○			
9	Truck pushed into Cooler No. 9.	○	55		

Portion of a Process Analysis chart of an ingredient, regular pork trimmings, in the manufacture of a frankfurter. From the article, "Work Simplification," by W. C. Zinck, in *The Encyclopedia of Management.*

EXHIBIT W-3   Man-Machine Analysis

				○ AN OPERATION ○ A TRANSPORTATION ▽ IDLE □ AN INSPECTION

ELEMENT NO.	DISTANCE	MAN NAME Luther W _____, Jr. WHAT - HOW - WHY RECORD HERE THE FACTS AND THE KEY POINTS OF WHAT YOU ACTUALLY SAW THE MAN DO	ELEMENT SYMBOL	CYCLE TIME 20 Sec. — VALUE ADDING TIME	MAN	M/C IDLE	ELEMENT SYMBOL	MACHINE TYPE Grinding Machine SPECIFICATIONS 12" Wheel, Bonded TOOL-FIXTURE DATA 12" Level Plate RECORD HERE WHAT THE MACHINE DID
1		Turns body to left					Idle
2		Picks up Casting					
3	18"	Carries casting to level plate					
4		Checks casting legs on plate					
5	12"	Carries casting to grinding machine					
6		Grinds casting legs		2		2	Grind
7	12"	Carries casting to level plate					Idle
8		Checks casting legs on level plate					
9	12"	Carries casting to machine (grinding)					
10		Grinds gates off casting		4		4	Grind
11		Turns body to right					Idle
12		Tosses ground casting into tote barrel					

Cycle Time - 20 Sec.
Machine Effectiveness - 30%
Man Effectiveness - 30%

Portion of a Man-Machine Analysis chart, showing present method, grinding legs and grinding gates on loader casting. From the article, "Work Simplification," by W. C. Zinck, in *The Encyclopedia of Management*.

EXHIBIT **W-4** *Operation Analysis*

							DIE MAKER FILE		
		LEFT HAND					**RIGHT HAND**		
ELE MENT	DIS- TANCE	DESCRIPTION OF ELEMENT	SYMBOL	VALUE ADD'G TIME	VALUE ADD'G TIME	SYMBOL	DESCRIPTION OF ELEMENT	DIS TANCE	ELE MENT
1		Picks up insert	◯			▽	Holds file		1
2	12"	To filing position	◦			◦	To insert	12"	2
3		Holds insert	▽		20	●	Files insert at hole to remove rough edge		3
4		Rotates insert	◯			▽	Holds file		4
5		Holds insert	▽		20	●	Files at hole		5
6		Rotates insert	◯			▽	Holds file		6
7		Holds insert	▽		20	●	Files at hole		7
8	12"	To container	◦			◦	To relaxed position	12"	8
9		Places insert in container	◯			▽	Idle – Holds file		9
		To pick up next insert	◦						
		Repeat					Repeat		

Operation Cycle Time   – 64 Seconds

Left-Hand Effectiveness – 0%

Right-Hand Effectiveness – 94%

Operation Analysis chart of filing a hole in a plastic clothes line insert, showing imbalanced use of hands. From the article, "Work Simplification," by W. C. Zinck, in *The Encyclopedia of Management.*

your department compare with accepted standards for those types of operations? Are there problems of glare? (See *Lighting.*)

2. If air conditioning is out of the question as too costly, where would comparatively simple ventilation changes improve working conditions?

3. Where are layouts or machine setups causing "operator acrobatics?" Are women employees struggling with controls that were positioned for men?

4. Should some employees be sitting instead of standing? Are posture chairs in use?

5. What elements of periodic change would you introduce into your most monotonous operations? Would such a change suffice in lieu of a rest period? (See *Fatigue* and *Rest Breaks.*)

6. With specific workers in mind, how important is it to preserve certain groups intact when re-layouts are made? Is the "social value" worth some slight departure from the most efficient engineering setup? (See the remarks about the answer to the puzzler in *Office Arrangements.*)

7. When do peaks in certain operations occur? Can any rescheduling or reshuffling be done in the interest of workers' convenience, without sacrifice of efficiency?

8. How fatiguing are the floors in your operating departments where workers are on their feet all day long? Have you noticed any areas especially cluttered up?

9. Is noise detracting from efficiency? Is the situation worth requesting a study? What relatively simple changes can you suggest to better this condition?

10. How expensive would it be to add color to some of your workplaces? What operations might be helped by heightening the color contrast between equipment and items being worked on?

11. Have you thought about suggesting that the effect of music be tried out in your department? Would music —say near the close of the day—help banish boredom? (See *Music for Employees.*)

WORKLOAD FORECASTING

The supervisor is concerned with two types of workload forecasting: (1) planning for current and immediately foreseeable routine work, and (2) the possible disruption of the existing workload that may result when a special project now being planned is undertaken.

For routine, repetitive operations, it is obvious common sense to keep up-to-date, complete, and accurate records of work scheduled and in progress in your department. Depending upon the scope of your responsibility for scheduling and assigning specific orders going through your department, you may want to set up some sort of planning board or other control to indicate loadings ahead for various individuals or lines. A widely used visual control is the Gantt chart developed during World War I by Henry L. Gantt. (See *Planning and Scheduling— 1. Progress Charts* and *Planning and Control Boards.*)

For special projects, always double-check on how realistic your time estimates are. Ask the following questions:

1. Have I allowed "elbowroom" for unexpected delays, interferences, or false starts?

2. Am I taking sufficiently into account the time for employees to get used to new methods—or the time to train green employees in the new work? (See *"Learning Curve" in Estimating.*)

3. How much of the performance on the new project

in my department will depend upon the co-operation of other departments over which I have no direct control?

4. Will special arrangements have to be made to get the kinds of records needed for the estimates? Are any spot checks possible?

5. Am I trying to kid anybody by putting rubber into the estimates? Are others trying to kid me? Are circumstances such that I *have* to kid somebody? (Be especially careful on this one!)

6. Will my estimating be helped if I think about three possibilities—"optimistic," "pessimistic," and most likely"?

Related Entries   *Employee Efficiency; "Learning Curve" in Estimating; Planning and Control Boards; Planning and Scheduling—1. Progress Charts; Planning and Scheduling—2. "Critical Path" and Other Network Plans; Rush Jobs; Seasonal Peaks.*

WORKMEN'S COMPENSATION

Workmen's compensation is a system set up by legislation whereby an employer is liable, *regardless of fault*, for medical care and specified monetary benefits to employees injured while working for him. In exchange for this liability, for which the employer can make provision through the purchase of insurance, the employer is protected against an unlimited amount of damages which could be recovered for injuries caused by his negligence or that of his agents.

There are workmen's compensation laws in every state, the District of Columbia, and Puerto Rico. About half of the state laws are compulsory, but even where they are not, most employers elect to operate under them, because if they do not they are deprived of certain legal defenses if an employee should sue them. The advantages to the injured employee are obvious: He does not have to engage in expensive litigation, he does not lose benefits even if his own negligence was the cause of the accident (or industrial disease), and he receives benefit payments promptly. Amounts of benefits are clearly set forth in the statutes in relation to temporary, permanent, total, or partial disability.

The supervisor is important in this whole matter, because the insurance rates which management pays are directly influenced by its accident experience. Therefore, quite aside from the human element of not wanting to have anybody hurt, a good accident record, which so heavily depends upon the vigilance and discipline of the foreman and upon his good induction and instruction procedures, can result in a reduction of many thousands of dollars paid out in workmen's compensation insurance.

Related Entries *See listing of entries related to labor laws under National Labor Relations Act.*

THE WORRIED EMPLOYEE

A worried employee is an employee who is very apt to make mistakes or to be involved in an accident. A supervisor should be alert to problem situations of this sort, and to help within appropriate limits. (See *Employee Counseling* and *The Mentally Disturbed Worker.*) According to the Michigan Industrial Mental Health Council, the following are signs and symptoms of the worried worker:

1. *Sudden change of behavior.* (John usually whistles a good deal. He hasn't lately. Why?)

2. *Irritability.* (Nowadays Jane is always in a squabble or is nagging about something. Used to be a sunny sort of girl. Why is that?)

3. *Sudden sadness.* (Ted seems to be down in the dumps. The corners of his mouth droop, and he is always going out for a smoke. What's the matter?)

4. *Preoccupation.* (Helen doesn't have her mind on the job. She couldn't keep up today, although she is a fast worker. When I asked her about it, she said, "I've got other things to think about, but I'll be all right." Only she isn't.)

5. *Too many mistakes.* (Bill used to be good, but he has become careless. Makes too many mistakes. I'll have to speak to him about it.)

6. *Increased accidents.* (Jake used to be careful and often cautioned others. Too bad he is hurt.)

7. *Increased absenteeism.* (Dorothy has missed so many days that we'll forget she works here pretty soon. She says she hasn't been sick, but that things at home are very complicated.)

8. *Increased fatigue.* (David's hours are not so bad, but he seems tired out all the time. He says he is worried about his boy. I guess this is tiring him as much as his work.)

9. *Excessive use of alcohol.* (I often wonder about Tom who is supervisor down the line from me. He is really a quiet, timid sort of man, but when he comes in slightly liquored up, he acts touchy and is very aggressive with his men. Too bad he seems to need liquor to make him able to face his job.)

Related Entries *The Alcoholic Employee; Emotional Reactions; Employee Counseling; The Mentally Disturbed Worker; Tensions and Stress.*

A GLOSSARY OF TRAITS, BEHAVIOR CHARACTERISTICS, AND RELATED PSYCHOLOGICAL TERMS

Listed here are traits, behavior characteristics, and related psychological terms and expressions which the supervisor is likely to hear at meetings of professional personnel-management groups he may have occasion to attend, or which he may come across in articles and books on the subject. Some of these he will also see on merit-rating or job-analysis forms. The terms are often bandied about loosely, and if a supervisor feels he should use any of them in a merit-rating or appraisal discussion, or in an employee counseling situation, he should be sure that he knows their meaning. (We define *trait* and *behavior characteristic* first. The rest are in alphabetic order.)

TRAIT. A *trait* is a distinguishing quality in a person, a distinctive, definable characteristic, a mark of individuality. A trait may be one predominant habit pattern, or a combination of a number of habit patterns or behavior characteristics. It is something you associate with a person as a continuing mark of difference from other people—not something of a temporary nature.

BEHAVIOR CHARACTERISTIC. A *behavior characteristic*, as distinguished from a particular action or instance of behavior, is a pattern which an individual sets up by habitual repetition—neatness in dress or in work habits, for example. In appraising employees, the terms "trait" and "behavior characteristic" are practically interchangeable.

* * *

Ability represents the power to perform, and is something which can be demonstrated and measured. It is distinguished from *aptitude*, which represents a latent capacity to perform after the necessary skills have been acquired. (*Skill* is a highly developed ability which expresses itself in superior performance.) Ability can be developed by training and practice, within the limits of an aptitude as discussed under that head.

Accuracy represents care in the use, interpretation, and and distribution of information; a habit of checking into sources of information and purported facts; and as a personal trait with respect to workmanship, it means that a person can be relied upon to follow instructions and specifications closely as regards tolerances, finishes, etc. (in appraisal, don't confuse accuracy with "truthfulness," since *willful* inaccuracies cannot be tolerated.)

Adaptability and Flexibility mean willingness to adjust a course of action or point of view or a habitual way of doing things to changing conditions, or to new instructions or new facts and interpretations. This appraisal point is relatively easy to apply to production and other rank-and-file workers. With respect to subordinate executives, judgment in appraisal is required by putting this trait into perspective with *decisiveness*, discussed below. Adaptability and flexibility should not be confused with a weather-vane inability to determine a sound course of action and sticking to it.

Aggressiveness. If you use this term in an appraisal, be sure all concerned understand whether it is used favorably or unfavorably. An aggressive person can be self-assertive, a follow-through, get-it-done good man to lean upon (favorable). Or he can be an obnoxious "pusher" (unfavorable). It may be best to avoid this term if possible in appraisal forms and memoranda. (*Note:* Psychologists use the term "aggression" as a general one applying to feelings of anger or hostility, often resulting from being frustrated as a result of not achieving a desired objective.)

Analytical Ability is the ability to think through a problem, determine data and information needed for solution, evaluate them, and arrive at a solution which considers indirect as well as direct factors. Analytical ability obviously rests on a high degree of intelligence, but it is worth considering as a separate trait because some kinds of jobs require considerable analysis, based on study and reflection, without necessarily calling for quick decisions under stress or emergency situations.

Anxiety, as a behavior characteristic (as distinguished from a concern about a particular situation) is a vague, chronic state of fear, which can be a symptom of deep-seated emotional problems, calling for professional help. One trouble sign is that such an emotionally disturbed person, if a particular thing about which he is worried is shown to him to be non-existent or exaggerated, will immediately latch on to something else to express fears about. The trouble is *inside of him,* and not with the thing he is worried about at the moment. (See the entries, *The Mentally Disturbed Worker* and *The Worried Employee.*)

Aptitude represents a latent capacity to perform after the necessary skills have been acquired. It thus refers to the ability to profit from training and practice. An aptitude seems to be something which is inborn, and which sets a limit upon the ultimate skill which can be attained.

Thus a person may have a pronounced aptitude for music, and under proper training may attain to a great ability in one or more forms of that art. On the other hand, a person with little aptitude for the piano may progress somewhat under training but will never develop professional skill. Psychologists do not measure aptitudes directly; they infer them from measures of ability. We all must get along with what aptitudes we have—we cannot acquire more, although some unsuspected ones may be revealed later in life. Psychologists seem agreed that even though a person apparently starts with no aptitudes at birth and acquires them as he gets older, he will have all he is going to have by the time he is 15 or 16. But perhaps the most important thing of all to know about aptitudes is that you should not be discouraged about your quota. The fable about the tortoise and the hare is applicable here: Most people do not develop their aptitudes to anywhere near the degree possible. It takes work.

Attitude. An employee's *attitude* refers to the way in which he responds, either positively or negatively (favorably or unfavorably) to the situation in which he finds himself, the people he works with, the company's or department's objectives, etc. Again, as a behavior characteristic, it refers to an habitual response, rather than to a specific incident or situation. Determination of employee attitudes is part of a supervisor's job—through the normal processes of upward communication (see *Listening,* and the two entries on *Suggestions*). Managements today often make surveys of employee attitudes through formal questionnaires and interviews, or through professional survey organizations.

Behavioral Sciences include any science that studies the behavior of man (and of the lower animals) by means of experiment and observation. The recognized behavioral sciences include psychology, sociology, and social anthropology. In recent years specialists in these fields have increasingly been turning to the study of human behavior in a working environment.

Character, when the term is used to describe a trait or behavior characteristic, means the basic code of conduct by which a person strives to live. He may fall short of it on occasion, but he does have a set of ideals by which he judges himself. Thus if we say a subordinate or another executive "has character," we mean he has a firm code of conduct and can be counted on to live up to it with fewer lapses than most people. High character has its roots in a person's very earliest associations—the influence of the home, the school, the church. (See the entry, *Integrity*.)

Creativity. See *Imagination*, below.

Culture. When people speak of someone as "cultured," they usually mean he is well educated, well read, well spoken, and usually that he enjoys such things as music, art, literature, etc. When a behavioral scientist or social scientist refers to a "culture," he means the customs, habits, and traditions that characterize a given social group, or nationality, or race. These are the kinds of things a supervisor must keep in mind in anticipating or judging the motivations and reactions of employees.

Decisiveness is the ability and willingness to determine a course of action and carry out a decision. A decisive person has the courage of his convictions. In a person of mature years this is not something that can be improved significantly by further training. You have to be careful in judging this trait, because a cocksure person may rattle off pronouncements and make snap decisions which later turn out to be half-baked. You have to work with a person a while before you can form an opinion. If there is evidence of indecisiveness, it may be well to see if there is a basic lack of self-confidence which can be overcome. (see the entry, *Self-Confidence*.)

Dependability is a characteristic that gives others a feeling that a person will not have to be followed up to be sure he gets a job done. This is more than an occasional demonstration of initiative—it is a pattern of consistent adherence to promises large and small. Dependability is definitely something that can be developed under proper supervision. (See the entries, *Delegation* and *Oversupervision.*)

Dominance. This term, when used in appraisal, can be meant in a highly favorable sense, indicating that a person has the capacity to act on his own initiative and responsibility, doing things without having to be told, and exercising leadership. The trouble is, the term can have negative associations—to *domineer* meaning to exercise power in an insolent or arbitrary way. It is best to avoid this term in favor of uniformly positive ones, such as *initiative, resourcefulness, leadership.*

Emotion is a stirring up, a departure from a calm state. It often results in an impulse to take some form of more or less violent action. As indicated in our entry, *Emotional Reactions,* it may also include pronounced physiological changes in breathing, blood circulation, glandular reaction, etc. You have experienced these yourself in states of fear, anger, disgust, grief, joy, surprise, and the like. Remember that emotions are desirable—they are a part of the richness of life. However, in a business environment, when we speak of someone as reacting emotionally, we mean it in a negative sense, that he is reacting instinctively—without really thinking and without much control. *Emotional stability* means the ability to stay on an even keel, especially under stress. An emotionally stable supervisor or employee does not "blow his top" in minor emergencies, or when his will is crossed. He is said to have *poise,* which means he is well balanced.

Habit is a way of behavior that has been acquired through frequent repetition. The older a person gets, the more ingrained these ways of acting or thinking become. Resistance to change is often due to inability or unwillingness to change habits.

Imagination and Creativity imply the ability to make new and beautiful or effective combinations out of separate ideas or things, which others have never thought of putting together in just that way. In business, imagination results in bold and original proposals and actions. However, in appraising employees and executives, understanding and interpretation of this term can swing widely. Try to use it in a way that will pin down the meaning— perhaps by citing examples of initiative and resourcefulness.

Industrial Psychology is concerned with methods of selecting, training, counseling, and supervising people in business and industry. An industrial psychologist is someone who has had formal training beyond the undergraduate level in psychological methods used to study human behavior, and is familiar with important findings of research in that field. He may work full time for a company, or as a consultant, or hold a teaching or research position in an academic institution.

Industriousness is the characteristic of being steadily and painstakingly active; not lazy. The trouble with using the term in appraisal is that while it is usually applied in a positive sense, a person can be "busy" without actually being productive. It is better to stick to discussing tangible performance results, as discussed in *Development of Subordinates—1. Development-Appraisal-Development.* If you want an appraisal term in this area, perhaps *perseverance,* defined below, may be better.

Initiative is the quality of being a self-starter, of getting things done without having to be prodded. It is usually coupled with *resourcefulness*—the ability to think of alternative ways of achieving an objective, to make do with the men and facilities available. Of course, a subordinate may display more initiative than you want him to, by going beyond the directives and authority given him. Keep in mind the soundness of action an employee has demonstrated by his self-starting. Without good judgment, taking action may merely be a demonstration of impulsiveness. As mentioned in connection with *decisiveness*, above, you have to work with a person a while before you can form an opinion on this trait.

Intelligence is the ability to grasp new ideas and deal with novel situations. It is a "general" aptitude, or combination of aptitudes, since it contributes to proficiency in a number of abilities, such as analytical ability and judgment. Keep in mind the distinction between intelligence and *knowledge*. The latter is something which a person has acquired through experience and training. Focus attention on how a subordinate has demonstrated a *capacity* to acquire knowledge, but remember that intelligence is more than the ability to sponge up information, but rather the ability to *use* it effectively—especially, as stated, under new and unusual conditions.

I.Q. (Intelligence Quotient) is a measure which was devised in an attempt to express an individual's relative standing, as regards intelligence, with other persons of the same age. Roughly speaking, it is the ratio between the number of questions answered correctly by a person on a given test devised for such measures, and the average number of questions answered by somebody of the same age as he is. The decimal ratio is multiplied by 100 to provide a more convenient measure. Thus an I.Q. of 100 would indicate average mental status, and above or below 100 would indicate corresponding above or below average mentality. However, the term came to be bandied about as a purportedly precise measure of intelligence, which in turn was implied to be a single attribute, rather than a combination of aptitudes and abilities. Moreover, the measure itself had little meaning when applied to adults rather than to children. Psychologists today look upon I.Q. as an outworn concept of a way of summarizing a person's mental status.

Intelligence Tests. See *Personnel Tests,* below.

Judgment is the ability to form a valid opinion, make a good estimate, or reach a sound conclusion from the facts and surrounding circumstances in a situation. It implies the use of good common "horse sense" and includes a good sense of timing and the ability to sift out the important factors from a host of less important or inconsequential ones.

Knowledge. Don't confuse with *intelligence.* See above.

Leadership is a person's ability to handle people so that they will be "for" him at all times, especially in an emergency. In a supervisor it is the ability to get others to work willingly and to win the confidence and co-operation of those who report to him. . . . to tell and instruct in such a way that people will *want* to do their work in the right way. (See entry, *Leadership.*)

Learning refers to the *change of behavior* as the result of experience. "Experience," of course, here means the experience gained in a contrived situation, such as a classroom, as well as experience on the job or in life in general. A *learning curve* is a measure of progress in learning. (See the entries, *Learning* and *"Learning Curve" in Estimating.*)

Maturity means completeness in growth and development. In adults, where physical maturity is taken for granted, it is applied against a general concept of how a healthy, well-adjusted adult should act and react. Thus it does not simply mean full development within his own limitations of someone obviously deficient in many of the aptitudes and traits which are associated with normal human beings. . . . Maturity is not a matter of age. Some people are fully matured in their early twenties, while others remain essentially immature all of their lives. (See the entry, *The Immature Employee.*)

Motivation is what makes people move—either physically, or in the way they think. You can make a person jump by sticking him with a pin, or stay overtime and perform an unpleasant task by the promise of a reward. By "employee motivation" we usually mean whatever makes employees behave in a way desired by management. The important thing for the supervisor is to realize the many ways of getting people to react favorably without sticking pins into them. (See the entries, *Motivation* and *Punishment*, and follow through by reading as many of the related entries listed as you have time for.)

Neurosis. See *Psychosis*, below.

Obsession is a fixed idea that constantly intrudes into a person's thoughts, but has no basis in the real situation around him. (See the entry, *The Mentally Disturbed Worker.*)

Paranoia is a mental disorder marked by extreme suspiciousness of the motives of others. Symptoms of such behavior—for example, when an employee insists someone is trying to "get him" when there is obviously no basis for such a fear—should lead a supervisor to see if he can get the person to seek professional help. (See the entry, *The Mentally Disturbed Worker.*)

Perseverance means stick-to-it-iveness. This should be an important appraisal point wherever a job involves tedious effort or where there is a high probability of disappointments and failure.

Personality is the sum total of a person's traits which he presents to the world. It is a short-hand word used to indicate how a person affects others. Thus a person may be characterized as having a "pleasant" personality, or a "cheerful" one, or an "unpleasant" one. If a supervisor is appraising a subordinate on this, he should be careful to be objective—to find out how *others* feel about the person in addition to his own reactions.

Personnel Tests may be *capacity or aptitude tests, proficiency or achievement tests,* or *personality and interest checklists or scales.* Aptitude tests are used in an attempt to predict success of an applicant on a job in which he has had no experience, or at most very limited experience. Proficiency tests measure skill or other occupational knowledge or ability. Interest and personality measures help provide an insight into the kinds of work a person will find satisfaction in doing, and the type of behavior to be expected from him. Tests commonly used are as follows: *Mental alertness tests* (*"intelligence tests"*) are designed to measure general intelligence. They may be referred to as verbal ability tests, verbal-linguistic tests, intelligence tests, classification tests, or simply "personnel" tests. *Clerical aptitude tests* measure speed and accuracy in perceiving numerical and verbal similarities and differences. *Mechanical aptitude tests* are available which are valid for a variety of mechanical jobs, but there is no measure of "general mechanical aptitude" which would predict success on *any* kind of mechanical job to which an employee might be assigned. In this class of tests are *mechanical comprehension tests* which measure ability to understand mechanical relationships, and tests which measure ability to perceive *spatial relationships* (as between disassembled geometric figures), and people who score high on these show aptitude for certain kinds of mechanical jobs. There are also certain *mechanical adaptability* tests which appear valid in measuring "knack" for mechanical, electrical and related activities. *Tests of manual dexterities* are available which measure arm-and-hand and wrist-and-finger dexterity, which can predict success in certain types of assembly, or packing and wrapping, or sorting jobs, and the like.

Manual dexterity tests should not be used as indicators of mechanical aptitude. *Vocational interest measures* measure basic interests which seem to be common among workers who are successful in specific occupations. Thus they are widely used in employee counseling, student guidance, etc.

Prejudice means prejudging something—leaning toward one side of a question for reasons other than those which should rightfully decide the issue—for example, reasons based on religious beliefs, personal likes and dislikes, selfish gain, etc. (See the entry, *Prejudices*.)

Psychosis is a mental disorder in which a person is suffering from so much anxiety, so many frustrations, imagined wrongs, etc., that his behavior becomes completely unrealistic to the point where he becomes dangerous and must receive professional and custodial care. (See *The Mentally Disturbed Worker*.)

Proficiency refers to the degree of ability already acquired—e.g., typing 120 words per minute, or being able to handle a certain machine operation without further supervision.

Rationalization means interpreting one's own behavior or attitude in a way that conceals the real motive (which may be a purely selfish one) and ascribing it to a motive which one considers more socially acceptable. It is usually unconscious in the sense that the mind doesn't want to probe for the real reason.

Resourcefulness is the ability to select alternative avenues for getting results, and to "make do" with the resources available. See *Initiative*, above.

Skill is a highly developed ability which expresses itself in superior performance. See the definitions *Ability* and *Aptitude*, above.

Tact is the special ability to deal with others without giving offense; sensitivity to the feelings of others; knowl-

Personnel Information Bulletin, published by the Office of the Assistant Administrator for Personnel, Veterans Administration, Washington 25, D.C.

If you are especially interested in personnel matters, a useful publication is:

Personnel Journal, monthly, 100 Park Ave., Swarthmore, Pa.

If you are an office supervisor or department head, you may want to secure membership in:

Administrative Management Society, Industrial Center, Willow Grove, Pa.

Systems and Procedures Association of America, 4463 Penobscot Bldg., Detroit, with many chapters throughout the country. This association publishes *Systems and Procedures Journal*, monthly.

Practical human-relations pointers are given in the following newsletters edited specifically for department heads, supervisors and foremen:

Administrative Officer, twice-a-month, published by Motivation, Inc., Springdale, Conn.

Assignments in Management, monthly, 307 Swiftwater Lane, Brookhaven, Chester, Pa.

If you want to pursue some of the more technical subjects alluded to in this guide, here are the names of books specifically written and edited for foremen and supervisors:

Dynamic Work Simplification, by W. Clements Zinck, Reinhold Publishing Corporation, New York, 1962.

The Foreman's Handbook, edited by Carl Heyel, 3rd ed., McGraw-Hill Book Company, 1955.

How to Control Production Costs, by Phil Carroll, McGraw-Hill Book Company, 1963.

Timestudy Fundamentals for Foremen, by Phil Carroll, 2nd
    ed., McGraw-Hill Book Company, New York, 1951.
What Every Supervisor Should Know, by Lester R. Bittel,
    McGraw-Hill, Book Company, New York, 1959.

On any subject having to do with management, you
can get a good overall view, in not too technical language,
by consulting the appropriate entry in:

The Encyclopedia of Management, edited by Carl Heyel,
    Reinhold Publishing Corporation, New York, 1963.

The *Encyclopedia* will give you further leads on all subjects, in the form of references to books, periodicals, and
professional associations active in the fields discussed.
Incidentally, the foreword to this encyclopedia offers a
"core-subject" reading guide, consisting of lists of entries,
and the sequence in which they should be read, to provide
a broad grounding in any one of 19 subject areas in the
field of management.